NEW ORLEANS STYLE AND THE
WRITING OF AMERICAN JAZZ HISTORY

JAZZ PERSPECTIVES
Lewis Porter, Series General Editor

Open the Door: The Life and Music of Betty Carter
By William R. Bauer

Jazz Journeys to Japan: The Heart Within   By William Minor

Four Jazz Lives   By A. B. Spellman

Head Hunters: *The Making of Jazz's First Platinum Album*
By Steven F. Pond

Lester Young   By Lewis Porter

The Last Miles: The Music of Miles Davis, 1980–1991
By George Cole

The André Hodeir Jazz Reader
By André Hodeir   Edited by Jean-Louis Pautrot

Someone to Watch Over Me: The Life and Music of Ben Webster
By Frank Büchmann-Møller

Rhythm Is Our Business: Jimmie Lunceford and the Harlem Express
By Eddy Determeyer

Lennie Tristano: His Life in Music   By Eunmi Shim

Lee Konitz: Conversations on the Improviser's Art
By Andy Hamilton

Delightfulee: The Life and Music of Lee Morgan
By Jeffery S. McMillan

*"Ellington Uptown": Duke Ellington, James P. Johnson,
and the Birth of Concert Jazz*
By John Howland

New Orleans Style and the Writing of American Jazz History
By Bruce Boyd Raeburn

OTHER BOOKS OF INTEREST

Before Motown: A History of Jazz in Detroit, 1920–60
By Lars Bjorn with Jim Gallert

John Coltrane: His Life and Music   By Lewis Porter

Charlie Parker: His Music and Life   By Carl Woideck

The Song of the Hawk: The Life and Recordings of Coleman Hawkins
By John Chilton

Let the Good Times Roll: The Story of Louis Jordan and His Music
By John Chilton

To Boyd and Ginnie

Authors of *Jazzmen* enjoying a "folk" moment in July 1941. *Left to right:* Charles Edward Smith, William Russell, and Frederic Ramsey Jr. (The Historic New Orleans Collection, accession no. 92-48-L).

New Orleans Style and the Writing of American Jazz History

BRUCE BOYD RAEBURN

THE UNIVERSITY OF MICHIGAN PRESS

ANN ARBOR

2012   2011   2010   2009   4   3   2   1

A CIP catalog record for this book is available from the British Library.

Library of Congress Cataloging-in-Publication Data

Raeburn, Bruce Boyd, 1948–
    New Orleans style and the writing of American jazz history / Bruce
Boyd Raeburn.
        p.   cm. — (Jazz perspectives)
    Includes bibliographical references and index.
    ISBN-13: 978-0-472-11675-1 (cloth : alk. paper)
    ISBN-10: 0-472-11675-4 (cloth : alk. paper)
    ISBN-13: 978-0-472-03321-8 (pbk. : alk. paper)
    ISBN-10: 0-472-03321-2 (pbk. : alk. paper)
    1. Jazz—Louisiana—New Orleans—History and criticism.
I. Title.
    ML3508.8.N48R34   2009
    781.65'3—dc22   2008032083

Contents

Acknowledgments

Having begun my jazz education in the womb, I have many people to thank. Mel Lewis told me that my mother, jazz vocalist Virginia Powell, was present at the auditions for her replacement in my father's band while she was carrying me, so I probably remained on the bandstand almost to term. My thanks therefore to the musicians who were with the Boyd Raeburn orchestra from Valentine's Day through November 13, 1948—I got the message. Over the next forty years I met many of the players that worked with Boyd, including Frankie Socolow, Dizzy Gillespie, George Handy, David Allyn, and Mel. I came to realize that the jazz world is full of special people.

This study began as a dissertation in history at Tulane University in 1988, and without the guidance of Bill C. Malone, Patrick Maney, and Wilfred McClay, it would never have been completed. But the assistance of others, beginning in the 1970s, was also crucial: Henry Kmen encouraged me to look closely at all New Orleans music; Al Rose exposed me to purism and its passions; Richard B. Allen taught me that research on traditional jazz is never easy and requires patience; Tad Jones showed me that New Orleans music was not just for old people; and the photographer Michael P. Smith helped me to see how neighborhood "cultural wetlands" nourish music in New Orleans. In the 1980s, William Russell, Alden Ashforth, Danny Barker, Larry Gushee, Bill Gottlieb, Fred Ramsey, Alan Lomax, Fred Starr, Barry Martyn, and James Lincoln Collier shared their experiences and expertise, deepening my curiosity about traditional jazz. Their comments (and especially those of James T. Maher) on the dissertation when it was finished in 1991 made it clear that I was only just getting started. By then I had become curator of the Hogan Jazz Archive, having worked my way up through the ranks, and while I was checking new books and journals one day, I encountered something interesting.

The appearance in 1991 of the special issue of *Black American Literature Forum* devoted to jazz, edited by Gary Carner, opened up new vistas of investigation, and several of the essays included in that volume have had a direct bearing on how this study has evolved. Since then I have met many of the scholars whose work has helped me, including Sherrie Tucker, Krin Gabbard, Thomas Brothers, Richard Sudhalter, William Howland Kenney, Scott DeVeaux, Thomas J. Hennessey, Charles Kinzer, Brian Harker, Burton Peretti, Gene Anderson, Charles Suhor, John Edward Hasse, Ron Welburn, Marcello Piras, and Walter van de Leur. Dan Morgenstern's and George Avakian's counsel has been invaluable. I am also especially grateful to the readers commissioned by the University of Michigan Press for their meticulous attention to detail and to acquisitions editor Chris Hebert and series editor Lewis Porter for their patience and sound advice. Of course, there are many whose work I value whom I have not yet encountered, but I assume that all paths in jazz cross eventually.

There were times when I thought this book would never get done, and the friends and loved ones whose support has sustained me made all the difference. My colleagues Jack Stewart and Michael White have juggled musical and scholarly careers, at times against seemingly overwhelming odds, and their insight has deepened my understanding of what New Orleans music is about and why it matters. Former and current members of my staff at the Hogan Jazz Archive—Lynn Abbott, Alma Williams Freeman, Dirk van Tuerenhout, and Kahne Parsons—have provided friendship as well as devotion to the cause of jazz preservation. I am also indebted to Alfred Lemmon, Marc Cave, Siva Blake, and Daniel Hammer at the Williams Research Center of the Historic New Orleans Collection for assistance with materials from the William Russell and Frederic Ramsey Jr. collections. Special thanks are reserved for Garnette Cadogan for his steadfast encouragement, which leads me to ask, "Who's mentoring whom?" Finally, I want to express my gratitude to my sister, Susan D. Raeburn, for pressuring me to finish this study, and to my wife, Linda L. Carroll, for not. Her dedication to scholarship inspires me.

Introduction

When visitors come to the city of New Orleans they will invariably ask, after they have had something to eat, where one might go to hear some "real" jazz—not the tourist music associated with the bistros of Bourbon Street but the *genuine article*. An honest answer, according to some local observers (especially in the aftermath of Hurricane Katrina), would have to be "nowhere, you're too late, it's gone," but the usual response is to direct them to Preservation Hall.[1] Often described as the "international headquarters" or "bastion" of "traditional" New Orleans–style jazz, the hall itself is frequently a source of disappointment for the uninitiated. Its dimensions are surprisingly modest, more like two connected cubicles than a "hall"; seating is limited to pews, with most of the patrons facing a choice of standing or sitting on the floor; the music is performed without amplification, there is no air-conditioning, and on a crowded night the overall ambience can become stifling, especially during the summer. Nevertheless, the lines to get in are usually long, and it is apparent that, affectation aside, many will forego creature comforts to participate in an "authentic" jazz experience. At Preservation Hall, no one ever asks, "How can you preserve a music that has ceased to exist?" The question is, why?

This book will attempt to answer that question by explaining how the concept of "New Orleans style" developed and by whom. The idea that one kind of jazz might be considered more authentic than another did not exist among New Orleans musicians when the idiom was first coalescing, in the years from 1896 to 1917; "hot" record collectors in major urban capitals such as New York and Paris developed it later, in the 1930s. Sasha Frere-Jones, the popular-music critic for the *New Yorker*, provides a convenient summary of this tendency to "purism": "Pop music purists invariably tell the same story about their favorite music. Whatever the genre . . . a purist will say that it was better at its inception, when the sound was an expression of something local and unique, before the terrible money came and strangers corrupted the music with their embrace." Understanding the source of this phenomenon in relation to jazz requires examination of an international movement of "hot" record collectors who sought to both validate and define American vernacular culture, positing a belief that issues of authenticity depended on a set of values that could be discovered through historical research and applied to all jazz performances. "Hot" jazz was defined as a performance style infused with "qualities of excitement, passion, and intensity," but as Eric Thacker has observed, "the term was used relatively vaguely to describe all types of band."[2]

The cadre of intellectuals who sought to provide such definitions was undoubtedly motivated by a music that stirred them emotionally, but in their desire to understand what it was and how it came to be, they could not resist the temptation to intellectualize, to move from advocacy to an often extreme ideology. Thus, while their efforts provided a catalyst that led to an interest in the history of jazz and to the general belief that American culture mattered in its own right, their devotion to ideological imperatives affected historical perspectives and entrenched biases in jazz historiography. In his review of the writing of jazz history, "Constructing the Jazz Tradition: Jazz Historiography," Scott DeVeaux identifies an "official version of jazz history" that emerged in the 1950s and continues to dominate jazz discourse by portraying the history as a "coherent whole . . . a skillfully contrived and easily comprehended narrative." While he applauds the utility of this "organic" approach in promoting academic acceptance of jazz as art, DeVeaux deplores the oversimplification "that begs as many questions as it answers." He is particularly concerned about control of definitions regarding the essential features of jazz and about embedded ideological agendas pertaining to ethnicity and economics that were initially useful in legitimizing jazz but now constrain further elucidation. "The time has come," he writes, "for an approach that is less invested in the ideology of jazz as aesthetic object and more responsive to issues of historical particularity. Only in this way can the study of jazz break free from its self-imposed isolation, and participate with other disciplines in the exploration of meaning in American culture."[3] Above all, DeVeaux's essay is a frontal assault on complacency in jazz studies.

The present study has similar aims. I intend it as an appeal for renewed scholarly interest in New Orleans jazz, conceived of broadly as a community-based continuum in which many types of jazz coexist, as opposed to an "official" jazz canon based on histories celebrating progressive stylistic evolution. One might argue that attempting to deconstruct the official history that has bestowed priority on New Orleans as the "birthplace" of jazz is not the best way to make that case, but as usual in such endeavors, my objective is not to tear down everything. What I hope to encourage is a better appreciation of where New Orleans style fits in the discourses relating to the apotheosis of jazz as art in the 1930s and to the writing of jazz history. Problematically, scholars infatuated with bebop and its ideology of artistic professionalism (the dominant paradigm since the latter 1940s) have discounted the discourses of the previous decade that favored New Orleans music. Other perspectives on professionalism are possible in jazz: New Orleans style was disqualified because it functioned as a form of entertainment, but entertainment and art are not mutually exclusive or incompatible.

Of the various "evolutionary" stages assigned in the "official" history of jazz, the only one that does not adhere to the concept of ineluctable progress as it is usually portrayed is the period covering jazz origins in New Orleans. Preceding construction of the "official" history was an "awakening of American jazz scholarship" from 1930 to 1950, a rather homespun pursuit of knowledge, peripheral to the academy, in which the identification and elaboration of the concept of New Orleans style were defining factors. As historical information became available through systematic investigation of jazz musicians' life stories and recordings during the 1930s, "hot" collectors refined generic jazz classifications based on polarities of "hot" (authentic) and "sweet" (ersatz), developed in 1930, and substituted a more precise terminology, based on the concept of New Orleans style embedded in Charles Delaunay's (1911–1988) *Hot Discographie* (1936). Lawrence Gushee defines "hot" jazz as "a style of small-ensemble jazz . . . that was for the most part learned and played by ear . . . and emphasized a continuous ensemble polyphony," but he also sees it in retrospect as "an interrelated group of performance styles with fixed instrumentation and a relatively restricted reper-tory."[4]

New Orleans style was conceptualized as a wellspring from which all other "hot" variants derived. "Traditional" New Orleans style was thus defined by its protagonists as an original, "pure" jazz archetype that repre-sented the unmediated creative potency of an underclass whose cultural products "trickled up" from the bottom of society, reversing the flow of cul-tural dynamics as it was then conceived. As such, it came to be regarded as "folk" music, despite its emergence in a market-driven urban environment. Since the study of jazz history encompassed the fundamental contributions of diverse peoples of African heritage to American vernacular culture, albeit qualified to some extent by peculiar regional factors in the case of New Or-leans style, racial considerations were intrinsic to the quest. Consequently, an interest in jazz history often meant that "hot" collectors found themselves in-evitably drawn to the political left in their pursuit of the "righteous cause" of jazz advocacy. While the objective of "hot" record collectors as writers in the 1930s was to control information on jazz in order to establish a consensus on its credentials as an American art form and to promote recognition of the music's roots in the African American experience, some New Orleans purists went further in arguing that authenticity in jazz was tied to race *and* to a specific regional culture, a distinctive environment that was at once represen-tative of American culture and an exception to many of its tendencies. The purist idée fixe that accompanied the "discovery" of New Orleans style within the "hot" threshold thus included a tendency to view all subsequent stylistic innovations skeptically as decadent forms, meaning that practition-ers of New Orleans style could be held accountable for observing what were thought to be its tenets in order to avoid contamination. Purist ideology ulti-mately imperiled communication between the advocates of New Orleans style and early jazz pioneers, their primary source of information about jazz origins, whose interests they sought to safeguard and represent.

The "construction" of New Orleans style by a cadre of sympathetic writ-ers involved shifting ideas about early jazz and meandered according to the vagaries of their application. This book follows these shifts chronologically: chapters are arranged in thematic couplets, with a lagniappe chapter ("a lit-tle something extra") at the end. Chapters 1 and 2 concern advocacy and ide-ology. The purists who moved from "hot" to New Orleans style required an ideological system to rebut the explosion of negative opinion that had accompanied the music's initial reception nationally. A review of the scholarly literature on this subject provides the backdrop for the book's later examination of the emergence of jazz purism in 1930.

The progenitor of jazz purism was Charles Edward Smith (1904–1970), a young writer who sought to define "hot" jazz as an authentic "folk" expression and a spiritually gratifying African American vernacular art. Smith's commitment to his "righteous cause" required appeals to Marxist, collegiate, bohemian, and eventually mainstream constituencies to consolidate opinion in favor of "real" jazz. In fashioning a vernacular (or organic) ideology, he drew eclectically from the sources that were available, including leftist ideology, his record collection, discography, and personal contact with musicians and fellow collectors. Smith benefited from the coalescence of an international network of "hot" record collectors engaged in critical analysis and historical research after 1934, a movement that he helped to launch with his article "Collecting Hot," published that year in *Esquire*. Affiliation with the network enabled him to sharpen perceptions, supplementing "hot" as a categorical imperative with "New Orleans style," a seemingly more precise term intended to describe the earliest jazz idiom and to situate it geographically. The concept became the historical and critical template for Smith, William Russell (1905–1992), and Frederic Ramsey Jr. (1915–1995) in *Jazzmen* (1939), a book that argued unequivocally that jazz was an art form originating in New Orleans and spreading by diffusion. Let me be clear: in retrospect, and despite some shortcomings, I believe that the foundational-origins theory presented in *Jazzmen* holds up pretty well, concentrating as it does on New Orleans as a distinctive regional culture in which jazz channeled community life, ethnic diversity, and joie de vivre. Yet many of the lessons learned by jazz historians between 1930 and 1939 and expressed in this book were subverted in the 1940s by the ideological distractions of revival and schism that dominated jazz discourses, a time when purism became virulent and unforgiving.

Chapters 3 and 4 explore the praxis phase of the ideological imperatives associated with the transition from "hot" to New Orleans style catalyzed by collectors. In order to document authentic jazz musicians who had been forgotten or overlooked by the record industry, collectors organized independent record companies to provide alternatives to big band swing, a popular version of jazz. "Hot" collector entrepreneurs such as John Hammond

(1910–1987) succeeded in infiltrating major record companies, using their superior distribution to expand dissemination of historical information and perspectives on jazz as art through the provision of liner notes on reissue albums. Others, such as the folklorist Alan Lomax (1915–2002), supplemented recordings of music with documentation of oral history, made possible by his affiliation with the Library of Congress. After 1940, New Orleans–style purists raised the stakes in attempting to rehabilitate the careers of the oldest and therefore most authentic (and atavistic) practitioners of New Orleans style through recordings and touring. Bunk Johnson (1889–1949) and Kid Ory (1886–1973) were brought out of retirement and became the patron saints of the New Orleans revival. Purists used their statements to codify standards of orthodoxy, increasing tensions between the revivalists and the proponents of swing, but they also learned lessons of lasting importance. William Russell's friendship with Bunk Johnson changed his life, narrowing his perception of New Orleans–style performance practices but widening his appreciation of the dignity of black musicians who used jazz to rise above segregation.

Chapters 5 and 6 track the progress of critical and historiographical conflicts occurring during the 1940s and their legacy. By 1940, New Orleans–style jazz had become a potent ideological weapon, linking jazz criticism and historiography and enabling partisans within the "hot" collector community to justify predilections based on a gradually unfolding definition of what that style was. The emergence of bebop during World War II intensified the animosity existing between proponents of the New Orleans revival and swing, redefining jazz modernism while traditionalists were trying to discredit it. For a while, it was total war. During the 1940s, jazz historiography was up for grabs within an intellectual minefield characterized by two antithetical versions of jazz history and aesthetics—one modern (representing swing and bebop), the other traditional (representing New Orleans style)—effectively smashing the consensus established with *Jazzmen.* New publications such as *The Jazz Record Book,* by Smith and Russell, and *The Real Jazz* (1942), by Hugues Panassié (1912–1974), set the stage for schism, marshaling support among purists in their fight against modernism and the cult of progress. The jazz polls administered by the modernist critic Leonard Feather (1914–1994) for *Esquire* in 1943–47 offered a convenient target for traditionalists and were ultimately consumed in the conflagration. Despite the appearance in 1946 of ultrapurist works such as Rudi Blesh's (1899–1985) *Shining Trumpets* and Mezz Mezzrow's (1899–1972) *Really the Blues*, however, a vociferously ecumenical movement restored a semblance of peace in the ranks, while also setting up some disturbing trends for the future of jazz historiography, evident in Sidney Finkelstein's (1909–1974) *Jazz: A People's Music* in 1948 and Leonard Feather's *The Book of Jazz* in 1957. Henceforth, the history of jazz would be conceived as an organic, evolutionary continuum of stylistic progress, privileging modernism at the expense of New Orleans style.

Chapter 7 traces public opinion on jazz in New Orleans from 1900 through the 1960s, focusing on the influence of the ideology associated with *Jazzmen* on the creation of a local jazz infrastructure that sought to boost economic development through cultural tourism. Although institutions such as the National Jazz Foundation, the New Orleans Jazz Club, the Archive of New Orleans Jazz, and Preservation Hall helped to preserve jazz in New Orleans, purism created special problems for the modern jazz musicians who lived there, excluding them from a tradition to which they had a birthright. In attempting to provide a "unifying theory" of early jazz, the writers who constructed New Orleans style and their adherents in the Crescent City often created division instead. Purism was therefore not only the a priori assumption that led "hot" collectors to construct a usable jazz history; it was also the impediment that precluded an accurate interpretation of the past.

What many of the advocates of purism failed to realize was that in the early days of jazz in New Orleans, there were no rules, except those attached to a seemingly moribund Eurocentric classical establishment and the formalistic pedagogical practices of Afro-French Creoles who despised American vernacular culture. New Orleans was a city where music was intrinsic to lifestyle, made possible by its unique situation in the nineteenth century as a crossroads for three omnipresent systems of culture formation: the trans-Atlantic world of Eurocentric art and popular music; a creolization reinforced by proximity to the Caribbean and the Gulf, which added *clave* to the "ring shout" practices of Place Congo (where African-derived musical sensibility could not only survive but flourish); and the American vernacular flow of "alligator horse ballads," work songs, minstrelsy, and especially blues along the Mississippi River. By the early twentieth century, this musical mélange fed a seemingly interminable calendar of festivities that included Carnival, debutante parties, lakefront picnics, train and riverboat excursions, social-aid and pleasure-club parades, church dedications, *soirées dansantes*, jitney and college "script" dances, theater vaudeville, sporting events (possibly at sporting houses), fish fries, and funerals. The "trick bag" of raw material available to New Orleans musicians was virtually infinite and precluded standardization, at least at first, because eclectic experimentation was how amateurs playing by ear achieved individual musical "voices," formed bands with varying skill or literacy levels, and learned to satisfy diverse clienteles. Even Buddy Bolden's (1877–1931) band (the ur-jazz prototype) offered waltzes, quadrilles, schottisches, and mazurkas to its older clients before midnight, reserving the low-down blues and slow drags for the "night people" who would keep the party going until dawn.[5]

The small-ensemble instrumentation of a "front line" (cornet, clarinet, and trombone) and a "rhythm section" (guitar, bass, and drums) of five to seven pieces engaging in collective improvisation that became the sine qua non of purists was by no means an absolute formula. In early New Orleans jazz, many configurations were possible, such as the accordion, cornet, clarinet, and valve trombone in the Accordiana Band (1899); or a pianist accompanied by a drummer; or string bands engaging in improvised (or not) polyphony without brass and reeds, such as the Six and Seven-Eighths String Band (1913). Gilbert "Bab" Frank (ca. 1870–1933) played "hot" piccolo as leader of the Peerless Orchestra in 1905; in that same year his brother Alcide (ca. 1875–1942), a violinist, led the Golden Rule Orchestra, which Johnny St. Cyr (1890–1966) described as "hotter" than Bolden's Band.[6]

Ethnic and racial diversity within working-class neighborhoods stimulated vernacular cultural development in the Crescent City. The prevalence of music in the streets via marching bands, wagon advertisements, and spasm bands meant that musical innovations coming out of the African American community were available to everyone within earshot, regardless of the strictures of segregation that sought to keep whites free from black cultural penetration. Tremé, the French Quarter, the Seventh Ward, Central City, the Irish Channel, and Algiers were "cultural wetlands" characterized by "crazy quilt" demographic configurations that predated the implementation of segregation in the 1890s, interspersing Creoles, Latinos, Jews, blacks, and whites side by side within blocks.[7] Demographics reinforced the predisposition already present among young people to embrace the "hot" dance music that came to be known as jazz, and not surprisingly, most jazz musicians came from these neighborhoods. Adding to the complexity was the reciprocal cultural exchange between the city and countryside, a factor never adequately addressed by the "hot" collectors who wrote the early jazz histories.[8]

Purists tended to undervalue the nature of New Orleans style as a system of performance practices grounded in experimentation and variegation. A comparison of the stylistic proclivities of New Orleans bands that worked in Chicago in the mid-1920s with those that mostly stayed home is enough to prove the point: New Orleans jazz musicians in Chicago exhibited the same penchant for pragmatism on recordings that guided their earlier trial-and-error experiences back home in cabarets and dance halls and on the streets. King Oliver's (1885–1938) Creole Jazz Band used only "head" arrangements for recording sessions, but Louis Armstrong (1901–1971) and his Hot Five combined occasional use of scores, "head" arrangements, and spontaneous ideas generated in the studio to enliven their recordings. Jelly Roll Morton (1890–1941) had his Red Hot Peppers rehearse with scores, but some players were expected to improvise in select passages, inserting their "voices" as Morton wanted. The recordings made in the Chicago region could all be considered variants of New Orleans style, but the contrasts were notable—each group was distinctive. In New Orleans, recordings made after 1925 by the Halfway House Orchestra, Sam Morgan's (1887–1936) Jazz Band, the Original Tuxedo Jazz Orchestra, the New Orleans Owls, and the Jones and Collins Astoria Hot Eight illustrate an equivalent variegation, yet none of them sounded like the New Orleans–style bands in Chicago. What these bands were doing was consistent with an open-ended musical approach that balanced tradition and innovation. Trying to apply a stylistic code of ethics to New Orleans music ignored its very essence.

Similar tendencies are apparent in the transformation of brass band traditions over the course of the twentieth century. When the market shifted toward jazz in the period before 1910, fully literate marching bands such as the Onward and the Excelsior had to adapt to "faking" or perish.[9] Over time, saxophones became increasingly prevalent within bands such as the Eureka and the Young Tuxedo, replacing baritone horns and putting pressure on clarinetists. Today, clarinets are rarely found among the new wave of brass bands such as the Dirty Dozen and the ReBirth, which emerged from Danny Barker's (1909–1994) Fairview Baptist Church Christian Band experiments in the 1970s, while traditionalists such as Dr. Michael White (1954), who also studied with Barker, continue to use them. Because Barker did not set limits on how his students could negotiate their stylistic identities, preferring instead to inculcate basic values such as discipline and self-respect, his plan to resuscitate what appeared to be a waning tradition succeeded. But rather than view the phenomenon as the *loss* of tradition (as some conservative brass band musicians have), one must recognize that Barker was conforming to a tradition of experimentation, which is precisely what has kept jazz-oriented brass bands alive and culturally relevant in New Orleans for more than a century.[10]

Even such basic distinctions as "hot" and "sweet" could distort historical realities by denying the range of tactics that New Orleans musicians used for various clienteles. Differentiation of "sweet" recordings made by Armand Piron's (1888–1943) New Orleans Orchestra and "hot" recordings made by Sam Morgan's Jazz Band became a truism among purists seeking to define stylistic polarities in the 1920s. Based exclusively on analysis of recordings, one can make this case. But oral history conducted with members of these bands contradicts such rigid distinctions. While purists characterized the Piron band as "foreign to the whole jazz concept," Piron advertised his group as "one of the foremost of all Jazz Orchestras in the country," and when asked in an interview if the band "ever played low-down blues," banjoist Charlie Bocage (1900–1963) replied: "If the occasion warranted it, such as for colored dances, although most of the band's work was as a society band for whites. The band's style didn't change for colored functions, except that the singing would be different . . . stomp-down blues such as a band would play at the Economy Hall [in Tremé]."[11] Bocage's brother Peter (1887–1967) said of clarinetist Lorenzo Tio Jr. (1884–1933), "He could play jazz, too, and he could play anything that you put up there in front of him, see?"[12]

The experience of Sam Morgan's Jazz Band shows how "hot" bands could employ "sweet" effects. Max Harrison's evaluation of their recordings stresses the commitment to variegation: "Comparison with the 1923 Creole Band suggests that Oliver took a rather conservative view of New Orleans jazz, and here the ensembles, the plangent sweetness of the saxophones notwithstanding, are more open, the rhythmic pulse lighter. The textures are extremely diverse, variation being achieved from one chorus to another by changes of density, volume, and so on. . . . The point is, however, that the

. . . Morgan recordings prove that New Orleans jazz was still blowing hot and strong, and was still evolving, even if attention had shifted elsewhere."[13] The commonality of bands that were defined as belonging to different categories is exactly what New Orleans–style purists failed to grasp in rendering their ideological constructions sacrosanct and immutable. By consequence, as Harrison states, attention ultimately shifted elsewhere, and the perception of New Orleans jazz as a vital art form diminished accordingly. Changing fashion with the rise of big bands and modern jazz was at least in part responsible for the transition, but the narrowness of purists seeking to freeze time was certainly a contributing factor.

Ironically, this inflexible posture was reminiscent of the resistance against which anyone interested in jazz had to contend throughout the 1920s, when the music was often characterized as a threat to American propriety. When New Orleans jazz first captured widespread public attention with the recordings of the Original Dixieland Jazz Band (ODJB) in New York in 1917, the issue of authenticity in jazz would have been inconceivable to most Americans. Jazz became a national sensation when the band's "Livery Stable Blues" sold widely for the Victor Talking Machine Company, but as competitors scrambled to find jazz bands of their own to record, the finer points of performance style were lost in the shuffle.[14] Beyond a small circle of practitioners from New Orleans, nobody seemed to know what jazz was. From the outset, jazz inspired controversy and confusion because of its novelty. For some Americans it represented a threat to middle-class morality and cultural values; others saw it as raw material capable of refinement; many merely danced to it or just sat and listened. Few Americans sought to understand how the music came to be or how it was connected to the culture of New Orleans. It was the proliferation of jazz that concerned most people in the 1920s, and in the ensuing struggle to promote or prevent jazz, the antagonism engendered did more to obscure understanding than to clarify it. A review of scholarly perspectives on the initial reception of jazz will therefore help to explain why "hot" collectors in the 1930s held the perception that the music they cherished was widely reviled as either meaningless or dangerous in the preceding decade.

Lawrence Levine's *Highbrow/Lowbrow: The Emergence of Cultural Hierarchy in America* explains why some Americans reacted negatively to jazz. Levine details the construction of an elaborate system of cultural control that was designed to categorize art and to segregate it from the masses. Accordingly, by the end of the nineteenth century, designations like "folk," "popular," and "art" were used to classify music and to erect a rigid hierarchy of cultural values that was responsive to manipulation by elites.[15] The definition that cemented the edifice was given by Henry F. May in his treatment of the "Custodians of Culture," which explains Culture as "not so much a way of describing how people behaved as an idea of how they ought to behave and did not."[16] Art music required cultivated tastes for proper appreciation and was reserved for those who enjoyed the educational benefits that wealth made possible. Popular music was ephemeral and disposable, a distraction for the middle and lower classes. Folk music was thought to be atavistic, recalling days of scarcity when people made music for themselves out of necessity. Its principal value was as raw material for proper thematic development in art music. In their attempts to control culture, the Custodians were doomed to failure, largely because they refused to recognize the forces at work all around them. What made jazz so threatening was that it did not fit comfortably into the scheme. As John A. Kouwenhoven (1909–1990) has observed, jazz was a product of "vernacular" culture, representing "the unselfconscious efforts of common people, in America and elsewhere, to create satisfying patterns out of the elements of a new and culturally unassimilated environment."[17] Vernacular culture was supremely eclectic and borrowed at will from folk, art, and popular genres, creating unity from diversity and transgressing the boundaries set up by the Custodians. Jazz was "out of control," and the attempts of critics, musicians, educators, and even record company officials to restrain it in the 1920s demonstrated the tenacity of hierarchical ideals.

In "Jazz and American Culture," Levine addresses the conflict that the emergence of jazz precipitated. Jazz was the antithesis of everything Culture represented, and its appearance at the very time when the Custodians were consolidating their system of classification made it a convenient target. If Culture was "traditional," then jazz was characterized as "the product of a new age." "Jazz was raucous, discordant," writes Levine. "Culture was harmonious, embodying order and reason. Jazz was accessible, spontaneous; Culture was exclusive."[18] In the face of Eurocentric Culture, jazz was a cultural Declaration of Independence from the Old World, drawing on the heterogeneity of American society to include the various racial and ethnic minorities as prime contributors to the nation's musical heritage, an inclusion the Custodians were trying to avoid. Given the racist implications of terms like *highbrow* and *lowbrow*, one can readily appreciate the reluctance of some Americans to see jazz as anything other than Pandora's music box.[19]

Yet if the appeal of Culture was exclusive, it was not always racially so. As Levine demonstrates, black music critics in the 1920s were often as prone to denigration of jazz as many of their white counterparts, primarily because they felt it conveyed all the wrong racial connotations. Maud Cuney-Hare (1874–1936) of *The Crisis*, Dave Peyton (ca. 1885–1956) of the *Chicago Defender*, and Lucien H. White of Harlem's *New York Age* all attacked jazz, especially when it began to incorporate melodies derived from sacred music into its repertoire.[20] White classical musicians and critics exhibited a similar hostility when elements from the European tradition began to be absorbed. But not all coverage of jazz was negative. Levine cites Henry Osgood's (1879–1927) *So This is Jazz!* (1926), Gilbert Seldes's (1893–1970) *The Seven Lively Arts* (1924), and conductor Leopold Stokowski (1882–1977) as recognizing jazz as a positive force in expressing and augmenting American culture, providing "new blood," "vitality," and "personal expression."[21] Jazz was "praised and criticized," depending on one's feelings about hierarchical Culture, and thus became attractive to many who were critical of Culture or felt alienated from it.

Predominant among those who sought a means of greater freedom of expression were young people. Levine mentions Milton "Mezz" Mezzrow, the collective membership of the Austin High Gang, and Hoagy Carmichael (1899–1981) as individuals who heard the New Orleans musicians associated with King Oliver in Chicago after 1918 and interpreted their music as a vehicle for personal expression. For some, inherent in the spirit of jazz was a tendency toward revolt, and for many young blacks, jazz provided a sense of "power and control." In time, whether the will to power or the spirit of revolt was foremost or secondary to strictly musical considerations, jazz succeeded in transforming the Culture that sought to exclude it. Jazz musicians were supremely eclectic and refused to make "absolute distinctions between the vernacular and classical traditions." In embracing an unbounded pluralism that ultimately included the full spectrum of world musical traditions, they were "revolutionizing not only music but also the concept of culture."[22] Following Kouwenhoven's cue, Levine sees this transformation as essentially complete by midcentury, by which time jazz was recognized as an art form internationally and, almost by default, at home.

Kathy J. Ogren explores the transformational power of jazz in greater depth in *The Jazz Revolution: Twenties America and the Meaning of Jazz,* which is especially rich in its treatment of the African American community's response to the music as a mode of communication. While writers like Claude McKay (1890–1948), Langston Hughes (1902–1967), and Zora Neale Hurston (1891–1960) found much to emulate in the spirit of jazz, others like W. E. B. DuBois (1868–1963), James Weldon Johnson (1871–1938), and Charles S. Johnson (1893–1956) were more interested in refinements that could bring black music into accordance with Eurocentric standards. In general, these writers of the Harlem Renaissance agreed on the value of jazz as a source of inspiration but differed as to what use to make of it. Jazz split the black community for the same reasons that it troubled many whites: associations with immorality; "primitivist" connotations inimical to Civilization; and concern over whether African American forms could, or should, be integrated into the American mainstream.

Ogren suggests that the association of jazz with immorality and "country ways" created problems for black intellectuals who were attempting to transcend prevailing racial stereotypes. Efforts "to move the debate about jazz away from the conventional moral and racial ground where critics, black and white, tried to keep it" were not entirely successful, precisely because the meaning of jazz went beyond purely musical considerations. As she affirms, "the essence of jazz was what disturbed white (as well as genteel black) critics, just as it was what attracted admirers of the new music."[23] The "participatory" nature of jazz was one of its most essential features, and when considered in terms of the usual "black performer/white audience" schemata, one can appreciate the revolutionary potential of the circumstances of jazz performance, content notwithstanding. "What is striking about the jazz controversy," states Ogren, "is that jazz communicated change across vast racial and cultural dividing lines, despite its development from a participatory and distinct black musical culture."[24] As one might expect, when white Americans debated the vices and virtues associated with jazz, they made strenuous efforts to curb this potential into safer channels such as Paul Whiteman's (1890–1967) "symphonic" jazz, a musical Pygmalion employing jazz soloists to enliven an otherwise huge and often ponderous concert orchestra. It never occurred to the "prudes" and "primitives" of the white world that blacks might have reasons of their own for eschewing white participation as a threat to African American cultural heritage.

Another approach to the problem of the "racial threat" was to claim jazz as a white creation. Given the primacy of the ODJB recordings and the fact that the black New Orleans jazz bands of Kid Ory and King Oliver did not record until 1922 and 1923, respectively, such arguments seemed plausible for many Americans and even persisted well beyond the 1920s.[25] Wishful thinking, along with ignorance of jazz history, accounts for Paul Whiteman's coronation as "King of Jazz" by 1923. Yet Americans had made the same mistake four years earlier, when James Reese Europe (1881–1919) was hailed as "King." White audiences knew Europe as the musical director for the dance team of Vernon and Irene Castle and as chief of the "Hellfighters" orchestra of the black 369th Regiment during World War I. His orchestra was not unlike Whiteman's and was known to carry as many as six pianists at a time. Alarmist commentary in the white press from critics, moralists, and educators usually connected jazz to African American cultural antecedents, often with the dubious corollary that every black American musician was a jazz expert. In an article for *Literary Digest* in 1919, Europe asserted that a New Orleans band led by "Mr. Razz" had started it all around 1904, and this article has been cited as an early example of jazz criticism.[26] However, as Ogren points out, no such band existed, and she speculates that this and a similar story about "Jasbo Brown" in Chicago probably refer to Tom Brown's (1888–1958) Band from Dixieland, which traveled from New Orleans to Chicago and New York in 1915.[27] Despite the speciousness of Europe's testimony, his comments are the only example given by Ogren from a participant in the jazz debates of the 1920s placing the nativity of jazz in New Orleans.

Jazz served the dual gods of communication and miscommunication, depending on the players and the audience. Among the views typical of the white perspective, pro and con, were those stressing the music's ability to "speed up" modern life into a sort of mechanistic frenzy with neurotic overtones; its significance in symbolizing a break with the prewar past; its stimulation of "primitivist" tendencies that were usually equated with sexual liberation; and its retrogressive effects on music education because it presented an "easy" alternative to classical training. Ogren states that by 1930 most Americans thought of jazz as the music played by Whiteman, a cultural "middle ground." In 1924, Whiteman's Aeolian Hall concert in New York showcased a version of what jazz "should be," attracting considerable interest from the city's music critics. Whiteman's strategy was to begin the program with "Livery Stable Blues," then build to the debut of George Gershwin's (1898–1937) "Rhapsody in Blue" in order to demonstrate how far the music had progressed. In his review of the concert, Olin Downes (1886–1955), of the *New York Times,* clearly preferred the "unbuttoned jocosity and Rabelaisian laughter" of the first piece to what followed, which he characterized as "polite."[28] But as Ogren affirms, Downes's peers did not share his views. Whatever the predilections of the combatants in the jazz controversies of the 1920s, the salient characteristic of debate emphasized absolute choices. What was lacking was any suggestion of a relativistic "pluralist" approach that would have allowed Americans to appreciate jazz on its own terms. Ogren sees the jazz controversy as abating by the early 1930s, when the Depression preoccupied American minds; syncopated rhythms became incorporated into the musical mainstream; performance sites shifted toward ballrooms and other, more decorous locations; and professional jazz critics emerged who regarded jazz as an art form.

Among the Custodians of Culture, the music educators of the Ivy League felt particularly threatened by the proliferation of jazz. As scions of the "better" universities, they felt responsible for the development of American music and sought to protect it from contaminating influences. In *Yankee Blues: Musical Culture and American Identity,* MacDonald Smith Moore focuses on the academic response to the jazz craze. Leading the opposition was Daniel Gregory Mason (1873–1953) of Columbia University, who provided grist for the mill of Culture in his formulation of the concept of "redemptive culture," a kind of musical "civil religion" that equated aesthetics with morality in an attempt to realize America's "spiritual potential." This was to music what the City Beautiful Movement of the turn of the century was to urban architecture, except that its xenophobic implications were extreme and exoteric. An essay by Mason entitled "The Jazz Invasion," included in *Behold America* (1931), argued that "jazz is so perfectly adapted to robots that one could be deduced from the other. Jazz is thus the exact musical reflection of modern capitalistic industrialism."[29] But this was only part of the threat. Jazz, as a product of African American culture, represented a sensual laxity that defied the discipline that was the backbone of Mason's Victorian principles. As Moore puts it, "Jazz represented the manifold paradoxes of modern life: hedonism and urban mechanism, the components of consumption capitalism."[30] Yet if Mason's characterization of jazz seemed compelling to the audiences that were disposed to hear it, it did little to account for titles like "Livery Stable Blues" that recalled a premechanical age, complete with the mimicry of barnyard animals by clarinet and trombone.[31]

With the appearance of a new generation of composers such as George Gershwin and Aaron Copland (1900–1990), who were receptive to jazz, Mason and others like him felt that control over America's musical destiny was in jeopardy. The ensuing search for scapegoats, handled in the manner of a witch hunt, was reminiscent of the underside of the Puritan heritage that many of the "Yankee" composers and educators shared. For them, the popularity of jazz was the product of a "Negro-Jewish" conspiracy. Moore describes the perception that "a radical romantic expressionism rooted in the undisciplined hedonism of the black jungle" had combined with the specter of "mechanistic civilization, based on the worship of things." As he states, "The Jewish nexus linked hedonism and mechanism in consumer capitalism through a concern with superficial creature comforts."[32] The use of "mechanistic" metaphors was intended to dehumanize jazz musicians as a prelude to their eradication, a necessary corrective to restore the nation's musical mission.

Yet for jazz lovers, who regarded improvisation as a form of spiritual catharsis, their music could hardly be equated with materialism. It was, instead, a means to avoid the dehumanizing implications inherent in mechanization, urbanization, and industrialization. During the Depression, when dehumanization became the companion of economic deprivation, the spiritual values associated with jazz seemed more important than ever, and the potential for anarchy transcended musical considerations, becoming virulently political with Hoovervilles and other forms of unrest. In the 1930s, jazz inspired a sense of mission that the "redemptive culture" of the ivory tower could not hope to match. Dreams of redemption were all but abandoned, and as if to compound ironies, Moore suggests that when this ideal resurfaced again in the 1960s, it was in the form of black claims that jazz represented the spirit of Black Nationalism in the concept of "soul"—an organic repository of African American identity—extrinsic to white contribution or comprehension.

Each of these historians is concerned with how Americans have succeeded, or failed, in coping with change. It would be a mistake, however, to conclude that historians initiated the analysis of jazz controversies in the 1920s. Sociologists first opened the door that historians only belatedly, though eagerly, transited. As early as 1947, Morroe Berger (1917–1981) led the way with "Jazz: Resistance to the Diffusion of a Cultural Pattern," in *Journal of Negro History*, which then became the basis for more comprehensive treatment by Neil Leonard (b. 1927), whose *Jazz and the White Americans: The Acceptance of a New Art Form* was published in 1962.[33] The strengths of Leonard's book are evident in the extent to which historical works previously cited have either borrowed or developed themes contained in his study.[34] Additionally, Leonard incorporates information on how the centralization of the entertainment industry acted to reduce or exclude access by the bands that later came to be identified as New Orleans–style. The "acceptance of jazz," in other words, was accomplished by dilution of the original impulse into forms like "symphonic" or "swing," more in keeping with what Leonard calls "traditionalist" values, which were also transformed in the process. In his conclusion, Leonard qualifies his thesis: once an innovation has been rendered safe and acceptable through adaptation, it may resurface "in its original state" and become "the basis or rallying point for the resistance to further innovation." It is then perceived as "static" and "formalized" by "modernists" seeking to create new modes of artistic expression. "The pattern of social response to esthetic novelty may begin anew," states Leonard, "often before the earlier innovation has become a fully accepted part of the dominant complex of values."[35] Revivalism is therefore an important part of the dialectic, yet it does not receive full consideration in Leonard's study. On many levels, Leonard's *Jazz and the White Americans* remains the most useful account of the jazz controversies of the 1920s, but subsequent works have added significant detail, especially regarding the response of the African American community and the participatory nature of the music.

What these various depictions of America's response to the proliferation of jazz following World War I show is that there was considerable confusion about what jazz was during the "Jazz Age." Preoccupation with threats to moral and aesthetic imperatives favored by upper- and middle-class Americans meant that jazz could not be regarded simply as a new musical form. Instead, it was dwarfed by its own implications. Paradoxically, jazz symbolized both "primitivism" and modern mechanization; it provided refuge for youngsters alienated from authority, and yet it also reflected the industrial capitalism on which authority was based; it represented the incursion of African American culture but soon became a product of white commercialism. Jazz "sped up" existence but reinforced trends toward increased leisure, driven by affluence and a consumer ethic. In the press, jazz was often associated with large Northeastern metropolises like Chicago and New York, while its Southern origin, particularly its New Orleans connection, was trivialized. This perception may have derived from its explosion upon the American scene via phonograph records, the production of which emanated from the Northeast. Consideration of the cultural context from which jazz had originally emerged, or of regional idiosyncrasies that were rapidly giving way to nationally oriented, centralized culture, was seemingly out of the question.

Of course, had anyone outside of the jazz community chosen to dwell upon the relation of jazz to New Orleans (and the issue was raised, if not widely recognized, because of the first records), local arbiters of taste were ready to do their best to deny it, as an editorial in the June 20, 1918, *New Orleans Times-Picayune* made abundantly clear: "In the matter of jass, New Orleans is particularly interested, since it has been widely suggested that this particular form of musical vice had its birth in this city—that it came, in fact, from doubtful surroundings in our slums. We do not recognize the honor of parenthood, but with such a story in circulation, it behooves us to be the last to accept the atrocity in polite society, and where it has crept in we should make it a point of civic honor to suppress it."[36] These words were prophetic, for the *Times-Picayune* did not reverse its editorial attitude toward jazz until 1961, making it truly the very last to recognize what has since come to be widely regarded as the city's most important contribution to world culture.[37]

It is easy to overstate the case for the social acceptance of jazz before 1940, and a few qualifications are necessary regarding one of the issues raised by Ogren, Leonard, and others—the establishment of "professional" jazz criticism and its salutary effect on the American public. Ronald G. Welburn's "American Jazz Criticism, 1914–1940" supports the contentions of the scholars mentioned above. Welburn states: "In the 1930s the jazz critic came into his own, writing about the major figures in jazz since New Orleans days which were not too far in the past. . . . Despite their individual and collective shortcomings they forged a jazz press of journalistic and aesthetic analysis and established a vocabulary for the critical scrutiny of jazz."[38] Certainly, the contributions of serious students of jazz such as Roger Pryor Dodge (1898–1974), Bernard H. Haggin (1900–1987), and Robert Donaldson Darrell (1903–1988) in the late 1920s were important and helped to prepare the way for the "hot" collector-writers of the 1930s. Dodge's essay "Negro Jazz," in the October 1929 issue of the *Dancing Times*, differentiated between Paul Whiteman's versions and the blues-derived black jazz that Dodge saw as the essential thrust of the new musical style. Writing in the *Nation*, Haggin argued that indigenous American music did not have to conform to classical rubrics to be great art; instead, "a composer must make his music out of the folk and popular music of his country which expresses the emotional character of his people." Haggin was alluding to an American dilemma that had been a concern at least since the early nineteenth century—the fear that the nation lacked an authentic American folk style (beyond slave tunes) comparable to those of most European nations—and he was proffering a remedy in jazz. Darrell, who wrote for *Phonographic Monthly Review*, was a champion of Duke Ellington and helped to institutionalize the record review as "the single most important contribution of jazz criticism to American music criticism."[39] The writings of Dodge, Haggin, and Darrell indicate that some critics were beginning to adumbrate a view of American cultural process consonant with Kouwenhoven's "vernacular" by the late 1920s, but all three were primarily concerned with music other than jazz, and their eclecticism cannot be considered the equivalent of "professional" jazz criticism.

Welburn contends that "the realization of a body of genuine jazz criticism can be understood as the point at which descriptive or analytical reviews of recordings appear in periodicals or newspapers on a regular basis."[40] He sees this development as occurring by the mid-1930s, which is the point at which John Gennari begins his more comprehensive study of the topic, *Blowin' Hot and Cool: Jazz and Its Critics*, with analysis of an excursion to Harlem's Savoy Ballroom undertaken in 1935 by John Hammond and Leonard Feather, the Promethean twin pillars of American jazz criticism. The English expatriate Feather and the scion of the Vanderbilt fortune Hammond ambitiously promoted recognition of jazz as an American art form and derided "the infantile state of U.S. jazz criticism" at the time, acting as "precocious adolescents, chafing against their class and ethno-religious pedigrees," while also being "caught up in an imagined sense of privileged intellectual and emotional communion with the music." Gennari gets to the heart of the matter:

"What's notable is that two ambitious, well-heeled young men would think of jazz not just as something pleasurable, but as something on which to build a career, something to which they could devote their lives. This music was not *just* fun, they insisted: it was serious, it had deep cultural and historical significance that had to be understood and honored, and it was an important force for positive social change."[41]

Within the appendix of *American Jazz Criticism* is Leonard Feather's notable answer to a questionnaire from Welburn. "It may be hard for you to realize," wrote Feather, "but the phrase 'jazz journalist' in 1941 would have seemed like a contradiction in terms, and I'm sure it was never used. I have *never* made my living just as a jazz writer."[42] If one views the gradual coalescence of standards to be the hallmark of "professional" status, it should also be remembered that jazz criticism did not provide its practitioners with a livelihood, so one must conclude that it was an avocation rather than a profession per se. What separates an avocation from a profession might be explained simply as a question of "commitment," particularly in American society, where "interest" is so often translated into monetary terms. Warren I. Susman's *Culture as History: The Transformation of American Society in the Twentieth Century* includes a chapter entitled "Culture and Commitment," which emphasizes the interrelation of these two ideas in the period between the world wars. Focusing primarily on "middle-class America," Susman explains how the linking of "culture" and "commitment" assisted Americans in coping with the experiences of depression and war, allowing them to "make their own world comprehensible" through their "self-conscious awareness" of the importance of these ideas. He clearly identifies with Americans' aspirations to find "a culture that will enable them to deal with the world of experience, and a commitment to forms, patterns, symbols that will make their life meaningful."[43] Within this context, jazz had great symbolic potential. Whether most Americans opposed or supported jazz during the 1920s is still unclear, but the writers who attempted to render jazz comprehensible, first aesthetically and then through the investigation of jazz history, nevertheless saw themselves as a part of an embattled minority.[44] Their sense of commitment carried political overtones, directed against what they construed to be a misinformed and reactionary public, thus placing many of them on the revolutionary left.

Yet, as Susman argues, during the Depression, the left tended to moderate, to gravitate toward the center in espousing tenets of "Americanism." In his discussion of popular arts, he maintains that "it was an era in which participation, or at least a sense of participation, became crucial, whether that participation was in sports, in block parties in urban communities, or in politics itself." Furthermore, Susman contends, "even the Communist Party by 1935 was ready to play its role in an era of adjustment. The Popular Front was no doubt dictated by international as well as national political developments. But in the United States the enthusiastic effort to link Communism and 'Americanism' created a firmer sense of belonging and involvement. The Party linked its movement to historic American tradition. . . . It put ideological conditions to one side and stressed its relationship to the American Way of Life."[45] Critical distinctions between authentic and ersatz jazz were important first steps toward a pro-jazz consensus among writers who linked a purist ethos with Americanism. If jazz was truly an American art form, and the first to be so recognized (constituencies for spirituals and other forms remained underdeveloped by comparison), then the story of what jazz was and how it originated had to be told. What the political left contributed to that undertaking was a sense of possibility through concerted cooperative enterprise, sustaining a belief that the search for America's musical soul had at last found its prize in jazz and that promotion of the music and elucidation of its history was a "righteous cause" deserving of total commitment.

CHAPTER 1

Hot Threshold: A Leftist Writer
and the Righteous Cause

The first American writer to attempt a detailed differentiation of an "original" jazz from subsequent derivatives was Charles Edward Smith, in "Jazz: Some Little Known Aspects," an article appearing in the October 1930 issue of *The Symposium: A Critical Review*. The *Symposium* was a "highbrow" literary publication that began as a "journal of philosophical discussion" but aspired to a broader purpose in attempting to instill "a critical tradition" among the "intellectuals—teachers, critics, etc." that comprised its readership. Its founder and coeditor (with Philip E. Wheelwright) was James Burnham (1905–1987), a professor of philosophy at New York University who was drawn to the left by his colleague Sidney Hook (1902–1989) and ultimately became a leading Trotskyite and theoretician for the Socialist Workers Party.[1] Burnham was still a critic of Marxism when Smith contributed his article on jazz to the journal (the only one it ever published), yet Burnham's 1933 conversion to Marxism may be read as a sign of the times and fairly typical of the intellectual climate of New York City at the time. Subsequent events suggest that Smith's gravitation to the left paralleled Burnham's experience rather closely.

Although Smith was born in Thomaston, Connecticut, he can best be appreciated as a perennial New Yorker, a denizen of the bohemian circles of Greenwich Village where jazz was fashionable. At the time of this publication, he was in his midtwenties and working as a freelance journalist. Unlike many of the other record collectors who began to concern themselves with "real" jazz in the middle part of the decade, Smith was not a college graduate. Jazz impresario Al Rose (1916–1993), who knew Smith in later years, names Carl Van Vechten (1880–1964) as one of his mentors. Like Van Vechten, Smith gained additional knowledge of jazz as a habitué of Harlem nightlife and intellectual circles.[2] As time passed, he became a prolific contributor to jazz letters, with credits such as *Jazzmen: The Story of Hot Jazz Told in the Lives of the Men Who Created It* (1939), *The Jazz Record Book* (1942), and *The Jazz Makers* (1957), along with numerous articles and reviews for publications as diverse as the *New York Times,* the *Daily Worker,* and the *New Republic.* In addition, he wrote scripts in the mid-1930s for *Saturday Night Swing Session,* CBS's first live network jazz program on radio, and collaborated with Frederic Ramsey Jr. in 1942–43 on *Jazz in America,* a radio series for the Office of War Information. He was awarded the Silver Medal for lifetime contribution by *Down Beat* in 1959 and was instrumental in founding the Institute of Jazz Studies, now a world-renowned special collection at Rutgers University. His most enduring professional association during the 1930s, however, was with the Luce Corporation, for *Time* and *Life,* which lasted until the early years of World War II.[3]

"Jazz: Some Little Known Aspects," sandwiched between essays on the poetics of Keats and T. S. Eliot in the *Symposium,* conformed to the rigorous scholarly format that the journal's editors required. In his article, Smith sought to correct what he considered to be the misconceptions surrounding jazz that had fueled previous debate. "It may be said, almost without qualification," he wrote, "that jazz is universally misunderstood, that the men of jazz, those of the authentic minority, have remained obscure to the last." America had misjudged jazz: "A wholesale popularization of what was, at its source, an original contribution to music, has left the world much too bewildered to perceive that this misunderstanding has sprung from essential goodness."[4] Smith continued by defining "popular" or "sweet" music as a banal derivative of "jazz" or "hot" music, ascribing the confusion between the two forms to American "self-consciousness" in the face of English and Continental culture. European recognition of jazz as Americana had led to Whiteman's entrepreneurial exploitation of the music, while "the real thing went on its quiet way, through the gamut of the white men who had inherited it from the early negro blues and, geographically, from New Orleans to Harlem, which today boasts the finest jazz in the country."[5] He saw the origins of jazz in black blues, a folk musical context that he described as "the projection of a people, and this would seem to be the only sensible definition," later stating: "It is no mere accident that folk songs are the touchstone of a people. Music is the medium for essence, as prose is for explanation."[6] In making connections among "hot" jazz, originality, and New Orleans, Smith was fusing aesthetics with historical perspective for the first time, thus introducing historicity into the jazz debates.

If jazz bore some similarity to folk music, this was due to the spiritual nature of improvisation, the vehicle by which a jazz musician revealed his essence. For Smith, solo improvisation was the music's essential feature, what made it "hot." Americans had failed to comprehend jazz, he argued, because original compositions are often objected to precisely on account of their originality, which transcends the limitations of conventional musical culture as it is generally understood. History could be used to illustrate the spiritual appeal of jazz, "so that the interested reader may know why the boys in Harlem sit near portable phonographs listening to choruses *ad libitum* by Bix Biederbecke [*sic*] and Jimmy Dorsey." Commitment to the music could explain "why a collector of this sort of Americana is reported to have paid one hundred and fifty dollars for a blues record of which the master had been destroyed."[7] The roots of jazz were an admixture of English folk ballads and African rhythms transmitted by "colored mammies," then the spread of sacred blends diluted through the "exploitation of the Chautauqua circuit," through the blues via composers such as "Williams, a negro composer [who] wrote *Royal Garden Blues*," to white jazz bands like the Wolverines, who "established a precedent in the rendering of this piece that has never been surpassed."[8] In describing Bix Beiderbecke's (1903–1931) band, the Wolverines (who, he notes, were called "white niggers"), Smith emphasized the "ad lib." chorus, "a tradition of uncertain origins in jazz bands," and marveled at the band's "fidelity to the medium," because "they themselves felt as a reality the spirit of the negro blues."[9]

Throughout the article Smith recapitulated the names and song titles of various white and black jazz bands but showed a curious propensity to categorize blacks as "blues" and whites as "jazz." Vic Berton (1896–1951) of the Red Heads, a white band, was "by far the greatest drummer in jazz," and a great deal of praise was lavished on Loring "Red" Nichols (1905–1965), the band's leader. Commercial considerations had increasingly forced such white bands to mix "hot" and "sweet" ("Wine and Water!"), and in a footnote Smith described blacks as affected as well: "Louis Armstrong, at present the only outstanding figure in jazz, succumbs more and more to the white man's notion of Harlem jazz. His record of *Ain't Misbehavin'* is a case in point. My contention is that when *hot* bands turn corny they are much, much worse than *sweet* bands could be. There is nothing so disgusting to the musical palate as a simulated ad lib. chorus."[10] Commercial compromise negated the integrity of improvisation and denied its spiritual essence. Even so, Smith hailed Louis Armstrong's studio group (the Hot Seven, which no longer existed) as "undoubtedly the most important band in jazz today," for "the Negro," he wrote, "if not thwarted, affirms life, exults in the simple, emotional joys of being."[11] This spirit was what white youths of the 1920s were trying to experience vicariously in dances like the Black Bottom and the Varsity Drag—an exercise in "excitation and sublimation." But Smith concluded by declaring that the dancing days of the 1920s were merely an interlude, "one glorious night," before the readjustments of the Depression set in. "Hot" jazz was now an endangered species.

Evident in "Jazz: Some Little Known Aspects" are two concepts that had great bearing on the subsequent development of early jazz histories. Intrinsic to the category "hot" was a purist impulse that became known as the "righteous cause" as the decade of the 1930s unfolded. The cause was "righteous" because it affirmed the spirituality found in sincere improvisation—the expression of feeling from the heart. The negative image of this concept was "sweet," the product of a commercialism dominated by Eurocentric standards. "Noncommercial" music (also including "folk") was therefore more representative of the American spirit, revealing the character of the people as they *were,* instead of as they *should be.* Purism was akin to cultural patriotism, with "hot" providing the threshold for the discovery of American character in jazz.

But if Charles Edward Smith was beginning to make these connections in 1930, he was still far from attaining the level of historical detail needed to understand the emergence of jazz in New Orleans. His *Symposium* article presents no evidence of any grasp of what came to be identified as New Orleans style. The improvisation he celebrated was not the "collective improvisation" that he would later extol as one of the hallmark characteristics of New Orleans–style jazz. He alluded to African rhythmic roots, which he characterized as "naiveté of rhythm," but showed little appreciation for the complexities of polyrhythmic syncopation or the dynamic subtleties associated with New Orleans bands. Most of Smith's treatment of jazz composition centered on whites like Leon Roppolo (1902–1943), Arthur Schutt (1902–1965), Elmer Schoebel (1896–1970), Hoagy Carmichael, and Red Nichols. While blacks like W. C. Handy (1873–1958), Joe Oliver, and Jelly Roll Morton were mentioned, reference to the composer of "Royal Garden Blues" as "Williams" (Clarence [1893–1965] or Spencer [ca. 1889–1965]?) suggests that this information was taken from the composer credit on a record label, where first names were rarely given. One must infer from the combination of omissions and emphasis on white and studio ensembles (with the occasional nod to their black counterparts on "race" records) that the better part of the research for the article was conducted on Smith's phonograph turntable.

In retrospect, one can appreciate how limited and haphazard Smith's exposure to New Orleans artists had actually been. The recordings of Armstrong and Oliver that were discussed tended to be those of the late 1920s, by which time both had all but abandoned the idiomatic style (much of it grounded in collective improvisation) that had characterized Oliver's Creole Jazz Band in 1923 and Armstrong's Hot Five in 1926. The classic performances of Jelly Roll Morton and his Red Hot Peppers for Victor in the period 1926–30, the work of Johnny Dodds's (1892–1940) Washboard bands and Black Bottom Stompers for various "race" labels in 1927–28, and the activities of Sidney Bechet (1897–1959) were either unknown to Smith or considered unworthy of inclusion. With the possible exception of Armstrong, all of these artists experienced difficulties in finding employment during the Depression, and while it is tempting to ponder the possibility that mention in Smith's article might have proved helpful, it is still unlikely that one voice crying in the wind could have made a significant difference.

Yet Smith had certainly heard enough to motivate further action, and his heart was definitely in the right place. He seemed to grasp the effect of commercial pressures on jazz artists, both black and white, and was clearly sympathetic to their plight. What reads as an undercurrent of resentment against "sweet" and "corny" tendencies in *Symposium* later emerged as leftist rhetoric in the pages of the *Daily Worker.* Of course, one of the most basic tenets of Marxism is that members of the bourgeois intelligentsia who have been converted to the cause should serve as educators and advocates of the proletariat in the class struggle. Accordingly, in "Class Content of Jazz Music," which he contributed to the October 21, 1933, edition of the *Daily Worker,* Smith gave jazz purism a Marxist tinge in a riposte directed against editor Michael Gold (1893–1967), offering an analysis that became the basis for the official position of the Soviet Communist Party on jazz as "the music of the proletariat." That a foreign government should take an interest in jazz was certainly a strange and unexpected development, especially considering the ambivalence of American attitudes. That the government in question should be that of the Soviet Union, which sought to use the music as an instrument of policy, underscored the idea that jazz could serve as a revolutionary agent of cultural change.

The story of Soviet Communist Party interest in jazz is ably reconstructed by S. Frederick Starr in *Red and Hot: The Fate of Jazz in the Soviet Union, 1917–1980,* a provocative survey of jazz in a most un-American environment.[12] Starr traces the growing popularity of jazz under pluralistic cultural policies until 1928, when Josef Stalin's First Five-Year Plan began to take its toll on the arts as part of a wider cultural revolution. Maxim Gorky's anti-jazz predilections became the gospel of the Association of Proletarian Musicians following a *Pravda* article in April 1928 that characterized jazz as "music of the gross," the epitome of bourgeois decadence. Unfortunately, the quest for a viable proletarian alternative proved to be more difficult than expected, and when the Nazis inaugurated a campaign to eradicate jazz from Germany, reconsideration of the Soviet policy was in order.[13] The solution to this quandary presented itself in the theoretical division of jazz into two parts—one bourgeois and the other proletarian—a perspective that was similar to the "sweet" and "hot" distinctions made by Charles Edward Smith in 1930. What resulted was a shotgun marriage that combined the dichotomization of jazz with policies proposed by the Sixth Congress of the Comintern in 1928 to recognize Southern blacks as an oppressed minority and to call for the establishment of a Black Republic of the South.[14] Starr concludes: "The Cultural Revolution had begun by condemning jazz and concluded by rehabilitating it. What remained to be seen was whether Soviet jazz would continue to develop 'from below' with a degree of spontaneity, or whether official vindication of jazz would prompt the regime to take it over and shape its further evolution 'from above,' along lines more compatible with recent

Communist puritanism."[15] As it happened, this was precisely the question Smith sought to address in "Class Content of Jazz Music," as a corrective to editorials written by Michael Gold.

Michael Gold (born Itzok Granich) is described by Irving Howe and Lewis Coser as "a raw, totally sincere, simpleminded radical," but Daniel Aaron provides a more balanced assessment in *Writers on the Left: Episodes in American Literary Communism*.[16] Gold's animosity toward capitalist exploitation of "African art" in the form of jazz informed poems such as "The Skunks of Jazz," which appeared in his "What a World" column of the *Daily Worker*.[17] Smith, in "Class Content," declared that "the conclusions on jazz music published in Michael Gold's column recently have not been as clear-cut as possible" and that he was therefore "permitted" to contribute his own views on the subject. Referring to previous comments by another contributor to the paper, Dale Curran (1898–1971), that jazz reflected black reaction to "white chauvinism," and that it was of American, not African, origin, Smith offered a "correct analysis" through the study of class relations. Citing resolutions from the Sixth Congress of the Comintern, he described how blacks were transformed from slaves to serfs and proletarians following the Civil War, by which time their original folk music had also been adapted into spirituals and work songs, the latter being the first music of proletarian content in America. The welding of these two strains with popular music brought forth the blues and, soon after, jazz, both of which exhibited "blue notes" and a decidedly folklike lyrical quality. No sooner had these forms been introduced by men of "diverse racial origins: Handy, Clarence and Spencer Williams, Russel Robinson, Rapollo, Callahan, La Rocca, Beiderbecke, etc.—than their spontaneous folk quality became designated in the realm of jazz by the term hot. This applied equally to slow blues and to very fast stomps. It referred not to tempo but to quality."[18] "Hot" jazz conveyed an originality of expression and sincerity that Comrade Gold should admire.

Smith found "hot" music in the dance halls of the proletariat and its origins in the "jug and washboard bands of the South," but it was not prevalent: "The hot element in jazz was then and continues to be an isolated phenomenon. This phenomenon has its basis in the class struggle. Hot jazz aims to be genuinely the folk expression of a people. It has its roots in the denial of the American Negro of 'the right of self-determination.' However, it is exclusively Negro music neither in origin nor in expression. To assert this would certainly be to fall into an extremist error."[19] "Sweet" music, in contrast, was "folk music from above" (a commercial manipulation of originally expressive material), pandering to shallow emotions, wish fulfillment, and stupefaction. It added "immeasurably to the dung-heap of bourgeois propaganda" and threatened to contaminate "hot" jazz. Ten years earlier, college boys "who could afford it" had collected "hot," aware that "hot jazz and hot musicians were usually of proletarian origin." If jazz was then decried as shallow emotionalism, they knew better. Attempts by "capitalist oppressors" to trivialize and commercialize jazz showed that the class struggle proceeds on the cultural as well as the economic front, and the survival of genuinely "hot" jazz indicated "the growing class consciousness of the masses," a prognosis that rested on shaky ground.

As Susman has convincingly argued, the very idea of culture that Smith was seeking to employ in the name of class-consciousness could undercut the ends that he envisioned. Despite a general movement to the left by the intelligentsia in the 1930s, the result was not intensification of class-consciousness or conflict in broad terms. While the idea of culture could be put to effective critical use, especially in calling attention to the "meaninglessness of an urban-industrial civilization," it was often conservative in its application. Searching for an "authentic" American culture "could become a new kind of nationalism" reinforcing conformist tendencies. According to Susman, the kind of culture patterns that became associated with concepts of "an American Way"—the development of public opinion; studies of myth, symbol, and folklore; and the proliferation of the mass media—"could and did have results far more conservative than radical, no matter what the intentions of those who originally championed some of the ideas and efforts."[20] If "hot" jazz was the equivalent of a "righteous cause" to be protected from capitalist manipulation by a handful of writers who sought to safeguard its folk virtues in the name of a proletarian ethic, it still remained a commodity that had to compete with other forms of music in an increasingly centralized American marketplace. No one realized this better than Joe Oliver, Jelly Roll Morton, Sidney Bechet, and especially Louis Armstrong, as they attempted to make ends meet during the Depression. Their stake in the survival of what Smith was calling "hot" jazz was second to none. With the possible exception of Morton, they chose adaptation over extinction.

In assigning class-consciousness to jazz musicians and their audience,

Smith was conforming to the Stalinist party line and ignoring the proclivity of many jazzmen to give the public whatever they desired, without regard to ideology, because they were paying for it. But Smith's views contrasted markedly with those of Michael Gold, whom Starr sees as more influential, especially on the question of jazz origins.[21] Gold emphasized a Negro-Jewish nexus in his explanation of how jazz originated and developed, characterizing the music as a common reaction to oppression.[22] For Smith, however, Gold had embraced an "extremist error," and the more pluralistic emphasis of "Class Content of Jazz Music" placed Smith at odds with the official position of the Communist Party. Furthermore, while Smith did identify "hot" jazz as "folk music from below," the definition of the term supplied in his *Symposium* article leads one to believe that if the concept of "vernacular" had been available, he would have used it. Indeed, it was the leftists' misfortune to be saddled with a terminology that had been co-opted by the Custodians of Culture, their fascist nemeses. The limits of terminology placed leftists at the same disadvantage as the Custodians in their attempts to make changing cultural patterns conform to an anachronistic categorical hierarchy.

Using Starr's *Red and Hot* as a touchstone, James Lincoln Collier has challenged the leftist perception of jazz as folk music in "The Faking of Jazz: How Politics Distorted the History of the Hip," a critique of doctrinaire jazz history published in the *New Republic* in 1985.[23] Both Starr and Collier argue that jazz was commercial from the outset (seemingly denying the possibility that jazz could be both folk and commercial), and Collier completely rejects the leftist notion that the music was "despised and neglected" by whites. He rightly points out that many of the first jazz bands to go North and West were contracted by white entrepreneurs as "novelty music for white audiences," not necessarily drawn out as a consequence of black migration, "as has universally been believed." Such experience applied to both white and black bands: "Freddie Keppard on the Orpheum circuit, King Oliver at jitney dance halls in California and elsewhere, the Original Dixieland Jazz Band . . . were all playing for segregated white audiences."[24]

Yet it is clear that Charles Edward Smith did not subscribe to the Communist view that jazz was *of* black culture and *for* black audiences alone, and Collier's critique of leftist jazz writers fails to take Smith's singularity into account: "[John] Hammond wrote for the *New Masses*, [Otis] Ferguson for THE NEW REPUBLIC, Charles Edward Smith for the *Daily Worker*, B. H.

Haggin for *The Nation,* and many of them were deeply involved in causes important to the left—the Pittsburgh coal strike, the Scottsboro trial, and black rights in general. These men were the primary writers on jazz of the time, and they were giving the music sensitive and perceptive coverage. They were also, however, altering facts to make them consistent with their political views."[25] For those who championed the cause of black rights and lamented the practices of record companies that relegated black artists to "race" markets in the 1920s, the opportunities provided by the leftist press were often the only viable outlets available to them.[26] Prevailing conditions, however, did not mean that leftist jazz writers were incapable of independent thought or that they were interested in jazz solely for ideological reasons.

The responses to Collier's *New Republic* article show that some writers felt no compulsion to make their musical preferences a political issue. B. H. Haggin's letter in the December 16, 1985, issue of the *New Republic* is a case in point. Referring to his past connections with "the Bliven/Cowley *New Republic*" and "the Kirchway/Del Vayo *Nation,*" Haggin denied ever having been asked to support particular political views by the editors, whose positions he often opposed: "I was not asked by the magazines to support . . . any view of the world of jazz. I wrote about what interested me in jazz, which was not the world around it but the music I heard in it." Haggin's conversion to jazz derived from hearing recordings by Armstrong's Hot Five in 1932—a didactic experience that "corrected the mistaken idea of jazz that Gilbert Seldes's writing in the 1920s had implanted." Seldes's enthusiasm for Paul Whiteman's "slick performances" had left Haggin unimpressed, but Armstrong's "improvisatory performances by small groups" had a telling effect. What the classically oriented critic found appealing in Armstrong was "the fascinating and exciting experience of moment-to-moment working of a creative mind with an inventive exuberance controlled by a sense for coherent developing form."[27] Collier's presumption of a kind of doctrinaire consensus among leftist jazz writers begins to break down when individual concerns are taken into account. Haggin, for example, liked jazz for simply musical reasons, but his feelings about the magazines to which he was contributing were contradictory and complex because he objected to their policy on Stalinism. When one discusses political categories like "the left" within the context of Depression America, even before the onset of Popular Front policies after 1935, assumptions asserting monolithic attitudes always create problems.

Even the question of black rights, which some leftist jazz writers, particularly John Hammond, turned into a kind of fetish, was not universally promoted by the political left. In an interview with Ron Welburn, Hammond commented on how differences within the ranks of leftist magazines affected personal and professional relationships. The editors of the *New Masses* had explicitly promised that his copy would not be tampered with when he signed on, but Hammond severed relations with the magazine in 1937 because it could not tolerate his attacks on left-wing labor unions that discriminated against blacks.[28] Collier states that "the political views of these men—and the papers they wrote for—forced them to regard the world of jazz around them in a particular way," but he seems to take for granted that their viewpoints were therefore consistent with political ideology.[29] At a time when ideological considerations were being relaxed in the name of the Popular Front, such inconsistencies were inevitable, and Hammond's commentary reinforces Haggin's contention that disagreements were openly tolerated, if not indefinitely.

Indeed, the House of Marx had many mansions. The fractious nature of American communism was, perhaps, its most evident characteristic.[30] On this subject, the experiences of Al Rose are particularly revealing, not only because of his lifelong intimacy with jazz as a cause célèbre but also because of his personal explorations within the environs of American communism.[31] Rose was born in New Orleans but left home at an early age to travel as a vagabond artist and jack-of-all-trades. In 1936, he was a student at Temple University when he began to produce a series of jazz concerts at the Philadelphia Academy of Music (well before Hammond's "Spirituals to Swing" concerts at Carnegie Hall) that put him into contact with New Orleans musicians, both black and white. In the same year, he became a Lovestoneite communist, eventually traveling to New York to receive his Marxist indoctrination at the New Workers School (which boasted murals by Diego Rivera, with whom Rose studied). He contributed to *Workers Age,* organized rent strikes in Harlem with Andy Razaf (1895–1973), and became involved with labor politics when he returned to Philadelphia.[32] With American entry into World War II, the right opposition disintegrated virtually overnight; Rose joined the Trotskyites, first as a member of Max Shachtman's (1904–1972) group and then as part of the alternative wing led by C. L. R. James (1901–1989), before being drafted. Although his affiliation with the left began later than that of Smith, Hammond, and Haggin, his path intersected with theirs on many occasions, and he knew Hammond and Smith personally. Like Smith, he emphasized the biracial development of jazz, a belief that set them both apart from Hammond.

According to Rose, the only jazz writers who were ideologically motivated were Stalinists such as Michael Gold and, later, Sidney Finkelstein, whose copy for *Jazz: A People's Music* (1948) "probably went through a political committee before it was submitted."[33] Trotskyites tended to have little interest in jazz (Rose was an exception). What was most noticeable about American communists who wrote on jazz was their overwhelmingly middle-class character: "You don't make a proletarian revolutionary movement out of petty bourgeois elements."[34] Rose describes their commitment to the music as "emotional," the product of enthusiasm, rather than "intellectual," in the guise of ideology. He consistently identifies jazz as the music of "a place and not a race" and depicts John Hammond as the archetype of young writers of the 1930s who sought to invert this relationship (carrying the torch lit by Carl Van Vechten) by emphasizing the special qualities of black artists, often to the exclusion of whites, who were therefore overlooked. In his interview with Welburn, Hammond reiterated that he was not a Communist Party member, unlike *New Masses* writers such as Jim Dugan (who was) and editor Fred Dupuy, who left the party to join the Trotskyites.[35] Rose supports this assertion, intimating that Hammond did not become a Communist until 1940, when the Stalin-Hitler Pact fell apart, although Hammond denied *ever* becoming a party member.[36]

Rose did not know Charles Edward Smith in 1933, when he was writing in the *Daily Worker*, but by 1939 Smith was decidedly "liberal" in his estimation (a Roosevelt Democrat). Perhaps, as for many leftists of the 1930s, Stalinist atrocities during the purges in the Soviet Union and in Spain had led to Smith's disenchantment.[37] Rose's experience with the Lovestoneites after Pearl Harbor seems to indicate that many leftists of the middle class sought the shelter of the middle ground, if not the far right, when the going got rough.[38] In his assessment of Smith, Rose paints a portrait of a man whose "whole fight was to try and stay sober," while other commentators depict Smith as "undependable."[39] On a more positive note, Smith is also portrayed as embodying a sort of Madison Avenue mentality, exhibiting the style of a writer who knew how to pitch to the preferences of the audience he was addressing. Such portrayals help to explain the stylistic divergence between Smith's *Symposium* essay, which is an appeal to former flappers, bathed in nostalgia, and his piece in the *Daily Worker,* which fashions a symbiosis between syncopation and class-consciousness. Yet whether his Marxism represented an evolution in his thinking or merely reflected the requirements of a new assignment, by 1933 Smith's ability to reach a broad range of readers in advocating for "hot" jazz was impressive, and he was just getting started.

As Collier freely admits, "to what extent the jazz writers were aware of the Comintern policy is impossible to know."[40] To be sure, Starr's and Collier's critiques of leftist jazz writers are helpful in providing a context for understanding their reaction to a society that seemed to discard the elements of jazz that were most worthwhile to them, but they are not very satisfying explanations of what attracted such writers to jazz in the first place. Smith, Hammond, Haggin, and Rose all opposed the Stalinist party line at times, and it is unlikely that dialectical materialism attracted any of them to a music whose appeal was primarily spiritual in their eyes. Certainly, if there is an explanation for Charles Edward Smith's dedication to the "righteous cause," it is not likely to be found in political ideology. One did not have to be a Communist to grasp the oppression confronting blacks in America, and Smith's belief that jazz originated in the hearts and minds of "niggers" of diverse ethnicities set his views apart from the those of Michael Gold and the Communist Party. As he slowly gravitated toward an understanding of the culture from which jazz had emerged, Smith came to realize increasingly how geography, chronology, and personality had intersected to create a rare musical beauty, worthy of commitment. If we really want to know from whence that commitment came, we can forget about Marxism and take a look at Smith's "hot" record collecting.

Pioneer jazz writers such as Charles Edward Smith were not only inspired to advocacy by their jazz records but actually derived power from them. Academics who have theorized the implications of white men collecting recordings of black music and the value of records as artifacts bear this out, albeit in very different ways. In "Revenge of the Nerds: Representing the White Male Collector of Black Music," Krin Gabbard describes "serial collecting" of jazz and blues records as a means of establishing masculine identity, "homo-social" networks, and power, noting that the collector "works at acquiring a commanding knowledge that can be carefully deployed in the right surroundings. The display of authoritative information, especially when it has been acquired outside of 'bureaucratized institutions of knowledge,' is a well established sign of masculine power in contemporary American culture."[41]

Gabbard is interested in the transracial mediation of identity that occurs when black music is collected by white men and how this relates to aesthetic preferences: "Insisting on the superiority of 'black' over 'white' styles allows the jazz fan to claim the moral and political high ground in a racist culture." Citing Scott DeVeaux's "Constructing the Jazz Tradition," he contends that "the well-established myth of jazz as an autonomous art is especially useful here because it shifts the debate into primarily aesthetic territory," thus allowing white collectors to sublimate the "homoerotic and voyeuristic" tendencies that are implied in expropriation of the black masculine identity of their musical heroes, against which they can never effectively compete. A more ecumenical appreciation of white and black artists, such as that exhibited by Charles Edward Smith, only serves to complicate (but not appreciably change) the situation for Gabbard, who sees such interest as "embracing the work of white men who have built their careers on appropriating the styles of black musicians." Gabbard's analysis of jazz record collecting in terms of the power it confers and the limits of that power is persuasive, but conditioning authenticity in jazz entirely on race can be problematical, as will be seen.

In considering jazz records as artifacts, Jed Rasula offers alternative insights into how record collecting relates to the writing of history and the conceptualization of jazz aesthetics. He sees jazz as "a unique subject for historians because of the nature and quantity of a certain kind of artifact, the sound recording," while also warning that "historians have tended to avoid theorizing the actual status and function of these artifacts."[42] Although Rasula's intent is to demonstrate how recordings challenge historians because of their variable utility in clarifying or distorting issues such as chronology, instrumentation, influence, composition, and extent of improvisation in performance practices, his primary target is the myth of progress, the same shibboleth that Scott DeVeaux decries in post-1950s jazz history surveys. The act of writing jazz history, with its teleological inclinations, is "positioned as a struggle between grapho-centrism and its phono-eccentric phantom." In short, writing jazz history is a white, Eurocentric approach that *confers* authority, while recordings are a black, Afromorphic medium that *contains* authority. As Rasula contends, "the customary approach in jazz history has been to submerge discussion of records in a narrativized package of sociological information in ways that obscure the fact that recordings are the actual subject, not the music as such."

Rasula's argument that jazz historians have both overestimated and underestimated the value of recordings as artifacts is certainly well taken. Yet, for those "hot" record collectors whose first knowledge of jazz came exclusively from recordings, the impulse to treat such objects as fetishes rendered them intrinsically *actual* in the sense that they were the only things that *made jazz real*. Charles Edward Smith's article in *Symposium* is a case in point. In addition, jazz records activated a sense of existential purpose that brought young white men into a reflexive relationship with black vernacular culture, permitting them to lose and then find themselves in the power of black music without risking much more than their preconceptions. (Of course, the next step would be to experience the music live.) Such objects could effectively serve the cause of Clio if one did not expect too much from them.

The power that Charles Edward Smith derived from his jazz record collection did not provide answers to the questions of jazz history, but it did impel him to do the work necessary to find those answers. Moreover, that work would not lead to teleological evolutionary perspectives in which the phonographic "evidence" could further seduce or mislead him; on the contrary, Smith and his "hot" collector colleagues set out to explore the pre-phonographic phase of jazz history in New Orleans in order to verify the jazz credentials of a cultural environment where "variegation, excess, deviance, and singularity" flourished within a decidedly eccentric and polyglot population. If Smith relied on his "hot" record collection for clues along the way, it was not to his detriment, because collecting records was merely the prelude to personal contact with a myriad of New Orleans musicians (white, black, and Creole) whose memories and attitudes about the origins and "evolution" of jazz would fundamentally change his understanding of what jazz was and why it was important.

CHAPTER 2

Discovering New Orleans Style:
The Writers of the Wax Wing

On May 7, 1982, there occurred at Tulane University's Dixon Hall an event that was at once culturally significant and obscure. Assembled before a half-filled auditorium was the panel of "The Jelly Roll Morton Symposium," a group that included several generations of jazz scholars who had either known Morton personally or had made him a focal point of their research. The graying "Young Turk" of the panel was Lawrence Gushee (b. 1931), of the University of Illinois at Urbana-Champaign, a Yale Ph.D. who would soon publish his findings on the nativity and early career of the composer/pianist.[1] William Russell and Richard B. Allen (1927–2007) were also present; together they had conducted nearly fifteen hundred reels of oral history interviews with assorted New Orleans jazzmen and had helped to found the Hogan Jazz Archive of Tulane University, the primary repository of documents for the study of New Orleans jazz. Al Rose was there, as was musician/writer Danny Barker, a New Orleans Creole who had worked with Jelly Roll and the only person of African heritage on the panel. Frederic Ramsey Jr. had worked with Russell and Charles Edward Smith on *Jazzmen* and was the man primarily responsible for its publication. But the participant who clearly dominated the discussion was Alan Lomax, the folklorist who had been Morton's first biographer, basing his work on the Library of Congress interviews he had conducted in 1938. Despite the individual differences revealed by the members of the panel as the program unfolded, it was clear that Lomax was acting as the unofficial spokesman for the group.

Such an illustrious assemblage of pioneer jazz experts was a rare occurrence, and in addressing the reasons why, Lomax made a point of mentioning that there was one individual whose presence was sorely missed: "There's been a tremendous opposition in this country to the study of American culture. . . . I'm making the point that the whole United States has only very gradually accepted the fact that we had a culture that was a legitimate thing to study. . . . This has been our history. We represent the first wave of criticism of an American musical tradition. We're almost all present; Charlie Smith, the dear boy, isn't here. But, after all, everybody here can tell stories about how little interest there's been in learning about how the first world musical language was invented in its capital here in New Orleans. And that's been typical of the attitude of the whole country toward its own native culture. It still is, by the way, it still is."[2] This was the message that Smith had spent the better part of his life trying to convey prior to his death in 1970, and Lomax did not refer to him inadvertently. The very fact that they were "almost" all there, talking about a thoroughly brilliant but disreputable piano player from New Orleans, meant that Smith's dedication to his "righteous cause" had not been entirely in vain. As Lomax was quick to observe, however, the war was far from being won. Sometimes a lifetime is not enough.

Individual effort, though often gloriously conspicuous, is rarely a match for a well-entrenched enemy, be it as tangible as a capitalist elite or as abstract as ignorance. In either case, there is strength in numbers, which is why historians study reform under the rubric of "movements" and advocate for ideologies. The movement to which Charles Edward Smith belonged has often been dismissed as a "hobby" or, worse, a cult. Like Smith, five of the eight panelists appearing at the Morton Symposium began their careers as "hot" record collectors, prospectors whose desire to learn about the lives and music of their favorite jazzmen led them to scour the countryside in search of the rare find. There was something about the ephemeral nature of a jazz performance once etched in wax but no longer commercially available that captivated the imagination. That such gems were considered to be little more than refuse by the merchants who had originally made them only increased their value in the eyes of collectors.

"Hot" record collecting resulted from the symbiosis of jazz with an incipient phonograph industry. The technology revolutionized consumption of music and permitted acolytes to experience jazz mechanically in their parlors, some achieving initial exposure as teenagers with ODJB records in 1917–18. Whatever the source, however, jazz could create controversy in bourgeois households because it was seen as antithetical to social order.[3] Although the producers of early jazz recordings, the Victor Talking Machine Company and the Columbia Phonograph Company, were eager to satisfy public demand for musical novelty, especially when the records sold well, they withdrew as jazz became controversial. The task of documenting innovation thus fell to small, independent companies such as OKeh, Paramount, and Gennett, which developed "race" series that enhanced the fetish appeal for youngsters intent on rebellion or vicarious thrills. "Hot" jazz records were the perfect fetish objects because they provided access to "forbidden" music without necessitating risky personal contact and were a commodity that could be possessed. Of course, in time, jazz record collectors were only too willing to abandon the parlor in favor of the nightclub and cabaret, but the phonograph always led the way. During the initial wave of jazz recording activity before 1926, African American and Creole musicians from New Orleans such as King Oliver, Jelly Roll Morton, and especially Louis Armstrong predominated in the independent catalogs before being picked up by the majors. Changing fashion, the rise of radio, and the implosion of the phonograph record market in advance of the Depression, however, acted to remove most of the New Orleans artists (except Armstrong) from record company rosters by 1931. Consequently, their discontinued recordings became exceedingly rare as collector's items. More to the point, stylistic developments, such as Armstrong's ascendance with masterpieces such as "West End Blues" in 1928, furthered recognition of jazz as art, making its documents valuable.

What began in New Orleans as "good dance music" now became the subject of intense scrutiny and analysis through listening to records—a key to American identity that emphasized the contributions of African Americans. As advocates of the "righteous cause," "hot" jazz collectors determined to control public opinion on jazz in order to defend black cultural achievement and counter the claims of conservative pundits, preachers, and prudes that it represented immorality, neurosis, and other forms of aberrant behavior. There was thus a ready audience for writers such as Charles Edward Smith, whose 1930 *Symposium* article not only established the outline for "hot" collector ideology but also disseminated it broadly within a youth market keen on combining amusing pastimes with a degree of social responsibility. By positioning themselves as critics, writers, and historians within a nascent "jazz press," collectors used the music's status as art to claim legitimacy, quell debate, and establish hierarchies of value based on areas of specialization that served their interests.

The origins of "hot" record collecting as an organized movement can be traced to the Ivy League college campuses of the 1920s, particularly Princeton and Yale. The Princeton cadre was composed of a professor and three students: Albion Patterson (1904–1996), Albert McVitty (1908–1980), Edwin "Squirrel" Ashcraft (1905–1981), and Augusto Centeno (1901–1965). They collected recordings by Bix Beiderbecke, the New Orleans Rhythm Kings, and Red Nichols. In 1927, Patterson and Centeno collaborated on *Boy in a Tuxedo*, a play that introduced successive characters by the playing of a different "hot" record for each. Their idea was rejected in favor of Shakespeare. Soon after, another student discovered some Armstrong records, adding him to the pantheon. At Yale, Wilder Hobson (1906–1964) and John Hammond led a parallel movement, but their preferences centered on black artists like Duke Ellington (1899–1974) and Fletcher Henderson (1897–1952). Although the Yale group came together after its Princeton counterpart, Hammond may have been the first to embrace jazz; well before his college days, in 1923, he had heard the Georgians at Lyon's Corner House in London.[4]

Charles Edward Smith's first "hot" experience came approximately five years after Hammond's, through the influence of a Princetonian who came to New York for a weekend visit. The record in question was the Red Heads' "Nervous Charlie," and Smith's account evokes F. Scott Fitzgerald: "This was at a Greenwich Village party which I also have occasion to remember because a couple mistook an upstairs room for a haystack and left the shade up. When the cops came we thought it was because of the hullabaloo and hooch and we hastily poured our prohibition booze into the house plants, making them really potted, and repaired in what dignity we had left to the speakeasy."[5] Smith returned the visit to his "hot" mentor at Princeton and listened to Armstrong's Hot Fives. Afterward, he began to prospect for records in Salvation Army warehouses and bought Gennetts "under the counter" because they were "race" labels. Derek Langridge, a student of "hot" collecting, describes the challenges confronting the prospectors: "To understand what collecting was like in those days (approximately 1925–1935) we have to imagine a time when the history of the music had not been explored, when there were no books as guides and above all no discographies. The early collector's knowledge was hard-earned, but he did have the exciting prospect of finding previously unknown recordings."[6]

Langridge provides a revealing portrait of the collector mentality. A dual impulse to classification and specialization inheres in the hobby—one creates order and establishes preferences rather than trying to collect everything. "The most fundamental distinction," states Langridge, "is between vintage collectors and the rest. Vintage collecting is not a precise category, because the antiquarian interest manifests itself in two ways. In the first place it consists of a preference for earliest forms of the music, and in the second place it includes an interest in old records as physical objects and particularly in first editions."[7] For vintage collectors, in-depth historical research is necessary to identify personnel, a prelude to the categorization and classification of styles that enables evaluation through charting of the music's history. Collectors had to write their own histories where none existed, and given their interests, purism would be an occupational hazard. In addition, the enhanced value (not always monetary) that accrues to an artifact when the culture that it documents has ceased to exist meant that collectors had an interest in investigating regional cultural context.

Given the ineluctable erosion of rural and regional cultures in the United States over the course of the twentieth century, one can therefore appreciate the nostalgic sense in which writers like Charles Edward Smith used the term *folk* to explain the origins of jazz. "Folk," "popular," and "art" were conceived as strictly defined categories predicated upon hierarchical social relationships tied to dichotomies like rural-urban, professional-unprofessional, and commercial-artistic. "Folk" was therefore defined as rural and unprofessional, as though each category existed beyond the effects of time or change. But in the twentieth century, the American folk were changing, undergoing radical transformations accompanying the urbanization, mechanization, and conglomeration of their environment. After all, what "folk" really meant was "of the people," wherever they might be found. Although the broad-based term *vernacular* was not being applied to culture in the 1930s, in retrospect one can see that collectors were moving toward it by a process of elimination. In attempting to understand a musical phenomenon tied to lifestyle like a New Orleans brass band funeral, the appellation "folk" is much more appropriate than "popular" or "art." The "second line" dancers who surround the brass bands that play "by ear" exemplify folk traditions that are "time-honored," yet they subvert the propriety and order with which hierarchical concepts of Culture are infused—they are uninvited guests. Arms and legs akimbo, the throng of the "second line" creates organic unity out of diversity. The relationship of the brass band to "second lines" is a functional one, a key that unlocks static cultural categories, because musicians will go where the market leads them, categorical imperatives notwithstanding.[8]

One can argue, as Al Rose did, that jazz (in its initial incarnation, at least) is the functional music of a people and a place, not blacks or whites but Orleanians, which replaces racial explanations with cultural and environmental ones. The fact that so much music takes place in the streets means that even those who try to avoid it are not immune. Langridge understands this: "Any discussion of jazz as folk music must give special attention to the music of New Orleans. Whatever the truth about its place in the creation of jazz, New Orleans is certainly unique in the length of time for which it retained a distinctive style of functional music. Regional styles were not very distinct even in the earliest days of jazz recording and by the mid 'thirties they could hardly be said to exist. From the evidence of records, however, the music of New Orleans has always had a distinctive flavor of its own. Very few recordings were made there before the 'forties, but the bands of Oscar Celestin, Louis Dumaine and Sam Morgan do not sound like anything recorded in Chicago or New York during the same period. . . . Many criticisms of New Orleans music are invalid because they use the wrong criteria. It must be seen as a form of near-folk music and judged accordingly. New Orleans provides an experience unique in jazz and a good subject for specialization."[9]

Moreover, New Orleans bands fulfilled a multiplicity of functions that spanned racial divisions within their own regional culture. Thus, Oscar Celestin's (1884–1954) Tuxedo Bands played to black audiences at the Pythian Roof Garden and to white audiences at the New Orleans Yacht Club in the 1920s. Sam Morgan's bands played for black dances in Bay St. Louis and for white audiences on the Streckfus steamers.[10] Repertoire might shift a little from site to site, but the bands were prepared in advance to satisfy audience demands in any case. The funeral of clarinetist Alphonse Picou (1880–1961), which was captured on film, illustrates how multiple functions and audiences could be satisfied at a single event. Several black brass bands were in attendance, and the endless trail of "second liners" was mostly black, but engulfing the entourage was a polyglot sea of locals moving en masse with the procession. Different levels of participation were open to all elements of society, which were not reticent in their participation.[11] Cultural imperatives designed to separate races and classes could be enforced at private parties or segregated cabarets, but no controls were capable of rationalizing the action in the streets. Although his account is brief, Louis Armstrong provided an early clue to this tradition in an autobiographical sketch of street parades contained in *Swing That Music* (1936).[12]

Yet beyond "secondhand" stories such as Armstrong's, "hot" record collectors who had never been to the "city that care forgot" were not in a position to know about jazz parades, "second lines," and other unique facets of New Orleans street culture. When New Orleans–style bands like those of King Oliver, Kid Ory, or the ODJB performed in cities such as Chicago, Los Angeles, or New York, they were removed from the regional environment that had nurtured their style and were forced to adapt. Some New Orleans players, like Ory, Jelly Roll Morton, and Sidney Bechet, sought to remain true to a conception of New Orleans style as they envisioned it, but others, like Armstrong, seemed to accept change without compunction. The records told the story, but they were not necessarily easy to decipher. Consequently, "hot" collectors derived different messages from them. More information was needed.

But for those who were willing to learn, all roads led to New Orleans. The tendencies that Langridge describes ultimately transformed vague conceptions like "hot" into more circumscribed terms such as "New Orleans style." When an international network of "hot" collectors devoted to research, trade, and teamwork took shape in the mid-1930s, new paradigms became inevitable. Although "hot" collecting never grew to the level of a popular pastime like baseball, it exercised an influence beyond its numbers, enlarging the scope and depth of jazz appreciation through strategies that contrasted markedly with trade magazines like *Down Beat* that sought to cash in on the jazz craze with photographs of scantily clad women and tips on how to "make it" in the music business.[13] Charles Edward Smith once again played a noteworthy role by publicizing the collecting underground.

Having shared his views on jazz with the "highbrow" readers of *Symposium* and the self-consciously "lowbrow" readers of the *Daily Worker,* in 1934 he reached a general readership with "Collecting Hot," for *Esquire* magazine.[14]

As Stephen W. Smith wrote a number of years later, in *Jazzmen,* after "Collecting Hot" appeared, "the stampede was on."[15] Two examples demonstrate how "Collecting Hot" solidified collector consciousness and promoted "hot" jazz advocacy across the United States. Archie Green (1917–1985), who grew up in San Francisco and became one of the nation's most dedicated chroniclers of American folk and labor songs, cites Smith's article as an early source of inspiration: "During high-school years, 1933–35, I first noticed advertisements for recorded music in newspapers and journals. . . . Also, at that time, I began to read magazine articles pointing to an analytic stance on musical subjects. Charles Edward Smith's 'Collecting Hot' gave me a sense of jazz as a subject for discourse. As well, Smith made me want to go junking for rarities."[16] On the East Coast, Merrill Hammond (1906–1997), who began collecting in 1920, had a comparable awakening: "Read 'Collecting Hot' by Charles Edward Smith, in *Esquire*. Realized I, too, was a 'hot' collector." In college, Hammond had played in jazz bands with students from Harvard and Johns Hopkins, earning extra money and touring New England and Europe during vacations. He got his degree in business administration from Johns Hopkins in 1932 and became a stock-market analyst, an officer in the U.S. Navy, and a specialist in industrial relations for an oil company. His realization, after reading Smith's article, that he was a part of a movement had a telling effect: "I began a correspondence and association with other collectors. Since then, contacts have become worldwide. Today, I am principally interested in encouraging the study of jazz as an art form. In this manner, it is my hope that the music will gain public acceptance as a worthy American contribution to the culture of civilization."[17] Jazz advocacy drew people together, creating a myriad of associations as "hot" collecting attracted a cross-section of young people, yet there were few African Americans.

Smith began his overview of jazz collecting with an exegesis of Creole sagacity, naming Sidney Bechet: "Bechet plays a New Orleans clarinet. . . . Among jazz collectors he is a venerable person, not in age but in experience." At age thirty-six, Bechet had been playing for twenty-nine years and had "the further distinction of having taught Larry Shields (Original Dixieland clarinet) and Leon Roppolo, a *hot* musician who remains unsurpassed in the jazz world."[18] Roppolo's Gennetts, with the New Orleans Rhythm Kings, were lauded ("the cream of the jazz crop") before Smith went on to discuss the vagaries of pricing in the form of a collector parable. Smith told the story of a college student who had invested over a hundred dollars in a vintage blues record whose master had been destroyed, precluding reissue. With the onset of the Depression, the "ardent collector" was offered seventy-five dollars "spot cash" for the record, which was summarily rejected. But this was not the end of the matter: "The pay-off came when the prospective purchaser, himself a collector, picked up a clean copy of the same record in a remainder pile for the sum of ten cents!"[19] Smith's didacticism was that of a veteran collector to the novice, and in fact, he was nearing his thirtieth birthday. But he soon made it clear that "hot" collecting was not for those who were in it for the money. The indispensable tools of the collector were patience and knowledge, and Smith lamented the lack of reference tools. Reiterating his now familiar distinctions among "hot," "sweet," and "corny," Smith argued that what was genuine had "the quality of folk music," a flavor transmitted to bands like the ODJB, which "had, perforce, to assimilate the Negro's music," thus suggesting a clear line of influence from black to white. If the novice collector wanted to know the history of the music, "a *hot* collection tells the story audibly."[20]

Smith stated that he followed "the historical path," although not all collectors did. Certainly this preference did not mean much in 1934, for no jazz histories were available. Hugues Panassié's *Le Jazz Hot* appeared in France that year, but it was not published in English translation until two years later.[21] Further, Robert Goffin (1898–1984), a Belgian lawyer and poet, had brought out *Aux Frontières du Jazz* in 1932. Yet neither of them had ever set foot in the United States, and both works were flawed as historical studies—Panassie's because it was a critical commentary based on limited knowledge of jazz history and black culture, Goffin's because it was fanciful and erratically researched.[22] Charles Delaunay's *Hot Discographie*, published in 1936, was another matter. Since it was a chronology of names and dates, language was not a barrier. And even if it had been written in Swahili, such was the need for a basic listing of discs and personnel among American collectors that they would have welcomed it anyway. In addition, its format introduced a new idea into the "hot" collector discourse—the notion that New Orleans jazz should be segregated from other variants as a discrete playing style—thus contributing effectively to the development of a purist ethos fixated on New Orleans style.

Henry Pierre Charles Delaunay had been born in Paris on January 18, 1911, the son of the celebrated Orphist painter Robert Delaunay (1885–1941) and the designer Sonja Delaunay-Terk (1885–1979; née Sarah Ilinitchna Stern). Although Delaunay's scheme of organization in *Hot Discographie* was eventually revised, the first edition arranged jazz records by "musicians who belonged to the same musical family; say the musicians of New Orleans, it was better to have them all together."[23] Delaunay's first exposure to jazz had come in 1926, in a sickbed, when he found recordings by Duke Ellington, Bix Beiderbecke, and Jelly Roll Morton in his parents' record collection during a six-month convalescence, allowing him ample time to study the records carefully. Morton's "Black Bottom Stomp" appealed to him because it "sounded like country dance music, like folklore." He began to compare the interaction of cornet, clarinet, and trombone, noting their respective roles, "and little by little these three came together clearly." Delaunay was thus the first to grasp "front line" collective polyphony, which came to be considered a fundamental element of New Orleans style.[24] His discographical work thus drew attention to the limitations of "hot" as a system of historical classification. It was not always easy to find a copy of his work, however, and for some it served as a kind of bible.[25] Prior to *Hot Discographie,* the only printed sources for collectors had been record company catalogs, which were often unreliable or purposefully misleading in that many records were not listed.[26]

Delaunay's collaborations with Hugues Panassié furthered the awakening of American jazz scholarship and contributed to a consensus paradigm of jazz history and aesthetics. Like John Hammond, Panassié had been born into wealth, Panassié in Paris on February 27, 1912, but he grew up at the family's Château de Gironde in the Midi-Pyrénées. He discovered jazz in 1926 when he was recovering from polio (which left him partially crippled) and was writing about it at age eighteen. Panassié's article in the prestigious French journal *La Revue Musicale,* in June 1930, provides an interesting parallel to the opinions expressed by Charles Edward Smith in *Symposium* four months later. In "Le Jazz Hot," Panassié declares that "any new form of art doesn't fail to raise violent opposition" (just as Smith had) and then goes on to make the case for "hot" jazz—"the real and unique form of jazz"—as art. Like Smith, Panassié concentrates on jazz as spontaneous solo improvisation, while also expressing appreciation for white and black artists based on their abilities. "It would be a mistake," he writes, "to believe that white jazzmen are inferior to black ones. They play so much in the style of the black players that one can easily be mistaken."[27]

Panassié and Delaunay built the Hot Club de France in 1932, and in March 1935 they unveiled *Jazz Hot,* the club's official organ. This magazine was the first of its kind, tracking new jazz releases, providing interviews with American musicians traveling in Europe, and carrying columns by members of the American "hot" collector community. Most of the text was in French and English, rendering it quite accessible to an American audience. But it was also dominated by Panassié, who took command of the magazine and the organization, thus earning for himself the title "self-chosen Pope of Jazz" (in 1934 he was appointed president "for life").[28] His magnum opus, *Le Jazz Hot,* expanded on themes contained in his earlier articles and is often cited as the first "serious" study of jazz, meaning that it was the first full-scale critical work to attempt to consider the music comprehensively from an analytical perspective. In his review of the book in *Jazz Hot,* beaux-arts critic Georges Hilaire (1900–1976) observed that "the great value of Hugues Panassié's work resides in the utter loyalty the author has shown, in his properly scientifical spirit of investigation, in his instinctive application of Descartes's methods. Panassié, who knows three thousand Jazz records, who can identify any American musician by listening to a record, who can recall by heart the choruses of all the principal hot recordings, could have written, even better than Robert Goffin, a personal treatise, a work hermetically his own. He could have given us *his* theory of Jazz; [instead] he has written *the* theory of Jazz."[29] One can see in these remarks how "authority" was conferred within the "hot" record collector community, through a series of skill tests not unlike the Boy Scout merit-badge system, but the rigor of the work was nonetheless exemplary for its time. The jazz critic Whitney Balliett has referred to *Le Jazz Hot* as "a singular work of musical criticism," although scholars such as Ted Gioia and John Gennari place it within the 1930s French discourse on "primitivism" because of its romanticized view of innate black creativity.[30]

Nevertheless, *Le Jazz Hot* represented an emerging jazz discourse and demonstrated that despite geographical distances, a jazz network of international scope was taking shape by 1935. Common interest in jazz was building a Franco-American entente, enabling trans-Atlantic friendships and communication. John Hammond's "Lettre D'Amérique" column in the first issue of *Jazz Hot,* in March 1935, preceded his personal appearances in France three months later, during which time he conferred with that nation's "Collector-in-Chief," Hugues Panassié. As advocates, they were "brothers in arms" dedicated to the proposition that enlightened cognoscenti could influence public opinion on jazz, but they were also contributing to the construction of an ideological scaffolding deriving from the premises upon which "hot" record collecting was based. Despite a number of errors and imperfections, especially with regard to historical fact, *Hot Discographie* and *Le Jazz Hot* became models for Americans wishing to write about jazz. Panassié and Delaunay shaped perceptions not only of what jazz was but also of why it was important, proffering Old World approbation for the fledgling American art form at a crucial time. These works served to goad American "hot" collectors, compelling them to bolster their musical tastes with historical research and suggesting, in the case of *Hot Discographie,* that New Orleans–style jazz might be worth considering in its own right.

Back in the United States, as the jazz-collecting population began to expand, the glory days of finding rare issues at Salvation Army warehouses, furniture stores, and junk shops became a thing of the past in large urban areas like New York and Chicago. Because so many recording companies had studios in the Loop section of Chicago or were located within the Great Lakes region, OKehs, Paramounts, Brunswicks, Autographs, Gennetts, and Columbia's "race" issues had been in plentiful supply in the Windy City throughout the 1920s. The market for records along the southwestern tip of Lake Michigan was probably the most voracious in the world, owing largely to the interest engendered among the local population by the successive waves of New Orleans artists who brought jazz to the region.[31]

George Hoefer Jr. (1909–1967) wrote about this phenomenon in his "Hot Box" column in *Down Beat.* Hoefer had begun collecting "hot" in 1922 in Chapel Hill (his father was a professor at the University of North Carolina), and after taking a degree in engineering there in 1930, he moved to Chicago. Early in the Depression, there was a thriving business in secondhand records in Chicago, especially on Cottage Grove Avenue, south State Street, and the

Maxwell Street market section. According to Hoefer, "Cottage Grove Avenue from 35th to 47th streets was one solid mass of junk shops door to door. These shops had victrola records stowed away in every imaginable corner . . . and more were coming in each day." Southsiders, mostly blacks, were selling their phonographs and records for pennies, taking what they could get. Sometimes they would burn the records for fuel on cold days. Several years later, conditions had changed, and "the collector was forced to resort to the single, out-of-the-way, used furniture store or Salvation Army–Goodwill dump."[32] Within a few years of Smith's "Collecting Hot," even junk shops had been picked clean. Stories of house-to-house canvassing of black neighborhoods in Chicago and New York began to circulate, and one disgruntled collector commented, "Man, if I could only go through those flats with a search warrant."[33] Meanwhile, "disks that once sold at junk-shop prices of from one to five cents could bring forty or more dollars if they were rare."[34] The end result was that entrepreneurs arose to help fill the demand created by rising prices, scarcity, and the reawakening of interest in jazz occasioned by the popularity of Benny Goodman and other matinee idols of swing after 1935.

Perhaps the first to hear the knock of opportunity was Stephen W. Smith (1909–1992), an illustrator of Western magazines who opened the Hot Record Exchange with William Russell in 1936. Located on Seventh Avenue and Fifty-third Street in New York City, the Hot Record Society (HRS) shop, as it was alternately known, became a gathering place for collectors of all descriptions before it began to specialize in New Orleans style near the end of the decade. Its clientele included sportswriter Heywood Hale Broun (1918–2001), Charles Edward Smith, Jerry Wexler (1917–2008), African American illustrator for *Esquire* E. Simms Campbell (1912–1991), drummer George Wettling (1907–1968), and "people who listened to the music . . . enjoyed the music and had a lot of fun with it."[35] Besides serving as a clearinghouse for collectors, it also functioned as the headquarters for the group of writers who ultimately compiled *Jazzmen,* a work often referred to as "the first historical study of jazz."[36]

Almost immediately, competition developed with Milt Gabler's (1911–2001) Commodore Record Shop, at 144 E. Forty-second Street. Gabler's father had first opened the Commodore Music Shop in 1926, but a decade later it had fallen on hard times. Milt had the good fortune to discover a cache of rare OKehs at the record company's Bridgeport, Connecticut, warehouse after its parent company, Columbia, had succumbed to the Depression. During his weekend at the OKeh warehouse, Gabler inspected almost one hundred thousand records and, according to one account, "cornered the market" on rare OKehs. Since the records were thought to be almost worthless, he was able to buy twenty thousand discs for a dime apiece. It took great patience to dispose of them, for the market for resale was limited, but the deal was ultimately profitable, with each record fetching between thirty-five cents and a dollar. Gabler's friend Gilbert Millstein (1915–1999) found that some in fact did much better: "A number of them, changing hands among collectors, have since sold for as much as thirty-five dollars."[37] This fortuitous discovery, along with a "March of Time" feature prepared by James H. S. Moynahan in 1937, allowed Gabler to operate at a deficit he could live with, and his selfless style of business is illustrated by Eddie Condon's (1905–1973) comment on the shop: "It's a shrine . . . the crummiest shrine in the world."[38] Condon's "mob" became "regulars" at the Commodore Record Shop, along with a number of Columbia University collectors like Eugene Williams (1917–1948), Ralph Gleason (1917–1975), and Ralph de Toledano (1916–2007), as well as Marshall Stearns (1908–1966) from Yale. Russell Sanjek (1916–1986), a collector who began with Commodore but soon defected to the HRS shop, described the difference between the two: "The Commodore people were all very serious. You know, you couldn't speak when somebody's solo was on. That was too serious to me. To me jazz was fun and that wasn't my idea of how to listen to jazz."[39]

Sanjek referred to "a kind of Montague-Capulet situation" between the two factions: "You walked down the street, you'd have to cross to the other side if you didn't want a confrontation."[40] The feud intensified when both groups began to reissue out-of-print records and launched "little" magazines—the *HRS Society Rag* and *Jazz Information,* the former appearing intermittently from July 1938 and the latter from September 1939, both in reaction to the excesses of "trade" magazines like *Down Beat.*[41] What separated these "hot" factions was a mixture of differing personalities and preferences, and examination of their magazines' respective editorial policies and viewpoints will be undertaken in due course. For the moment, however, other 1936 events must take precedence, for that year's publication of Marshall Stearns's "A Short History of Swing" in *Down Beat* (a twenty-part series commencing in June 1936 and continuing until April 1938) brought jazz history to the fore and presaged a wave of feuds to come.[42] Especially interesting was reaction to a particular article from the erstwhile leader of the ODJB, Nick LaRocca (1889–1961).

Marshall Stearns was a well-educated individual. Having graduated from Harvard University in 1931, he had spent two years at Harvard's law school before beginning graduate studies in English literature at Yale. His training in cultural anthropology and musicology was extensive, including courses with Melville Herskovits, George Herzog, and Henry Cowell. With Milt Gabler and John Hammond, he helped to establish the United Hot Clubs of America in 1935 and was president of the Yale Hot Club. His interest in jazz dated from 1924, and as an undergraduate he had played drums, guitar, and saxophone with various groups. Besides his writings for *Down Beat* in 1936, he also contributed articles to *Yale Review, Variety, Metronome,* and *Tempo,* making him one of the most prolific jazz writers of the time. In his "Short History of Swing," Stearns suggested that the Original Creole Band might have been the first to play jazz and portrayed the New Orleans Rhythm Kings as "borrowing" their style from black jazzmen.[43] Lawrence Gushee, in *Pioneers of Jazz: The Story of the Original Creole Band,* has since done everything possible to substantiate the view that this band (which never recorded) played jazz on their tour of vaudeville theaters across the United States and Canada in the period 1914–18, and he makes a convincing argument.[44] Given his own personal investment as a player in the early days of jazz, however, Nick LaRocca was quick to take issue with Stearns, hastily flooding the jazz press with letters and articles claiming that the ODJB were the *only* creators of the music and that all subsequent styles had been copied from them.[45] Although one scholar has characterized this exchange as "healthy," there is reason to doubt that either side approached the issue dispassionately.[46]

LaRocca's band was in the midst of a "comeback" that turned out to be ill-fated, and while they were at the Earle Theater in Washington, D.C., LaRocca received a letter from Stearns, dated January 11, 1937, that revealed how the line separating advocacy from ideology could be easily blurred in the heat of debate, especially on the issue of race: "Dear Nick: I have all your records from 'Livery Stable,' to the recent discs. I like the earlier ones better. Between you and me, our last argument should furnish you with plenty of publicity. I do think, however, that you failed to give colored musicians a break; and that is why I exaggerated the other extreme, since the public is inclined to believe you and musicians of your opinion. There is nothing I should like better than to see your scrapbook, however I am still in school and will be teaching next year. If I ever get a chance I shall certainly drop by and say hello. Let's keep up the battle. Sincerely, M. W. Stearns."[47] Stearns would later write the first great academic survey of jazz history, *The Story of Jazz* (1956), arguably the model for "official" jazz historiography, but at the time, his admission that the debate with LaRocca should generate "plenty of publicity" was a bit callow. In "exaggerating the other extreme," he had also allowed aesthetic predilections to influence historical judgments, yet he clearly felt that it was right to do so. A protégé of John Hammond, who has been accused of jumping to unsubstantiated conclusions regarding racism in the death of Bessie Smith (1894–1937), Stearns was a staunch advocate of social justice for African Americans.[48] But his inclination to dismiss LaRocca's testimony in favor of that of the Rhythm Kings, a band formed several years after the ODJB's success, was presumptuous, given the information at hand, even though subsequent investigation of the career of cornetist Charles "Buddy" Bolden by "hot" collectors showed in retrospect that Stearns was on the right track.[49]

The debate over jazz origins occasioned by Stearns's articles concentrated attention on the New Orleans roots of the music, but as the title of the series makes clear, the basic frame of reference was still swing, a form of jazz that was most closely associated with Benny Goodman (1909–1986). John Hammond, referred to by Irving Kolodin (1908–1988) as the "number one swing man," had engineered Goodman's success as "the King of Swing."[50] As a talent scout for Columbia, he had the necessary connections to "make or break" jazz musicians, and evidence suggests that he did both or at least attempted to do so.[51] Hammond's primary interest in black musicians has already been established, but it should be noted that he exhibited little interest in the New Orleans style of playing. His preference for James P. Johnson (1894–1955), Fats Waller (1904–1943), Count Basie (1904–1984), and "boogie-woogie" pianists precluded attention to someone like Jelly Roll Morton. Kolodin's estimation of Hammond's power in the mid-1930s is only slightly hyperbolic: "'Johnny' hears someone, and 'Johnny' tells someone. Presently that someone is being discovered, analyzed, and canonized (or perhaps, in an odd instance vilified) by the intelligentsia of dance music from coast to coast." The new interest in dance music associated with the Swing Era had created a demand for musical idols, and John Hammond's ability to supply them led Kolodin to observe that "an arbiter of fashions in that field is understandably one of America's more important private citizens."[52]

Hammond's 1938 "Spirituals to Swing" concert at Carnegie Hall, presented under the auspices of the *New Masses,* consisted entirely of black artists, but only Bechet and trumpeter Tom Ladnier (1900–1939) were familiar with New Orleans style.[53] Not long after this show, Hammond used his influence to help launch Barney Josephson's (1902–1988) Café Society in Greenwich Village, an example of a "social-minded night club," which was inspired by Earl Browder (1891–1973), head of the American Communist Party.[54] Helen Lawrenson (1907–1982), the "unofficial hostess" of the club, observed that Hammond "was mad about Negro music: blues and boogie-woogie, not spirituals or intellectual jazz, but the black gutbucket music from the whorehouses, honky-tonks, and gin mills of New Orleans, Chicago, Kansas City."[55] But although clients of Café Society like Raymond Moley (1886–1975) are mentioned along with Billie Holiday (1915–1959), Lena Horne (1917–), and Big Joe Turner (1911–1985), not one New Orleans artist is named. It appears that Hammond, like many New York musicians, considered the old-timers of New Orleans to be passé.

Given the musical trends of the mid-to-late 1930s, the title of Charles Edward Smith's article for the February 16, 1938, issue of the *New Republic* might seem misleading. "Swing" was not so much a tribute to Benny Goodman as an attempt to place him in historical perspective, and it furnishes an excellent example of Smith's growing sophistication in his grasp of New Orleans style. Previously, in "Heat Wave," published in the *Stage* in September 1935, Smith had amended his definition of jazz as "folk" in discussing the background of the ODJB: "Jazz was an outgrowth of the urbanization of folk music. . . . It is significant, therefore, that the predecessors of the Dixieland band were the street bands of urban America. From these bands (which were usually crude and musically blasphemous) the Dixieland inherited and developed a spirit of tempestuous improvisation; they fused it with the breakdown themes which in their sporadic outbursts were the true ancestors of King Jazz, related, as they so definitely were, to American folk music in general and American Negro folk music in particular."[56]

Smith was transforming his concept of "folk" from static to dynamic and moving toward an environmental perspective of jazz origins. LaRocca's reemergence on stage and in the jazz press, though brief, had not gone unnoticed by Smith, and the information included in the erstwhile bandsman's vituperative articles added to what Smith had obtained through correspondence, to be put to good use by calmer heads. "Swing" began with a quote from LaRocca ("We played from the heart, what we felt") and then discussed the blending of Anglo-American folk songs, ballads, and hymns with African American spirituals, blues, and work songs; the music's translation into urban environments; and how such changes affected instrumentation.[57] He referred to the "ear-music festival" that occurred in New Orleans, its multiracial character, before placing the ODJB within a plethora of "christenings, neighborhood dances, prize fights, picnics at Milneburg and so forth." "What made their music so sensational that it won a name of its own?" he asked rhetorically and then answered: "The instrumentation was novel, but what counted most was what they were able to do with the instruments. They carried on in the tradition of the folksong, they 'ad-libbed.' The tune itself was the jumping-off place for a solo flight—or flights in complex formation."[58]

This was Smith's first reference to "collective improvisation," and in the comparison he made between the ODJB and Oliver's Creole Band, he demonstrated a new understanding of the dialectic that fused band chemistry with what Jelly Roll Morton would call "plenty rhythm," the key to the style's raw power:

> The most important difference between them lay in the style. The Dixieland style assimilated breakdown, military and ragtime themes; its counterpoint was staccato and many-voiced, the patterns, seemingly wide open, floated on a rhythmic base. Cadenzas and importunate novelty effects found a resting place in the Dixieland's melodic pattern. The Creole band took over the nostalgic blues themes. Players worried the melodic line in turn; their counterpoint was close-knit and distinguished by overlapping patterns and a rolling, rocking rhythm. There was a definite forward surge that drove inevitably toward a finish—a definite swing.[59]

In his conclusion, however, Smith broke through to an insight on the functional nature of New Orleans music that is comparable to Derek Langridge's, mentioned earlier:

In such a short summary as the present it would be improvident to attempt to correlate present-day jazz with its environment, but it would also be unfair to the reader not to point out that a great deal of the swing genre, while technically excellent, is shallow and devoid of any but a purely instrumental virtue. Because this output has a superficial brilliance and a certain following, it encourages musicians to "fake," particularly on trumpet. Since many of the more talented improvisors have succumbed to this tendency as they lost touch with their own background, it seems possible that environmental relationships are a highly significant factor and might, to some extent, explain the difference between creativeness and brilliant sterility. Such a theory would not argue for retrogression, of course, but for an identity with the surrounding environment comparable, in more urban terms, with that experienced by the folk musician.[60]

Before the year was out, Smith was refining this theory in *Jazzmen* with William Russell, Steve Smith, and Frederic Ramsey Jr. The research was more of a modern American odyssey than a strictly scholarly undertaking, for the strategy was to seek out surviving New Orleans pioneers dispersed from coast to coast and get to know them. Charles Edward Smith received his first taste of New Orleans during the February 1939 Mardi Gras season, when he arrived to interview Willie Cornish (1875–1942), a former member of the Buddy Bolden band. The discovery of Bolden, who had previously gone largely unnoticed outside of New Orleans, was a major find that revolutionized jazz chronology and dramatized the need for a reassessment of jazz history from the ground up.[61] Louis Armstrong had previously discussed Bolden in some detail in 1936, in *Swing That Music*, but "hot" collectors failed to investigate fully until Bunk Johnson came to William Russell's attention via a tip from Armstrong, during the research phase of *Jazzmen*.[62] Bunk became an abiding presence in Russell's life, and as a consequence he exerted considerable clout in establishing Bolden's fame (and his own) in the pages of *Jazzmen*. After 1939, Bunk Johnson served as a kind of Sphinx of New Orleans style, and Russell spent the rest of his life trying to figure him out.

Smith was not the first of the *Jazzmen* authors to make the pilgrimage to New Orleans, and to understand the circumstances that allowed William Russell to claim that honor, one must return to New York, to the Hot Record Exchange. Russell had been born William Russell Wagner in Canton, Missouri, in 1905.[63] He grew up on the Mississippi River, and his first memorable musical experience came while he was still a teenager, hearing the calliopes of the excursion boats that plied the river, some of which carried jazz bands. He received a bachelor's degree from Culver-Stockton College in Canton and went on to study music at Columbia Teacher's College and the University of California at Berkeley and Los Angeles, where he developed specialties in Haitian, Chinese, Cuban, and various forms of atonal and avant-garde music. (In 1981, he received an honorary doctorate from Tulane University, but he divulged that information only reluctantly.) His conversion to "hot" collecting came when he was teaching school on Staten Island: a student had left Jelly Roll Morton's "Shoe Shiner's Drag" behind, and intrigued by the title, Russell sampled it and was never again the same.[64] By 1935, he was also a serious Armstrong collector, and his collaboration with Steve Smith the following year was the equivalent of matriculation to graduate school in "hot" studies.

Russell met Smith at the main Salvation Army store in New York while prospecting, and they decided to make a business of their mutual hobby. While teaching at Columbia in 1934, Russell had joined an itinerant puppet theater known as the Red Gate Shadow Players, largely because of his interest in Asian, African, and other "exotic" musical forms. He remained with them until 1940, and while traveling with the troupe he scoured the countryside for records with which to keep Smith well supplied back in New York. Clothed in Chinese attire, Russell played various gongs and "moon guitar" and on one occasion earned the enmity of the other players when he was late for a performance for Franklin Roosevelt's grandchildren, Sistie and Buzzy Dahl, because he had been out hunting for records at the Quality Music Store in Washington, D.C.[65] In 1937, on his thirty-second birthday, he arrived in New Orleans after traveling from Pensacola, where the Shadow Players had given a show. Unfortunately, he failed to hear any music due to a tight schedule and lack of a local guide, but he recalled staying up all night, "looking around the city, walking around all the streets he had heard of from records, like 'Canal Street Blues,' 'Basin Street Blues.'"[66] He returned twice that fall with Park Breck (1914–1997), a jazz writer and collector from Philadelphia, and met Tom Brown and Raymond Burke (1904–1986), among others. Russell and Breck also journeyed through Texas looking for collectibles, but Orleanian Orin Blackstone (1907–1980) had already "cleaned out" that state.[67]

Because of his mobile lifestyle, William Russell came to know most of the "hot" collectors of the 1930s on a first-name basis, and his recollections of these men provide a valuable source of information. George Beall (1911–1999) of Detroit, the scion of a ball-bearing manufacturer, became famous for uncovering a cache of rare Paramount records in a jewelry store and for writing about the New Orleans Rhythm Kings. John Steiner (1908–2000) of Chicago was a chemist whose knowledge of the intricacies of recording technology became legendary; he and Hugh Davis (1910–1986), an engineer, later went into the record-manufacturing business after acquiring the Paramount catalog, adding to their already extensive collection of "live" recordings. Bill Love (1918–1992), a civil engineer for the Louisville and Nashville Railroad, compiled a "Collector's Directory" in the early 1940s and was a founding member of the International Association of Jazz Record Collectors. Merrill Hammond, Marshall Stearns, John Hammond, and Charles Edward Smith were all identified as "leading collectors" by Russell, but perhaps the most singular individual mentioned was Hubert Shelby "Hub" Pruett (1900–1982), who had worked his way through medical school at St. Louis University and had pitched for the St. Louis Browns in 1922: "He wasn't a great pitcher but he was an enigma to Babe Ruth and he had the high sign on the mighty King of Swat. Babe was supposed to have said that if he had to face Pruett every day he wouldn't have been in the league."[68] People of diverse talents and interests populated the world of "hot" collecting, and Steve Smith described Russell as "the David Harum of hot collectors."[69] Together Smith and Russell created an informational network of remarkable proportions.

The importance of such a network to understanding the history of a music that had been documented primarily on recordings cannot be overestimated. If one was to locate "old-timers" who had long since passed from public attention, some leads had to be found. In New York, everyone turned to Herman Rosenberg (1909–1978), who seemed to be the only person who could transcend the rift between the Hot Record Exchange and the Commodore Record Shop. Russell Sanjek described him as "the man who was in both places. . . . He was in effect an information gathering system for both *Jazz Information* and for the *Rag*. He knew where the stories were."[70] Feuds notwithstanding, examination of the early issues of *HRS Society Rag* and *Jazz Information* demonstrates a cooperative distribution of historical and discographical information pouring into New York from all areas of the country in 1938–39. Orin Blackstone gave details on New Orleans musicians who had recorded at home in the 1920s; Charles Edward Smith wrote a piece about Bolden, based on an interview with Louis Armstrong; Walter Schaap and Margaret Kidder provided reports of jazz happenings in Europe; and numerous portraits of critics and collectors, usually sympathetic, filled the pages of both magazines.[71]

These were the bonanza years for the collection of jazz information, a time when American jazz scholarship became broadly assertive. Whatever the individual preferences of jazz collectors and enthusiasts, everyone could applaud the first major American studies of jazz in those years. Two of these works, Winthrop Sargeant's (1903–1986) *Jazz: Hot and Hybrid* (1938) and Wilder Hobson's *American Jazz Music* (1939), offered what was, in effect, a synthesis of critical and historical writings within the "hot" collector community up to that time, setting the stage for a new consensus-based paradigm that would more fully emphasize the importance of New Orleans style with *Jazzmen.*[72] Although there was some similarity in these books' analytical approach to the music, there were also differences that reflected the predilections of their respective authors. Both Sargeant and Hobson emphasized the importance of understanding the structure or "language" of jazz and how it differed from the European tradition, but while Hobson provided considerable historical detail, Sargeant's treatment focused on a critical analysis of the music, without much historical context. Sargeant's work therefore has little to contribute to the present discussion of an emerging jazz historiography.[73]

Wilder Hobson was a Yale man who worked at *Time* before he became editor of *Fortune.* An advertisement that ran in *HRS Society Rag* summed up the intent of his study: "*American Jazz Music* is the first book by an American to deal with the subject as a whole, in its technical as well as its historical aspects." The advertisement also mentioned Hobson's contention that jazz was "a *language* and therefore cannot be defined" and provided details on the relation of jazz to "Southern Negro music," including spirituals and blues, and on the emergence of jazz from New Orleans to Chicago and New York, leading to the appearance of swing.[74] Frank Norris noted that Hobson was a "hot" collector whose tastes were "catholic," meaning that he was also a devotee of Delius, Debussy, and even Beethoven ("which, by the way, is several blocks past where I get off").[75] By the time it was published in March

1939, *American Jazz Music* had undergone a thorough editing at the hands of John Hammond, Milt Gabler, and Steve Smith, but not Charles Edward Smith and William Russell, whose work in *Jazzmen,* published soon afterward, would render its historical content obsolete.[76]

In his chapter "From New Orleans Northward," Hobson told the story of New Orleans origins, while also relating that "prior to 1914 the jazz language was likely to be heard wherever there was the combination of an American Negro and a musical instrument . . . but there were no bands or soloists with more than a local reputation."[77] Hobson made the connection between regional culture and playing style but downplayed its relation to New Orleans, while also proffering what would now be described as an "essentialist" characterization of jazz prowess as innately racial. While his description of brass band funerals in early chapters was based on observer accounts by New Orleans trumpeter Joseph "Wingy" Manone (1900–1982), Hobson erroneously identified Jack Laine's (1873–1966) Reliance brass bands as "colored musical organizations," and Fate Marable's (1890–1947) riverboat bands were placed in the period "long before" 1917.[78] The mention of eccentric New Orleans characters like Buddy Bolden and Emile "Stale Bread" Lacoume (1885–1946) added flavor to coverage of the city's music scene, but Hobson had no real grasp of the full extent of the community-based musical context of New Orleans and of its history as a regional music capitol, even though he did have some familiarity with the regional nature of Southern culture at the turn of the century. Hobson's history of jazz origins does not begin to make sense until he gets to the story of the ODJB after 1917—a familiar tale to anyone who had been following the jazz press from the mid-1930s on. Up to that point, his characterization remains disconnected, largely due to the lack of anything resembling "a sense of place." This was the prime ingredient that *Jazzmen* would supply when it was published in October 1939, positing a fully developed cultural and environmental thesis for jazz origins in New Orleans.

The key figure in the publication of *Jazzmen* was Charles Frederic Ramsey Jr., a native of Pittsburgh who, at age twenty-one, graduated from Princeton into a job with Harcourt, Brace Publishers in 1936.[79] He went on to a career as a jazz writer and researcher that would eventually lead to the Guggenheim, the Ford Foundation, and the National Endowment for the Humanities underwriting his numerous projects, but in 1938 his goal was to persuade his bosses at Harcourt, Brace that a book on jazz under his direction was needed. He recruited William Russell on the strength of an article on boogie-woogie that had appeared that year in *Jazz Hot*; Charles Edward Smith, of course, was a natural choice for coeditor because of his well-deserved reputation as the first American to write analytically on the subject of "hot" jazz.[80]

Russell and Charles Edward Smith did most of the actual interviewing of New Orleans pioneers, and Steve Smith's wife, Lee, devised an elaborate procedure for the exchange of notes and transcriptions that kept the nine contributors abreast of the latest findings. Because of his special arrangement with the Red Gate Shadow Players, Russell was the most mobile, and he began to reaffirm previous acquaintances with musicians such as Johnny and Baby Dodds (1898–1959) in Chicago; Jelly Roll Morton in Washington, D.C.; and the players he had met in New Orleans the year before. Nearly a hundred musicians or close relatives were contacted either in person or through the mails in gathering materials for the book, and as the raw data was hurriedly collated and circulated, a new perspective on the origins of jazz and its variegation began to take shape. As Russell later recalled, "New Orleans musicians, colored and white, seemed more friendly, less commercial than the New York so-called 'Dixieland' musicians, the Fifty-second Street crowd in the Village." He found that "New Orleans musicians living in Chicago like Johnny and Baby Dodds were more friendly, too. Maybe it was something about the city and the music."[81] In conversations with Warren "Baby" Dodds, Russell learned that one of the great principles of New Orleans jazz was working together and helping each other: "That's the spirit which has made New Orleans music what it is. The ensemble style as opposed to the solo style illustrates this. . . . As Baby Dodds says, 'You have to be friendly and you have to be happy.'"[82] One might find cause to doubt such a rosy characterization, given the proliferation of musical "cutting contests" and other battles among New Orleans musicians that ultimately graced the pages of *Jazzmen*, but the profound effect of Dodds's words on Russell's perception of New Orleans style remains undeniable.

Other musicians interviewed by Russell for *Jazzmen* included Bill Johnson (ca. 1874–1972), who in 1939 was one of the oldest living New Orleans players on the planet. He had begun his professional career in 1890 as a guitar player but was best known as the leader and bassist for the Original Creole Orchestra, the first New Orleans jazz band to leave town in "1911" (Lawrence Gushee later confirmed that the date was actually 1907–8). It was Johnson who lined up the job at the Royal Garden and invited Joe Oliver to front the band in 1918. When Russell found him, he was running a sandwich shop on Thirty-eighth Street in Chicago, around the corner from the musicians' union. During the 1930s, he had worked occasionally with Lil Armstrong (1902–1971) in Milwaukee and Chicago but was essentially inactive when Russell interviewed him.[83]

Another Chicago discovery was Narcisse "Buddy" Christian (ca. 1895–ca. 1949), who had started in Storyville as a piano-playing "professor." To collectors, he had become famous for his banjo and guitar work on Clarence Williams's Blue Five recordings in 1924–25, which had included Louis Armstrong and Sidney Bechet. He had previously worked with Peter Bocage at the Tuxedo Dance Hall in 1912–13 and with Joe Oliver at Lala's Café in 1915–16, before leaving New Orleans in search of fame and fortune. Johnson and Christian supplied details about the early days in New Orleans and contacts to other players, and Johnson gave Russell a vintage photograph and a business card from his days with the Creole Band, which graced the pages of *Jazzmen*. For verification, Russell checked the dates and anecdotes against the files of the *Chicago Defender*, which yielded further information. For Russell, the interviews that he conducted for *Jazzmen*, like his first hearing of Jelly Roll Morton, were turning points in his life. Henceforth he dedicated himself to the collection of information on New Orleans jazz musicians with a persistence that won him worldwide admiration and yet another title: the "grand lama of jazz."[84] His contributions to *Jazzmen* included pieces on Armstrong and on boogie-woogie and a chapter entitled "New Orleans Music," which was ostensibly written with Steve Smith but for which Russell deserves the greater credit.[85]

In the introductory passage to the book, Ramsey and Smith state the purpose of *Jazzmen*: "to relate the story of jazz as it has unfolded about the men who created it, the musicians themselves."[86] These they divided into two groups, New Orleans pioneers and the inheritors of their tradition, the musicians of Chicago and New York. From the outset, the relationship of New Orleans style to its derivatives was plainly stated, which meant that the conceptualization of New Orleans style as an ur-jazz that was "hot," but also something more, had come to fruition. Russell's essay was primarily about the context from which jazz had emerged, and his emphasis was on black and Creole traditions and their interaction. Throughout his treatment, the "sense of place" lacking in earlier works was everywhere apparent. Russell provided plenty of "local color" in an account of the "ring shouts" at Congo Square, including details on topography, Houmas Indian background on the plot, its then-current appellation as Beauregard Square, and descriptions of the instruments played and dances performed there. Congo Square established the survival of African musical rituals in New Orleans as a foundation for further developments occurring with Emancipation, providing a specific site for discussion of how African musical sensibility could influence vernacular cultural developments in an American urban environment. After the Civil War, freedmen began to commingle with Creoles of color and adapted the wind and string instruments used by Creoles and whites to their own devices: "Such instruments were already widely used by the Creole Negroes, most of whom, though skilled in written music, were not so close to the blues background. The latter were improvisational in character. Soon Negro groups, having learned to play by ear, were engaged to play for dances and by 1880 were found on some of the packets on the Mississippi River. On the boats the Negroes worked as porters, barbers, and waiters during the day and entertained the passengers with music at night."[87] The lack of formal instruction for all but a few blacks made "faking" the rule. When applied to the popular music of the day, a kind of simplification resulted because of black preference for "endless repetition of short motifs," appurtenant to their African musical heritage. Improvisation was fundamental to musical expression in New Orleans, and those blacks with no improvisational ability "fell by the wayside."

This context of musical creativity was already the hallmark of New Orleans music before the rise of Buddy Bolden, who became its first identifiable jazz exponent. Russell felt that such experimentation was partially the result of chronic underemployment of blacks and the lack of "restraining tradition and supervision." As he pointed out, the musical freedom afforded the black population of New Orleans led to innovations that were impressive by any standards: "The fact that these men were not primarily note readers also explains, when collective improvisation was attempted, the origin of the characteristic New Orleans polyphony, which in its more complex manifestations became a dissonant counterpoint that antedated Schoenberg."[88] The extraordinary capabilities of New Orleans' black musicians were apparent in the

Bolden Band, which played in "barrel-house" taverns, for lawn parties at Miss Cole's, at picnics and private parties, or at dance halls like Perseverance or Tin Type. During Mardi Gras, white clubs such as the Buzzards, the Mysterious Babies, and the Fourth District Carnival Club provided employment. The functional imperative operative in New Orleans was also manifested in Russell's discussion of some of the dives in which Bolden played: "The tougher the dance the more raggedy was the playing."[89] Readers within the band, like Willie Cornish, helped the others to master quadrilles, polkas, and other "traditional" dances that were in demand at more refined venues. New Orleans concepts of "professionalism" meant that musicians must be prepared to satisfy a variety of tastes if they wanted to keep working, and as Russell related, even Bolden was considered to be expendable when he began to miss engagements. Bolden was a legendary figure even among those musicians who knew him well, and his "nervous breakdown" in 1906 created a vacuum at the top that required a successor.

Bolden's influence on young New Orleans musicians was implicit in much of Russell's commentary. Freddie Keppard (1890–1933), for example, switched from violin ("alley fiddle") to cornet to achieve more power, a Bolden trademark. According to Russell, Keppard was a Creole who could not read music, and he became the "hottest thing" in New Orleans after Bolden. Like that of his comrade Sidney Bechet, Keppard's story showed the influence of black "uptown" style on the younger generation of Creoles, underlining an assimilation of musical techniques between blacks and Creoles. Keppard later became a member of the Original Creole Orchestra under Bill Johnson ("the first important group to leave New Orleans") after a period with the Olympia Band, the rival of Bolden's organization. Russell mentions that the Victor Company had offered the Creole Band a recording date in 1916, but Keppard was adamant in his refusal, fearing that other players could then steal his style. The value of recording as a money-making tool may have been appreciated by professionals in music-industry centers like New York, but to New Orleans musicians at this time it held no real attraction. The Creole Band toured the country from "1911 through 1918" (actually, 1914–18), when defections from the ranks scattered its members throughout the nation—some came home, while others relocated to California and Illinois.

Meanwhile, former members of the Bolden Band re-formed into the Eagle Band, setting the stage for the introduction of Bunk Johnson. Bunk's name had come up in an interview with Louis Armstrong that Russell had conducted in preparation for *Jazzmen*. By writing to "Bunk"—General Delivery, New Iberia—Russell had established an initial contact that would prove fortuitous. Johnson had retired from music many years before and was a dependent of the artist Weeks Hall (1895–1958), the owner of "The Shadows on the Teche," in New Iberia. He worked occasionally as a handyman, but his main function was to regale the family with accounts of his musical exploits in New Orleans. In his letters to Russell, he played the same role, feeding him information about Buddy Bolden and early jazz as if pouring water into a sponge, much of which later turned out to be specious. Nevertheless, the thrill of discovery was sufficient to earn Bunk a prominent place in Russell's essay, and he accepted Johnson's dating of the Bolden photograph without question as 1895, which later proved to be about ten years early and skewed *Jazzmen*'s chronology.

Within the Eagle Band saga, Johnson was said to have had "the most refined taste and finished execution of all cornetists," even though he was from a "tough uptown" neighborhood, the Irish Channel.[90] He had "an unprecedented sense of swing" and infused his blues and "gutbucket" style with "a tone unrivaled in its beauty." It was supposedly Bunk who had brought Bechet into the band, playing parades by day and halls like the Masonic at night. Such activities included funerals for the numerous fraternal orders that served as insurance, recreation, and burial societies for the black population. On the way back from the graveyard, the inevitable "second line" would gather, daring the band to get "hotter" and rejoicing in the pandemonium. Other venues such as ball games, balloon ascensions at Washington Park, lakefront parties at Milneburg and West End, and river excursions provided numerous opportunities for "ratty" bands, and the competition was fierce. Dance bands riding around the streets on large furniture wagons engaged in "cutting contests" to advertise a job or to obtain one. Spheres of influence (blacks uptown, Creoles downtown) could figure prominently in the outcome of such events, but even hostile neighborhoods occasionally bowed to a superior musical display by "intruders" if they deserved it. The Eagle Band was said to be unassailable on their own turf, inspiring fear in the hearts of downtown "Frenchmen."

Following his discussion of performance sites, Russell described the characteristic or "traditional" instrumentation of New Orleans dance bands, eliminating violin from the mix with a quote from Jelly Roll Morton ("violinists weren't known to play anything illegitimate, even in New Orleans"):

> For dance jobs practically every New Orleans group used seven pieces. The cornet, playing the melody most of the time, was considered the leader. The clarinet played a faster moving part, usually of legato runs and arpeggios, and filled in at the end of phrases with characteristic "breaks." The trombone, which at times supported the others with a sort of rhythmic bass, also took its own countermelody in the best style of New Orleans music, and supplied a moving melodic line, or "slides," when the other parts were stationary. . . . The rhythm sections consisted of drums, guitar, and string bass. The absence of pianos in New Orleans orchestras could be explained, in part, by the difficulty of fitting them into the wagons so often used for street advertising.[91]

Pianists like Tony Jackson (1876–1921), Jelly Roll Morton, Richard M. Jones (1892–1945), and Clarence Williams found plenty of work in the brothels of Storyville, along with a selection of "nine cabarets, many 'dance schools,' innumerable honky-tonks, barrel houses, and gambling joints." After 1910, the Tuxedo Dance Hall and District cabarets such as 101 Ranch, Big 25, and Pete Lala's all had bands. In reference to Billy Phillips's 101 Ranch, Russell stated that "here could be seen the future members of the New Orleans Rhythm Kings, the Original Dixieland Jazz Band, and the Halfway House gang, whose first impressions of hot were received while listening to the older Negro musicians."[92] Indeed, the primacy of New Orleans blacks in the inception of New Orleans style was basic to Russell's treatment of jazz origins, and when Jack "Papa" Laine, leader of the Reliance bands and early employer of LaRocca, was questioned on the validity of the cornetist's claim to have "invented" jazz, he found it hard to take the question seriously.[93]

In his conclusion, Russell pointed out that Storyville was "kind to hot music." "With dozens of bands, many trios, and other musicians employed every night," he stated, "it is little wonder that jazz first sprang up and flourished in New Orleans." But it was a tough way to earn a living: musicians worked from "eight until" and earned $1.00 to $2.50 a night.[94] The closing of the District in November 1917 set in motion a musical diaspora that increased the emigration that had started with the Creole Band. Riverboats carried New Orleans musicians upriver to Memphis, St. Louis, and Davenport. Part of this exodus resulted from the shifting of blacks to the manufacturing centers of the North with "changing industrial conditions," but Russell saw the principal reason (erroneously) as the fall of Storyville.

A letter from the Hot Jazz Society of San Francisco to Bill Russell, granting him "a No. 1 honorary lifetime membership card," described him as "the author of the most vital and interesting portion of the best book ever written on jazz, 'Jazzmen.' "[95] In an interview conducted many years later, Russell conceded that the book had numerous errors, but in contrast to preceding efforts, his characterization of jazz origins was a quantum leap forward. For the first time, New Orleans style was clearly differentiated from its derivatives and placed within a discrete geographical and chronological setting. The city's variety of indoor and outdoor performance sites, overlapping correspondence of brass and dance bands, functional aspects of festival and funeral traditions in which music acted to define community and lifestyle, and racial and ethnic diversity were all integrated in his essay. Furthermore, the standard format and specialized roles of certain instruments in collective improvisation were specifically explained. Saxophones, the most popular jazz symbol in the 1920s, were not even mentioned. Pianos were not initially included in the instrumental equation, but in towns like Chicago and New York they were expected, so New Orleans bands like the ODJB and King Oliver's Creole Jazz Band departed from the tradition accordingly. Russell's insights, based on his interviews with "the musicians themselves," put the pieces of the puzzle together, providing a foundation for future efforts. Subsequent scholarship would demonstrate that Russell had overstated the duration of Congo Square, the effect of Storyville's collapse, and the pervasiveness of collective improvisation and "faking" among early jazz bands, while also succumbing to Bunk Johnson's version of chronology. But he had made great strides in penetrating the riddle posed by the Sphinx of New Orleans style, even as he was seduced by it. Sorting this out would be a life's work.

In what might best be seen as a "preamble" to Russell's article, a section by Charles Edward Smith delivered a rather personal and impressionistic portrait of the city of New Orleans that nevertheless emphasized its importance as a musical capital and the salutary effects of racial and ethnic diversity:

Every writer makes his own city. The city of fine living and free spirit, woven into the dream of a poet. The city of brass bands and military marches, grand balls and rowdy lakefront parties. . . . You have to think of New Orleans the band city or it will be hard to understand why it couldn't have happened on the levee at Memphis, on the waterfront of Savannah, or on the Gulf Coast with the deep, sobbing blues . . . Cajun or Creole, black or white, the others heard. They heard because their lives were part of that life, and because the music didn't draw a color line. White or black or a shade between, they listened hard when the Bolden Band pointed its horns towards Lincoln Park, because that was the King.[96]

Smith's first trip to New Orleans in early 1939, like Russell's almost two years before, had created an indelible impression on a willing subject. In addition to his editorial responsibilities, he made two contributions to *Jazzmen*: "White New Orleans" and "Land of Dreams," the former a complement to Russell's piece and the latter a cameo of his trip to the city. The division of coverage on origins was the probable result of respective sympathies vis-à-vis the role of race, for Smith had been consistent from the beginning on the polyracial character of the music, while Russell was inclined to credit the inspiration of uptown blacks. Such differences did not diminish their mutual commitment to the identification and exploration of New Orleans' special place in jazz history.

Smith used the term "Dixieland" to distinguish the white jazz tradition that began with Jack Laine's Ragtime Band and extended through the ODJB and its worldwide impact after 1917–19, although he admitted that such terminology was usually applied "loosely." Laine was born in 1873 and, like most youngsters in the city, grew up idolizing the brass band musicians who had been prevalent since before the Civil War. Musically active by the early 1890s, he took full advantage of the musical opportunities that existed in New Orleans before the advent of radio, cinema, and other mechanical media. On one level, Smith agreed with Russell as to the root inspiration for jazz: "Improvised music, introduced into New Orleans white music through the influence of the uptown Negroes, had by the latter part of the nineteenth century become as traditional for some groups of white musicians as had brass band music."[97] But as his story unfolded, it was clear that he saw special genius in the work of men such as Leon Roppolo, who, like his Creole counterparts Bechet and Keppard, had to withstand the disapproval of classically trained elders (especially in Italian and German families) when youngsters neglected "reading" in favor of "faking." As he stated, "it should be emphasized that white New Orleans contributed its own background to jazz, and since this background was different from that of the Negro, 'Dixieland' music was bound to show differences."[98] (By this point, his "environmental thesis," alluded to previously in "Swing," had reached full maturity.) The entrepreneurial nature of Laine's musical activities, however, meant that he could field several outfits simultaneously, and Smith noted that African American trombonist Dave Perkins (ca. 1871–1931), who was light enough to pass for white, was a regular in the Laine lineups, along with Creoles like Achille Baquet (1885–1956) on clarinet and men of "Latin American" lineage like Lawrence Veca (1889–1911; actually of Sicilian heritage) on cornet. Laine's band played quadrilles until the public began to demand "rags," which were then incorporated into the repertoire. "Rehearsed until improvisation fused with written music learned by ear," stated Smith, "it [rags] made a solid contrapuntal core that changed white New Orleans, almost overnight, from traditional round dances to white imitations of Negro shags and trots."[99] In other words, Laine's Reliance bands followed a parallel and in many respects identical course to that which had driven the Bolden Band, working out the music that dancers wanted in "head arrangements."

Laine's bands became the incubators for young white talent in New Orleans. Nick LaRocca, Henry Ragas (1897–1919), Eddie Edwards (1891–1963), and Tony Sbarbaro (1897–1969) of the ODJB; George Brunies (1902–1974) of the New Orleans Rhythm Kings; and Emile "Stale Bread" Lacoume of spasm band fame were all affiliated with Laine units. In addition, "most New Orleans musicians, white or black, used only superlatives in talking about Veca."[100] This meant that blacks and whites were hearing each other, largely because it was impossible to segregate what musicians were exposed to when so much musical activity was occurring outdoors. Perkins played with Bolden *and* Laine at different times in his career, serving as a mediating influence, which helps explain how jazz moved so quickly throughout the ethnic and racial spectrum. When he married a black woman who had nursed him back to health after a protracted illness, the white union considered withdrawing his card, but up until that point, near the end of his career, he had worked "both sides of the fence" without being confronted about it.

The "Dixieland" bands that left New Orleans for Chicago in 1915 and 1916 were white organizations, but the context from which they had emerged in New Orleans was many-hued. With mixed-blood Creoles teamed with blacks *and* whites, not to mention Latinos like Martin Abraham (1886–1981), who was known as "Chink Martin," any attempt to assign racial connotations to style would be relative. When Laine assembled his bands, he did so not primarily on the basis of color but according to musical ability (entailing obvious risks in a segregated society when Creoles and light-skinned blacks were employed). The risks were justified: exciting and superior musicianship provided a competitive advantage and more work. Although Smith does not state this explicitly, this impression is easily derived from his handling of the subject.

In his discussion of the successes and failures attending "Dixieland" bands in Chicago and New York, Smith recounted the swapping of players among groups. Clarinetist Larry Shields (1893–1953) served with both Tom Brown and the ODJB, and his "classic" renditions of tunes like "Tiger Rag" became the basis for imitation by Northern musicians who heard him live or on the recordings. Leon Roppolo was perhaps even more influential as a member of the New Orleans Rhythm Kings in Chicago, in the early 1920s. Roppolo came from a long line of musicians. His grandfather had been a clarinetist of note in Sicily, and he began instruction on violin with Professor Carrie, who was black, when he was ten. But Roppolo's father's clarinet (he too was a player) beckoned to him. He practiced surreptitiously until his father found him out and sent him to Professor Santo Giuffre. At fourteen Roppolo ran away from home to join Bee Palmer's (1894–1967) show on the Orpheum Circuit, and by 1922 he was in Chicago. Roppolo's career was short-lived due to a nervous breakdown; like Bolden's, his path led to the sanitarium. Before ending his essay with the fall of Storyville, Smith put Roppolo, and "Dixieland," in perspective:

> Because the musicians in New Orleans started out early in life, the city was flooded with child prodigies. Out of these a few were really gifted and were to leave their mark on jazz development. The Rhythm Kings were to make important contributions for they were in themselves creative and technically uninhibited, as the Dixielanders had been before them. To acknowledge the influences that contributed to their music is

not to deny its originality. No music is without antecedent. The Negro himself, coming to America, traded his own instruments for those identified with western music, assimilated in his folk music the strains of English and Continental folk song, assimilated the Spanish-American music which was already a mixture of Negro, Spanish, and Indian. To ignore these influences, and the backgrounds from which they spring, is to fail to grasp the significance of the music itself.[101]

In this single statement, one can see the culmination of nearly ten years of research and reflection. The equanimity with which Smith approached the question of race and jazz origins was rare for his time and distinguished him from other writers like Hammond, Stearns, and even to some extent Russell, who were much more emphatic in claiming exclusively black origins. As the letter from the Hot Jazz Society attests, Russell was the one who emerged from the *Jazzmen* experience as the preeminent authority on New Orleans style, but Smith's even-handedness was also a notable achievement. Although the editors' decision to differentiate between black and white origins was very likely intended to establish relative degrees of authenticity, positing black creation and white imitation, Smith's contributions helped to qualify that orientation by suggesting that musical ability was the proper criterion for evaluating historical significance, regardless of race.

Although not directly tied to the issue of jazz origins, Smith's "Land of Dreams" is a necessary companion to "White New Orleans" because of the way it qualifies certain statements in the other piece and because of the sense of disillusionment pervading it. At the conclusion of "White New Orleans," Smith gave the impression that the closing of Storyville led to the end of an era, but in "Land of Dreams" he affirmed that there were other, more significant reasons. Storyville, to a New Orleans musician, was only part of the picture: "If you asked him what killed the music business in that town he'll tell you any one of a number of things—the radio, the talking picture, the filling in of the lake front, poverty."[102] Perhaps Smith should have entitled this piece "Land of Nightmares," for his visit to New Orleans revealed to him not the musical Mecca he had imagined, but a town where talent went unappreciated and underestimated. The players were there—he met many of them—but local outlets were more attracted to national "name" bands, so major venues were denied to local musicians. His judgment of the city's musical culture in 1939 would sound familiar to New Orleans residents today: "Although New Orleans continues to be a musician's city, with the lessening of jobs there has come an inevitable lessening of young talent. There isn't the economic incentive, for one thing. The youngster knows, or is duly warned by his parents, that choosing music for a profession is a shortcut to poverty. Moreover, he will not hear as much good jazz in New Orleans as formerly. But this isn't because there are no musicians. It's simply because the city can't support them."[103] Within the black underworld of the city, jazzmen like "Big Eye" Louis Nelson (1885–1949), Walter "Fats" Pichon (1905–1957), Burnell Santiago (1915–1944), and John Brunious (1920–1976) could still be heard, and maybe twice a week, if they were lucky, they worked the nightclubs of the French Quarter. Henry "Kid" Rena (1898–1949), who had come up with Bunk, Joe Oliver, and Louis Armstrong, was recovering from a long illness, yet he was fortunate to be working seven nights a week in a dance hall catering to locals. Smith portrayed the New Orleans music scene in dire terms, and when the discussion abruptly shifts to non-Orleanians like Chick Webb (1909–1939), Mary Lou Williams (1910–1981), and the expatriate Sidney Bechet, there is a palpable sense of relief.

The Swing Era was often hard on New Orleans musicians who sought to preserve "traditional" New Orleans style. Whether at home or abroad, their big band peers tended to objectify them as relics. Jelly Roll Morton, whose success in the 1920s came to an abrupt halt in the Depression years, when Victor dropped him, was ridiculed and even vilified by jazz musicians in Harlem in the 1930s. Yet others, like clarinetist Barney Bigard (1906–1980), a featured soloist with Duke Ellington, had no difficulty fitting in. The Luis Russell (1902–1963) Orchestra in New York, composed primarily of Creole, African American, and Latino New Orleans transplants, produced marvelously innovative swing arrangements that reflected New Orleans style. Bob Crosby's (1913–1993) Bob Cats (a combo within a big band) matched fresh arrangements of New Orleans–style classics with the more "contemporary" material recorded by the orchestra. In New Orleans, the big bands of Herbert Leary (1911–1988), Sidney Desvignes (1893–1959), and Walter Pichon found work, but musicians who wanted national recognition had to leave the city, as exemplified by Don Albert (1909–1980), a Creole who toured widely after moving to San Antonio in 1930.[104]

Smith discusses this perception of alienation in relation to Sidney Bechet, apropos of the difficulties he encountered in merging with contemporary swing musicians who lacked a grasp of New Orleans style. He quotes Bechet's reaction to the band in which John Hammond placed him for the "Spirituals to Swing" concert at Carnegie Hall: "It didn't feel quite right. I wanted the band with me. They put the rhythm section up on the platform."[105] For those unfamiliar with the specifics of New Orleans style, such comments would be unintelligible, but any musician who had left the city to try his luck elsewhere would know exactly what Bechet meant, for they had experienced similar problems. That is why Joe Oliver sent for New Orleans men as replacements for his bands in Chicago, why Jelly Roll Morton was so careful in picking sidemen for his recording sessions, and why both of these men ended their careers in despair when the supply of New Orleans talent began to dwindle during the Depression. Like Russell, Smith came to appreciate the importance of New Orleans style to the musicians who practiced it and the way in which it differed from a "hot" style that now seemed less distinctive, a generic category that had outlived its usefulness. Of course, Smith would be accused of hopeless antiquarianism by many of his contemporaries. Given the title and content of "Land of Dreams," he would have gladly pled guilty, for he knew that without new blood to carry on the tradition, the diminishing ranks of New Orleans stylists meant eventual extinction.

Frederic Ramsey's piece on King Oliver made this point dramatically. Oliver's death, in April 1938, practically demanded a panegyric, and Ramsey supplied it. In choosing Oliver, he knew he had a tragedy on his hands, and he decided to make the most of it, because in a sense it encapsulated what had happened to New Orleans style. Although a good deal of Ramsey's information on Oliver's early years was erroneous, the letters that he obtained—especially those having to do with the last years of his life—were particularly poignant.[106] More than any of the other contributions to *Jazzmen,* Ramsey's was a literary rather than a strictly historical account, especially noticeable in the instances of dialogue attributed to Oliver. Some of the hyperbole may have resulted from the use of Bunk Johnson as a source, but it is also clear that the "mytho-poetic" treatment of Oliver was intentional.[107]

As portrayed by Ramsey, Joe Oliver had to fight his way to the top echelon of New Orleans cornetists, overcoming obstacles related to his youth, "slow learning," and the jealousy of established heroes like Freddie Keppard and Manuel Perez (1873–1946). After one night at "Aberdeen's Bar"

(Abadie's) in Storyville, when Oliver blew "clear as a bell, crisp and clean," the tables were turned—he was crowned "King."[108] With the closing of the District, he headed for Chicago, where he became a sensation.[109] As Ramsey said, "Every week brought a new triumph for Oliver."[110] Tales of gargantuan displays of consumption—like eating a dozen pies at one sitting on a bet—are commonplace in his account, and in Los Angeles, Oliver turned down "the highest salary ever offered to anyone" because he missed Chicago. With the arrival of Louis Armstrong, Oliver's Creole Jazz Band reached the level of magic: "No one understood how Joe and Louis could play together without looking at each other, or without written music at all, yet run through a break and not clash on a single note."[111] Somewhat reminiscent of Keppard's reaction to the Victor offer, Ramsey depicts Oliver cutting the titles off the music his band used to prevent other bands from stealing his repertoire. The band recorded for Gennett, OKeh, and Columbia, but the boys "that put jazz on the map" with these recordings for Oliver soon betrayed him. Ramsey saw this occasion as the turning point for "King Joe." The defection of Johnny and Baby Dodds with Honoré Dutrey (ca. 1887–1935), followed closely by Lil and Louis Armstrong, was a harbinger of bad times to come: "Before this date, Joe had never had particularly good luck. But by sticking close to his idea of being 'a band man, and a band man only,' he had managed to reach the top of his profession, and to gather together an orchestra that deserved all the fame and money that came to it. Henceforth, he was trailed by misfortunes which dogged him and pulled him down. This never stopped him; he went on trying to organize one band after another, sometimes meeting with fair success, only to have someone else come along and draw the musicians in his orchestra away from him. Whenever everything seemed to be going fairly well, there was sure to be some particularly unfair blow from an unexpected source."[112] A fire on the first night ruined a propitious debut of a bigger and better band at the newly refurbished Lincoln Gardens. Oliver went to work for Peyton's Symphonic Syncopators at the Plantation Café as a featured sideman, a step down, even if he was billed as "the world's greatest jazz cornetist."

In 1925, he formed the Dixie Syncopators with a New Orleans crew that included Edward "Kid" Ory, Barney Bigard, Albert Nicholas (1900–1973), Luis Russell, and Paul Barbarin (1899–1969). Two years later, Oliver was still playing at the Plantation and "holding office hours" as a composer for music publishers when the club closed for remodeling. The alternative was touring, and while on the road, Oliver inaugurated an unsuccessful letter-writing campaign to try to lure Bunk Johnson away from the South. Lengthy touring meant increased attrition, a problem that became recurrent as jobs became scarce. Increasingly, Oliver found himself at the mercy of unscrupulous booking agents, a bus that kept breaking down, and recalcitrant bandsmen, and then his teeth began to bother him—he lost them all. By 1937 he was stranded in the South, where few people had heard of him, and before his death he was reduced to the role of pool hall attendant in Savannah, Georgia. Family members arranged to have him buried at a plot in the Woodlawn Cemetery in New York, but no money remained for a headstone. As Ramsey attested, by the time *Jazzmen* was published, Oliver's legacy was all but forgotten: "His name is disappearing fast; music that derives from his Creole Jazz Band is played today by musicians who know nothing of King Oliver. Only his family, and his old friends from New Orleans and Chicago, remember him now; men like Bunk Johnson, to whom he once wrote: 'I too would like to see you, so we could sit down and talk about old times.' "[113]

The tragedy of Oliver's career after he left Chicago was in stark contrast to that of Louis Armstrong, his erstwhile protégé. While Oliver was continually plagued by bad luck or victimized by poor judgment as a businessman, Armstrong's experience was just the opposite. William Russell's "Louis Armstrong" showed how someone was always there to help Louis when he needed it, including Oliver. When "little Louis" was arrested for firing a pistol in 1913, the resulting time spent in the Waifs' Home provided instruction on cornet by bandsman Peter Davis (ca. 1880–1971).[114] The golden opportunity to join Oliver in Chicago led to marriage with Lil Hardin, a pianist who had attended Fisk University. Her interest in his "improvement" sharpened Armstrong's reading skills and provided the guidance that launched his solo career and superstar status with Fletcher Henderson's orchestra in New York. But Russell's explanation of Armstrong's rise to the top of the entertainment world did not attribute it to luck but, instead, to unmitigated talent, "which was developed in a harder training school than that of which most jazz musicians of today have to go through."[115]

One of the qualities Russell admired in Armstrong was his endurance. "His physique, lung power, lip control, and throat relaxation, which enable him to obtain such fullness of tone throughout his entire range," impressed

Russell. Such qualities "were developed by many a long march under the semi-tropical New Orleans sun, and by long nights of playing in Storyville's cabarets."[116] Moreover, his showmanship, for which he was often criticized, was also rooted in the environment from which he had emerged:

> So many critics and too-serious purists among the hot fans who object to the showmanship, facial contortions, and bodily antics of the New Orleans musicians forget that in the public eye they were only entertainers, along with the "dancing girls," and their livelihood depended on their comic as well as musical ability. . . . We should be under no illusions about the artistic aspirations of those who worked in Storyville; the musicians were trained to entertain the customers of brothels and barrel-houses. In this amusement business the gift of gab in kidding the patrons had a telling effect when the players came down from their balcony to pass the hat.[117]

Recording sessions for the Hot Five in the mid-1920s were "the height of informality," once again demonstrating the nonchalance of New Orleans musicians, who frequently ruined "takes" with outbursts of laughter and other spontaneous tomfoolery.[118] Armstrong's use of glissandi, delayed attack to achieve rhythmic "swing," and excursions away from diatonic scales into modal blues scales embellished with chromatic runs all testified to the extent to which New Orleans players had departed from European conventions. Russell described Armstrong as a singular and unique performer but also stressed his indebtedness to a distinctive musical environment. Although the imperatives of the music industry did influence the subsequent direction of Armstrong's career (Russell followed it to about 1931), Russell's account left the impression that a little bit of New Orleans remained in everything Armstrong did.

Other chapters in *Jazzmen* described the dissemination of jazz to Chicago and New York, recounting tales of Bix Beiderbecke, the Austin High Gang, Red Nichols, and the phenomenon of Fifty-second Street. The significance of Stephen Smith's "Hot Collecting" has already been mentioned, while Roger Pryor Dodge's "Consider the Critics" sketched the history of writers who had shown an early interest in jazz. But it was the section on New Orleans that not only provided the most in the way of new information on jazz origins but also emphatically claimed priority and distinction for the products of that musical culture. What the authors of *Jazzmen* liked about New Orleans was that it was a city where music was used for enjoyment rather than edification. Although there was perhaps too strong a distinction made between African American "fakers" and musically literate Creoles, such pervasive factors as interest in the blues among young people of diverse backgrounds, experiments in instrumentation designed to explore the expressive power of small bands engaging in polyphony, and the widespread inclusion of "trap" drummers to intensify rhythm for dancers were sufficient to argue that New Orleans jazz musicians shared a common style.

Positing New Orleans style as the beginning and focal point of jazz history, *Jazzmen* established a consensus paradigm on what jazz was and how it had come into being, refuting the stereotypes that had elicited so much confusion in the 1920s. In addition, it provided a foundation for subsequent versions of jazz history that remains largely intact, subject to only minor tinkering here and there. One must therefore ask how the book has fared among the historians who have responded to Scott DeVeaux's call for a dismantling of the "official" history that *Jazzmen* helped to launch. DeVeaux refers to *Jazzmen* as a "landmark" book that was essentially "biographical," adding that "there is little by way of formal argument in [its] highly anecdotal narrative. . . . The one most consistently and vividly represented [narrative] in *Jazzmen* is The Tragic."[119] While DeVeaux's appreciation of the biographical component honors the desire of the authors of *Jazzmen* to allow the musicians to "tell their own story," he overlooks the cultural/environmental argument in the New Orleans chapters completely. Further, while Fred Ramsey's treatment of Oliver certainly qualifies as "Tragic," Russell's chapter on Armstrong does not. DeVeaux's characterization misses much of what makes the book important.

Others dismiss the theoretical implications of the book as well. Although Guthrie Ramsey celebrates Sargeant's *Hot and Hybrid* for adumbrating interest in "the transformation of African cultural practices into American ones . . . that would begin to blossom in the 1940s," he incorrectly excludes the authors of *Jazzmen* from those who were "sensitive to that notion," beyond the mention by Frederic Ramsey and Charles Edward Smith that "the Negroes retained much of the African material in their playing." For him, the salient feature of the book is the misguided belief that "the uniqueness of jazz, especially during the New Orleans period, was the result of musical illiteracy, a condition these authors considered a virtue."[120] Like DeVeaux, Ramsey fails to address the implications of the cultural/environmental arguments made by Russell and Smith, especially with regard to what must be construed as an abrupt break with the tendency to explain jazz origins in terms of racial essentialism (present to some degree in Hobson's *American Jazz Music,* published only months before). Cultural explanations that played down the idea of innate racial and ethnic behaviors and focused on common, regional, culture-building processes allowed the "hot" collector community in general to get beyond this type of thinking. Congo Square had "Africanized" the New Orleans music scene long before the emergence of jazz. Although such insights relating to the "discovery" of New Orleans style had been present in germ since publication of Delauany's *Hot Discographie* in 1936, their presentation as a fully developed theory of jazz origins in *Jazzmen* in 1939 had a formidable and immediate impact.

John Gennari appreciates this impact fully. After quoting jazz critic Nat Hentoff on how the book dramatically changed his life upon first reading, he explicates *Jazzmen*'s thematic content, noting how it parallels developments "chronicled in 1930s urban proletarian literature and ethnographic journalism" and concluding that "*Jazzmen* featured intelligent musical analysis of lasting value."[121] He argues that the narrative thread is not so much Tragic as it is informed by a kind of Heroic Romanticism and reads the book as folklore, "an epic full of larger-than-life heroes and unforgettable places that cohered into a new national mythology."[122] Gennari also recognizes that "*Jazzmen* was replete with . . . examples of powerful cross-racial cultural exchanges and affinities[;] even as in its most politically progressive moments it reckoned honestly with the jazz world's own racism [in which] Charles Edward Smith took the lead." He situates *Jazzmen* correctly in connecting it to the exploration of American folklore but does not seem to fully grasp how such "exchanges and affinities" were specifically predicated on the cultural peculiarities of New Orleans as a discrete regional environment.[123]

The most emphatically "Tragic" narrative within *Jazzmen* does not pertain primarily to the diminuendos of once great musicians who had been laid low by adversity but to the plight of America's regional cultures, although these stories were related. The threat posed to the regional jazz culture of New Orleans by the consolidation of the American entertainment industry in Northeastern urban centers (and later West Coast cities) is the specter that haunts the book most tellingly. As DeVeaux suggests, "the general enthusiasm for swing did not necessarily translate into appreciation for, or even awareness of, the jazz that stemmed from New Orleans. . . . Swing brought both a new musical language and a new economic basis for the music which threatened to make the earlier style obsolete."[124]

Appreciating the symbiotic connection between regionalism and the vernacular arts that informed *Jazzmen*'s exposition of New Orleans music is essential to understanding its significance as a jazz history. As Arthur F. Wertheim has shown, the association of regionalism and vernacular culture was typical of the intellectual climate existing during the Depression. Wertheim remarks of folklorist Constance Rourke (1885–1941) that "her interest in the relationship of folk and popular culture to regional traditions led to the discovery of neglected aspects of Americana."[125] In essays on Paul Bunyan and vaudeville in the *New Republic* in the 1920s and in *American Humor* in 1931, Rourke devalued the influence of European culture in the shaping of national trends, thus celebrating the integrity and vitality of America's indigenous culture. Intrinsic to Rourke's approach was a repudiation of the notion that Northeastern urban control over the economy and the arts had been the salient feature in the nation's cultural development. Like the authors of the New Orleans section of *Jazzmen*, Rourke looked upon regional cultures nostalgically, venerating traditions that were being effaced by the dual impulses of technology and national consolidation. For such scholars, whatever national culture America could boast derived from the wellspring of regional cultures that had nourished it. Rourke's writings were political in the sense that they emphasized the need to preserve what remained of regional culture and raised public awareness of the issue. Like Charles Edward Smith and William Russell, she was an advocate for a vanishing America. The sense of urgency that infused her writings was certainly understandable at the time, and it may be related to contemporaneous attempts at preservation of local culture evident in New Deal programs like the Federal Art Project and other facets of the Works Project Administration (WPA).[126] All in all, the motives and methods that inspired Rourke's work and the New Deal programs were much the same as those within *Jazzmen*.

The discovery of the circumstances that had given rise to New Orleans style was thus part of a larger crusade to document and understand the role of regional cultures in the building of an American national culture. That these regional variants underwent transformation and even distortion when exported beyond the confines of their cultural context made their identification and preservation urgent, but it did not necessarily mean that derivative forms lacked artistic merit or integrity, although some surely did. Some of the content of *Jazzmen* was based on misinformation, yet the realization that New Orleans style was distinctive and endangered enhanced the sense of urgency and purpose that had motivated authors like William Russell, Charles Edward Smith, and Frederic Ramsey Jr. Subsequent scholarship could correct dubious "facts."[127] After *Jazzmen* was published, however, interest in writing extensive histories dwindled to some extent among the New Orleans purists associated with it. What became increasingly important to them was the preservation of what remained of New Orleans style among old-timers like Bunk Johnson, Henry "Kid" Rena, Jelly Roll Morton, Kid Ory, and Sidney Bechet, none of whom were flourishing when *Jazzmen* was finally published in October 1939. Saving the style thus became a matter of rehabilitating the musicians themselves and providing them with the wherewithal to practice their art in an environment that would be conducive and sympathetic, at least in theory.

The essentially passive role of the collector-turned-historian now took on new meaning, bordering on social activism. Initial attempts to infiltrate major record companies (which began to take an interest in reissues of old stock when the records' renewed marketability became apparent in the late 1930s) ultimately led to collector-inspired independent efforts emphasizing decidedly communitarian imperatives. During the 1940s, the lessons learned in the previous decade were actively applied in a valiant crusade directed against what the purists saw as the commercialization and intellectualization of jazz. To men like Russell, Smith, and Ramsey, keeping jazz "down to earth" was a labor of love completely consistent with their social views, but as ideology began to ripen, it also grew more rigid, leading to miscommunication among the New Orleans musicians and their benefactors. Yet if successes were matched by failures, the legacy of commitment and action deriving from the efforts of New Orleans–style purists to turn back the march of time would be a documentary record available for all to hear. In this regard, it remains a testament not only to the musicians but to the producers as well.

CHAPTER 3

A Declaration of Independents: Noncommercial Music and Collector Discology

By 1940, American jazz writing had undergone two major phases of development. From 1917, a first phase of controversy opened a floodgate of opinion concerning the transformational power of jazz. Some of this writing was hopeful, seeing the music as a means to revitalize a European cultural tradition that was already being Americanized. Much of it sought to exploit the fear of change, blaming jazz for the decline of morality, cultural decadence, the rebellion of youth, and encroachment by racial and ethnic minorities. Little attention was given to the origins of jazz, except for speculation concerning the historical derivation of the term. The rush to judgment all but precluded the development of historical sources, making reliable information sparse and erratic. During the 1920s, commentary from music educators, journalists, preachers, outraged parents, and press agents represented a random and extremely diffuse cross-section of opinion.

Beginning with Charles Edward Smith's *Symposium* article in 1930, and couched to some extent in the favorable record reviews of R. D. Darrell, B. H. Haggin, and Roger Pryor Dodge, a second phase of consolidation emerged that redirected the course of jazz writing. Henceforth, jazz opinion tended to be shaped by supporters of the music, who formed a consensus on the implicit value of jazz as art. As record collectors, writers, and scholars, they promoted the "righteous cause" for fun and profit. In response to a legacy of misinformation and confusion, they sought to establish order. Reformist zeal marked the writings of Charles Edward Smith, William Russell, Frederic Ramsey, Marshall Stearns, John Hammond, Hugues Panassié, and Charles Delaunay, indicating awareness of past debates, but it was most apparent in their attempts to educate the public on the history of jazz. A concomitant of collecting, discographical research yielded ever-expanding lists of jazz personnel, often leading to interviews with musicians. In the course of a decade, jazz scholars penetrated beneath the record label to reveal historical realities mirroring larger social concerns of racism, the commercialization of art, and the nationalization of culture. Given their interest in these issues, and considering the political polarization occasioned by the incidence of the Depression and the magnetic pull of fascism and communism, many jazz writers inevitably gravitated to leftist publications like the *Daily Worker, New Masses,* and the *New Republic.* But from the middle of the decade on, opportunities provided by specialty magazines like *Down Beat,* as well as broad-based circulations such as *Esquire,* enabled these writers to influence opinion by establishing their own agenda. The inclination of publishers to market "serious" books on jazz strengthened the trend toward mass acceptance, and the appearance of *American Jazz Music* and *Jazzmen* in 1939 consolidated jazz opinion around a set of discrete historical issues, completing the definition of parameters in a combination of criticism, discography, and history, roughly in that chronological order.

John Gennari and Ron Welburn argue that critical standards reached a stage of maturity by 1940, with Winthrop Sargent's 1938 *Jazz: Hot and Hybrid* the first important musicological synthesis of jazz. While 1939 was a watershed year for jazz history, however, what of discology?[1] Phonograph records were the first sources for all jazz scholars, and the relationship between collectors and manufacturers of phonograph records figured significantly in the gathering of discographical information. From the vantage of collectors, the main issue was access—to company listings and session logs, to masters of out-of-print recordings, to recording contracts for preferred artists—and when access was curtailed, many of them responded by forming recording companies of their own. At the heart of this issue was the belief that manufacturers, whose primary interest was profit, could not be relied upon to fully document or preserve the art form. During the late 1930s and 1940s, passive discography gave way to militant discology in a movement to resurrect New Orleans–style jazz and preserve it, usually referred to as "the revival." Not surprisingly, the only two works devoted exclusively to this phenomenon are both discographies, and in order to appreciate how the revival influenced jazz writing and history, it will first be necessary to explore the methods collectors employed to preserve the phonographic record of jazz.[2]

The history of the recording industry is especially fascinating because of the variance between its initial aims and its present ones.[3] As originally constituted, Edison's North American Phonograph Company and its affiliates were in the business of selling phonographs to corporate America to aid stenographers. As testimony given at the 1890 convention of Edison affiliates affirmed, recordings of music were sometimes used for demonstration purposes but tended to subvert the sales pitch directed at businessmen.[4] Large-scale production of recorded music for a consumer audience was never seriously considered in the early 1890s, partially because of the limits of technology but also because of an entrenched bias against popular entertainment as unlikely to yield much profit—an attitude that soon changed. When the phonograph was adapted to public use in the form of a lucrative nickel coin-slot cylinder player (installed in drugstores and cabarets), affiliates like the Louisiana Phonograph Company began to realize the potential for profit in recording music and marketing it to consumers.[5] But a hostile takeover battle, pitched against Edison by the rival American Graphophone Company, caused the first chapter of the recording industry's saga to end in bankruptcy in 1896, and reorganization of the industry's corporate structure in the early twentieth century led to predominance by two companies, Columbia and Victor, locked in competitive struggle.

A patent pool in 1902 on lateral-cut phonograph technology, and the switch from cylinders to discs, allowed Columbia and Victor almost complete control over the production of phonographs and sound recordings in the United States prior to the patents' expiration. By 1912, the recording industry included only three companies: Victor, Columbia, and Edison. As patents expired, a national mania for dance records created the first boom period for the phonograph, in 1913, and by 1916 forty-six manufacturers were in the business.[6] One year later, the ODJB demonstrated a huge demand for jazz records, but the response of manufacturers was conservative. As Chris Sheridan has observed, "Before 1920 the companies grossly underestimated the possible market for jazz, especially among the black population, none of whom, it was erroneously believed, could afford the equipment to play back records."[7] Throughout the 1920s, the recording industry was controlled by manufacturers who packaged "jazz in Chippendale" to consumers, using 75-cent records to entice buyers to invest up to $2,000 in record players.[8] Between 1914 and 1919, the value of phonograph production jumped from $27,116,000 to $158,668,000, and the number of manufacturers swelled to nearly two hundred.[9] Overproduction and a contracting market in 1920 forced many of them into receivership, coinciding with a business depression in 1921–22. Ultimately, however, record sales began to compensate for failures in the marketing of phonographs. In 1921, 100,000,000 records were produced (a dramatic increase over the 1914 figure of 25,000,000), and two years later production remained high at 92,000,000. Roland Gelatt attributes this prosperity to the demand for jazz, which was responsible for keeping the dance craze alive.[10] In little more than thirty years, the phonograph industry had expanded its market to include the home-listening-and-dancing audience, but the subordination of music to machinery remained constant.

The cautiousness of major companies like Victor and Columbia was evident in their reluctance to expand jazz releases and in their failure to exploit the black market. Several independent record companies, such as the "race" labels Gennett, Paramount, and OKeh, became the prime sources for the documentation of jazz. Because of their success, the policies of the majors changed. Prior to 1926, Victor's artists and repertoire (A&R) director was Eddie King (1895–1974), whose dislike of "hot" music and abandonment of plans for a "race" series in 1921 put the company at a disadvantage in the growing jazz market. His replacement by bandleader Nat Shilkret (1889–1982) enhanced the Victor jazz catalog, adding Jelly Roll Morton, Duke Ellington, and King Oliver to the roster between 1926 and 1930.[11] From 1927 to 1930, Victor's commitment to the documentation of jazz became even more convincing when the company made field recordings of jug bands in Memphis. By the beginning of 1929, the company had inaugurated a "race" policy with the V-38000 series. Shortly afterward, however, Victor was taken over by Radio Corporation of America, and the "race" series was discontinued in 1930. Due largely to competition with radio, record sales began to decline even before the Crash of 1929, reducing annual totals from almost 100,000,000 in 1927 to 6,000,000 in 1932. Phonograph sales also declined, from 1,000,000 to 40,000, in the same period.[12] Implosion of the recording market caused severe retrenchment and removed independent labels from the industry. Yet in retrospect, it was apparent that the independents had set trends that major recording companies followed in the 1920s. Fred Wiggins (1881–1968) of Gennett had recorded Jelly Roll Morton with the New Orleans Rhythm Kings in 1923, and along with King Oliver's Creole Jazz Band, Bix Beiderbecke and the Wolverines also gained early recognition as a result of their connection with Gennett. Columbia's 13000-D and 14000-D "race" series had come early, in November 1923, as an attempt to copy OKeh's success with Mamie Smith and Oliver. Columbia was so taken with OKeh, in fact, that the company acquired it in November 1926.[13] OKeh's maxim of recording good jazz wherever it could be found was transferred to the major, which made recordings in New Orleans of Celestin, the New Orleans Owls, and Sam Morgan's Jazz Band in the period 1925–27. Like the independents, the majors saw the need to expand the documentation of jazz, including regional variations, by the end of the decade.

The man whose work most fully embodied the documentary spirit within the record industry from 1917 to 1929 was Ralph Peer (1892–1960). As an A&R man for Columbia in 1917, he had arranged the ODJB's audition in January 1917. Unfortunately for Columbia, however, company executives scoffed at the results, and the spoils went to Victor.[14] By 1924, Peer was with OKeh, scouting the territories for musical talent, and in March of that year he arrived in New Orleans, leading to the first jazz recordings ever made in that city, including Johnny DeDroit (1892–1986) and his New Orleans Jazz Orchestra, the S. S. Capitol Orchestra, Johnny Bayersdorffer (1899–1969), A. J. Piron, and the Original Crescent City Jazzers. In January 1925, Peer returned to record Celestin's Original Tuxedo Jazz Orchestra; Abbie Brunies's (1900–1978) Halfway House Orchestra; the New Orleans Rhythm Kings; Billy and Mary Mack with Ernest "Kid Punch" Miller (1894–1971); and the Midnight Serenaders, featuring "Papa" Jac Assunto (1905–1985). When Columbia absorbed OKeh, Peer joined Victor and continued his roving recording activities, returning to New Orleans in 1927 to capture Louis Dumaine (ca. 1890–1949) and his Jazzola Eight, Ann Cook (ca. 1888–1962), John Hyman (1899–1977) and his Bayou Stompers, and Richard "Rabbit" Brown (ca. 1880–1937). It was during this excursion that he also reached Bristol, Tennessee, to record pioneer "hillbilly" performer Jimmie Rodgers (1897–1933) and the Carter Family for the first time; he would maintain a strong interest

in cowboy songs, Cajun ballads, and other folk music throughout his trav-
els.[15] Ralph Peer's journey through Columbia, OKeh, and Victor helped to
establish a broader perspective among recording companies as to the kinds of
music that were suitable for recording.

Peer's progress in documenting bands outside of the main recording centers in New York and Chicago was permitted by technological innovation.
By 1925, electrical recording was beginning to replace acoustical techniques,
greatly enhancing fidelity and allowing mobile units to engage in field recordings, which were still being made on cylinders.[16] Despite his catholic tastes,
Peer's field recordings were intended to expand markets by featuring local
talent, largely to induce further sampling of the general catalog. He could
have recorded Henry "Kid" Rena, Buddy Petit (né Joseph Crawford;
1887–1931), and Chris Kelly (1891–1929) in New Orleans but was presumably
unaware of them or unsure they would sell.[17] Other A&R men who organized sessions in New Orleans occasionally let the economic incentive rule
their relations with local bands. Benjie White (1901–1987), of the New Orleans Owls, remembered a Columbia official excluding most of the band's
repertoire in favor of songs that he wanted to plug, most of which they did
not know. It was also a Columbia man who instigated the famous "hot" renditions of hymns like "Sing On" and "Down by the Riverside" by Sam Morgan's Jazz Band in 1927, insisting that they should be recorded in dance
tempo. The band agreed to record his versions but refused to incorporate
them into live performances for fear of offending audiences.[18] Most A&R
men preferred to "develop" jazz talent, making changes in the artist's performance whenever they thought it might improve the product. Their very involvement defeated the cause of objective documentation of undiscovered,
regional music and furthered the nationalization of culture that the recording
industry and radio were promoting.

Recording with minimal tampering, however, was occurring beyond the
confines of the record industry. In 1920, Robert Winslow Gordon
(1888–1961), a folklorist trained at Harvard, made field recordings of folk
music on cylinders. Gordon wrote of his findings in *Adventure* magazine
throughout the 1920s, and in 1928 the Library of Congress hired him to establish an Archive of American Folksong. Although Gordon was interested
in the influence of popular music on folksong, he did not record any jazz. But
he did help to provide an alternative approach to the commercialism of the

record industry.[19] The folklorist sought to preserve the music as he found it, remaining ever vigilant for regional variations. Rather than exploiting the music for profit, he wanted to understand it. Armed with anachronistic cylinder recorders, folklorists learned to make do with limited budgets and technology, relying on the purity and expressiveness of the performance to reward their efforts. Given shared ideology, it was no wonder that "hot" collectors used folklorists as their role models and accordingly treated jazz as folk music, despite the problems this approach entailed.

Gordon's recordings built on the work of John Avery Lomax (1867–1948), the collector of cowboy songs who, along with his son Alan, succeeded Gordon as director of the Archive of American Folksong in 1933. Alan was still a teenager, but his appetite for field recording was expansive. In 1935, he accompanied Zora Neale Hurston on an expedition to Florida, where he sometimes donned blackface to avoid trouble with white authorities.[20] Lomax's fascination with black folksong, particularly the blues, led him to the periphery of jazz, but for many years he considered it too commercialized to warrant serious attention. He may have inherited this opinion from his father, for his first ventures into field recording were at John Avery's side, in 1932, while collecting for *American Ballads and Folksongs* (1934). The elder Lomax had started his career interested in cowboy songs (*Cowboy Songs and Other Frontier Ballads* was published in 1910), but by 1932 he was collecting work songs, blues, and spirituals from the rural South, recording in lumber camps, small towns, and prisons. As a witness to black poverty and tribulation, Alan undoubtedly formed opinions about social injustice that were later reinforced by subsequent experience.[21] In addition, he found that field recording could serve the cause of social justice directly by focusing attention on a gifted performer. In 1934, father and son proved this point with Huddie Ledbetter (1889–1949), better known as Leadbelly, who became an instant celebrity after the Lomaxes recorded him at Angola Penitentiary, negotiated his freedom, and took him to New York.

Leadbelly, whose paternal grandparents had been murdered by the Ku Klux Klan, was perfectly suited for conveying a message of epic proportions relating to the plight of blacks in the South. He was an itinerant musician who had worked in the bawdy houses of Shreveport, Louisiana, by the time he was sixteen and had been in and out of prison numerous times, usually for violent crimes stemming from battles over women and whiskey. Leadbelly was probably the only convict ever to sing his way out of prison twice. Texas governor Pat Neff pardoned him in 1925 after he took advantage of a gubernatorial visit to sing a plea for mercy. Nine years later, the Lomaxes arranged for his second pardon, from Governor O. K. Allen of Louisiana. Following his release from Angola, Leadbelly accompanied John Lomax on a tour of Southern prisons, helping him to gain the confidence of inmates for recording purposes. After a journey covering six thousand miles, Leadbelly was brought to New York City to entertain the intellectuals and artists of Greenwich Village, where he became the hit of the party circuit. In these environs, jazz enthusiasts like Charles Edward Smith and John Hammond mingled freely with folklorists like the Lomaxes, and Leadbelly's triumph in 1934 was a precursor of Bunk Johnson's reception a decade later. Folklorists provided a frame of reference for jazz collectors on several levels. Their field recordings embodied the documentary spirit, and they offered an example of committed scholarship with more than a tinge of social activism. In due course, the convergence of interest between jazz researchers and folklorists could not be denied, and it was Alan Lomax who first bridged the gap by recording Jelly Roll Morton for the Library of Congress in 1938, a feat that was accomplished through force of personality, although not his own.

Lomax, in fact, did not recruit Morton for the sessions. According to Bill Russell, jazz writer Sidney Martin persuaded Morton to go, uninvited, to the Library of Congress because it was recording folk artists.[22] Lomax later described his first meeting with Morton: "He came there with some friends of his who knew him and said he wanted to correct the history of jazz. Well, at that time jazz was my worst enemy. It was wiping out, through the forces of the radio, all the music that I cared about—American traditional folk music—and I looked at him with considerable suspicion, but I thought: 'Well, I'll take this cat on and see what he can do.'"[23] The urbane and vociferous Morton was the antithesis of the folk artists whom Lomax had been interviewing, but given "hot" collector attitudes about jazz as a folklike music and the added potential for gaining information about the itinerant musicians with whom Morton had consorted, there was plenty of reason to audition him. The test was "Alabama Bound," which Morton played with such sensitivity that Lomax was immediately converted. In a burst of enthusiasm, he obtained permission from his superiors to use fifty blank aluminum discs and quickly returned to Morton with a bottle of whiskey that he had been keeping for a special occasion. He placed the bottle on the piano and sat at the pianist's feet with a crystal microphone, not exactly sure how to proceed. Morton began to play and started talking, reticently at first, but the music seemed to boost his confidence, and soon "he realized that he had been given an opportunity to make his statement in full." Perhaps for the first time in his life, "he felt he had the kind of recognition he knew, in truth, he deserved."[24] The sessions, which began in May, lasted several weeks and were resumed briefly in December, during which time Lomax was given the essentials of jazz history according to Jelly Roll Morton.

Like many jazz pioneers, Morton had thrived during the 1920s, riding the record boom and publishing his compositions with the Melrose Brothers.[25] With the collapse of the boom, he fell upon hard times, and his career came to a full stop when Victor decided not to renew his contract in late 1930. By 1938, he was living in Washington, D.C., working at the Music Box, a shoe box of a nightclub in which he was said to have an interest. Once "hot" collectors located him, pilgrimages by Bill Russell, Charles Edward Smith, Al Rose, Sidney Martin, and others became frequent.[26] Given his penchant for self-promotion, Jelly made no secret of his interviews with "the Librarian of Congress," as he called young Lomax, and was pleased that he had been recorded at great length, while most other interviews had been short.[27] Morton had already shared his story with various collectors and had written some vitriolic articles for *Down Beat,* but the extensive coverage bestowed upon Lomax surpassed existing sources, in both quality and scope.[28] What Lomax had fallen into was the first important oral history session ever recorded.[29] Not until 1947, however, when Rudi Blesh's Circle Records released an abridged version of the interviews in a twelve-album set for $125, did the content of the session gain broad circulation among collectors. Three years later, Lomax's *Mister Jelly Roll* was published, complete with a discography, and it was greeted as a major contribution to jazz letters.[30]

Bill Russell was able to gain access to the recordings early on, and there were complaints that the primitive Presto recorder that Lomax had used distorted the pitch of Morton's voice and piano. But the interviews afforded a wealth of new detail on New Orleans origins, particularly on the role played by Creole musicians.[31] Morton provided insights into family history, fraternal organizations, "second lines," "Mardi Gras Indians," and jazz funerals. Although his recollection of dates struck Lomax as haphazard, his memory of personalities like Tony Jackson, "Black Benny" Williams (ca. 1890–1924), and Game Kid was vital and highly anecdotal.[32] In reaction to the popular misconception that jazz had to be loud, raucous, and fast, Morton opined: "Jazz music is to be played sweet, soft, plenty rhythm. When you have your plenty rhythm with your plenty swing, it becomes beautiful. To start with, you can't make crescendos and diminuendos when one is playing triple forte. You got to be able to come down in order to go up. If a glass of water is full, you can't fill it any more; but if you have half a glass, you have the opportunity to put more water in it."[33] Morton also added insights on how popular tunes of the day had been reworked into New Orleans style: "We had our own way of doing. When we'd buy the regular stock arrangements, we would familiarize ourselves with the melody and then add what *we* wanted till we sounded like we had special orchestrations. Then we'd cut off the names at the top of the music in order to throw everybody off the scent. It used to make the music publishers so mad they wanted to tear up the sidewalk. But what could they do?"[34] By the time *Mister Jelly Roll* reached print, Lomax had supplemented the original material with information provided by interviews with Johnny St. Cyr, Bunk Johnson, and "Big Eye" Louis Nelson Delille, touching on subjects that Morton had avoided, such as segregation.[35] He had become a major presence in the community of jazz scholars. Never one to mince words, Lomax saw in Jelly's tale the same evils he had encountered in his attempts to preserve American folksong: "Maybe no music, no fresh emanation of the spirit of man ever spread to so many people in so short a time. Jazz, in this sense, is one of the marvels of the century—a marvel that has spawned a monster—a monster entertainment industry feeding upon jazz, growing gigantic and developing a score of interlocking colossal bodies whose million orifices pour out each week the stuff of our bartered dreams."[36] The music was a response to oppression: "It is within the folk life of these Creoles that the emotional character of hot jazz is to be found, for their music was not only an Afro-American offshoot, not merely a complex of many elements, but a new music of and by New Orleans—a wordless Creole counterpoint of protest and pride."[37] Lomax's emphasis on Creole contributions supplemented perspectives in *Jazzmen,* forging an important link in the chain of events that brought American jazz scholarship to a new level of maturity by 1940, but Lomax also improved on *Jazzmen*'s methods: the interviews with Morton showed how recording technology could preserve not only the music of jazzmen but also their life stories.

A growing awareness of these lessons was occurring within the academic community, particularly among historians. At the December 1939 meeting of the American Historical Association, the agenda was the study of culture through interdisciplinary methodology, focusing primarily on the work of anthropologists. In 1940, the proceedings of this meeting appeared as *The Cultural Approach to History*, and discussion of source materials included essays by folklorist Ben Botkin (1901–1975) and ethnomusicologist Charles Seeger (1886–1979).[38] Botkin affirmed the necessity of subjecting jazz history to scholarly analysis, adding that historians should be receptive to collecting "oral sources of local anecdote and personal reminiscence."[39] Seeger encouraged the expansion of source materials to include "the phonograph and the photograph, and still more the sound film," as well as other unwritten and nonverbal sources.[40] Together, they made a strong case for the incorporation of oral history techniques in the study of social history and argued convincingly for greater attention to popular and folk music as a legitimate source for historical study.

Of course, "hot" collectors had long been aware of the value of phonograph records as cultural artifacts. Many of them had started their collecting careers at the end of the 1920s, when the phonograph record market was in decline, but by 1934, when collecting had begun to proliferate, it seemed as though "authentic" jazz had died out with the bull market.[41] The great independent labels were no longer in business, and jazz heroes like Oliver and Morton were no longer making records. The men and women who promoted the New Orleans revival sought to redress this situation by combining the most enlightened aspects of the work of record industry pioneers like Ralph Peer with the purity of intent witnessed in the documentary spirit of folklorist field recordings. What resulted from this union was a concept of "noncommercial" music that became a rallying point for collectors interested in the history of jazz. Simultaneously, retrospection within the record industry accompanied rising record sales with Franklin Roosevelt's inauguration in 1933.[42] RCA Victor reintroduced a "race" series under the subsidiary Bluebird label during the summer of 1932, reducing prices to thirty-five cents per record and marketing the product through the Woolworth chain. Besides the contemporary recordings of artists like Fats Waller, Earl Hines (1903–1983), and Artie Shaw (1910–2004), Bluebird also rereleased classics by Jelly Roll Morton and the Jones and Collins Astoria Hot Eight and even brought out previously unissued material.[43] Encouraged by these trends, jazz record collectors sought to work with the major record companies, lobbying for more reissues and, especially in the case of John Hammond, infiltrating companies such as Columbia in order to make them more jazz conscious. With recovery as the foremost imperative for the industry, company executives were willing to experiment. In particular, two men who had served apprenticeships with Brunswick-Vocalion, Edward Wallerstein (1891–1970) and Jack Kapp (1909–1949), brought new attitudes to the forefront of the industry.

By 1934, Wallerstein had taken command of Victor's Record Division and was promoting the catalog through large advertising budgets. In September of that year, RCA introduced the Duo Jr., a small turntable/pickup unit that could be attached to radio sets. By the late 1920s, many Americans had opted for radio over phonographs, and phonograph sales had declined sharply by 1930. Roland Gelatt has written of this strategy's impact on the consumer: "Despite its limitations, the Duo Jr. reproduced records tolerably well when attached to a radio set of adequate size and power. Moreover, though it carried a list price of $16.50, it was practically given away with the purchase of a certain number of Victor records. RCA's Duo Jr. was not only made as inexpensively as possible but was sold at cost. Its low price helped to overcome the national resistance to phonographs and converted tens of thousands of Americans into record collectors. This writer was one of them."[44] In the early 1920s, free records were given away to promote phonograph sales; now the manufacturers were giving away free phonographs to promote records. The subordination of recordings to phonographs in the majors' policy had been reversed completely, submitting to the pressure of a buyer's market. Under Wallerstein, Victor cashed in on the swing craze with Fats Waller, Lionel Hampton (1908–2002), and Benny Goodman. Wallerstein later went to Columbia when it was revived in 1938 (following discontinuance in the United States in 1933) and helped to launch an extensive reissue program under the supervision of John Hammond and George Avakian (1919–). Although he continued to believe that "serious" music lovers were the backbone of the record market in the 1930s, once William S. Paley (1901–1990) of the Columbia Broadcasting System decided to acquire and revitalize the Columbia label, Wallerstein acted quickly to lure Benny Goodman and Duke Ellington away from Victor. At Hammond's suggestion, he also placed Count Basie under contract. Thus, in the course of less than a decade, he had not only managed to resuscitate Victor but had also restored a condition of intense competition within the industry by resurrecting Columbia. Based on increased advertising within the market, the benefits of jukeboxes for promotion, and price cuts, record sales reached 127,000,000 in 1941, a return to prosperity in which Wallerstein's guidance had been crucial.[45]

Jack Kapp's influence on the industry was similarly impressive. Kapp had recorded Jelly Roll Morton for Vocalion in 1926 and knew how to relate to jazz musicians.[46] In 1934, backed with the capital of London stockbroker E. R. Lewis, he started the Decca Record Company in the United States, named after its English counterpart. Kapp also realized the possibilities of bold advertising and inexpensive products, and his strategy was to offer "name" artists such as Bing Crosby (1903–1977), Fletcher Henderson, and the Mills Brothers at discount prices. Unlike Wallerstein, Kapp had no interest in classical music, preferring instead to build catalogs squarely on sweet and swing, and Decca enjoyed considerable success as a result. With artists like Louis Armstrong and Bob Crosby's Orchestra added to his roster, Kapp built Decca to second place, behind Victor, within five years.[47] In 1941, Decca bought Brunswick from the American Record Company, including the Vocalion and Melotone catalogs (six thousand masters), and Kapp hired Milt Gabler to put his acquisition in order. Gabler eventually became the supervisor for Decca's "hot" jazz sessions, working for Kapp from Monday through Friday and tending to his own business on weekends.[48] By 1943, Decca was supplementing its contemporary listings with reissues from the Brunswick catalog, keeping the collectors satisfied with historical material. Despite the willingness of Decca, RCA Victor, and Columbia to make out-of-print records available by the early 1940s, collectors were not entirely satisfied. While the majors had certainly made great strides in their appreciation of the demand for reissues during the 1930s, the revelations of jazz scholars had significantly broadened the expectations of the collector community. Jazz collectors applauded the reissue programs, but they distrusted the profit motive that had discriminated against important pioneers, and they knew that reissues would be deleted if they did not sell. In the end, they realized that the only way to fully document New Orleans–style jazz and other "noncommercial" music was to do it themselves.

The emergence of a new breed of independent labels dedicated to documentation of "authentic" jazz can be traced back to the coteries of "hot" collectors in New York City in 1934 and to Panassié and Delaunay in the Hot Club de France. Once again, the French were one step ahead of the Americans. In the spring of 1937, Delaunay established Swing to document the musicians who were available to him and to license new American releases. Pathé-Marconi (affiliated with EMI) handled production and distribution, and the artists recorded included Django Reinhardt (1910–1953), as well as visiting Americans such as Coleman Hawkins (1904–1969) and Benny Carter (1907–2003). It was the best situation conceivable, giving Delaunay complete artistic control.[49]

In the United States, Milt Gabler was the first to initiate independent reissues, a path to contemporaneous documentation, and a 1941 pamphlet for his Commodore Record Company explains what motivated his decision to enter the field:

> Jazz collectors have had a hard row to hoe for at least two decades. Great jazz recordings, items that give satisfaction with repeated playing, have been few and far between. About five percent of the total output of the major companies' waxings live through the years. Of course, in this year 1941, there are countless fine recordings to build a collection with, the only trouble being the inaccessibility of these masterpieces. For years, the recording companies that mothered these jazz classics ignored their value, they were not interested in anything as non-commercial as righteous jazz. Mainly through the tireless efforts of the Commodore Music Shop's clientele, was this field revived. The Commodore re-issued its first records early in 1934. It founded the United Hot Clubs of America and began its accompanying label in the summer of 1935. Many of the superlative records in this leaflet were re-issued over five years ago. Now with the field developed, the major companies are interested in these jazz masterworks, and without too much effort you can find SOME of these same records listed on their lists also. However, the couplings are different from ours and in many cases their masters are second choices, giving you different solos to enjoy or not, as the case may be. In spite of claims to the contrary, we have a feeling, based on our many years of experience in

these matters, that the manufacturers will again discontinue these great jazz items when their revenue has diminished. To them it is strictly a business; to us it is our first true love.[50]

Gabler's first releases came from a leasing arrangement with the American Record Company (ARC), which controlled the masters of the defunct OKeh, Brunswick, and Vocalion labels. The United Hot Clubs of America (UHCA) label emerged "out of a haze of Tom Collinses" during a discussion with Marshall Stearns at the Commodore Record Store, also relying on the tacit support of John Hammond and Hugues Panassié.[51] Although the Hot Clubs envisioned in the plan did not thrive, over the next five years Gabler reissued fifty-seven jazz classics on UHCA, including the names of musicians on the labels according to instrument. Every effort was made to satisfy collectors, such as designing labels that looked good while spinning.[52]

The genius of Gabler's scheme lay in his ability to deal with ARC on its own terms. For years, record companies' standard procedure had been to delete any item that did not sell more than one thousand copies. Well familiar with the demographics of the collector community, Gabler knew that it could absorb roughly that amount, probably in about two years.[53] By limiting his market to UHCA members, he was able to match collector demand with record company minimums, working the margin to the economic benefit of all by charging one dollar per record. Since ARC did the pressing, production expenses were negligible, consisting primarily of labeling and distribution. The first UHCA release (his fifteenth reissue) was a Charles Pierce recording from 1927 featuring Muggsy Spanier (1906–1967) and Frank Teschemacher (1906–1932), two Chicagoans, and throughout the series Gabler tended to favor Chicago style. But he also offered Bessie Smith, King Oliver's Creole Jazz Band, the Wolverines, Jack Teagarden (1905–1964), Louis Armstrong, and the New Orleans Rhythm Kings. Jam sessions organized by Eddie Condon were held at the Decca studios to promote the reissues, which soon sold out. Most of the musicians who played at these events had not recorded for a number of years, and that fact, combined with Gabler's inability to purchase the masters or the rights to them, influenced a change in strategy. If a revival of the market for "authentic" jazz was to be sustained, it had to rest on contemporary recordings of jazzmen still active in the field. Condon agreed, arguing that many of these musicians had improved since their early recordings.[54] In addition, despite some success, Gabler was only breaking even, and by late 1937 he realized that the only solution was to launch his own record company.

On January 18, 1938, Commodore Records was born with the recording of a Condon-led group at the "bleak but technically excellent" midtown studios of ARC. Condon generated publicity through his friend Hank Brennan (1910–1992) at *Fortune* magazine, who enlisted the services of Alexander King (1900–1965) at *Life* and Charlie Peterson (1900–1976), a jazz-informed photographer. Peterson's photograph of Pee Wee Russell (1906–1969) got a full page in *Life,* which ran a spread on Commodore; the musicians (including New Orleans trombonist George Brunies); and Nick's Bar in Greenwich Village, where the band was employed. Although the piece did not appear until August, the public response surpassed all expectations and helped to launch the label. Gabler opened a second location on Fifty-second Street, and his mail-order business increased.[55] Commodore began documenting stars of the big bands in small, improvisational groups, including Lester Young (1909–1959), Coleman Hawkins, Chu Berry (1910–1941), and Billie Holiday. In particular, Holiday's "Strange Fruit," recorded in 1939, became a sensation, fetching high prices among collectors in England and elsewhere.[56] The success of Gabler's enterprises, from reissues to an independent label, created a precedent that invited others to follow suit. Given the dearth of New Orleans talent on Commodore, opportunities were beckoning to New Orleans–style purists.

In 1937, Stephen Smith of the Hot Record Exchange, Gabler's closest competitor, inaugurated the Hot Record Society label, based on an agreement with ARC and Decca similar to Gabler's. The company lasted nine years, about as long as Commodore, and generally followed Gabler's strategy, beginning with reissues and gravitating toward recording sessions in August 1938.[57] As one might expect, given the rivalry between the Hot Record Exchange and the Commodore Shop, and Bill Russell's feelings about the Condon clique, there was some dissension. In the January 1939 issue of *HRS Society Rag,* Smith took notice of a slight attributed to Gabler under the banner "Commodore Classics in Swing???": "We have just learned from LIFE magazine that Milton Gabler was the source of their misinformation concerning the fact that King Oliver's *Dippermouth Blues* was not available, either on the original OKeh label or on a re-issue, and that either the Commodore or Brunswick might re-issue it soon. Since so many regard Milton as the collectors' friend, we are sorry to hear this. We are quite ready to forgive any blow to our pride however, because we realize that he makes more money out of his own efforts than he does from ours."[58] "Dippermouth Blues" was listed on HRS, and it seemed improbable that any self-respecting collector, especially Milt Gabler, would have been unaware of this. Even so, the UHCA and HRS repressings never duplicated each other, despite shared preferences for artists like Bessie Smith, Louis Armstrong, King Oliver, and Bix Beiderbecke.[59] At HRS, a board of renowned critics and collectors handled reissue selections. Panassié and Delaunay were members, as were Charles Edward Smith, John Hammond, Marshall Stearns, Wilder Hobson, Bill Russell, and Park Breck.[60] Hammond, Stearns, and Hobson, in particular, were allied with Gabler, yet the general composition of this group was such that it could readily avoid conflicts by considering the desires of the collector community as a whole. *Jazz Information* advertised HRS products regularly, and a sort of mutual self-interest seemed to govern the relations between the Smith and Gabler labels.[61] Both companies peddled an eclectic assortment of vintage jazz reissues, although the HRS placed a greater emphasis on New Orleans.[62] This tendency became obvious when original recordings were undertaken. Smith recorded Rex Stewart's (1907–1967) Big Seven and Jack Teagarden's Big Eight, but the "biggest of the big" were the Bechet-Spanier Big Four records made in March 1940.[63] The Creole bassist Wellman Braud (1891–1966) was on the session, and Smith described the intent behind the session in the liner notes: "The genius of Sidney Bechet and Muggsy Spanier is a fact attested to by every critical work on the subject of jazz as an American art form. The H.R.S. records by the BECHET-SPANIER BIG FOUR, the only ones ever recorded of these two giants of jazz playing together, are a contribution to these critical essays."[64] In a second volume, Smith drew directly from *Jazzmen* in extolling "the same exciting collective improvisation, the same abundance of solos of unusual warmth and imagination, and the same careful choice of evergreen melodies"—which he had apparently chosen.[65]

The Bechet-Spanier Big Fours were recorded at General Records' studio in two sessions.[66] General is best known for Jelly Roll Morton's last recordings in 1939–40. Morton had contacted Charles Edward Smith about "a subject of mutual benefit," which turned out to be an offer from General to record "an album of the old New Orleans favorites."[67] Altogether, some twenty-four sides were released, including a predominance of piano solos, along with sextet and septet renditions. According to Lomax, General's attitude was reflected in the band sides: "The stand-out side, of course, was *Mamie's Blues,* which, everyone agreed, was not 'commercial.' Nevertheless it has kept the album in print ever since, and has been called the most beautiful of all jazz piano records. When General went on to make some 'commercials' with a swing band . . . the records died fast."[68] In an advertisement that appeared in *HRS Society Rag,* the *New York Times* referred to Morton's recordings as "a historical document which reflects a period and locale that gave birth to jazz."[69] Discographer Brian Rust has characterized the General catalog as "aimed at the connoisseur of jazz," and in the company's Morton issues one can readily appreciate the influence that UHCA and HRS had in redirecting the market toward a more documentary, retrospective approach.[70] Increasingly, subgroups within the ranks of consumers were being identified not so much by race as by taste, engendering new categories within the record industry in the 1940s. Although General did not make many jazz recordings, the company had been sufficiently impressed with Morton's Victor releases following the publication of *Jazzmen* to warrant giving him a try. The movement of majors such as Victor and Columbia toward historically minded recordings was a signal for smaller companies to follow suit, yet the original impulse had come from the collector community through its writings and independent recordings. After the infiltration of majors by Hammond and Gabler, emphasizing reissues, other collectors began to form companies that subordinated out-of-print classics to original issues by contemporary musicians who played in a traditional style.

The trend toward stylistic pluralism was evident in Blue Note Records, which began operations in January 1939 after its founder, German expatriate Alfred Lion (1908–1987), attended Hammond's "Spirituals to Swing" concert at Carnegie Hall. A statement of purpose accompanied Blue Note's first brochure in May 1939: "Blue Note Records are designed simply to serve the uncompromising expressions of hot jazz or swing, in general. Any particular style of playing which represents an authentic way of musical feeling is genuine expression. By virtue of its significance in place, time and circumstance, it possesses its own tradition, artistic standards and audience that keep it alive. Hot jazz, therefore, is expression and communication, a musical and social manifestation, and Blue Note records are concerned with identifying its impulse, not its sensational and commercial adornments."[71] Lion's first recordings were of boogie-woogie pianists Albert Ammons (1907–1949) and Meade Lux Lewis (1905–1964). The details behind this session provide an illustration of how the collector community operated. Lion had started collecting jazz records in Germany in 1925, when he was sixteen. From 1926 until 1930, he lived in the United States, building a record collection that was the envy of the Continent when he returned to Europe. In 1938, he returned to the United States "in order to escape the right-wing Nazi domination of his homeland and to be close to the source of his passion—jazz."[72] Lion encountered Hammond in a post office shortly after his arrival, and after an exuberant exchange of jazz tales, Hammond gave him two complimentary tickets to the concert at Carnegie Hall.[73] The thrill of that night was propulsive: Lion saw Ammons and Lewis at Café Society the following week and asked if he could record them. Upon learning that they would actually be paid for the session, they readily agreed. During the recording, Lion created "an atmosphere of respect, appreciation, and warmth that brought out the best in these men," producing a set of recordings that Blue Note's Michael Cuscuna has described as remarkable: "Lion pressed some fifty copies of 78s by each of them. Either out of innovation or naiveté, Lion let them play each number so long that the records had to be pressed on 12" discs. This was a format reserved primarily for classical music at the time. . . . A few small orders began to trickle in as these first few records received glowing reviews. Alfred didn't exactly run out and quit his day job, but at least Blue Note was in business."[74] Gabler and Smith also employed twelve-inch format for their best issues, the rationale being that the three-minute limitation of ten-inch 78s constricted extended compositions or improvisation, but it was Lion's Blue Note debut that led the way.[75] The shift from ten-inch to twelve-inch format was significant not only because it freed jazz musicians from strictures imposed by record companies (for financial reasons) but also because it symbolically placed them on an equal footing with classical artists in terms of respect.

Blue Note offered many innovations during its long and varied career. It inaugurated a series of "night-time" (four-thirty A.M.) sessions with the Port of Harlem Jazzmen, adapting to the habits of musicians, who often played best at such hours because of the routine of "after-hours" jam sessions. Later, Sidney Bechet joined this group and became a mainstay for Blue Note; his recording of "Summertime" was the label's first big seller, although Victor had rejected Bechet's suggestion that he record the piece because it was "unsuitable" for him.[76] Like "Strange Fruit" for Billie Holiday, "Summertime" was a signature tune for Bechet. In October 1939, Lion's lifelong friend Francis Wolff (1907–1971), who was also fleeing Nazi tyranny, joined him. Recalling his association as a photographer and producer with Blue Note in 1969, Wolff described the reasons for the label's success: "By 1939, jazz had gathered enough momentum so that an experiment like Blue Note could be tried. We could not round up more than a handful of customers for a while, but we garnered a good deal of favorable publicity through our uncommercial approach and unusual sessions like the Port of Harlem Jazzmen and the Edmond Hall Celeste Quartet. Somehow we set a style, but I would have difficulty to define same. I remember though that people used to say 'Alfred and Frank record only what they like.' That was true. If I may add three words, we tried to record jazz 'with a feeling.'"[77]

Such feelings were the product of innovative "dream sessions" combining the talents of top players left to their own devices. The Edmond Hall (1901–1967) Celeste Quartet was a case in point. Hall was a New Orleans–style clarinetist who had worked in a variety of bands in New York since his arrival in 1928. Like many of his New Orleans peers, he preferred the anachronistic Albert system clarinet to the newer Boehm models. Lion and Wolff teamed him with Meade Lux Lewis (on celeste!), Charlie Christian (1916–1942; a proto-bebop guitarist), and Israel Crosby (1919–1962; he had worked with Albert Ammons, on bass). The format was that of a chamber group, perhaps a nod to Artie Shaw's earlier experiments with string quartet some years earlier.[78] While Commodore was the first to organize "dream sessions" with the Condon recordings, Blue Note was far more daring in translating the concept. Gabler and Smith were staunch supporters of Blue Note, and when Alfred Lion was drafted in July 1942 and sent to El Paso, Texas, Gabler ran the company until he returned.[79] As Wolff later told jazz critic Ira Gitler (b. 1928): "With the war, the record business immediately picked up. The soldiers wanted them—the Army wanted them. Records became hot, and Commodore sold a lot of them, mail and wholesale. Shellac was scarce, and only people who had been in the business before the war could get a priority."[80] Revenues accrued during Lion's absence allowed Blue Note to resume recording activities in November 1943. From that time on, Lion and

Wolff entered what has been called their "swingtet" phase, documenting the proliferation of small bands that resulted from the decline of swing. One of the players on these recordings, saxophonist Ike Quebec (1918–1963), ultimately served Blue Note as an A&R man, establishing a connection that led to the label's interest in modern jazz after 1947.[81] Giving a jazz musician that much control over the fate of a record company was unheard of within the industry, but for Blue Note the choice was consistent with the approach Lion had applied from the beginning.

The contrast between Blue Note's flexibility and the rigidity of RCA Victor was demonstrated at the Jelly Roll Morton sessions in September 1939. According to Fred Ramsey, Victor had renewed interest in Morton because of his mention in *Jazzmen* and sought to capitalize on the book's publication by releasing some new recordings. Actually, the company had already begun to move toward New Orleans "old-timers" at the behest of Hugues Panassié in October 1938. This was Panassié's first visit to the United States, and he was determined to "make some New Orleans–style records, as this type of jazz was not being recorded anymore."[82] He teamed Sidney Bechet and Tommy Ladnier with Mezz Mezzrow (a mentor to Hugues since the mid-1930s), along with various New York sidemen, much as Hammond did several weeks later at "Spirituals to Swing." Panassié wanted to revitalize the New Orleans tradition: "Jazz then was right in the middle of what has been called the 'swing era' with big bands much in evidence. And there were plenty of good ones: Duke's, Basie's, Lunceford's and others—all full of first-class soloists. I was very fond of them, but they were very successful, making a lot of wonderful records; they did not need my help at all."[83] The Panassié sessions laid the groundwork for Morton's record dates, not only in pushing the idea that New Orleans style could be commercially viable but also by including a celebrated jazz expert on the production team, certifying the records' "authenticity." In addition, this was the first example of a recording session strategically underwritten with the idea of instigating a New Orleans revival.

This was the context from which the idea of packaging record albums with liner notes emerged.[84] Major record companies could aid the circulation of historical information through liner-note booklets, even if they were only doing so to exploit the proliferating market for publications on jazz. The authors of *Jazzmen* appreciated the boost that RCA Victor could give to Morton's career (not to mention book sales), and whatever reservations they had in general about the policies of the majors, they were eager to experiment. Ramsey took notes during the sessions, which later appeared in an appendix to *Mister Jelly Roll*.[85] This account was a fairly straightforward description of the musicians, rehearsals, and recording that only hinted at some of the problems that attended the sessions. In later years, at the Jelly Roll Morton Symposium, he was much more revealing.

Ramsey recounted the circumstances of his first meeting with Morton and the decision to approach the major: "He blew into the Hot Record Shop on 7th Avenue with an idea to make a record, or several. . . . Naturally, we all started making plans. We had a book that was about to come out in October, that was the one called *Jazzmen*, and so we whipped up this deal by going to RCA Victor, and on the strength of a book coming out we could have Jelly Roll Morton's New Orleans *Jazzmen* make a sessions or two."[86] The honeymoon was brief. Ramsey identified trouble during the sessions related to the "absolutely restrictive, fascistic controls of the music industry on the music."[87] In particular, A&R man Leonard Joy (1894–1961) had a number of encounters with Morton. It soon became apparent that Morton's arrangements were too long for standard ten-inch issue, so sections of the musicians' choruses were scrapped arbitrarily. On one song, Morton played a "pickup," and immediately red lights started flashing from the control booth. Joy did not like the pick-up, asking "what's wrong with it?" Morton replied that it was an "E-flat diminished seventh," adding, "Don't you know your music?" Joy was duly silenced, but on the second date, when Morton requested the recording of some quartet sides, he was refused because the titles were not on the playlist. Throughout the sessions, between takes, Morton played "brilliantly and compulsively," and Ramsey lamented the failure of the engineers to capture any of it.[88]

The second, and perhaps greater, problem had to do with dissension within the band. As leader, Morton had very specific ideas about how the musicians should play. He had requested New Orleans men, and Sidney Bechet, Zutty Singleton (1898–1975), and Albert Nicholas were recruited on somewhat short notice. Sidney de Paris (1905–1967) played trumpet, and Claude Jones (1901–1962) was on trombone (Morton wanted Ory, but his address was unknown). Conflict between Morton and Jones over style led to his replacement by the second session; Morton was dissatisfied with de Paris's phrasing on "Climax Rag" and let him know it. Ramsey suggested that the trouble between Morton and the "non–New Orleans men" was more than a matter of style—it was a reflection of the running feud between Morton and various Harlem musicians who disliked his bravado.[89] In his *Mister Jelly Roll* account, Ramsey stated that "nobody ever drinks at Jelly Roll's dates," but at the Symposium he related how he had seen the musicians in a bar just prior to the session. They were complaining about Morton's "authoritarian" ways and "conspiring" against him. Ramsey concluded that the second session had been "scotched by the attitude of the non–New Orleans musicians who were there."[90] To many New York musicians, the New Orleans style that Morton wanted was simply "old-fashioned," and they were not about to submit to lectures by a man whose career had died with the Depression. Added irony came late in the second session, when Ramsey was handed a note with Ory's address in San Francisco, implying his availability. Bechet had made the first session "come alive . . . it soared," the result of his basic understanding of what Morton was trying to do.[91] Without him on the second session, Jelly was outnumbered—thus his plea to Leonard Joy to reduce the band to a quartet of New Orleans men. Ramsey's testimony illustrates the reasons for the complaints against the majors that were so conspicuous in the independent label's manifestoes, and it shows the difficulties facing New Orleans musicians seeking a "comeback" with "historical" recordings. Yet within the majors, some officials occasionally did their best not to obstruct but to facilitate such recordings, as occurred when Sidney Bechet was assisted by one Victor agent who was "a friend of our music and our race," named John D. Reid (1907–1974).[92]

When Reid first met Bechet in late 1939, it was to record him at the Log Cabin in Fonda, New York, for Leonard Joy, who had been duly impressed on the Morton dates. Reid was an admirer of Bechet's gifts and enthusiastically promoted him to Joy, who signed him early in 1940, after he had detached from Blue Note.[93] He was to record twenty-four titles, with accompaniments by Jelly Roll Morton, Fats Waller, Duke Ellington, Charlie Barnet (1913–1991), Tommy Dorsey (1905–1956), Lionel Hampton, and others that would have teamed him with Victor's jazz elite. As John Chilton has shown, however, the rising tide of revival caused the original plan to be jettisoned: "By the early months of 1940 the jazz 'revival' had moved a stage nearer and more people were asking for recordings of 'authentic' jazz, by which they usually meant a line-up of trumpet, trombone and clarinet playing material from yesteryear. RCA Victor was in business to sell records, so naturally went with the market trend; thus the majority of Bechet's recordings for the company featured a traditional line-up (though Bechet did play soprano saxophone on several occasions). Sidney was originally encouraged to record tunes associated with the 1920s, but later, in an effort to tap the juke-box market, he made various novelty themes. At the very time that Bechet was to be recorded in contexts worthy of his talents as a star soloist, a revival of interest in the music that he had played such a part in creating denied him his big chance."[94] Given Bechet's earlier commentary on his discomfort at "Spirituals to Swing," one might wonder if he would agree, but Chilton is certainly correct in characterizing the revival as a double-edged sword, capable of restraining a broad talent such as Bechet's by confining it to traditionalist repertoire.

While Morton preferred New Orleans–style musicians whenever he could get them, Bechet's meanderings in the Northeast and Europe had broadened his horizons to instill catholicity akin to Armstrong's, and he was not shy about experimentation.[95] Under John Reid's direction, he made the first multitracked "one-man band" recordings in April 1941, utilizing a technique devised by Reid that enabled him to use six instruments recorded separately and then rerecorded onto a master disc.[96] These records generated plenty of publicity, but as Chilton observes, Bechet's contract with Victor "did not make him rich." Yet Reid administered what money he did receive: "He was granted a royalty of one cent on each side recorded, and there was an advance payment of 720 dollars. By now John was getting to know Bechet pretty well, and he deemed that it would be in his friend's interest to receive payment in 12 monthly installments of 60 dollars each. That way, he reasoned, Bechet would not get involved in any madcap business schemes. Bechet trusted Reid and went along with the idea, but this did not stop him from using all the money he had saved during his residency in Fonda as an 'investment' in a mink farm. . . . His business luck ran true to form and he lost all his money."[97] During the mid-1940s, Bechet also attempted to start a music school at his residence in Brooklyn that was similarly ill-fated, at least from the financial standpoint.[98] Reid gave Bechet lifelong friendship and guidance, transcending contracts or other financial ties.[99] Although he was a Victor official, his friendship with Bechet was more representative of attitudes within the collector community than it was a matter of company policy. In his devotion to Bechet, Reid went well beyond the call of duty.

In an interview in 1962, Bill Russell provided some interesting insights into the measure of Reid's devotion: "About 1943, I also obtained notes on Bechet from John Reid, who got them before 1941 in Philadelphia when he was connected with RCA. Reid was also a Jelly fan and got some of the unissued masters from Victor files, some of which were issued by New York 'bootleggers' like Sam Meltzer or [Dante] Bolletino. These men were called 'bootleggers' because they sort of pirated the records. They would issue them on all sorts of labels like Biltmore or British Rhythm Society, one was even called Jolly Roger. Sometimes, Victor would even press them, not realizing they had indirectly stolen Victor rights, taken the records off and copied them, and were issuing them on another label."[100] Russell also mentioned Bechet's summer sessions at Camp Unity in Allaban Acres, Wingdale, New York ("which had the reputation of being a communist camp or at least a left-wing camp"), where Reid and his friend Mary Karoley (1908–1993) recorded him.[101] Over time, Reid compiled a personal collection of field-recordings and other masters on Bechet, Bunk Johnson, and Earl Hines that was donated to the Arkansas Arts Center in Little Rock in the 1960s. In later years, he became an executive vice president of American Radio & Television, before taking a comparable position at Baldwin Electronics, both in Little Rock. During World War II, like Ramsey and Charles Edward Smith, he worked for the Office of War Information (OWI), recording "Big Eye" Louis Nelson, Alphonse Picou, Peter Bocage, and Paul Barbarin in New Orleans in the summer of 1944.[102] Reid's dedication to the documentary spirit, his "collector's conscience," was at odds with his corporate commitment to RCA, but it is easy to see which side prevailed. As it did for many other collectors, the "righteous cause" became for Reid a higher calling that allowed him to pursue a socially conscious role in preserving the music, while also rehabilitating its practitioners.

At Columbia Records, John Hammond held a similar position, except that his exploits earned him notoriety unparalleled in the record industry, and for good reason. The shift from "race" markets to stylistic pluralism had been accomplished largely because of his success in selling black artists in Britain while he was with English Columbia and Parlophone, beginning in

1933. He later recalled the circumstances under which he had entered the music industry:

> The record business was a very important factor in preserving jazz, but in 1928 radio came in and this was the beginning of the end, it looked, for the record business—first the radio, then the 1929 financial collapse. . . . Since jazz was extremely marginal as far as profitability was concerned even in those days, the first kind of records they stopped making was jazz. It might have been a permanent casualty if it hadn't been for the acceptance of jazz in England. It's quite amazing how much England fashions American tastes in music. In 1931, when no jazz was being recorded in this country, the three biggest labels in England all had very active jazz series of the great American jazz artists, both Black and White. They were just screaming for more products, and nobody would give it to them. This is more or less how I came into the record business.[103]

Hammond also referred to "the White folks and the reactionaries that supervised the record business in those days," but he further admitted, "The record companies have done more I think than any other part of the amusement business to break down prejudice, but there's a whole lot more to do."[104] Hammond's ability to sell racially mixed bands for Benny Goodman reoriented market approaches while recovery was occurring. He rode that wave of success into A&R positions with Columbia in 1937 and 1939–43, beginning a long association that brought such talents as Count Basie, Bob Dylan, and Bruce Springsteen to public attention.[105] But in 1939, the task at hand was organization of a major reissue campaign, a matter requiring some delicacy, given the access that had been granted to labels like UHCA and HRS. It became Hammond's job to smooth relations with the collector community when Columbia entered the reissue field, a move destined to adversely affect the independents.

Collector reactions to the Columbia reissues appeared in the pages of *HRS Society Rag* from November 1940 through February 1941, during which time it became apparent that the HRS reissues would cease.[106] In one editorial, Heywood Hale Broun discussed how reissues had affected the collector community: "When the re-issues, HRS and UHCA, began there was a slight but noticeable falling off in the admiration for certain records, to wit, the ones re-issued. . . . Now Columbia has begun to dig into its extensive jazz library and matters have come to a crisis. To many collectors this is good news—they like jazz music, like to have it available at fifty cents a record, but to too many others it is like finding one's special, little-known novelist in a popular edition of Womrath's."[107] Columbia controlled the OKeh catalog, as well as its own 13000/14000-D series, thus representing the lion's share of early "race" recordings. But the collector wish-fulfillment fantasy—complete access to all vintage jazz classics—was now seen as problematical because it decreased the relative value of rare finds and brought newcomers into the field in increasing numbers. For others, however, the involvement of Columbia, Victor, and Decca in the reissue field meant an opportunity to spread the music via major distribution systems, an improvement over the mail-order tactics of the independents. Broun made this clear in relating news about the Columbia program after meeting with Hammond:

> In fairness to Columbia it must be said that the UHCA received full compensation for masters used by Columbia, although rumors to the contrary were at one time current, and that the HRS as stated above will also be compensated. The HRS and UHCA worked hard for the cause of jazz when such help was most needed, keeping it alive and increasing the field of interest until it became a profitable venture for the large commercial companies. We feel that Columbia can do a good job of it. We have made criticisms of their policy in certain specific instances and probably will in the future but there is some justice to Columbia's idea that the reissues should not cater to collectors alone but should attempt to bring new fans up by easy stages, some of those easy stages being records which full fledged collectors may not like.[108]

Hammond responded: "Columbia welcomes suggestions from hot fans. All letters are read by everyone from the President down to Hammond, and several re-issues have been made as a direct result of these requests." The public was now "educated," and Hammond gave credit to the collectors: "We are grateful for the work of the HRS and the UHCA. Without their work in educating the public we would have had a thousand more headaches."[109] He also made remarks that seemed inappropriate for an A&R man at a major record company. In outlining plans for original recordings, Hammond revealed, "We are working at digging up some good little bands for this series, which we hope will produce good solid uncommercial music."[110] These "Hammond Specials" gave official notice that the majors had incorporated more than a historical reissue consciousness. With John Hammond at Columbia, "noncommercial" music was about to become company policy.

Columbia's reissues were extensive and utilized tactics developed by the independent record companies. The "Hot Jazz Classics" carried personnel listings on their labels and were packaged in albums with liner notes by John Hammond, George Avakian, or "both" (Avakian's notes were sometimes issued under Hammond's name). Avakian was born in the Soviet Union but spent most of his life in New York City. He began collecting "hot" in 1934, when he was fifteen, and in 1937, while he was at Yale, he started contributing articles to *Tempo* as a substitute for Marshall Stearns.[111] His first project as a producer was *Chicago Jazz* for Decca in 1939, and before he received his degree from Yale in 1941, he was already working with Hammond at Columbia. True to Hammond's statements on the educational thrust of "Hot Jazz Classics," the notes that accompanied the music of Armstrong, Smith, Henderson, Beiderbecke, and Ellington provided a synopsis of the artist's place in jazz history, along with discographical information. Occasionally Hammond (or Avakian?) could not resist revealing his prejudices, as seen in a comment on Frank Teschemacher: "one of the very few improvising jazz musicians who never sold out to the blandishments of sweet commercial jazz." But in general, the tone was neutral and only slightly didactic.[112] Contemporary recordings of Bechet and Ory were also undertaken as part of a "Jazz Masterworks" series. The use of such terms as "Masterworks" and "Classics" illustrates the degree to which the major record companies had come to regard jazz as an art form by 1939.

By the mid-1940s, all three major record companies had adopted the reissue concept from the collector-owned independents, and they had incorporated provision of liner notes in the process. While Columbia relied on Hammond and Avakian, Decca and Victor employed Charles Edward Smith on a freelance basis. In 1940, he contributed a booklet to a set of records featuring Louis Armstrong, Henry "Red" Allen (1908–1967), Zutty Singleton, Johnny Dodds, and Jimmie Noone (1895–1944). Decca entitled the album *New Orleans Jazz*, and Smith provided historical details on Bolden, Storyville, "hot" intonation, collective improvisation, and "correct" instrumentation. Although this was not a reissue package, the intent behind the project, with its educational approach, was no different from Columbia's "Hot Jazz Classics," and Smith injected a similar didacticism into his notes:

Like folk music jazz in its earliest form—that is, New Orleans jazz, has its own traditions. If Igor Stravinsky, Shostakovich, and Maurice Ravel (among others) have been able to understand various phases of this process, there seems little reason why Americans, too, should not approach jazz on its own merits, at least in those periods where it is comparatively free of the influence of popular music as such. One of the widespread fallacies about it is the belief that jazz of more than fifteen years ago was necessarily backward and that the good things were added thereunto in the Broadway refineries! You don't find this belief very strong in New Orleans.[113]

Later reissue projects for Victor's "Hot Jazz" series credited Bill Russell and Stephen Sholes (1911–1968; a Victor A&R man who had worked with Morton and Bechet), along with Smith, now identified as the "foremost authority on American jazz."[114] The collectors' association with the majors provided new outlets for their writings and represented a consensus-based educational strategy emphasizing jazz history and appreciation. But it was no coincidence that the vast backlog of jazz classics aimed at the collector-inspired revival market corresponded with the first American Federation of Musicians strike against the record companies, allowing them to withstand the ban for more than two years.[115]

Despite infiltration of the major record companies and proliferation of reissues, the hunter had not been captured by the game. Wartime demand for recordings (including 8,000,000 V-Discs, which were pressed at company plants), the awakening of American jazz scholarship with its attendant revival market, and the rise of vocalists (who were nonunion) at the expense of big band musicians combined to provide sufficient profits to underwrite major technological changes in the recording industry before the end of the decade.[116] Favorable market conditions benefited the majors and the independents alike, but only the majors had the distribution capabilities to fully exploit the situation. Independents in the 1940s led the way as they had two decades earlier, and the major companies continued to monitor their progress, adapting new ideas to established commercial practices. The mutuality of interest between collectors and the major labels that existed during World War II consolidated opinion on the value of the jazz heritage and helped to identify and promote its major heroes, providing a kind of folkloric "great man theory" approach that was ultimately superficial, intended more as an introduction than as an elaboration. As a solution to the problems of preserving and documenting New Orleans–style jazz, the actions of the majors were thus insufficient. Even the New Orleans–friendly independents such as Hot Record Society had failed to address the most pressing imperative: the "discovery" this time not of style but of the originators of that style, sage musicians who could still be recorded. Within the general revival of small-band, improvisational jazz (which had New Orleans, Chicago, Kansas City, and New York variants), a reinvigorated, almost militant, concentration on New Orleans style and its "unsung heroes" began to develop among certain collectors in 1940, giving rise to a more ideologically articulated and strident "purism" that was destined to unleash forces that would fracture the consensus on jazz history and criticism so deftly accomplished with *Jazzmen* only months before.

CHAPTER 4

Reviving New Orleans Style:
What Did Bunk and Ory Say?

The New Orleans revival was largely a response to the discovery of Bunk Johnson by the authors of *Jazzmen* and the attempt to use him as an example of what jazz must have sounded like prior to its commercialization—for Bunk claimed to have played with Bolden, had never recorded, and had been musically inactive for a decade. His assertion that he had been the primary influence on the young Louis Armstrong had started the ball rolling, eliciting the belief that Bunk must have been at the center of jazz in its formative phases, serving as a kind of fountainhead. For better or worse, the fascination with Bunk Johnson created a cause célèbre that lasted for nearly a decade and extended from coast to coast. Appreciation of his artistry became the test of the true believer (and within the broader jazz world, there was plenty of debate on the issue), creating division within the collector community in many cases and narrowing "purist" sensibilities to the point of militancy. Bunk's obscurity was his key to success, appealing as it did to veteran collectors who were not likely to be overly impressed with the reissue efforts of Decca, Columbia, and Victor. In the wake of Bunk, pioneers like Kid Ory and newcomers playing in the old style, particularly the Yerba Buena Jazz Band, attracted increased attention to the West Coast, establishing a "quadrangular trade" relationship among New York, Chicago, New Orleans, and San Francisco–Los Angeles. The New Orleans revival sought to complete the movement from commercialism to authenticity that the collector-owned independents had inaugurated.

The first attempt to record Bunk Johnson was a successful failure. Heywood Hale Broun ventured to New Orleans in August 1940 to document Bunk but found that commitments to a WPA teaching program in New Iberia prevented the trumpeter from making the recording. Charles Edward Smith had put Broun in touch with Dr. Leonard Bechet (Sidney's brother, a dentist), who arranged for a band led by Henry "Kid" Rena to attend the session, scheduled at WWL, a downtown radio station. As Broun later described the experience in a report for *HRS Society Rag*, the parade of elderly musicians wound through the station's corridors "amid a sea of shocked and disapproving expressions."[1] The session yielded eight sides, which became the single offering of the Delta label. Among the musicians who recorded were Alphonse Picou and "Big Eye" Louis Nelson Delille on clarinet and Jim Robinson (1890–1976) on trombone. When Bill Russell reviewed the Delta album in October, his approval was evident. He prefaced his remarks with the observation that "considerable confusion still exists in regard to the question of 'authentic,' 'classic' and even 'recreated' New Orleans Jazz" but went on to proclaim that "hot fans who have wondered just how a full New Orleans jazz band, playing in the traditional style, would sound, at last have that opportunity."[2] Kid Rena, "who like Armstrong and Oliver learned the blues from Bunk," led the band "with a lack of precision in ensemble and section playing," which Russell viewed as the very essence of "the rough and ready, knock 'em down and drag out style of music which we call New Orleans hot jazz."[3] As surely as Bunk, Kid Rena's Delta Jazz Band could serve to illustrate the precommercial prototype: "Many of us will probably never know what the great King Bolden's band was like, but this album gives the first chance we've had to hear the nearest thing to it. If we don't like these Deltas we'd better stop yelping about the New Orleans classic style and go in for Kansas City style, if there is such a thing, or is it just the Red Bank, N.J. style?"[4]

When the records were later reissued on Rudi Blesh's Circle label, Blesh referred to them as "many things at once": "They are historical: the first recordings of pure New Orleans jazz made in modern times. They are—or were, until the issuance of this album—among the scarcest of all jazz records. They are the only records to include the playing of certain of the great artists of the classic period of jazz. . . . There has been lots of talk about pure, uncommercialized jazz, much has been written about its history and origins, but it remained for Broun to demonstrate that it wasn't all history, that the music, itself, and many of its great founding players were still alive."[5] This was jazz "as it sounded in its first flushes of classicism, before it left New Orleans for the vicissitudes of commercialization and destructive 'improvement' that were to follow." It was music "that money couldn't buy . . . the music of the men who stayed home, the men who loved to make music for its own sake; the men who never lost their faith in pure melody that speaks to the heart."[6] Until recently, the Kid Rena Deltas had never been issued in large enough quantities to gain widespread circulation (except among collectors), but they set the stage for Bunk Johnson's reception, which was destined to achieve a considerable amount of attention, and set in motion a collector steeplechase to determine who would be the first to record him, since Broun had failed to do it.

Subsequent investigation has called into question much of the information that Bunk Johnson supplied to the authors of *Jazzmen,* including his date of birth and the Bolden connection, but collector faith in his credibility remained strong throughout the 1940s, despite challenges from within the ranks.[7] The circumstances of his retirement from music after 1931 were enough to gain for him a special place in the estimation of revivalists akin to martyrdom. While on the bandstand with the Black Eagle Band in Rayne, Louisiana, in November 1931, he had witnessed the murder of bandleader Evan Thomas (ca. 1890–1931), and in the resulting melee his instrument was crushed and his teeth knocked out. When he began to play again seven years later, it was as the beneficiary of a new set of teeth, a trumpet, and a cornet, provided by various collectors who had learned about him from the pages of *Jazzmen.*[8] Weeks Hall, the reclusive painter and owner of Shadows on the Teche, described the pilgrims who came to visit Bunk while he was employed there to Edmond Souchon (1897–1968), his physician, who later recalled his comments. According to Souchon, Hall found the many "jazz connoisseurs" who came to inquire about Bunk bothersome and occasionally impolite. He also distrusted them and "was suspicious of what they might write, especially from a Jim Crow angle. . . . Recognition, he did not want, nor any publication of his goodness to these old musicians on their last legs in New Iberia."[9]

Reports that Johnson had appeared as a guest with Louis Armstrong's orchestra in New Iberia began to circulate in mid-May 1941, feeding speculation that his "lip" might be returning, enabling him to finally record.[10] Mary Karoley accomplished the first recording of the legendary trumpeter with a portable recorder supplied by John Reid. The session occurred at Johnson's New Iberia home on February 2, 1942, and was never intended for commercial release, instead serving as an audition of his playing ability and an opportunity to record a message for his friends in New York. This "field trip recording" included a rendition of "Maple Leaf Rag" and a dialogue between Bunk and his admirer that was later transcribed by Paul A. Larsen for his article "Bunk Is History!" On the recording, Johnson does most of the talking, with encouragement from Karoley ("Tell 'em, Bunk!!"), and in his salutations to Louis Armstrong, Sidney Bechet, Bill Russell, Herman Rosenberg, and Hoyte Kline, he insists on his need for a new and better trumpet, while proffering thanks for past donations. Of Bill Russell, he says that "he has done wonderful for me, he helped me in every instance," adding: "I do not have a better friend than Mr. Bill Russell. I receive messages . . . mail . . . and also money from him at times, he sends me lots to help me along, and I want to thank him and let him know how proud I was to meet his mother, his father, and two brothers during the holidays on their way going back home. They stopped in New Iberia and chat with me a long while and I learned to know them and feeled as if I had known them all my life."[11] Bunk was just as adamant about being primed to play the cabarets of New York, and he included a special message for record company officials: "I can play well, and play all the old time music—just what you all want, I really have what the 'RCA' wants—if I can only get there to explain it and something to explain it with."[12] In time, Bunk got his wish, but his next recordings, the first to reach commercial release, came later that year in New Orleans, when two teams of collectors converged on that city with the aim of documenting the legend.

Representing the New Yorkers were Bill Russell and Eugene Williams. Williams had been coeditor of *Jazz Information,* with fellow Columbia graduate Ralph Gleason, until it ceased publication in 1941, and from 1940 on he became more absorbed with his Jazz Information label, a reissue project intended for limited-edition circulation of early Oliver, Armstrong, Henderson, and Smith.[13] He wanted to enter the field of original recordings with Bunk, following the trail blazed by other independents before him, but in a spectacular way. Bill Russell's original intention was to record Bunk "just to hear what he sounded like," and there was no thought of commercial release.

During the war, Russell was working for a transformer company in Pittsburgh, and the recording session had to be organized on vacation time. The night before he left for New Orleans, he heard from Dave Stuart (1911–1984) and learned that he was heading to New Iberia to make a recording: "All Dave had in mind was to record him for his own enjoyment. . . . Gene decided to go along and talk it over with Dave."[14] Dave Stuart was the proprietor of the Jazz Man Record Shop in Los Angeles (established in 1939), which also produced original recordings on the Jazz Man label. He had journeyed to New Orleans in early 1940, when "Big Eye" Louis Nelson had autographed his copy of *Jazzmen,* and had been the only white man at Jelly Roll Morton's funeral.[15] On this trip he was accompanied by two West Coast collectors, Bill Colburn (1907–1965) and Hal McIntyre, and together with Russell and Williams, they set about the task of deciding who would record Bunk and who would release the records.

Stuart had several aces up his sleeve: Jazz Man had a wider distribution and an ample supply of shellac, a crucial factor, considering wartime shortages.[16] But Bill Russell had already made arrangements for the formation of a suitable band, and the obvious course of action was collaboration, a wise decision given the obstacles that the project encountered. Bunk did not want to work with union musicians, who were not inclined to get involved anyway because of potential fines, so drummer Paul Barbarin and banjoist Johnny St. Cyr were eliminated from the list of first choices. "Big Eye" was ill, and Russell had doubts about his forcefulness. When Johnson arrived in New Orleans, he suggested "George" for clarinet, who turned out to be George Lewis (1900–1968), located with the help of Jim Robinson, the trombonist. Lawrence Marrero (1900–1959) on banjo, Walter Decou (ca. 1890–1966) on piano, Austin Young (ca. 1885–ca. 1954; Lester Young's uncle) on bass, and Ernest Rogers (1891–1956) on drums made up the rhythm section. Local recording facilities were not available to blacks, so arrangements were made with an employee of Grunewald's Music Store to use a piano storeroom on the third floor. With a single microphone and a box of steel-based acetates, the documentation of Bunk Johnson was finally accomplished on June 11, 1942, on a Presto recorder. Rogers worked at a foundry and arrived only three hours before the store closed, providing little margin for error.

Of twelve acetates available, three were spoiled as the result of poor microphone placement, but the rest of the session went well, although when the

masters were sent to Los Angeles for processing by Jazz Man, the engineer almost discarded them on the basis of inferior sound quality. Even so, as one of
Bunk Johnson's biographers has argued, "From the standpoint of the quality
of studio recordings of the time they are certainly crude, but it is still possible to get a lot of joy out of them, and in the circumstances it is remarkable
that they sound as good as they do."[17] Christopher Hillman describes the
musical results of this session as an indication that the project had accomplished its objectives:

> This is jazz reduced to its fundamentals, played by men whose styles were
> comparatively unaffected by the preceding 20 years, and recorded on
> equipment that emphasized raw vitality at the expense of subtlety. The
> music, however, is by no means primitive. Some of its excitement derives
> from the fact that it is a collective activity shaped during conception and
> not predetermined. In this it may be labeled a folk music, as it is a prod-
> uct of a common social heritage in which the listener has as active a part
> as the performer. Bunk, Lewis and the other members of the band were
> playing against, as much as with, each other. The resulting heterophony
> leaves no doubt that this spontaneous, clashing sound must have been a
> part of New Orleans music since the time of Buddy Bolden.[18]

Their mission accomplished, the five collectors who had masterminded
the session went their separate ways. The reception given the Jazz Man
recordings was mixed, but in the *Record Changer* (which became the preferred collector magazine in 1942, following the demise of *Jazz Information*
and *HRS Society Rag*), Nesuhi Ertegun (1917–1989) proclaimed that "the
outstanding jazz records of 1942 have undoubtedly been those issued on the
'Jazz Man' Label . . . courageous and uncompromising."[19] Jazz Man had also
issued the first recordings by Lu Watters's (1911–1989) Yerba Buena Jazz
Band, a San Francisco revivalist group, and some unissued Mortons, which
Ertegun had brought with him from Washington, D.C., when he relocated to
the West Coast to begin his affiliation with the Jazz Man Record Shop and
his fascination with Kid Ory.[20]

Although Jazz Man had won the Bunk Johnson sweepstakes, Bill Russell
and Gene Williams also profited from the trip. On his way to New Orleans,
Russell had detoured to Iowa in order to interview Buddy Bolden's widow,
Norah, who yielded details on Bolden's family and friends.[21] In addition,

Russell's association with Bunk was directly responsible for his decision to enter the recording field with the American Music label in 1944, and his experience in recording Johnson on substandard equipment—his baptism under fire—prepared him for the future. Williams returned, undaunted, to document Bunk again in October and released six records on Jazz Information, using a band similar to the one employed in June.[22] While in New Orleans, he dashed off a short note to his friends at the *Record Changer:* "There isn't any good jazz, strictly speaking. Just the smell of it. But I like that and talking to Bunk. . . . He told me plenty, and he can remember almost anything that ever happened to him."[23] Besides activating his nostrils, Williams's jaunts to New Orleans also set his pen in motion, and he contributed liner notes to the Jazz Man project in the form of a brochure. In it he lamented the fact that "the city which was the home of jazz offers no modern recording facilities at all," but he further stated that "Bunk's records may require this explanation, but they need no apology." Also available were spoken-word recollections by the sage trumpeter, available in limited edition.[24] The Jazz Information releases were better recorded than the Jazz Man sides, and Hillman believes that these recordings "reflect Bunk's outlook better than those of the earlier date, when he was restricted to numbers that his sidemen could play at short notice."[25] Milt Gabler's Commodore label undertook distribution of the records for Williams, who later worked at Decca with Gabler while also devoting himself full-time to Bunk's career. In the brochure that came with the discs, Williams affirmed that the discovery of Bunk Johnson was "undoubtedly the most important event in recent jazz history" and that the recordings were made for "historical interest."[26] He went on to state: "The performances are arranged, as much as possible, the way Bunk wanted them: which is with few solos, emphasizing the creative strength of the old-style New Orleans ensemble. Bunk's thrilling lead, and Lewis' busy variations, lead the band through the fine old melodies in a way which will make many jazz enthusiasts furious at the circumstances which deprived us, until now, of so much great music."[27] Within months of Bunk's first recordings, an unself-conscious militancy was becoming apparent in the promotion of his rediscovery. The unnamed villains were, of course, the major record companies. In time they would all demand a piece of Bunk, but for the moment they preferred to play a waiting game. Subsequent events kept them beguiled, if not always amused, with Johnson's burgeoning popularity, evident in a series of ventures that took him to San Francisco, Boston, New York, and Chicago between 1943 and 1947.

During the 1940s, the jazz scene on the West Coast began to rival New York's, adopting similar modes of focus and organization, witnessed in the Jazz Man Record Shop's growing visibility in the world of "hot" collecting. In addition, San Francisco became a hotbed of revivalism through the efforts of Lu Watters's Yerba Buena Jazz Band, a shifting clique of younger, white musicians who had grown disenchanted with swing and had come to regard New Orleans style as the last refuge of musical integrity. The band was organized in 1940, holding forth at Big Bear, in the Berkeley Hills, before opening its own "cooperative" venue at the Dawn Club on Annie Street in San Francisco. Watters was worried that the inevitable call from Uncle Sam would scuttle the band before it could make the most of its initial success, "so about five guys and myself formed a corporation to operate the Dawn Club. That way we would pick up right where we left off."[28] By 1942, the popularity of Watters's crew had created a ready market in the Bay Area for personal appearances by Bunk Johnson, and early in 1943 Rudi Blesh (whom Hillman describes as "on the fringe of the movement associated with the book *Jazzmen*") arranged for Bunk to accompany him at a series of lectures at the San Francisco Museum of Art, to be held in March. Johnson finally arrived in April and was joined by Bertha Gonsoulin, a pianist who had worked with King Oliver. The reception afforded them was noted in a report in the *San Francisco News* entitled "Hot Jazz Lectures Have S.F. Popeyed." Writer Emelia Hodel found the turnout for Bunk impressive, with seventy people attending the first lecture, seven hundred at the second, and "standing room only" thereafter. Her description of the crowd revealed the diversity of the audience: "Many of the audience were young folk—hep to jazz. But there were just as many adult and even elderly folk—all of them completely engrossed in this novel series."[29] Hodel went on to call Bunk Johnson "the granddaddy of all jazz, the originator of New Orleans 'low-down' blues music, and the teacher of Louis Armstrong," before quoting Rudi Blesh to the effect that "San Francisco has become the hot jazz capital of the world within the last three years." Blesh discounted the value of revivals in other cities with "Chicago-style" bands, dismissing that style as "white men trying to play like Negroes." The problem with Chicago stylists was that "they tampered with the instrumentation, and replaced the trombone with the saxophone, which can't begin to give the rhythmic impulse that the trombone has to give."[30] Blesh's definition of jazz, as given by Hodel, was also revealing: "a music of the American Negroes going back to African racial origins, with rhythmic, melodic and harmonic characteristics uniquely racial in character."[31] The article ended with the news that Blesh and Bill Colburn were planning a special concert featuring Bunk Johnson and Kid Ory with "Papa" Mutt Carey (1891–1948) at the Geary Theater on May 9. Bunk was being "held over."

The success of that concert can be gauged by its coverage in *Time,* under the banner "Bunk Johnson Rides Again." The groundswell of support was still growing: "The most historic jam session in the annals of jazz took place one day last week in San Francisco's Geary Theater. Some 1,500 devotees thronged to hear it from all over northern California, from Los Angeles, even from the East. They raised the roof—but in a solid manner: they were no mere swarm of jitterbugs buzzing before the latest of the many swing band sensations. They were mostly seasoned jazz tasters who had gathered to sample vintage New Orleans music produced by a group of the Negroes who had been in that city when jazz was young."[32] The concert was broadcast by the NBC Network in part, and the OWI rebroadcast it by shortwave to servicemen throughout the globe.[33] Following his engagement at the Geary Theater, Bunk began a series of weekly sessions for the Hot Jazz Society of San Francisco with sidemen from Lu Watters's band. Over the course of several months, Bunk charmed the society members and their guests, including the national press, at the "Chamber Jazz Room," a Longshoreman's Union hall on Golden Gate Avenue.

The society's weekly newsletter delighted in the publicity Bunk's presence had brought to its proceedings, its reporter reiterating Blesh's remarks about San Francisco becoming the center of the jazz universe and noting the favorable responses from the many musicians who attended the sessions. The consensus of opinion was that "our sessions are not only more authentic than the jam sessions of New York, Chicago and Los Angeles, but the audience participation makes those other hamlets sound flat in comparison."[34] In subsequent issues, mention was made of celebrity guests who attended the sessions. On one occasion, bandleader Count Basie was there and was quoted as saying: "That Bunk hasn't lost a thing, and he was the best then [1930] . . . and to think of my young trumpet section always complaining of 'beat lips.'

We can all stand a lesson from Bunk!"[35] The August 4 bulletin announced the participation of Nesuhi Ertegun and Marili Stuart (née Morden; 1919–1988), of the Jazz Man Record Shop, and the August 8 column by Virgil Thomson (1896–1989), famed composer and music critic for the *New York Herald Tribune,* devoted considerable space to the society's sessions: "Persons not members of this society can join at the door if properly introduced. Last Sunday there were perhaps 500 people, a youngish but not adolescent audience consisting of well dressed working people, professors, a goodly number of service men, both enlisted and commissioned, and one pretty young lady in a welder's uniform, complete with metal hat. Dancing was permitted in the back of the hall, and drinks were available in the adjoining bar."[36] Thomson's evaluation of the music lent further support to the cause. He described "New Orleans style" in detail, observing that the instruments engaged in no "fancy work." Improvisations were characterized by "the greatest freedom but also with an astonishing sobriety." Special superlatives were reserved for Bunk, who was "an artist of delicate imagination, meditative in style rather than flashy, and master of the darkest trumpet tone I have ever heard." Thomson's overall impression was that "this sort of music is as cultural an activity as any and more than most." The purity of Bunk's playing compared favorably with "the symphonic stuff," and that was not the only point in common: "Both kinds of music, of course, are deplorably commercialized these days. Its purity, nevertheless, a non-commercial quality, is wherein any music's cultural value lies."[37] Bunk's star was ascendant, and he remained in California until July 1944, when he returned to New Orleans to record for Bill Russell.

Russell had originally planned to record Bunk in New Orleans in the spring of 1943, but when he learned about the San Francisco trip, he diverted there to help organize the Geary Theater date. In a 1979 interview with George Kay for the *Mississippi Rag,* he explained how he made the most of the situation:

> The next year I decided to go back but I decided the working conditions were bad and material and recording equipment were still in short supply. My brother, who is an electrical engineer in Pittsburgh, fixed up a little home recorder for me. The whole thing cost about $60 including amplifier, cutting head, and microphone. When I went to New Orleans,

George Lewis got a band with Kid Howard on trumpet and Jim Robinson on trombone. We recorded the band on a Sunday afternoon at the Gypsy Tea Room located at St. Ann and Dumaine. The place was run by Louis (Massena), who also promoted boxing. I sold the records to Blue Note. At that time there were no records being issued because of the Petrillo ban. Alfred Lion was in the Army and Frank Wolfe [*sic*] was running the business for Blue Note. Wolfe bought all sides of the 12-inch records and released them on the Climax label. . . . Wolfe liked "Climax Rag" so well that he named the label after the tune.[38]

Russell was interested in recording as much New Orleans music as he could, and Avery "Kid" Howard (1908—1966) provided an alternative to Bunk, but over the next few years the focus was nevertheless on Johnson. Russell's decision to start his own record company came during the next summer in New Orleans, while he was recording Bunk in July and August. As he told George Kay: "Then I decided to go into the record business to be sure that I could feature Bunk and his music. I managed to get vinylite pressings from the Muzak Company but on 12-inch discs only. I sold my records mostly by mail order."[39] Having made his commitment, Russell began to consider his recording projects more seriously, especially since some of the recording Bunk had done on the West Coast had turned out quite well.[40] As the site of the weeklong session, Russell selected the San Jacinto Hall in Tremé (adjacent to the French Quarter), a structure described as having a "warm resonance . . . ideal for sound purposes."[41]

Alcide "Slow Drag" Pavageau (1888–1969) on bass and Baby Dodds on drums were added to the front three of Johnson, Lewis, and Robinson, with Lawrence Marrero on banjo. Russell paid considerable attention to the placement of the musicians on the bandstand, but as he learned, this was a problem that New Orleans musicians had worked out long ago:

Ordinarily, the old time dance halls had balconies above the main floor. The bandstands generally stretched across the end of the hall and were long and narrow. The band would set up in a straight line. At the far left would be the drums, then the trombone, then the trumpet, the clarinet, the guitar or banjo, and the string bass at the far right. Baby Dodds told me that this setup was not accidental but was the result of a lot of experimentation and thought. They felt that the band was better balanced that way. The string bass was used more like a rhythm instrument, with a lot of slapping and big tone as Pops Foster played it. There were also a lot of chords in the bass line to emphasize the rhythm. . . . Not only were the drums and guitar rhythm instruments in the old New Orleans bands. Everybody in the band played rhythm with the lead instrument playing melody.[42]

Russell recorded nearly fifty tunes, and when John Hammond (who was stationed in New Orleans) stopped by the hall one evening, he assured Russell that these sides were "the best recordings ever made in New Orleans." According to Christopher Hillman, "That may be putting it a little strongly, but after 40 years it is possible to say that they are among the very best and owing to the time at which they were made, undoubtedly the most influential."[43] Others have gone so far as to include the American Music releases as among the "three most important series of recordings by an organized band in the history of New Orleans jazz," along with Oliver's Creole Jazz Band and Morton's Red Hot Peppers.[44] Armstrong's Hot Fives would certainly seem to warrant inclusion as well, but there was widespread division among New Orleans purists over Armstrong, who had long since committed himself to following the swing trend with big bands. Russell returned in May 1945 to record the same band again and "made history" with the first "documentation" of a New Orleans brass band, led by Bunk and "Kid Shots" Madison (1899–1948), as well as a recording of "Wooden Joe" Nicholas (1883–1957), another New Orleans trumpeter who had never been recorded. In fact, the band was a simulacrum intended to demonstrate anachronistic performance styles of the early twentieth century, attempting to revive a tradition that was thought to be on the verge of extinction.[45] By this time, Bunk had expanded his horizons with a trip to Boston to join Sidney Bechet, and Kid Ory was riding the crest of the revival wave in California.

Bechet had wanted to work with Bunk again since 1940, when he had promoted the idea of including him in some of his RCA Victor sessions, envisioning him as a replacement for Tommy Ladnier, who had died in 1939. In his autobiography, *Treat It Gentle,* Sidney blamed Gene Williams especially for the failure of his plan.[46] In an article for *Footnote,* Mike Hazeldine has identified the discrepancies in Bechet's account through a skillful reconstruction of events based on correspondence among Bill Russell, John Reid, Gene

Williams, and Wynne Paris. By way of explanation for the hard feelings, he offers this observation: "All this should be seen against the background, that by the 40s, Sidney's career was not making progress. He was not achieving the star billing that he felt should be his. By the mid 40s, Bunk was media news—Sidney no doubt felt he should capitalize on this. Bunk knew this too!"[47] Bechet and Bunk had their reunion under strange circumstances in January 1945. The occasion was a national radio broadcast emanating from the Municipal Auditorium in New Orleans as part of a three-way linking that also included New York and Los Angeles concerts, all designed to showcase recent *Esquire* poll winners. The New Orleans concert was promoted as a celebration of the "return" of Basin Street (renamed North Saratoga after the demise of the District), and Bechet was part of an "all-star" band under the direction of Louis Armstrong, with whom he had been feuding as the result of a Decca-session clash in 1940.[48] Bunk Johnson was brought out to play the final number with the band, but only part of his rendition of "Basin Street Blues" with Armstrong and Bechet was broadcast, and much of that was obscured by the closing announcements.

Arrangements were made for Bunk to be featured with Sidney's band at the Savoy Café in Boston the following March, but before he left town, he was engaged to make a recording of background music for a film being shot by the OWI on the visit to New Orleans by members of the French Resistance, including Jean-Paul Sartre.[49] He then met Bechet in New York, where they recorded for Blue Note. Eddie Condon interviewed Bunk on a radio program for CBS the same day, and on the next he took part in one of Jack Crystal's (1909–1963) famous Sunday Jam Sessions at Jimmy Ryan's Club.[50] Despite this auspicious beginning, the mood quickly soured. During the Blue Note recording, Bechet had used a clarinet in order to complement Bunk in the traditional way, but for years he had relied on the soprano saxophone for its more strident tone (which enabled him to compete more forcefully for the lead), and this was the instrument he chose for the Savoy Café. Inevitably, Bunk and Bechet began to grapple with each other, and the results were at best uneven. Gene Williams was working for Decca, which kept him in New York for the first week of the booking; when he did finally manage to get to Boston, his assessment of the band was that it was good when Bunk was playing but even then could not be considered an example of New Orleans style.[51] On April 8, Bunk ended his association with Bechet and returned to

New Orleans, to be replaced by Johnny Windhurst (1926–1981), a local favorite of the Boston Jazz Society and later a member of Bob Wilber's (1928–) Wildcats.[52] Venerable New Orleans trumpeter Peter Bocage, who had formed his own Creole Serenaders after parting ways with Piron, was then imported, but he soon tired of Bechet's ways and left the job to Windhurst. After his experience with Bechet, Bunk determined never again to join a band he could not lead.

As had been the case in San Francisco two years earlier, jazz enthusiasts thought nothing of traveling long distances to hear "New Orleans style," or the closest thing to it. When Gene Williams made his trips from New York to Boston, he did not go alone: with him were Ralph Gleason, Jean Gleason, and Sam Meltzer. Jean Gleason's (née Rayburn, 1918–) insightful account of Bunk's reception in New York derived from her attendance at the Ryan's session:

> Bunk's first appearance here created an atmosphere of expectancy and excitement unlike anything within memory. Although no announcement had been made to the effect that Bunk would be present at the Sunday Session, news of his arrival in town on Thursday had spread sufficiently to cause a large turn-out. . . . The crowd came as much to see and meet Bunk as to hear him play, for the stories of his greatness as a personality are as numerous as those which concern his incomparable trumpet playing. . . . Under the handicap of playing with a band that did not play his style of music, that is, traditional New Orleans ensemble style, Bunk, nevertheless, proved his mastery in a sensational manner.[53]

"Meanwhile," she concluded, "there will be a general exodus in the direction of Boston over the weekends." Bunk's troubles with Sidney did not prevent him from consolidating his following in the Northeast as he had on the West Coast; if anything, they allowed him to claim the purist high ground and increase his notoriety.

In letters to Bill Russell, whose schedule prevented him from attending until the bitter end, Williams related details of events both on and off the bandstand, alluding to Bunk's complaints, crowd reaction, and the composition of the audience. The Savoy did not permit dancing, but that did not prevent large crowds, and the place was "jammed with white and colored every night." The band played nightly, a demanding schedule, for which Sidney was paid $550 and Bunk $100. The long hours and the discrepancy in pay were taking their toll on Bunk, who was having trouble with his "lip." Williams felt that Sidney was playing too much soprano, which subverted the New Orleans concept and thwarted Bunk's supposed leadership of the ensemble. The discord was obvious and disconcerting: "Sidney plays standing up with his soprano thrown into the air in his dramatic showman way; Bunk slouches in his chair most of the time, looking disgusted and playing, when he does, right into the back of the piano."[54] Sidney was fuming because Bunk was ignoring him on the bandstand, refusing to take cues. He was also jealous of the applause directed at the old man, who did little to deserve it in his opinion. Williams felt that Bechet had "a very genuine grievance" against Bunk, whose behavior was "driving him crazy." In private conversation with Williams, Bunk admitted that he was about to quit because "the band didn't play the tunes right, the tempos were too fast."[55] John Reid also wrote to Russell concerning the conflict. He was impressed with Bunk's playing ("better than I had expected from the records") but worried about the deteriorating situation within the band. Reid saw only one solution: "I wish you could be here now, as together I think we could smooth things out. I'll try the best I can with Sid, but I'm in no position to talk turkey with Bunk."[56]

Russell finally made it to Boston for the final performance, and he later wrote to Wynne Paris about his feelings concerning the Boston fiasco. He prefaced his assessment with an admission that "I'm about as bad as Bill Colburn in believing that everything I know I learned from Bunk, but the actual truth is that just about anything I know that's worth knowing, I did learn from Bunk." Russell intimated that the trumpeter's lip problems were probably a ruse and that he was just being "evil" in his thinking, as Sidney maintained. Yet whatever the psychosomatic implications of Bunk's behavior, the root difficulty derived from his feeling that Bechet was not playing according to the "rules" of New Orleans style, by which a clarinet or saxophone should play a supporting, obbligato role to the trumpeter's lead in ensemble passages. Everyone knew that Sidney had been breaking those rules for years, so one must marvel at the naiveté of Bunk's handlers. On his last night in Boston, with Russell in the audience, Bunk had engaged in "all that pantomime . . . in which he'd do so much pointing and making various gestures." He was sending Russell a message: "You see what I meant when I said yesterday & this afternoon that this kind of music & this kind of band are all wrong?"[57] But Russell's faith in "the word of Bunk" was no mere contrivance, as he explained to Paris: "It's easy to see why people think I'm as crazy as Bill Colburn when I say that I honestly think Bunk is not only the best musician I've ever known, but the wisest man I've ever met, but it would take a long time to go into all of that. But don't be fooled by the way he can act so dumb, for he's one of the quickest thinkers I ever saw. As he once said 'while the white man is talkin' I'm thinkin, & before the white man is through talkin' I have the answer.' And that month-long act he put on in Boston doesn't mean that he didn't know at the 1st rehearsal in N.Y. that the band was hopeless, musically."[58]

What Russell appreciated in Bunk was the way he could reduce a melody to its essence in order to magnify the emotional intensity of the ensemble: "Bunk just picks out three or four notes out of a tune and hits away on those. He really simplifies the tune. This is what my teacher, Arnold Schoenberg, used to call 'reducing' a tune. Reduction rather than elaboration of the melody."[59] Favoring elaboration, Bechet often came on too strong for Russell's taste, milking the material for dramatic effects that seemed contrived. Rather than viewing the difference as due to respective predilections within the realm of New Orleans style, Russell preferred to follow Bunk's lead and blame Sidney for breaking the "rules." Russell was also infatuated with Bunk's power and penchant for variegation, which he described in the fall 1942 issue of *Jazz Quarterly*: "For several years descriptions of Bunk's playing had led us to expect a softer, 'sweeter' style—one in which a beautiful tone was used with great delicacy, and a style depending more on melodic subtlety than driving force. . . . A predominant characteristic of Bunk's style is simplicity . . . but Bunk's music is never so simple that it lacks distinction or imagination, and his 'variations,' often subtle, are ingeniously constructed. . . . Often when Bunk's band first announces the theme of a simple chorale-like number . . . all the parts are played in a sort of pseudo unison, or at least the parts are in similar rhythmic values. Of course they never are in true unison nor are they hit off rhythmically together, and naturally almost every sin known to European musical culture is committed—lack of precision, out of tunefulness, smears, muffs—in other words we have with us once again the well known 'sloppy New Orleans ensemble'—but an ensemble whose unpredictable rhythms, vitalizing accents, and independence of parts (even when playing isometrically) are more thrilling than any symphonic group."[60] For Russell, the Boston trip demonstrated that New Orleans style was not negotiable or capable of being modernized. Bechet's career had taken him a long way from his musical roots, to the point of incompatibility with a player such as Bunk Johnson, whom Russell saw as dedicated to the original style. Curiously, the trip had also shown that many members of the audience could not tell the difference and were quite content to accept what they heard as the "real" thing. While the New Orleans revival, by 1945, was becoming quite broad, it was not very deep. Even Russell, who was widely acknowledged as the most expert student of New Orleans style, was, by his own admission, just beginning to understand. Bunk's lessons, and their relation to New Orleans style, were not only musical—they were ontological.

Meanwhile, during 1944–45, revivalism in California was shifting its locus from San Francisco to Los Angeles. With Bunk back home, attention was increasingly focused on Kid Ory, whose personal history resembled Bunk's in some respects and differed dramatically in others. Edward Ory had relocated to the West Coast in the fall of 1919, persuading several New Orleans musicians to accompany him. In June 1922, he led the first black New Orleans jazz band to make a recording, for a small Los Angeles company called Nordskog, upon whose product Reb Spikes (1888–1982), the mastermind of the session, quickly superimposed his own name. The trombonist retaliated by pasting his own sunshine label on the discs. Ory built a following in Southern California with live engagements (enhanced by radio broadcasts), but in late 1925 he left the band to trumpeter Mutt Carey in order to join King Oliver in Chicago, where he recorded simultaneously with Armstrong's Hot Five, Oliver's Dixie Syncopators, and Morton's Red Hot Peppers. After Oliver moved to New York, Ory returned to California in 1929 and reassembled his old band, but work became scarce with the onset of the Depression, and by 1933 he was employed by the Postal Service as a sorter and running a chicken ranch—out of music altogether.[61] Nesuhi Ertegun recalled the occasion that brought Ory out of retirement: "He was found in the early Forties, leading a quiet, comfortable life in Los Angeles. When Marili Morden of the Jazz Man Record Shop took a photographer to trumpeter Mutt Carey's house for some pictures of Mutt and Ory, she asked Ory to bring his trombone, so that action shots could be made. Ory ran through a few choruses while the photographer worked. This was the first time he had played the trombone in nine years."[62] Following Barney Bigard's departure from Ellington in 1942, Ory worked with him as a sideman; although Bigard's outfit was not a New Orleans–style band, it provided the incentive for Ory to refurbish his technique and reorganize his own band with Carey, Bud Scott (ca. 1890–1949; banjo/guitar), Buster Wilson (1897–1949; piano), and Ed "Montudie" Garland (ca. 1885–1980; bass).

The Geary Theater concert in 1943 provided considerable momentum, and in early 1944 Ory was approached by Orson Welles (1915–1985) to perform on his radio show. Liner notes to a later release of these broadcasts on Folklyric Records tell the story: "Those war years of 1943–1944 were relatively good ones for casual musicians and in the Hollywood–Los Angeles region there was not only good money around, there was also the combined attraction . . . of the movie studios and the network radio studios."[63] Welles was famous after his *War of the Worlds* stunt and the success of *Citizen Kane,* and his decision to move his Mercury Theater broadcast to Hollywood in the early 1940s had special implications for the New Orleans revival. He commissioned Marili Morden to find a suitable band "that would reflect the original sounds of jazz." Ory's band was hired and augmented by the addition of Jimmie Noone on clarinet and Zutty Singleton on drums. When Noone dropped dead from a heart attack on the morning of the April 19 show, Wade Whaley (1895–ca. 1968) was brought in as a temporary replacement before Bigard was employed to finish the thirteen-week engagement.

According to Nesuhi Ertegun, Kid Ory's All Stars were an instant hit: "Mail poured in from everywhere, asking for more music by the New Orleans All-Stars."[64] Orson Welles later commented on his experience with the revivalists: "There's something of the opium eater in your jazz cultist. His enthusiasm affects him like a drug habit, removing him, it seems, from the uninitiated and less paranoid world about him and encouraging many of the attitudes of full-blown megalomania."[65] Bill Russell has suggested that, despite Welles's personal popularity, his radio show was the victim of falling ratings and was about to lose its sponsor when the decision to hire Ory was made.[66] Given his comments quoted earlier, Welles must have seen Ory as the Pied Piper who could solve his problem by engaging a new audience. Ory also did broadcasts for the Standard (Oil Company) School Broadcasts in the spring of 1945, with Bill Colburn and Hal McIntyre (who narrated). These were weekly programs designed for schoolchildren in the Western states and included printed syllabi provided by Standard Oil for students and teachers alike.[67] Colburn's connection with the series was mentioned in George Montgomery's "Jazz in Los Angeles" column in the *Record Changer* in April 1945: "Bill Colburn, the nomadic apostle of New Orleans music in general and Bunk Johnson in particular, came to town toward the end of February and right away things started to happen." On March 1, Colburn brought Ory's band to NBC for a Standard School Broadcast, the airing of which was postponed when Franklin Roosevelt's address to Congress ran past schedule. Taking advantage of a "captive audience" of schoolchildren and members of the Los Angeles jazz colony, Ory performed the full program. "Then," Montgomery reported, "to the delight of the fans in the studio, Colburn played some tests of the Bunk Johnson records which Bill Russell is issuing."[68]

Jazz revivalists welcomed all opportunities for public relations, but they were especially determined to expose young people to the New Orleans tradition. An article on "New Orleans Jazz" by Marili Ertegun (she and Nesuhi had been married for "some time" before announcing it in mid-1946) applauded the efforts of the Pasadena Jazz Society: "While this band, made up of teen-agers, is not yet technically adept, its spirit and understanding of the form is at once evident. All such efforts by young musicians should be applauded and supported in every possible way if we are to make up for the lean years mentioned above. Such young bands are insurance against the time when the pioneers of the style shall have retired."[69] Kid Ory benefited considerably from the radio spots of 1944–45, although they were aired only in the Western part of the country.[70] The broadcasts brought Ory's band to the attention of recording interests; as usual, revival-inspired independents were the first to take advantage of the Kid's neglected status.

In August 1944, Nesuhi Ertegun recorded Ory's band in Los Angeles, releasing the four sides on the Crescent label—"Crescent" a double entendre referring to his Turkish ancestry and to the Crescent City. A limited edition of fifteen hundred records was made available through Morden's Jazz Man Record Shop and soon sold out (later released again with a second run, in November 1945).[71] In advertisements, the responses of critics were highlighted. *Down Beat*'s "Jax" called the records "the righteous stuff itself," and Frederic Ramsey, writing for *Jazz Record*, noted their technical quality: "Here is a big jazz event. . . . For the first time in jazz history, we have high fidelity recording of a New Orleans jazz band. . . . It is a triumph for the style known as New Orleans."[72] Comparisons between Ory's recordings and

Bunk Johnson's were unavoidable. Writing for the April 1945 *Record Changer*, Gene Williams defended the American Music issues: "Most of the arguments about the merits of Bunk Johnson and his music come from people who don't know what New Orleans music is and who have never heard a New Orleans band. Now they can hear one. And even more strikingly than Kid Ory's recent recordings, these new Bunk Johnson records prove how much dynamite still remains, after fifty years, in the music of the New Orleans Negro."[73] Ironically, in 1946–47, Williams spent a considerable amount of money promoting Ory's career in the West, to the neglect of Bunk Johnson, who later remarked that if Gene had spent the money on the New York audience, he would not have lost it.[74] In general, however, most revivalists sought to nurture the fortunes of both men, who reigned as dual monarchs of the New Orleans movement.

In February 1945, Dr. Fred B. Exner, a collector specializing in New Orleans style, recorded Ory for his Exner label. Exner flew to Los Angeles from San Francisco, underwent some anxious hours awaiting union clearance and procurement of a studio, and finally recorded Ory on Lincoln's birthday.[75] The following month, the band attained major-label status with a session for Decca in Los Angeles. Late in 1946, Columbia joined suit, and Rudi Blesh's Circle label released an album of a broadcast done for his *This Is Jazz* program for the Mutual Network in 1947.[76] Many of these recordings included Creole songs, sung in dialect, which Ory recalled from his early days on the Woodland Plantation in his hometown of LaPlace. Like Bunk, he provided insight on the specifics of New Orleans style for his disciples. Al Otto and Ben Marble, publishers of the Los Angeles–based *Clef* magazine, ran "What Did Ory Say?" in the March 1946 issue. When asked if Bud Scott's guitar was "out of place" in a New Orleans outfit (as opposed to banjo), Ory responded: "Don't you believe that stuff. Bud Scott is one of the most genuine, authentic New Orleans musicians of the bunch. He played guitar long before the banjo came into style. It was guitar first, then banjo, then a five-string instrument called a banjo-guitar which had some guitar features but possessed the drumhead of a banjo, finally returning to the guitar, which is just what real New Orleans jazz started out with."[77] The writers concluded their essay on a philosophical note: "We live and learn, which is just what Kid Ory and his Creole Jazz Band are doing; for although they play in the real jazz style of bygone days, they stack up instrumentally with the best of today's younger artists. It isn't because they're content to rest on their laurels."[78] Recordings and other media took Ory's traditionalist message well beyond the West Coast. In liner notes accompanying the Circle album, performances at the University of California at Berkeley and at Carnegie Hall in New York are mentioned, as well as soundtracks for the motion pictures *New Orleans* and *Crossfire.*[79]

Proximity to film studios allowed Ory's band to reach the moviegoing public, an important market that was denied to Bunk Johnson, and in the 1950s Ory made two trips to Europe, which Bunk never did. By the 1960s, he was essentially retired, but he appeared at the annual Dixieland concerts held at Disneyland, which were televised, and had an engagement on the *Ed Sullivan Show* in 1965.[80] Ory's role in the revival of New Orleans style was indispensable during the 1940s; Bunk's tour of California in 1943–44 had ignited the fuse of first discovery, but Ory's band kept the fire going once Bunk had abandoned the scene. Whereas many critics felt that Bunk Johnson had undoubtedly been a master musician in his youth but had declined, Ory was seen as reaching his peak as a player during the 1940s.[81] When Ory placed eleventh in the 1946 *Esquire* poll, observers did not fail to notice that the "kid" was doing quite well for his age.[82] Nevertheless, in retrospect one can see that historical attention has often emphasized Bunk's role in the revival at the expense of Ory: while Mike Hazeldine and Barry Martyn, Austin Sonnier, and Christopher Hillman have provided biographies of the legendary trumpeter, a biography of Edward "Kid" Ory has yet to be published. Despite the growth of Los Angeles as a media capital during the war years—a process that reflected wartime demographics—New York remained the center stage of the entertainment industry throughout the decade, and it was there that Bunk Johnson concentrated his efforts.[83]

Even before the Bechet episode, Bill Russell and Gene Williams had been laying plans to bring Bunk to New York City. In September 1945, their hopes were realized with a booking at the Stuyvesant Casino on Second Avenue.[84] Gene financed the trip with a family inheritance and boarded the band in his large apartment on Washington Square. A pianist, Alton Purnell (ca. 1911–1987), was added to the usual lineup of Lewis, Robinson, Marrero, Pavageau, and Dodds for the Stuyvesant, where the men were kept working six nights a week. The band was well received; on opening night about four hundred people attended, many of them musicians. But the band was somewhat puzzled by the response, for this was a listening, not a dancing, crowd.

As Hillman has pointed out, "in their home surroundings appreciation of the playing was expressed in movement by the dancers, not by passive intellectual absorption, and they thought that they must be doing something wrong."[85] But Hillman is also careful to distinguish between interest and detachment in the behavior of the audience:

> Comments by those who heard them show that, however motionless their response may have been, the people in the audience were experiencing a vitality and color, a sheer naturalness in the music, that was like nothing they had heard before. From this communal exposure to such a direct celebration of the life force grew up a whole new movement towards "purity" in jazz, expanding on the romance expressed in *Jazzmen*. In the long run a good deal of damage was done, even to Bunk's own cause, by such over-reaction, but we must accept at least that the music that gave motivation to such a crusade was of tremendous appeal. It expressed a freedom from neurosis and artificiality that made a great impact on the sort of intellectuals and middle-class college students who made up the bulk of its subsequent following.[86]

This observation contrasts markedly with Welles's assessment of the jazz cult, which suggests that many revivalists may have fallen prey to the very demons they thought they were escaping, a case in point being the tragic circumstances of Gene Williams's death.[87] Despite the fanfare afforded the band at its debut, crowds began to dwindle, and the group was moved to a smaller hall in the same building. Favorable press reports brought in more people, reestablishing Bunk at the main hall and reducing Williams's losses. Because of the exposure afforded at the Stuyvesant Casino, Decca recorded the band in November, and Victor did two sessions the next month. Ralph Gleason wrote voluminous notes for the Victor album, which gave the history of Bunk's early career and rediscovery, as well as insights into the response of New Yorkers to Bunk's music: "*Time* magazine called his band the 'hot jazz sensation of the year,' his picture was in the papers, his name on all New York's lips." Further details of opening night and subsequent activity were also given: "They were an immediate sensation. *Time*, the *New Yorker*, *Pic*, *Mademoiselle*, *Cue*, *Vogue*, *Junior Bazaar*, and *Esquire* and the New York papers ran photographs and interviews." In addition, Bunk made the rounds of the radio studios to promote the band and prepared for a special New

Year's Day (1946) concert at Town Hall, with Orson Welles presiding as master of ceremonies. As *Time* Magazine put it, Bunk "was about to discover that there was money in his music!'"[88] Gene Williams was certainly hoping for as much, but problems within the band became increasingly disruptive as the engagement wore on. The strict schedule of playing six nights a week naturally took its toll, especially on New Orleans musicians who felt out of place in New York City, unaccustomed as they were to being away from home.[89] But Bunk was dissatisfied with the playing of some of his sidemen, a factor that became a bone of contention between the leader and his managers.

In *New Orleans Music,* Barry Martyn interviewed Harold Drob (1923–1999) on his association with Bunk Johnson, revealing the inner workings of the New York collector community. Drob had been inducted into the army on his twentieth birthday, January 26, 1943, which he remembers as the day he heard his first Bunk Johnson recording at the Commodore Record Shop. While he was in the armed forces, friends back home kept him informed about the proceedings at the Stuyvesant Casino: "I went into the army and was in for three years, and I was in Europe when Bunk opened at the Stuyvesant. I had friends here in New York who were writing to me and telling me how wonderful it all was. The day I got out of the army, the first thing I did was find some civilian clothes and go right down to the Stuyvesant. So the day I went in I heard the first records and the day I got out I saw him for the first time."[90] He had been collecting jazz records for a number of years, with a preference for Jelly Roll Morton and Bessie Smith, and when he was exposed to Bunk Johnson, the music "really fitted my image of what was needed—what I was missing."[91] His experience as a collector ("we really got to know our records when we bought them because we had so few new ones") made him sensitive to the subtleties of Bunk's approach and the methods of New Orleans players when he caught the band in its final week at the Stuyvesant Casino: "This is another thing I had realized about him, and Mutt Carey, whom I heard a lot, and some other New Orleans players—they didn't give you everything they got every time. Now most of your players, from Louis Armstrong on down—their triple forte—they're giving you everything they've got every time they come out. These guys were always holding something back; they always had some little surprise. The same with Jelly. You get an alternate take of a Jelly record and suddenly he's playing something surprising on the piano."[92]

Bunk's problems with the band members arose from his attempts to control them and his exasperation with their limitations, particularly the lack of reading skills. The leader felt restricted musically, and the accommodations at Williams's apartment led to the same result physically:

> Drag came in there because of George. I knew Bunk would have never recommended Slow Drag as a bass player. As a matter of fact, I saw George tune up the bass for Drag. I don't know if the guy knew whether he was playing in tune or not. That was a big part of the problem: Bunk didn't hire them. When he was dissatisfied with Baby, he couldn't fire him. He wanted them to send Baby home and they wouldn't do it. . . . In the case of Baby Dodds, they thought, how could he possibly want to get rid of the world's greatest drummer? (So he didn't understand where they were coming from and they didn't understand where he was coming from.) The guys in the band didn't understand where anybody was coming from. Here were all these people packed together in this apartment. Although it was a big place, some of them had to share rooms, and it was just not comfortable all around.[93]

Russell's and Williams's ideological expectations regarding how New Orleans musicians should behave were in perpetual conflict with what their charges actually wanted. Over the course of the revival, the limitations of classifying traditional jazz as folk music became increasingly apparent as the practitioners of New Orleans style revealed their desire to be regarded as competitive among their contemporaries in popular music. Recognizing this predicament, Drob encouraged Bunk to select his own musicians for the "Last Testament" sessions for Columbia, made on December 23–26, 1947, for which he served as the producer—it was the only time Bunk was afforded complete freedom in a recording studio.

But Drob is also clear about the sincerity of Russell's and Williams's intentions. When asked about their roles and motives, he replied:

> It was pure love of the music. Well, you know Bill, money is the most meaningless thing in the world to that man. He couldn't possibly have intended anything but to promote the music. It was the same with Gene. They were two of the nicest, sweetest people I've ever known. Gene gave up a well-paid job at Decca Records to do this. . . . (Bill was there during

the first engagement, but wasn't around that much during the second trip.) He would come in for a day or two, sit there and meticulously write down the name of every tune they would play, and then go on his way. He had nothing to do with the promotion. Gene was technically Bunk's manager; he had an agreement with Bunk.[94]

Before the booking ended on January 12, several V-Discs had been made, and although Williams lost three thousand dollars on the band's New York stay, the Stuyvesant's proprietor, Ben Menschel, was convinced of the band's potential for success. When Williams went west to see Ory at Bill Colburn's urging, Bunk was free to strike his own deal with Menschel. He returned on April 10, 1946, with Lewis, Robinson, and Pavageau, with Kaiser Marshall (ca. 1899–1948) on drums and Don Ewell (1916–1983), a white, Mortonesque player, on piano.

Ahmet Ertegun (1923–2006) Nesuhi's brother, reported on Bunk's return, which lasted until the end of May, in the *Record Changer,* noting the release of the Victor recordings to coincide with the visit and the imminent issue of the Deccas. Ertegun did have some objections: "It is regretted that Williams-Russell-Gleason are not in charge of the dances any more. Further it is hoped that the present manager will see his way clear to sending Marrero carfare up to New York."[95] During this second Stuyvesant engagement, Leadbelly came to sit in with the band on several occasions. Bunk did not seem to care for him and referred to him as "Mr. Heavy Belly."[96] Russell came up to record Bunk in a trio with Ewell and drummer Alphonse Steele (1895–1983) in April, his last Johnson session for American Music. In the final days of the second Stuyvesant stint, Russell was quite active in New York. He met with Alan Lomax to discuss the Morton manuscript; joined the Gleasons and the Reids to toast Bunk and his wife, Maud (Menschel had brought her up to keep Bunk in line) at the Stuyvesant; and shopped for sheet music. According to Russell, weekends at the Casino usually attracted three hundred customers or more (sometimes six hundred), and the band was doing well financially. Gene Williams reported brisk sales of the Victors and revealed information on Nesuhi Ertegun's negotiations with Avakian to sign Ory to Columbia with a fifteen-hundred-dollar advance. Gabler had approached Bunk with an offer from Commodore, but when he insisted on using Pee Wee Russell and George Wettling, his regular session men, instead of Bunk's picks, the offer was rejected.[97] Apparently no one suspected that the best days were now behind them.

The Decca recordings by Bunk did not come out until 1947, as part of the album *New Orleans Revival,* which contained four sides by Johnson and four by Ory. Gene Williams prepared the liner notes in the spring of 1946, while expectations were still high. In them he revealed his perception of the essentials of the New Orleans revival: "When it was brought, finally, before the public, the music of New Orleans turned out to be truly revolutionary. It was different not only from all the imitations, but also from what its discoverers had expected." The music of "the New Orleans Negro" had taken fifty years to reach the public in its "pure" form, and it was now recognized to be neither crude nor primitive. Yet it remained a "simple" music, played "with the honest intention of pleasing those who paid to hear it." New Orleans style was dance music, designed to make people feel happy, and "to tired, confused, half-desperate Americans of the first post-war year, it was a promise of something genuine and solid."[98] Here was a simpler, gentler music to soothe the anxieties of a violent, complex time. In a world numb from six years of global conflict, New Orleans style offered a return to feeling—a celebration of life and, perhaps, a way of coping with the memory of lives lost.

Such significance, however, could be a heavy burden to bear, and subsequent appearances by Bunk Johnson in Chicago in September 1946 and in New York the following year created more anxiety rather than less. By the time Bunk arrived late in Chicago for the concert at Orchestra Hall, $250 had been refunded to disgruntled members of the audience (many of whom reentered for free when he finally took the stage).[99] *Down Beat* ran the story under the title "Bunk's Concert a Miserable Mess: His Ork Hall Bash a Complete Snafu." Writer Don C. Haynes tried to be as kind as he could: "A review of Bunk Johnson's Orchestra Hall concert Sept. 6 turns out, tragically, an almost impossible task. Bunk was a good two and a half hours late for his own concert, and once he did appear on stage his lip was in such bad condition that he could not play coherently. . . . The picture of the old trumpet player . . . was a pitiful and tragic one. For those who were there and could see and hear, the name Bunk Johnson lost its magic and its meaning."[100]

In November 1947, Bob Aurthur (1922–1978) voiced a similar opinion in *Jazz Record* regarding the New York appearances: "It is a pitiful thing to watch a tradition crumble into something that is almost laughable . . . that is, if it weren't so sad." Johnson's performances at Town Hall and Jimmy Ryan's were interpreted as the product of a hoax, because everything went wrong. Bunk had arrived for the Town Hall concert late, an hour before the show, and then only after the concert manager had sent last-minute airfare. He came without an instrument, and "he had no lip." The performance was disappointing, and Aurthur was seeking scapegoats, blaming the "crackpots and lunatic fringe in jazz" who had rediscovered him: "They had to sell Bunk, and in order to do this, they had to build him into something he never was. They had to take an old man in baggy, un-pressed pants and an ill-fitting coat and make him into a god."[101] The adherents of noncommercial music were now being accused of commercialism! Although he failed to attend Town Hall—"because I had a feeling that something was going to happen that I didn't want to see or hear"—Aurthur did make it to Ryan's, where it was "old home week" for New Yorkers who remembered Bunk from the Stuyvesant:

> But somehow or other, most people managed to drift out to the sidewalk while Bunk was on the stand until it got so crowded that a cop had to chase them all back in again. They made a lot of money that night at Ryan's, but I just can't help think of the looks on the faces of some of the people who had never heard Bunk play before. . . . The illusion is destroyed. The fact that Bunk is one of the great surviving historical figures is almost forgotten. It is wondered whether he ever did play trumpet to anyone's delight when deep down we know he was one of the giants. But the prophets have their profits, and I hope they're satisfied.[102]

In December 1948, George Hoefer contemplated Bunk's career in his own "postmortem" for *Down Beat,* only months before the trumpeter's death in New Iberia, in July 1949. Hoefer's judgment was by now a familiar one:

> The tragic part of it all was that Bunk was exploited by purists who misinterpreted the horn man's own feelings toward jazz. Bunk just wanted to play for persons enjoying themselves while dancing. Some of his mentors went so far as to say his way of playing was the key to saving the world. There were a few seasons of concerts, none of which proved to be financially successful or a musical sensation. Bunk was at his best and happi-

est while playing for dancing at the Stuyvesant casino in New York. This was probably the longest and most successful musically of all his New Orleans Revival meetings. His last chore was recording 12 sides for Bob Stendahl in New York a year ago. These sides have not been released as yet. Since last Christmas Bunk has gone back into obscurity and has been forgotten completely by the entrepreneurs as well as by the general jazz public.[103]

On one point Hoefer was certainly mistaken: Bill Russell had not forgotten his hero. He was with Bunk during his last days, shaving him, running errands for him, and when the time came, he helped to bury him.[104] The charges of commercial exploitation that were leveled against Bunk's "managers" were certainly undeserved. Ever since the second Stuyvesant Casino booking, if not before, the management of his career had largely been in his own hands, as a letter from the Orchestra Hall concert promoter John Schenck to Bill Russell makes clear.[105] Both Russell and Williams had invested a considerable amount of time, energy, and money in Johnson's comeback, and whatever rewards accrued to them tended to be spiritual rather than material. Anyone who really knew Bunk grasped the fact that he was nobody's pawn, and from the very beginning it was he who had exploited the opportunities that Armstrong, in a moment of deference, had fortuitously provided. The patience of his benefactors had been strained even more than their finances at times, and yet they stood by him to the bitter end.

Yet it was Bunk who gave them the means to persevere. Russell, Williams, and Colburn ultimately derived much more than knowledge from their affiliation with Bunk Johnson, for they found in him not a god but a guru with a simple message—"Be happy today, and tomorrow will take care of itself." Albeit vicariously, they came to appreciate the celebration of life as an antidote to oppression, experiencing catharsis in Bunk's blues. Over the course of their association, they achieved an intimacy with a number of New Orleans musicians that came from experiences beyond the bandstand: rent parties; communal dinners of red beans and rice or Chinese food; forays to the jazz clubs of New Orleans, San Francisco, New York, Los Angeles, Boston, and Chicago; and, sometimes, quiet conversation.[106]

In a silent home movie (made in Chicago in 1947), a relaxed and playful Bunk reveals a side of his personality with which his later critics were apparently unfamiliar. The film begins with the "old man" sitting in a chair beside a phonograph, playing his trumpet so that his fingering can be observed. A pretty young lady places an unidentified record on the turntable, but Bunk is not amused, so he gets up, grabs the record, and smashes it, laughing. First one, and then several, pupils join him, darting in and out of frame during the jam session. The young lady, accompanied by two friends, is inspecting the various instruments lying around, smoking a cigarette, peering down the bore of the trumpet, and laughing. Bunk now has a bottle of whiskey; he pours it down the bell of the trumpet and then drinks, first from the trumpet and then from the bottle. He listens to another record, plays along with it, and then feeds the dog that has been lying at his feet. He is enjoying himself.[107] The insouciance revealed in Bunk's "performance" could be humorous when captured on film, but the experiences with Bechet in Boston, and his later tardiness and general unreliability, showed the negative side of such an attitude. But Russell, Williams, and Colburn were determined to factor Bunk's peccadilloes into the management equation. The flouting of such "show business" conventions as showing up on time duly outraged critics and customers, but ever mindful of Bunk's sermons, his "managers" always did their best to take it in stride.

Because he was so ideologically invested by supporters and detractors alike, everything Bunk did could be interpreted as controversial. Divisions within the jazz world among critics and musicians over his performance skills and demeanor revealed the dual impulses that were reconfiguring jazz aesthetics in the 1940s. One "camp" was based on the critical assumptions evident in *Jazzmen*, postulating New Orleans style as a musically uncontrived, yet multifaceted, art form that was anything but "primitive"; the other was tied to teleological ideals of Progress in which newer, more sophisticated artistic styles such as swing and bebop organically evolved from earlier, "primitive" variants. Jazz critics judged Bunk Johnson according to the set of values to which they subscribed. Accordingly, French critic André Hodeir (1921–) used Bunk as an example of the "primitive" New Orleans stage of evolution in *Jazz: Its Evolution and Essence* (1956): "The praises of toothless and winded cornet players have been sung by zealous partisans of early jazz, for whom old time jazz is necessarily better than classical, and primitive jazz better than old time. . . . It is true that some great soloists lent their talents to this New Orleans renaissance; and it is thanks to them that the movement does not appear altogether as a fossilized vestige of a dead era."[108] Stanley Dance's (1910–1999) evaluation of Johnson was also dismissive: "Bunk's years of absence from active music-making showed in all his playing. He could do little more than suggest his former ability, while his colleagues rather proved that, after the best musicians left New Orleans in the '20s, jazz had indeed stagnated there. Nevertheless, the records made under the names of Bunk, George Lewis and Kid Rena had a certain historical value in that they illustrated details of repertoire, tempo and routine, but musically they suffered greatly in comparison with the masters who had gone out from the city many years before."[109]

No wonder then, as Jed Rasula observes, that New Orleans–style purists used the revival as a strategic weapon: "The sectarian vengefulness of Dixieland revivalists in the 1940s was a protest against the evolutionary perspective. The revivalists [such as Bunk and Ory] could declare in a fiat of authenticity (they were there!) that jazz was not an evolutionary form; it was not born, it could not die, and above all it could not 'evolve.' It could only *be*, and they were there to demonstrate the pure existence of the thing."[110] Bunk Johnson's status as the avatar of New Orleans style made it easy to ridicule him. Yet his fall from grace did not diminish the potency of the New Orleans revival, and his recordings still sell and occasion debate.[111] The collectors who organized record companies like Delta, Jazz Man, American Music, Circle, Crescent, and Exner made this possible, insuring that the music of the New Orleans revival would be available for generations to come. These companies functioned like cooperatives, in which profits were used to further distribution, not vice versa. Purists heard what Bunk and Ory were saying in their music, and it drew them toward a socially responsible approach to the documentation of vernacular culture—that is, when ideology did not get in the way. Unfortunately, it often did. The New Orleans revival exposed troublesome ideological contradictions within the purist ethos, and in truth, the recordings by Bunk's Brass Band made by William Russell in 1945 seem as heavy-handed as Columbia's recordings of "hot" hymns by Sam Morgan's Jazz Band in 1927 had been—although the intentions were certainly different. Had Russell chosen to record brass bands that were then active in the social life of the Crescent City, such as the Eureka and the Young Tuxedo, he would have been on firmer documentary ground, but then the heuristic point he was trying to make would have been lost.[112]

Or so it seems. In actuality, the idea of making a brass band recording "without saxophones" came from Bunk. According to Russell: "Every parade band I'd ever heard the past three years in N.O. had from 1 to 3 saxes. I was practically resigned to hiring one if necessary to make it authentic 'according to present day N.O. standards,' but Bunk sez, 'No, none of the saxes are any good in a band.'"[113] Russell's mistake was in trying to extract a universally applicable maxim from what were essentially one man's peccadilloes. Russell's faith in the word of Bunk remained unwavering throughout his lifetime, and at times he became a victim of the awe in which he held the master. What mattered most, however, was the maturation of their relationship, which enabled Russell to finally appreciate Bunk as a self-directed and articulate musician in the present, rather than as an intuitive curiosity representing the past. Under such circumstances, broad allusions to the pervasive power of essentialist racial ideologies that "appointed white men as those who could best classify and judge jazz" in early jazz discourses come into question. Yet, as Russell freely admitted, it took him four years of knowing Bunk to realize that he was the student and Bunk was the teacher.[114]

Had Hodeir and Dance been equally receptive, they might have heard what Bunk was saying a bit differently. This is why Harold Drob's "Last Testament" session became so important in retrospect—it afforded Bunk respect and control. Yet it also became apparent that documentation of early twentieth-century New Orleans–style practices could not be achieved after the fact, no matter how well-intentioned the motivation might be. In the wake of the New Orleans revival, the expectation that "expert" packaging of vernacular culture could entirely avoid the pitfalls endemic to entertainment-industry exploitation turned out to be increasingly hard to sustain. Furthermore, while the revival of New Orleans jazz had a tremendous and largely positive impact internationally after World War II, in the United States it laid the groundwork for a rupture within the American jazz community that resulted in an identity crisis from which it has yet to recover.[115]

CHAPTER 5

Jazz Schism: The Perils of Intellectualization

Despite the desire of many jazz researchers to keep the study of the music "down to earth," by 1940 the theories of a growing number of critics and historians had greatly intellectualized the field. Recognition of jazz as an art form—a basic tenet of the collector community that had been transferred by John Hammond and others to the promotional strategies of the record industry by 1940—was tantamount to a declaration of aesthetic independence, conferring a sense of intellectual legitimacy on American vernacular culture. The New Orleans revival was therefore not an exercise in nostalgia, as revivals are often expected to be. It was instead constructed as a contemporary alternative to big band swing and to promote an ideological imperative, that New Orleans–style jazz possessed an aesthetic purity not apparent in derivative, commercialized forms. It was also intended to demonstrate the validity of diffusionist premises that had been built into the conceptualization of jazz history offered in *Jazzmen*.[1]

While the revival helped to establish a niche for traditional jazz in the marketplace, it did not alter the industry's basic orientation toward novelty, which rested on a belief in Progress tied to an evolutionary perspective.[2] Indeed, the major record companies marketed the revived New Orleans style as a novelty, a cult item, in an increasingly pluralistic bid for consumer dollars. In order to preserve and sustain New Orleans style, the revivalists themselves had to detach it from its regional cultural context, which meant contradicting the thrust of *Jazzmen* as a celebration of regional culture. New Orleans style became a commodity because selling it seemed to be the only viable alternative to extinction. As a result, distinctions among folk, popular, and art music were accordingly blurred, for the recordings that fueled the revival were examples of a quasi-folk style, recognized as an art form, competing in the popular music market. New modes of categorization were needed, and the events of the 1940s supplied them.

The New Orleans revival set into motion a chain reaction that fragmented the consensus exemplified by *Jazzmen,* dividing the jazz community into mutually hostile camps of traditionalists and modernists. The debate centered around the diametrically opposed theories of diffusionists and evolutionists, although acrimony often obscured the clarity of respective positions. The battleground was the jazz press, such as it was, pitting a cross-section of the established jazz literati against perceived newcomers, whose affiliation with the collector community was limited. The catalyst for this crisis was the appearance of popularity polls in magazines like *Down Beat* and *Esquire*—the former a reader's plebiscite, the latter a critic's choice. Although the polls were little more than publicity stunts, they created more dissension than goodwill, imposing a value-laden, hierarchical structure on an increasingly heterogeneous musical community. The polls tested the elasticity of jazz as a concept to the breaking point, forcing the development of terms like *traditionalist* and *modernist* to differentiate among widely divergent styles. Centrifugal force exacerbated the problem. While the New Orleans revival attempted to turn the jazz clock back as far as it could go, the self-conscious innovations of bebop and progressive jazz adumbrated the future.[3] A reconstruction of jazz aesthetics thus became inevitable, with historiographical implications of major proportions when modernists began to challenge the idea that jazz had been born in New Orleans.

The split between traditionalists and modernists absorbed, and to some extent clarified, another dualism that was also present in the jazz community. In assessing the ideology of the New Orleans revival, comparison with the history of religious revivalism in the United States reveals some striking parallels. During the Great Awakening of the eighteenth century, schismatic forces divided congregations into "New Lights" and "Old Lights" in much the same way as traditionalists departed from modernists. The primary issue was purity of religious experience, but the lines of division were based on a conflict between sensibility and rationality, with the end result that American

Protestantism was bifurcated by the time of the Revolution into "the camp of folk religion and that of intellectual Calvinism."[4] The "New Light" revivalists emphasized emotion, and the New Orleans revivalists were their equivalent in desiring to return to a simpler, purer jazz experience, free of intellectual mediation or explanation. Folk music, like folk religion, required initiation rather than education—it was immediately accessible to its participant audience. Modernists, in some ways like the "Old Lights," demanded an educated public that could appreciate the technical virtuosity of modern jazz and its subtleties. Purists believed that modern jazz did not invite participation. They saw its practitioners as distancing themselves from the audience, operating as an elitist avant-garde that was always one step ahead of the musical masses.

Recalling once again the commentary offered by Sanjek and Russell on the attitudinal differences between the Hot Record Exchange and the Commodore Music Shop, it is clear that the respective positions of the two cliques ("good time" versus "serious" jazz appreciation) correspond to an emotion-versus-intellect differential. When Bill Russell lauded the "imprecision" of Kid Rena's approach to collective improvisation on Broun's Delta recordings, he was stating a preference for "feeling" over "technique" that reflected the predominant ethos of the Hot Record Exchange. The contrast between the editorial policies of *HRS Society Rag* and *Jazz Information* is also evident. Whereas *Jazz Information* maintained a decidedly serious intellectual tone throughout its existence, *Society Rag* supplemented its coverage of jazz news and history with collector fables, burlesques of critics, and other humorous pieces that were specifically designed to amuse as well as inform.[5] Such distinctions, however, must not be overemphasized, for feeling and technique, emotion and intellect, were intrinsic to all jazz. Nevertheless, the distinctions were real, and questions of degree could assume great importance when politicized within the context of the traditionalist/modernist debates.

Despite the overriding antagonism that governed relations between traditionalists and modernists, each had affinities (which were largely ignored) that should be noted before closer examination of respective ideologies is undertaken. Both groups shared an underlying dissatisfaction with big band swing, which was the predominant force in the popular music market in the early 1940s.[6] Because big bands required disciplined section work, guided by the conception of an arranger, opportunities for solo expression were limited,

reducing many players to the level of cogs in a well-oiled machine. Individu-
alists who felt they had something to say were constrained by the regimenta-
tion of the big band format and sought to escape from it by returning to
smaller combinations that allowed greater personal expression. This was
why Lu Watters formed the Yerba Buena Jazz Band, sparking the traditionalist revival in San Francisco, and why beboppers like Dizzy Gillespie
(1917–1993) and Charlie Parker (1920–1955) ultimately sought refuge in
smaller groups after dabbling with big band experiments in modern jazz with
Earl Hines and Billy Eckstine (1914–1993).[7] Traditionalists and modernists
alike abandoned the status quo in search of greater personal freedom and
creativity (and perhaps to flee teenage jitterbugs with a less cerebral interest
in jazz). They were headed in opposite directions, but bound for collision.
Yet the means by which they sought to build constituencies were virtually
identical. Just as Watters depended on Jazz Man to bring his music to a wider
audience, Parker and Gillespie relied on Dial Records, another Los Angeles–based independent organized by Ross Russell (1909–2000), a traditionalist turned modernist.[8] It was the devotion of the small independent labels
such as Dial, Manor, Guild, and Savoy that nurtured the nonconformist
"modernists" until the major record companies had seen enough to take a
chance.

When *Jazzmen* was published in late 1939, the ideological tension between New Orleans style and "modernism" in the form of swing was already
apparent, but "modern jazz" was not yet a viable term, at least not in the
ideological sense in which it was used after 1944.[9] *Jazzmen* achieved international distribution within months of its publication, and a pocket-sized edition was distributed to American servicemen gratis, as part of a jazz arsenal
that also included V-Discs and radio programs broadcast by the Office of
War Information and Armed Forces Radio Service.[10] Copies of *Jazzmen* arrived in Britain early in 1940, and its appearance there and elsewhere
strengthened the resolve of opponents of Nazi tyranny, for jazz came to be regarded as a symbol of freedom par excellence during the war years.[11] Its impact on the home front made collectors of a new generation of young Americans, but only briefly—scrap drives ended the prospecting phase of hot
collecting abruptly in 1942, as patriotic young men and women dutifully
handed over their old records to Uncle Sam, who needed shellac.[12] With the
passing of the golden age of collecting, the stature of old-guard collectors

such as Bill Russell, Charles Edward Smith, and Fred Ramsey was duly enhanced, particularly in the eyes of novices, and their future collaboration was thus assured, at least for a few more years.

In 1941, Smith and Russell were asked to submit an article on New Orleans style to *Modern Music,* a quarterly published by the League of Composers, indicating the growing acceptance of jazz as an art form within academic circles. The article contained many of the insights and the errors of the New Orleans section of *Jazzmen* but went into greater detail on instrumental techniques in New Orleans style, explaining that "as each instrument explored its own role in the ensemble, it developed its own characteristic features. And so a most idiomatic orchestral usage was perfected."[13] Smith and Russell described how wind and percussion instruments in small bands replaced the predominance of string orchestras in what amounted to a musical revolution. The introduction of a folk-derived blues feeling and the adaptation of "expressive vocal features, including vibrato," changed the way musicians played together:

> A new kind of dynamics was needed. This involved more natural tone production and less attempt to adjust or modify the natural dynamics and volume. Each instrument was forced to find its most telling style. A transparent polyphony gradually replaced the massive sonorities of European orchestras. With the application of solo style to the ensemble there was no longer a need or a place for the doubling of parts, union passages, exact repetition of motives, nor even the much over-stressed precision of performance. A rich and frequently dissonant polyphony resulted.[14]

Kid Rena was given as a recorded example of lead trumpet, with numerous references to Armstrong, Ory, and Johnny Dodds, and the influence of New Orleans style on the development of jazz bands in Chicago, Kansas City, and throughout the Midwest via diffusion was unequivocally stated. The article concluded with a swipe at the swing bands of Basie and Goodman, in which "choirs of instruments began to replace the one-of-a-kind setup": "Actually this new 'big-band' jazz utilized fewer of the technical features of 'the real old jazz' than is generally supposed. To some extent it even represents a dilution."[15] While the commercialism that resulted from the competition of big bands in the popular dance music market did not necessarily preclude a "worthwhile product," Smith and Russell made it clear that jazz was usually debased in "the tattered, soiled garments of popular dance music." Because radio tended to favor ersatz jazz, and because the record companies had confined great talents like Armstrong's to the "race" market, the true heroes of jazz achieved recognition belatedly, or not at all. The message to the academicians was clear: it was time to set the record straight. In fact, there were indications that music educators had already responded to the call.

Earlier in 1941, Louis Harap's (1904–1998) "The Case for Hot Jazz" had appeared in the *Musical Quarterly*, a journal known as "the musicologist's bible." Harap put forth a synopsis of the ideas that had emanated from the collector community throughout the 1930s, reiterating the anticommercial arguments of Smith, Russell, and others.[16] He accused academicians of succumbing to musical myopia: "Musically speaking, a culture that is favorable to improvisation is not less sound artistically than one in which performance keeps composer, executant, and audience discrete. For a musical culture of the former kind requires that the music really live in and through the people, that the music be as natural an expression as the idioms of speech, and that the musical idiom be therefore expressible by a large part of the people."[17] He also lauded the singularity of New Orleans style, using King Oliver and his Savannah Syncopators as an example, adding that it was necessary for such groups to be "limited in number so that each musician can hear the others, and, furthermore, there must be mutual familiarity with one another's style of playing."[18] But while the perspective of academic music scholars was being broadened by Harap and Virgil Thomson in the 1940s, serious analysis of jazz as an art form did not become integrated into general surveys until the appearance of Gilbert Chase's *America's Music: From the Pilgrims to the Present* in 1955.[19]

In 1942, the collaborative efforts of Charles Edward Smith, William Russell, and Fred Ramsey continued with the publication of *The Jazz Record Book* by Smith and Durrell, a New York firm that patronized jazz scholarship in the 1940s.[20] Although this project was essentially a guide designed to familiarize the uninitiated with a judicious sampling of jazz recordings, a survey of jazz history preceded the record listings. *The Jazz Record Book* was a cooperative enterprise, with John Hammond, Stephen Sholes, Milt Gabler, Stephen Smith, George Avakian, R. D. Darrell, Hugues Panassié, Charles Delaunay, George Hoefer, Eugene Williams, and Alan Lomax all thanked in the acknowledgments. The book was dedicated to Jelly Roll Morton, whose passing was sorrowfully noted.[21] The preface was Smith's, and his statement that "the New Orleans style, contrary to a widespread notion that it is mainly limited and technically rigid, represents considerable variety and fluidity" reveals his continued equanimity on the subject, but Russell, whose primacy in the field was now considered to be beyond question, wrote most of the discussion of the "parent style."[22]

Russell borrowed heavily from the *Modern Music* article (some passages were repeated verbatim), but overall coverage was more comprehensive, and the stylistic analysis was more detailed and incisive. While noting that the New Orleans scene had lost much of its former glory, he maintained that "there are upwards of fifty known names in jazz who still live in or who have returned to the city whose music they helped to develop."[23] Yet the days of regional insularity were now long gone: "New Orleans music, of course, has long since ceased to be a local phenomenon. Today, as everyone knows, it is the core of American jazz."[24] The correlation of the maturation of the recording industry with the rise of jazz bands was also mentioned—"the emergence of instrumental jazz from its status of a somewhat regional music coincided with the development of the recording industry itself"—as was the confusion of terminology that had accompanied the development of the music in its infancy: "For a time the word *Creole* meant jazz, just as the word *ragtime* had been used (erroneously) to designate this type of music some years earlier." Russell went on to explain that "the word jazz is now used to designate generally the field of popular music. We limit its use to the hot music field, which is both proper and saves adjectives."[25] The music that was New Orleans style had been called many things, from "raggedy uptown" to "hot," but recognition of its nativity in New Orleans was by this time considered to be a fait accompli: "At present it is doubtful if anyone seriously disputes the claim that New Orleans is the birthplace of instrumental jazz. Innumerable facts in support of this theory have been put forth and subjected to proof. But even the most intense regional culture could hardly account for such a phenomenon. Its background is anything but simple."[26] While jazz drew on American Negro folk roots derived from African traditions (spirituals and blues), which were then "transformed by urban development" in Southern cities, it was only in New Orleans (according to Russell's informants, "veterans of the early phase of jazz") that all the necessary elements were specifically combined.[27]

Russell devoted an entire section of his coverage of origins to the relationship between jazz and dance, and it is here that he addresses the issue of African survivals in New Orleans music. While noting the correspondence of African dance and the descriptions of rituals in Congo Square, he concluded that such connections were often overemphasized: "The fusion of African and European-American elements took place over a long period of time. It is possible to say of specific musical creations that one or another element predominates, but it is not so easy to find what one might call a 'pure' survival. Those who take the long jump from African tribal music to jazz indulge in fascinating, but unscientific, hypothesis. Similarly, it is possible only for purposes of classification to isolate this or that phase of Negro music from its cultural setting."[28] Information on how the foxtrot had derived from the French quadrille, and on folk-derived dances such as the shag, the grind, the twist, the belly rub, the drag, and the creep, provided detail that had not been included in *Jazzmen*.

Sections on Storyville, ragtime, and the spread of jazz all went well beyond Russell's earlier writings, and material stemming from Lomax's interviews with Morton was also put to good use.[29] Following the historical survey was a detailed examination of the elements of New Orleans style, with specific sections devoted to rhythm, scalar structure, harmony, form, tone (intonation), and instrumentation. Russell discussed the roles of individual instruments, including saxophone (which came later, adapting the New Orleans reed style based on clarinet to the needs of larger aggregations) and piano (which functioned primarily as a rhythm instrument in the collective ensemble format).[30] Subsequent passages in *The Jazz Record Book* dealt with how commercialization of jazz had adversely affected the careers of numerous New Orleans pioneers, suggesting that the difficulty of finding adequate employment had, in many cases, shortened their lives. Kid Rena was given as a contemporary frame of reference for "authentic" New Orleans style, and the authors' hope that the careers of surviving jazzmen could be salvaged was made clear: "Revival of interest in New Orleans jazz may, ultimately, benefit some of these men who lost out in the jazz boom because they chose to stay in the city of its origin!"[31] All in all, *The Jazz Record Book* provided a wealth of additional information on New Orleans origins and style, surpassing *Jazzmen* on many levels. Surprisingly, while *Jazzmen* still finds its way into many bibliographies, *The Jazz Record Book* is rarely cited.

Smith and Durrell also published Hugues Panassié's *The Real Jazz* in 1942, largely because its chances for seeing print in France were nil during the war but additionally because Panassié was widely respected by influential members of the jazz literati in the United States. The manuscript had been smuggled out of France and handed over to Charles Edward Smith and Bill Russell for correction, indicating the extent to which Americans had come to dominate the field of jazz history and criticism since the mid-1930s.[32] American jazz scholarship had surpassed that of the French, whose original contributions served as an incentive to excellence but who were now clearly the junior partners in the Franco-American "hot" jazz entente. The French, of course, are a proud people (Panassié particularly so), making Panassié's admission of major errors in *Le Jazz Hot,* stated in the preface, all the more noteworthy.[33] As in his previous works, Panassié's thrust was primarily aesthetic, but *The Real Jazz* contained a good deal of historical information that reflected the influence of American scholarship. Yet what is significant in this work, as it relates to the present study, was the way in which Panassié interpreted the history, for he had imbibed at the font of purism in the manner of Russell and Smith. In doing so, he eschewed the myth of Progress: "Another unfortunate error made by jazz musicians was to suppose that progress was necessary and that their art must be in continuous motion. They asserted that the musicians of 1920 played very well 'for their period' but insisted that such a recording, or even a recording made in 1925, had become in 1930 obsolete and hopelessly outmoded. 'It's not modern' was their disdainful cry when they listened to an old recording or to an excellent musician who had not modified his style for several years."[34] And the "superstition about progress, allied to a desire to dazzle," created a preference for technical virtuosity that undermined the essence of "real jazz," which was *feeling:* "Many musicians, possessed of fine instrumental techniques, stressed that technique to the detriment of their strictly musical work. They attempted to play the greatest possible number of notes with a maximum speed and tried to increase their range to abnormally high registers. . . . Briefly, virtuosity became too often an end in itself, instead of remaining only a means. It is only too easy to see what harm such a disastrous conception could have on jazz music."[35] Placed in perspective, New Orleans style was thus aesthetically superior to much of what had been derived from it, which lacked coherence: "In the New Orleans orchestras the instruments were combined in excellent balance from the point of view of tonality as well as accentuation." In Panassié's estimation, New Orleans stylists remained cognizant of their "duties," respecting the needs of the ensemble even as they engaged freely in improvisation. They became a mutually reinforcing unit—a study in balance. In modern orchestras, it often seemed that the primary emphasis was on the individual soloist, to the detriment of the group as a whole, and the balance was lost. The distinction between strong and weak beats became obscure, and melodic clarity was sacrificed: "As a result the improvisation of an ensemble gives the impression of being a group of individual solos played simultaneously rather than a homogeneous, and well-knit work."[36] Of course, Panassié was here referring to those big swing bands that had done some good in employing older jazzmen as soloists but were now deemed inferior because they substituted technique for feeling, a distinction that the followers of the "swing fad" were incapable of grasping.[37]

The appearance of *Jazzmen, The Jazz Record Book,* and *The Real Jazz* showed the degree to which New Orleans–style purists had established hegemony over jazz scholarship by 1942, but one might well inquire as to how typical such views were of the collector community as a whole. A consideration of the demographic configuration of the "hot" jazz collector community in absolute terms is probably out of the question, but there are sources that provide insight into who some of these collectors were, where they lived, how they supported themselves, and what their preferences were. William C. Love, Max Kaplan, and Alderson Fry's *Who's Who in Jazz Collecting* was compiled to alert interested parties who did not already know that there was an extensive private network of collectors throughout the United States and Europe (information on the latter was minimal, due to the German occupation). While the idea for this project was first conceived in 1940, wartime disruptions and its ambitious nature delayed the book's completion until almost two years later. The compilers listed details on the collections of 242 respondents and gave the names of an additional 287 collectors, representing a significant sample, on which conclusions about the composition and tastes of the community as a whole can be based. Some statistical data was supplied in the preface to the listings, but it is also clear that the editors had neither the time nor the inclination to exhaust all the possibilities for profiling this group.

The average age of the collectors was given as 26.8 years, and the average number of years collecting was 6.5, leading to the conclusion that record collecting was most prevalent among young adults, most of whom had entered the field in the mid-1930s, when magazines like *Down Beat* and *Esquire* were developing a jazz readership and the record industry was experiencing recovery.[38] The average size of collections was 1,075 records, representing a range from fewer than 100 to as many as 12,000; the actual number of "hot" jazz collectibles was judged to be about 5,000 by the compilers, so larger collections were assumed to include records that would not be considered "real" jazz. Favorite recordings became a problem for the compilers, because 325 different records received votes, so only records receiving 5 or more votes were listed. As a general rule, however, records by Louis Armstrong were preferred (147), while Bix Beiderbecke came second (65), Duke Ellington was third (51), and Muggsy Spanier was fourth (44). In some cases, a record by Lill's Hot Shots, a band led by pianist Lillian Hardin, would score as well as one by Louis Armstrong (her former husband), Clarence Williams's Blue Five, or Johnny Dodds.[39] The correlation of these record preferences with the reissue catalogs of UHCA, HRS, and Commodore was not mentioned in the survey, but it is nonetheless significant. Judging from the statistical averages offered by Love, Kaplan, and Fry, a majority of the collectors polled preferred bands such as King Oliver's Creole Jazz Band, Armstrong's Hot Five, Clarence Williams's Blue Five, and the Chicagoans who were inspired by them.

The statistical generalizations given in the preface to *Who's Who in Jazz Collecting* show that purist sensibilities were paramount in the collecting community in 1942. When one moves beyond the preface into the directory listings, this conclusion becomes even more apparent. While some collectors (particularly women, it seems) were attracted to the records of swing matinee idols like Benny Goodman or Artie Shaw, the ubiquity of New Orleans artists is what commands attention.[40] But the sample offered is capable of yielding much more than insight into collector preferences. The list of 242 respondents gives occupations and addresses, except when a collector decided to withhold them. By subjecting this material to analysis, information on the demographics of the collector community, especially social characteristics and spatial distribution, can be obtained. One can also differentiate according to gender: although their numerical representation was relatively low, women exerted a considerable influence within the collector community disproportionate to their numbers, as will be seen.

Collectors who worked as laborers will be defined as "blue-collar," and a few of the occupational responses given should suffice to convey what is meant by this term: teamster, service station manager, sheet metal worker, paint jobber, mill worker, bottler in a winery, and door factory worker. "White-collar" usually refers to professionals working in a service industry: attorney, librarian, group chief at the Census Bureau, novelist, bank president, stenographer, chiropractor, jeweler, and meteorologist. Because of the difficulties of classifying occupations such as musician, student, and soldier, these respondents are treated separately. Listings in the directory, when quantified according to these categories, show the following: 64 percent were white-collar, 12 percent were blue-collar, 12 percent were students, 10 percent were musicians or worked with them in some capacity (such as a record store owner or a jazz writer), and 2 percent were members of the armed forces. The predominance of white-collar professionals is overwhelming. Of the group sampled, names were used to determine gender, with men numbering 225 and women 15 (two names were excluded because gender was not apparent). Educators and clerks were numerous among white-collar occupations, while blue-collar occupations tended to vary widely. Broadly speaking, the middle-class composition of the collector community is indisputable, as is the preponderance of males compared to females (a ratio of 15 to 1).

Analysis of spatial distribution is also revealing. Because the list of miscellaneous names of known collectors who did not respond to the questionnaire is included in the compilation, this sample numbers 529. In sectional terms, by far the largest concentration of collectors was in the Northeast (from New Jersey through New England, and including Pennsylvania), with 205. The Great Lakes Region (Illinois, Michigan, Wisconsin, and Minnesota) had 90; the Midwest (Ohio, Iowa, Indiana, Missouri, and Kansas) had 76; the Far West (California, Oregon, Washington, and Arizona) had 63; and the South (including Texas, Washington, D.C., and the border states) trailed, with 55. Jazz record collecting tended to be an urban phenomenon, with New York City ranking first, with 51 collectors (a number that does not include suburbs in New Jersey and Connecticut, which would have pushed the total much higher), followed by the Boston metropolitan area (35), Los Angeles (25), Chicago (23), and San Francisco (20). While states like Ohio (49), Michigan (34), and Pennsylvania (24) had relatively high totals, these collectors tended to be dispersed statewide. In 1942, then, the "typical" American jazz record collector could be described as an urban professional, usually male and financially comfortable, who lived in a large city near the East or West Coast or in the Great Lakes region. Judging from the variety of preferences witnessed in *Who's Who in Jazz Collecting,* one might add that collectors were a highly individualistic lot, joined together in a loosely knit confederation organized around general principles like "jazz is art."

This generalization is supported by the responses of collectors to a question about their objectives: 50 percent of the respondents collected "serially" within or without specialties, using terms such as "comprehensive," "complete," "all," and "every"; 20 percent were content with "representative" collections; 17 percent said they collected primarily for "enjoyment" or "pleasure"; and 13 percent collected to obtain "knowledge." Individual responses were sometimes revealing. John Hammond stated that he collected for "pleasure and escape." Timothy Leary collected "to get all the good records there are, of course, but excluding the type of record that stinks except for two bars by some great, probably." One collector wanted to "have more than 500 records," while another was more concerned with "keeping the number of my records down so that I know each one individually." Perhaps the most honest response was, "I buy records because I like jazz and enjoy arguing about it."[41] During the embattled 1930s, the righteous cause of jazz acted to hold this coalition together: prospecting and partisanship forged a chain of cooperation. But when the recognition of jazz as an art form became pervasive and supplies of old records began to dry up, the idiosyncracies contained within the community came forth like jinn from a bottle.[42]

And there were plenty of idiosyncracies from which to choose. While Krin Gabbard's fascination with "collector nerds" and John Gennari's depiction of John Hammond and Leonard Feather as "white guys without dates" is offset to some extent by the broader demographic range informing *Who's Who in Jazz Collecting,* such scholarly interest in "hot" record collecting as an exercise in purposive masculinity tempts one to explain the jazz schisms of the 1940s as an exercise in runaway testosterone. Yet these characterizations also suggest that "hot" record collecting might qualify as an example of what

Sherrie Tucker calls the "feminized, devalued sub-genres" prevalent in jazz, especially since the national jazz market of the late 1930s was so completely dominated by swing.[43] Tucker's unwavering insistence upon recognizing women in jazz certainly justifies a closer inspection of how female "hot" collectors negotiated for power within homosocial networks dedicated to analysis of the music of black men.

The women of "hot" collecting were, in fact, quite powerful, and they have already made their presence felt in this study. Lee Smith, the wife of the proprietor of the Hot Record Exchange, had been a key member of the *Jazzmen* team. Although she acted primarily as a stenographer, anyone who has ever attempted to transcribe, collate, and index oral history interviews knows that such work is not easy. While extremely absorbing, time-consuming, and tedious, it is crucial to the advancement of knowledge in a field as dependent on oral testimony as jazz scholarship. John Reid's confidant Mary Karoley was the first to record Bunk Johnson, serving as a purist plenipotentiary sent to check his credentials. The future of the New Orleans revival was riding on that trip, and her diplomatic skill ("Tell 'em, Bunk!") was of paramount importance. Jean Rayburn became Mrs. Ralph Gleason in 1941, after the duo had worked together to launch *Jazz Information*. Rayburn began as circulation manager and rose to the rank of coeditor when conditions warranted it.

Dave Stuart's wife, Marili Morden, ran the Jazz Man Record Shop in Hollywood, had every record ever made by Bessie Smith (she was a serial collector) and enjoyed widespread respect for her jazz and blues expertise. She was also highly sought after for her connections, deriving from friendships with black musicians throughout the Los Angeles area, such as Kid Ory and T-Bone Walker. In other words, she controlled access not only to "hot" records but also to many of their creators, which was like being in charge of the food supply, only better. Morden wrote in virtually all of the "little" magazines associated with "hot" collecting—advising young male collectors on collecting strategies, which allowed her to shape their minds. One might even go so far as to say, without too much exaggeration, that all of these women "collected" collectors, with Morden taking top honors for the biggest collection. After she separated from Stuart (probably in 1942), she maintained a secret marriage with Nesuhi Ertegun before going public. Given her oft-cited beauty and insouciance, one might imagine that the "pretty young lady in a welder's uniform, complete with metal hat," described by Virgil Thomson at a Bunk Johnson concert in 1943 might have been her, but that is probably too much to hope for. Whoever that young lady was, she certainly lends credence to Gabbard's claim that female jazz record collectors could adopt masculine postures and use them advantageously.

Women who collected "hot" were not only to be found in large urban areas. Mary Teresi was a student from Milledgeville, Georgia, and listed her interests in *Who's Who in Jazz Collecting* as "music (jazz, classical), dress designing, traveling, prize fighting, dogs, and people" (presumably not in that order) and let it be known that, "I collect records only for the music, not for a hobby."[44] Her interests in "hot" collecting were transmitted to her friend Richard B. Allen, who later became one of the founders of the Archive of New Orleans Jazz at Tulane University. Clearly, female "hot" collectors wielded an authority that ordained them with the power to influence men, a product of their knowledge and commitment to the cause.

When "masculine" strategies employed by women came into conflict with the power plays of men, however, such authority could diminish rapidly, exposing the vulnerability of females in the face of male bonding and domination. The experience of New York jazz enthusiast Rita Temple, who became embroiled in the fight between Bunk Johnson and Sidney Bechet at the Savoy Café in Boston in March 1945, should suffice as an example. Gene Williams, who was ostensibly Bunk's primary manager at the time, came to Boston on two consecutive weekends (March 16–18, March 23–25) to support Bunk and hear the band. His friend Rita Temple came up with Sam Meltzer, a bakery sales clerk and amateur saxophonist, on March 17 and returned to New York with Williams on the early train two days later. The following weekend, she accompanied Williams as a traveling companion. Bechet had booked the job, so it was supposed to be his band, but Bunk was attracting most of the attention and refused to obey orders, which angered Bechet. There was trouble on the bandstand when Johnson failed to come in on cue and resisted Sidney's leadership in less polite ways, which quickly infected the social activity surrounding the engagement, such as dinner parties that included Temple and Williams.

Bechet blamed Williams for Bunk's behavior, but rather than confronting him directly, he chose instead to cast Temple in the role of Mata Hari and the manager as her pimp:

Gene came after [Bunk] with a girl, let's call her Lorraine. Bunk had a girl he was going around with, but Gene brought this Lorraine around and they took him across the street to a drinking place. Gene paid for everything; they got Bunk plenty full of liquor and he was really going. And Gene kept telling him he should go home with this girl. . . . This Gene, he'd made an arrangement with her; she had been hired to stand up in front of Bunk in a way of speaking, show herself off for Bunk, persuade him to leave me and go with Gene.[45]

Sidney claimed elsewhere in the book that he was having an affair with Temple and that she had divulged the details of the plot to him while in his room.[46] Bechet's failure to control Bunk required a scapegoat, and given his well-documented struggles with misogyny (such as his deportation from England following charges of attempted rape), his side of the story probably reveals more about his demons than it does about Rita Temple's alleged foibles. Williams's account, as given in lengthy letters to William Russell at the time, completely exonerates Temple, whose sincere wish to see the discord within the band resolved for the sake of the music was evident in her every action.[47] Bechet used that empathy against her in order to portray himself as the aggrieved party because, as a man, he could: Temple was a "temptress," and most men would therefore accept his version of the story.[48] Ironically, when Williams and Temple attempted to book lodging (in separate rooms) at Sidney's boardinghouse, they were rejected as "white trash," but Bunk's landlady accepted them because "after all we were supposed to be fighting a war for democracy and she was opposed to segregation, so she would give us the rooms."[49]

The decisive actions of women were fundamental in the planning, execution, and reception of the New Orleans revival. In the inevitable debates that attended its promotion, they served not as cheerleaders on the sidelines but as fully engaged combatants, but it was nevertheless men who claimed most of the publicity. Prior to 1943, the revival was still in its incipient stage. The purists who had recorded Bunk Johnson in New Orleans in 1942 were busily engaged in preparing their products, and his appearance in San Francisco with Rudi Blesh was entirely unexpected. Blesh seized the opportunity for promoting Bunk's cause as his own, and he published the lectures he gave on Bunk's behalf at the San Francisco Museum of Art privately in the spirit of a magnum opus. Collectively entitled *This Is Jazz,* they began with a quote from Bunk Johnson: "Playin' Jazz is talkin' from the heart. You don't lie."[50]

Blesh was throwing his hat into the ring as a bid for the crown of purism, and his opening remarks tended to undervalue the impact his predecessors had made on the record industry, academia, and the public:

> Continuous controversy not infrequently acts to bring out the real nature of the object. In this case, however, it has tended consistently to misrepresent and obscure. This process has gone so far, and the misconceptions to which it has led have become so widespread and so deep, that real Hot Jazz is now an esoteric subject unknown in its essence to the vast majority of people, and we must include by far the majority of legitimate musicians, composers and critics. Thus obtains the almost astounding fact of a native art requiring basic definition before it can be discussed before a native audience.[51]

His description of the work of purist writers also ignored their dedicated scholarly approach and the extensive nature of their research. According to Blesh, "much of the argument has been carried on by people who don't even know what they are arguing about." Jazz writers had been forced "to assume the role of crusaders," giving rise to "apologetic" or "belligerent" attitudes. "I do not propose," he promised, "by taking either attitude, further to feed the flames of controversy."[52] He borrowed liberally from *Jazz: Hot and Hybrid, Jazzmen,* and *The Real Jazz* (no mention of *The Jazz Record Book*), and had he read Harap's "The Case for Hot Jazz," he might have qualified his wholesale indictment of those who had been laboring to understand jazz, both within and outside of academic circles. As it was, his position was far more extreme than that of the authorities he chose to cite.

Blesh's lectures displayed that extra touch of vehemence that a latecomer to a battle often musters, and the quotations from *Jazz: Hot and Hybrid* were used to attack Winthrop Sargeant, denying the possibility that jazz could fuse with other forms of music: "Basically Jazz is too vital and too fundamentally different from European music to hybridize with it at all."[53] Throughout *This Is Jazz,* the distinctive features of the music were explained according to a racial thesis, the first musical example a record of "Babira Songs" from the Belgian Congo, played in rapid succession with an American spiritual.[54] Blesh was trying to show the survival of pure Africanisms in jazz: "Note that this is collective improvisation on a theme with remarkably complex and extended rhythmic figures which recur according to a pattern *felt* by the singers. This is a good example of *participative* music. Substitute musical instruments and would this not be Jazz, or a development very close to it?"[55] Comparisons of "Negro" and "white" playing abounded in the audio demonstrations, usually with pejorative commentary directed against the latter, such as the claim that the New Orleans Rhythm Kings' "Tin Roof Blues" was stolen from King Oliver's "Jazzin' Babies' Blues."[56]

Blesh's belittling of Paul Whiteman exposed an essentialist view of race employed for inflammatory purposes, despite his disclaimer to the contrary: "His last name *White Man* may well stand as a symbol of what a white man, classically trained or even classically conditioned, will do when he sets out to develop and improve artistic material to which he is racially alien and the true nature of which he fails to understand."[57] He employed similar arguments in denigrating "Chicago style" and swing, using thirty-six recorded examples to illustrate how Europeanization always diluted the potency of African American music (*"Improve it! White men cannot even play it!"*).[58] Despite detailed discussion of jazz history and technique, however, *This Is Jazz* was essentially a synthesis that did not really add anything new to jazz scholarship, except, perhaps, Blesh's own particular brand of vehemence. So heavily did Blesh rely on the previous work of Hugues Panassié, Charles Edward Smith, William Russell, and Wilder Hobson, that the lectures remind one of the venerable practice of "argument from authority." As a vehicle for the transmission of information on jazz origins and appreciation, the lectures may have sufficed, but the biases that pervaded them did nothing to serve the cause of true understanding.

Considered in the light of Blesh's *This Is Jazz* dicta, an article by Jake Trussell Jr., a Texas collector, appearing several months later in the British journal *Jazz Music*, illustrated the growing rift between diffusionists and evolutionists prior to the rise of bebop. In "Why Fusion?" Trussell had this to say: "There is a horrible schism developing amongst the more intelligent critics of Jazz, the American critics that is. When we realize that there are very, very few intelligent Jazz critics to begin with, we can begin to see the horrible implications of this small nucleus splitting up into raiding parties loaded down with intellectual tomahawks and time bombs. The split has been lurking around the hot corner for some time, skulking back in the dark licking its chops for the final bloody and devastating kill. It finally popped out into full and horrifying bloom directly after Duke Ellington took his band into Carnegie Hall and rendered his *Black, Brown, and Beige.*[59] Ellington's experiment in the fusion of jazz and the classics had evoked a variety of responses; Trussell was against it, but because Ellington was highly revered "on two continents," many critics applauded it in the manner of indulging the Duke's "new clothes." When John Hammond condemned the piece in the *Jazz Record,* "a vitriolic personal attack" followed from Leonard Feather in *Jazz Magazine.*[60]

In order to fully appreciate the ironies so apparent in retrospect in this exchange, one might refer to Hammond's "About the Author," later appearing in Feather's *The New Edition of the Encyclopedia of Jazz:* "Leonard Feather's first visit to America was in 1935, and I recall being on the pier waiting for the *Normandie* to dock." Hammond helped Feather forge important connections, and "within a few days, he had combed Harlem, placed some songs with Clarence Williams, and arranged to become (gratis) the London correspondent of the *New York Amsterdam News.*" Feather crossed the Atlantic many times over the next four years, gaining experience in both the British and the American jazz scenes. He became a "confidant and press agent" to Duke Ellington, wrote tunes for Irving Mills (Ellington's publisher), and contributed to "every conceivable musical publication here and abroad." In 1943, he joined *Esquire*'s staff when that magazine expanded its jazz coverage to capitalize on increased interest apparent during the war years, and soon after he was "directly responsible" (with Robert Goffin) for the annual polls organized by *Esquire.*[61] Feather eventually became widely recognized as the dean of American jazz critics, but in the 1940s, his penchant for championing whatever was considered to be innovative or daring made him an antagonist to the "hot" jazz collector community. One might even go so far as to claim, with only slight exaggeration, that without Leonard Feather, there would never have been a war between traditionalists and modernists about the nature of Progress or, at least, that its character would have been far different from what ultimately transpired.[62] In his influential position at *Esquire,* and as coeditor with Barry Ulanov (1918–2000) of *Metronome* (a classically oriented trade magazine that was seeking a new audience, which the pair delivered with bebop), he was very much the thorn in the side of jazz purism.[63]

The dissension that was becoming evident within the jazz world reflected the larger stresses and strains that seemed endemic to the American scene in 1943. Max Jones's (1917–1993) "U.S. Commentary," in *Jazz Music*, reported the occurrence of race riots in Los Angeles; Mobile; Beaumont, Texas; Detroit; Collins, Mississippi; Mariana, Florida; and Harlem during the summer months. As Jones averred, "It is a disgraceful story, and the Government's connivance at this unique brand of southern Fascism makes nothing more or less than a mockery of the nation's claim to be the arsenal of democracy." Now, after eight years free from overt racial violence, "the northern states have succumbed to southern propaganda (disseminated through the industrial centers by southern Klansmen engaged in war work) and become dissatisfied with existing race relations."[64] Whatever the status quo had been, both within the world of jazz and without, it was now falling apart. Under such circumstances, the defense of African Americans, and the purity of their arts, must have seemed all the more critical. Reports of jazz musicians, white and black, receiving beatings at the hands of servicemen during the war years sent an unmistakable message to the jazz community as well.[65] Jazz could still be used to scapegoat select racial or ethnic groups as deviants, sometimes with dire consequences. The potency of jazz as a symbol for the struggle against intolerance and oppression thus had meaning on the home front just as surely as it did abroad. As traditionalists and modernists squared off in the 1940s, each side saw itself as defending what was essential in jazz, and therefore in American vernacular culture, thereby preparing the path for its survival in the future.

Nonpartisan elements within the collector community registered their distress with the worsening and increasingly polemical situation in the jazz press, which was not without racial overtones. In November 1943, Edwin Hinchcliffe's "No Laughing Matter" appeared in *Jazz Music*, Hinchcliffe complaining that "what is in essence a simple folk art is in danger of being buried under a mass of pretentious verbiage."[66] Hinchcliffe was careful to clarify that he "was not a jazz expert, not even a jazz critic," but he was a fan of the music, and the favorite records that he listed read like a page from *Who's Who in Jazz Collecting.*[67] His was an appeal for greater tolerance: "Jazz enthusiasts have become the Calvinists of music—so intent on heresy hunting that the fundamentals of their religion (jazz really seems a religion to them) have been forgotten in the pursuit of schismatic quarrels." Jazz criticism was becoming a mixture of "bigotry and pedantry" in which "partisanship carried to the extreme" predominated: "Black jazz, White jazz, and never the twain shall meet! And all carried on with the most owl-eyed solemnity."[68] Threats to jazz were not to be found in fusion with other musical forms but rather in the narrow-mindedness of its purist defenders:

> I cannot subscribe to that cheap inverted form of snobbishness—one of the more disquieting tendencies of modern life—that disparages the intellectual workings of the mind in favour of the judgment of the emotions. For that reason, I find it hard to understand this apparent fear of the jazz accent being adapted to the forms and purposes of art music. In what does this fear lie? Apparently in the idea that through this usage, jazz itself will be absorbed into art music, and as we know it now, will disappear. . . . What is likely to lead to sterility in jazz is this bitter partisan warfare that would shut it into watertight compartments—Black or White, Chicago, New Orleans or Kansas City—with each separate band of sectarian supporters denying the genuineness of all but their own particular brand.[69]

Hinchcliffe's words proved prophetic, for the controversy over Ellington's adventures in fusion was nothing compared to the general escalation of hostility that was directed against swing and bebop, which was already in its formative stages. Similar arguments for a latitudinarian approach to jazz by R. G. V. Venables had led to ridicule and derision, as his "In Self Defence," contained in the same issue of *Jazz Music*, made clear.[70] If the growing acceptance of jazz by the intellectual establishment amounted to aesthetic independence, it was now becoming apparent that it was merely as a prelude to cultural civil war.

The appearance of the first *Esquire's Jazz Book,* in early 1944, was heralded as a sign that pacification remained possible, and the introduction provided by Arnold Gingrich (1903–1976), the magazine's editor, was assiduously optimistic: "There are exciting things happening on the jazz front. Not the least exciting of them, we hope, is the issuance of this book." Gingrich cited the Jazz Concert at the Metropolitan, the "consensus" reached by sixteen experts in the selection of an All-American Band, and the recognition of jazz as an art form as reasons for satisfaction: "A year ago nobody would have believed that you could ever get even six experts in this field to arrive at a clear-cut consensus, let alone sixteen."[71] The panel of experts did, in fact, avoid identification by stylistic affiliation, but Roger Kay (1921–2001), a contributor to *Orchestra World* (and thus an outsider of sorts), could not resist temptation:

> The three schools of thought represented by the judges are: the *traditionalists,* who claim that the only authentic, pure jazz was at its peak in the nineties, and that its best examples are on records made prior to 1925. Their idols are either dead or sound as if they might die any minute. The *modernists.* Justly disgusted by the attitude of the former group, they bend over backwards to oppose traditionalist views. To them, most musicians over thirty are venerable fossils, and a "mad riff" will "send" them, while a dramatically beautiful, exquisitely musical solo by, say, the great Reinhardt on guitar, will be discarded as being "nowhere." Finally, the *perfectionists.* Whenever a solo with real ideas pleases or moves them, it's good. Whoever plays it. What's more, they dare claim that jazz is not a curiosity, or a precious relic of another age, but very definitely a living Art, constantly growing and improving.[72]

Kay declined to mention which group he belonged to, but presumably he would have chosen "perfectionist," for his interaction with jazz consisted largely of arranging violin accompaniments for recordings by notable soloists such as Barney Bigard.[73]

In point of fact, of the sixteen experts engaged for the poll, only two— George Avakian and Charles Edward Smith—could, by their choices, have been considered traditionalists. By far, the majority of the panel was staunchly committed to swing (including John Hammond), with Leonard Feather and Barry Ulanov of *Metronome* representing the ultramodernist vanguard. Abel Green (1900–1973), the editor of *Variety,* and Elliott Grennard (1907–1968), the editor of *Billboard,* also participated, but it is unlikely that any of the categories mentioned by Kay could have accurately applied to them. All of the winners of the 1944 *Esquire* poll (Armstrong, Goodman, Teagarden, Hawkins, Tatum, et al.) were known as swing musicians at the time, although Oscar Pettiford (1922–1960; the favored bassist) was already involved in the musical experiments on New York's Fifty-second Street that ushered in the bebop revolution.[74] While the *Esquire* poll did differ from the popularity contests conducted by *Down Beat* and *Metronome* (which began in 1937 and 1938, respectively), there was a certain amount of coincidence between them.[75] What Gingrich saw as consensus was in actuality less the product of general agreement than a process by which polar extremes cancelled each other out in favor of a majority committed to the industry status quo.

Gingrich had fallen victim to the oft-cited warning about mistaking the eye of a hurricane for the calm at the end of the storm, and purist responses to the *Esquire* poll and the All-American Band concert at the Metropolitan were not long in coming. Two articles appeared in the February 1944 issue of the *Jazz Record,* the collector-oriented magazine run by pianist Art Hodes (1904–1993) and printer Dale Curran. Private Bob Aurthur, USMCR, made his views very apparent in the title of his review: "The Great Enlightenment—Jump and Swing Held Forth at the Metropolitan and On the Air, But Jazz Was Nowhere at All." Aurthur began his piece with an anecdote about "a well-dressed gentleman looking like a church deacon" bringing a shopping list into the Commodore, "determined to be a hip collector." Subsequent investigation revealed that the gentleman's source was *Esquire's Jazz Book* and that his "enlightenment" was a caprice. The bitterness expressed in the article was born of defeated expectations: "Perhaps this would be the happy climax to the great rise in interest that we have seen in the last couple of years. Maybe with *Esquire's* great influence jazz would come out of the cellars . . . to move into the inner sanctums."[76] Aurthur's objections were based on his belief that *Esquire* had deluded the public into accepting swing as jazz. But the blame belonged to the experts, whose motives he impugned:

> The trouble, I think, lies directly with the experts who did the choosing. In order to be an expert in jazz these days you have to be slightly eccentric. In a poll such as *Esquire's* you might feel bound to pick the Names; then in direct protest you put down the men whose praises you have been singing, maybe just to be different, for years. Perhaps that's why Lim picked Eldridge and Dickerson who always play his sessions; or Feather picked Pete Brown who is on most of the aforementioned Feather's not even mediocre records; or Rosenkrantz picked Bill Coleman who played over in Europe for many years and is Timme's good friend. Not that these men aren't all great musicians—they are—but they are *not* the backbone of great American jazz.[77]

Perhaps it was Gingrich's expectations that were being defeated, for *Esquire's Jazz Book* had done more harm than good: "But if *Esquire* had to do it, if they felt it was their solemn duty to enlighten the peasants, why couldn't they have called it swing and left the fanatics where they were? We're happy!"[78] Private Aurthur's salvo was intended as a direct hit (and one would expect no less from a U.S. Marine), but just to make sure that a mortal wound had been inflicted, the *Jazz Record* added the extra firepower of one of its big guns.

In "Jazz at the Met," Frederic Ramsey provided further explanation of why the All-American Band concert had been doomed from the outset. His comments took a different tack, calling into question the value of "jazz extravaganzas" and arguing that the Metropolitan was not an appropriate setting for a jazz performance because it lacked the requisite intimacy. Included in the critique was the by now mandatory swipe at Leonard Feather, who had served as master of ceremonies for the event: "The Feather introductions continued in what might be euphemistically styled 'an informal manner' if one wished to conceal the fact that his presentations were lackadaisical, disjointed, and at times even insulting in their casualness."[79] Ramsey recalled a party he had recently attended, contrasting the spirit that had prevailed there to the pretentiousness he had witnessed in the performances at the Metropolitan:

> In New York, some of the best presentations of jazz have transpired at parties, like that of photographer Gjon Mili last summer. A big barn of a place, the studio still had pretty generous seating capacity and an easy, informal air. Musicians dropped in and out all evening long. This party, too, was given in conjunction with two nationally known magazines, *Life* and *Vogue*. But what a difference in spirit! And the music reflected the easier atmosphere. This party could well serve as a prototype for subsequent jazz get-togethers—although I don't know what Gjon Mili would have to say about their transpiring in his studio.[80]

Other examples of suitable venues were given: Art Hodes's sessions at Labor Stage, the Eddie Condon concerts at Town Hall, and the perennial Sunday-afternoon jam sessions at Ryan's. The *Esquire* concert marked "the apogee of interest to date in a great American idiom," but the lessons to be learned from the performance were not the ones that the sponsors had intended: "Jazz at the Met, then, was a milestone in a very real sense; it should serve as a warning to those who would like to see the present popularity of jazz channeled into healthy outlets. Because with jazz, the way of the spectacle, the super-colossal production, is the way to the end of an outstanding American art."[81] Taken together, Aurthur and Ramsey found little comfort in *Esquire*'s attempts to construct a united front within the jazz community, and their respective critiques of the jazz poll and the attendant concert reduced the lofty ambitions of that magazine to smoldering rubble. Yet it was not just *Esquire* on which their sights were fixed: Leonard Feather and Barry Ulanov were moving targets, and purist reactions to their writings in *Metronome* provide further evidence of the polarization of the jazz press that was occurring in 1944.

Alma Hubner, a Chilean who had expatriated to the United States during the war, attacked a Feather-Ulanov editorial that appeared in the February issue of *Metronome,* describing that magazine as "gloriously commercial."[82] In "Must Jazz Be Progressive?" she began with an extended quotation from the offending article: "Jazz is a great art because it accepts high standards of musicianship, because it is progressive. We are not with the lunatic fringe of jazz fandom and jazz critics who look merely for lameness, halting delivery and blind devotion to the jazz of thirty years ago in a jazzman. We are with and for the great jazzmen who look ahead, who are projecting their music and propelling this art to a brilliant future. We are not frightened because the men we like are famous, young and healthy."[83]

Hubner argued that *Metronome*'s use of the term *jazz* was a distortion of its true meaning, especially when attached to the adjective *progressive:* "Frankly speaking, there is no such thing as progressive jazz. Jazz has pioneered for a long time, and only lately has it come near to being accepted as 'art' by the public at large. We've known all along that it is an art, a great American musical art. As such, it need not progress to become something else, it must remain being what it is: just jazz."[84] The standards that mattered were the ones that had been present at the very beginning of the jazz revolution: "These men played jazz the way they felt it, they played for pleasure mostly, giving no commercial concessions. They weren't dazzled by flashy technical displays. They only admired the unusually brilliant imagination . . . simplicity and sincerity."[85] The modernists championed by Feather and Ulanov were, by contrast, "too much aware of their own importance," yet

Hubner doubted their powers of innovation, referring to them as "imitators" of players like Lester Young and Coleman Hawkins.[86] But the purpose of her article was less to chastise modern musicians than to defend jazz purism from the charges of "lunacy" proffered by the modernist critics: "Of course we're lunatics, but we like our jazz the way it is, we'll continue enjoying two-beat Dixieland, and we'll need no progress. Jazz doesn't need it as much as some jazz critics do. They're a hindrance, and it's folly to continue giving them this much importance."[87] Feather and Ulanov had attacked the cherished ideals of the "hot" jazz collector community and were characterized as interlopers who should be ostracized. With influence at *Metronome* and *Esquire*, however, they were firmly established and could not be so easily dismissed. Despite the blitzkrieg tactics of the combatants, the battle between traditionalists and modernists was destined to be a war of attrition.

The controversy surrounding the appearance of the *Esquire* jazz poll brought the divisions existing within the world of jazz into sharp relief. Particularly evident was the effect on the jazz press: traditionalists supported collector magazines like the *Jazz Record* and the *Record Changer*, while modernists controlled opinion at *Esquire* and *Metronome*, magazines that had only the slightest affiliation with the collector community. For years the war dragged on in a myriad of articles, letters to the editor, and record reviews, diverting a great deal of time and energy with little hope of (or desire for) resolution. Occasionally, minor skirmishes were won or lost. In the May 1944 issue of the *Jazz Record*, Pat Richardson noted in "Of Jazz and Intellectuals" the success of an Art Gallery jam session in which "the intellectuals were given a good example of what jazz is and why."[88] The following month, John Lucas (1917–2001) made his views on young modernists very clear with an article entitled "Young Cats Going to the Dogs—When Jazz Becomes a Lady and Soloists Play to the Gallery, the Future of Our Music Looks Dark," in which he bemoaned the lack of essential "understatement" in their playing.[89]

In the July edition of *Metronome*, a letter to the editor from Fred E. Glotzer applauded Feather's "What Makes a Good Critic?" which had appeared in May, adding that the traditionalist critics had done more harm than good: "I have met, during some of my lectures, many people who have come under the influence of emotionally-minded and nostalgic critics, and believe me they are a pretty hopeless crew."[90] Another letter championed the cause of Boyd Raeburn (1913–1966), a modernist big band leader, and elsewhere Feather's "Dizzy Is Crazy Like a Fox" drew attention to Gillespie's growing influence on modern jazz trumpet technique, promoting the Raeburn band in the process.[91] Although the term *bebop* was not used in the tribute to Dizzy, it soon gained general currency, thus escalating the traditionalist/modernist quarrel. Yet attempts to establish a neutral middle ground were made before 1944 ended. In November, Anton Stepanek's "Jazz and Semantics" sought to clarify the differences between Feather's and Lucas's use of *jazz,* suggesting the term *Dixieland* for a band such as George Lewis's New Orleans Stompers.[92] Stepanek might have saved himself the trouble, for in the next issue of the *Jazz Record,* Lucas responded with agreement on the need to standardize terminology but rejected Stepanek's choice of terms, supplying instead the stylistic categories that had been developed by the "hot" collectors, "the usage to which I am accustomed."[93] By the end of 1944, both traditionalists and modernists had been given ample opportunity to sharpen their stilettos, and they must have looked forward to the next *Esquire* poll with a sense of determined anticipation.

Gingrich's introduction to *Esquire's 1945 Jazz Book* was a stark contrast to the great expectations that had manifested the year before, but somehow his optimism remained intact. One reason for hope may have been the fact that the 1944 edition had broken all existing records for the sale of books on jazz: "Having accomplished its mission of extending the frontiers of jazz appreciation, which it did through a vastly larger sale than had ever before been achieved [by a jazz book] . . . the 1944 JAZZ BOOK promptly went out of print." Based on that success, *Esquire* had struck a publishing deal with Smith and Durrell for the present and future editions, thus joining *The Jazz Record Book* and *The Real Jazz* in "the fast-growing body of literature on the subject."[94] Yet Gingrich tempered his optimism in the face of certain grim realities with which he was only too familiar:

> Because of our interest, here at *Esquire,* in trying to accelerate the advancement of hot jazz to the status of a big-league factor in what our Gilbert Seldes first charted as the realm of the Lively Arts, we have tried to straddle, if not to reconcile, the two extremes of jazz ideology, and have been roundly cursed by both camps for the effort. So far, that has only added zest to our program of jazz-advancement, but it is probably only realistic to recognize the possibility that if anything can wreck that

program, further aggravation of the dissension between the two schools of jazz critics would be the one thing that could do it. Meanwhile, however, it is perhaps more fitting to save such dark forebodings for some gloomy Sunday afternoon when it's raining, and confine our comment here to the cheerful truth that the Board of Experts served well this year, if somewhat reluctantly in some instances.[95]

To be sure, *Esquire* had gone to great lengths to quell the complaints that had accompanied their previous effort: experts could no longer name their own productions among favorite records, and the award concerts were to be held simultaneously in New Orleans, New York, and Los Angeles. Furthermore, the panel of experts had been expanded from sixteen to twenty-two, allowing greater representation for the polar factions, at least in theory.[96]

Purist additions to the panel of experts included Bill Russell and Eugene Williams, but Charles Edward Smith was now classified as a "moderate," as was Robert Goffin, despite the fact that their choices were decidedly traditionalist.[97] In sum, the winners of the poll were more conspicuously modernist than they had been the year before, and Dizzy Gillespie was a winner in the New Stars category. *Down Beat* writer and collector Paul Eduard Miller (1908–1972) provided an article entitled "Fifty Years of New Orleans Jazz" for the *Jazz Book*, but the reactions from traditionalist magazines showed little tolerance for *Esquire*'s attempts at placation.

Nesuhi Ertegun's "Esquire 1945," in the *Record Changer*, recommended the *Jazz Book* for its photographs and musician biographies before launching a frontal assault on the poll, the concerts, and the articles contained therein. His opinion of the New Orleans concert was entirely negative, although Bunk Johnson had provided twenty-five seconds of true jazz amid a half hour that was otherwise a travesty. The trombone solos of J. C. Higginbotham (1906–1973), who was not an Orleanian but had worked with Armstrong and Henry "Red" Allen in the preceding decade, had abruptly drowned out Bunk's obbligato to Armstrong's vocal on "Basin Street Blues," thus ending the New Orleans portion of the broadcast on a very sour note. In assessing the damage, Ertegun did not mince words:

This half-hour program was presented to a vast radio audience as illustrating New Orleans jazz. Such falsification of reality, such a monstrous caricature of a beautiful form of music, is one of the most shocking events in the annals of jazz exploitation. All the readers of the *Record Changer* should write Mr. Arnold Gingrich, editor of *Esquire,* and ask him either to let New Orleans music alone or to present something which actually resembles it. We are sick and tired of such deliberate misrepresentations and willful distortions. Those who are interested in real New Orleans music cannot tolerate any more of these grotesque pseudo–New Orleans concerts.[98]

Based on the insights derived from his assistance in the production of the Welles broadcasts featuring Ory, Ertegun charged that the shabby treatment of Bunk had been by design: "A radio program on a coast-to-coast network is necessarily very carefully arranged. . . . I am therefore forced to believe that the scandalous way in which Bunk was treated by the organizers of the concert was deliberately planned out." He went on to decry the "poor quality" of the performances, stating that "the above-mentioned level is so low that not to be able to reach it seems an impossibility."

Ertegun reserved a special insult for his favorite target: "I must say, for instance, that I have never heard the Duke Ellington band sound so bad as when they played a composition by Leonard Feather known as the *Esquire Jump.*"[99] But lambasting Feather's compositions was not enough; he and Gingrich had stacked the deck in their selection of critics for the panel:

> The American public is misled when an incompetent jury makes a confused and haphazard selection of musicians, and *Esquire* presents this selection as a final verdict on the great men of jazz reached by an objective and well-qualified board of experts. Is it too much to hope that next year Mr. Gingrich will exercise more care in his choice of voting critics? As a gesture to those elements that Mr. Feather characterizes as "purist," William Russell, Eugene Williams and George Avakian were asked to take part in the voting this year. This obviously was a futile and meaningless step, as the votes of these critics, which went to New Orleans musicians, could not possibly alter the general trend of the voting. To insure this doubly, the number of judges was increased from sixteen to twenty-two, and Williams, Russell, and Avakian were drowned in a sea of jive lovers.[100]

As far as Ertegun was concerned, *Esquire* had been "invaded" by *Metronome,* with dire results. The poll was not merely a sham—it was a conspiracy.

Also included in the February issue of the *Record Changer* was George Avakian's "Philippine Philippic," a dissection of Feather's interview technique, as exemplified in a conversation with trumpeter Max Kaminsky (1908–1994) that had appeared in the September 1944 *Metronome*.[101] Avakian showed (by contrasting the full text of Kaminsky's answers with what had reached print) how editing could distort the replies to Feather's questions, thus bringing them into accord with the critic's own views. But even more germane were insights on how Feather's control of the *Esquire* poll questionnaires acted to reinforce personal prejudices concerning the credibility of certain critics: "Feather begins with the old chip on his shoulder. He puts himself on the side of the 'critics who, having had a little musical education, prefer their music to musicians,' which is a new line he is adopting to build himself up—he is a colorless pianist—and tear down critics who do not play professionally. He installed this line in a questionnaire which accompanied the ballot forms for the 1945 *Esquire* Jazz Experts Poll, which he is placed in charge of by the magazine."[102]

While Avakian's piece was intentionally satirical, assertions that Feather was unethical and venal were not part of the joke. Further along in the essay, Avakian provided an indictment of the modernist that became gospel to the purist community:

The assistant editor of *Metronome* dashed home and sat at his typewriter. First he patted himself on the back as "progressive and modernist," as though they went together, and called himself a critic instead of a paid publicity agent cagily keeping alive the people and business who hire him. Next he put Charles Edward Smith, Jake Trussell, Myself, "and the rest of them" (a fine, carefully flung dismissal, isn't it?) on the other side of the fence—and rightly so, for we are not professional publicists, and represent no interests which give us our bread and butter, and don't peddle ourselves for recording sessions, and don't write tunes for these record dates so that we can get royalties on them, and don't plug the records and the musicians on them so that they'll become popular, thus increasing royalties and prospects for repeat engagements. Nobody has ever sued us for $100,000 dollars; no negro bass player has ever hauled off on us; no musician's friend has ever beaten us up; no white cornetist has ever whaled the daylights out of us. I guess we are sorry characters, but we *do* have friends.[103]

Avakian's commentary was more fuel for the flames of vendetta, which showed no signs of abating. Articles appearing in the *Jazz Record* followed suit. Art Hodes's editorial for the February edition began by celebrating the magazine's second anniversary but soon turned nasty. Although no names were mentioned, his readers could not have mistaken the intended referents: "And then came the 'New Order.' We suddenly started making 'Progress.' What was once accepted as swing music began to be called jazz." Included in the editorial were charges of venality and Hitlerism, but Hodes concluded on a positive note: "This will be an important year for our kind of jazz. Let's hope we succeed in chasing the money changers out of the temple."[104] Elsewhere in the *Jazz Record* was a reprint of Rudi Blesh's criticisms of the *Esquire* concert, which had first graced the pages of the *New York Herald Tribune*. Its contents were virtually identical to the views expressed by Ertegun in the *Record Changer,* indicating how the polls and Feather's tactics affected a closing of the ranks within the purist camp, at least momentarily.[105]

Discussion of a united front among jazz purists to combat the machinations of Feather and Ulanov had, in fact, been raised several months earlier by Ralph Gleason, in an article for the September 1944 *Record Changer* entitled "Featherbed Ball." In it Gleason had outlined a strategy for putting forth the cause of righteous jazz that was later reiterated by Rudi Blesh in "Crawl Out of Bed—Winter Is Over," in the March 1945 issue:

> Combat the Feather-Esquire clique on its own ground with articles in popular magazines; get good musicians publicly playing real jazz and recording it on the commercial labels for wide sale; get jazz out on the air on every feasible radio source; write novels with fictionalized accounts or backgrounds of jazz; keep all the good small jazz magazines going; get the whole field of definitions straight and established in a scientifically accurate and universally accepted semantic; but write no more serious books explaining jazz to the still large and uninitiated public. All of Gleason's points are valid, I believe, except the last.[106]

Since Blesh was busily engaged in preparing a book of his own, his denigration of the existing literature, which Gleason felt was sufficient, was not surprising. In differing from Gleason, he defended his position vigorously: "Books cannot be proscribed, nor libraries and museums be forbidden to interest in jazz. The subject must not become self-consciously rough-house like the college-boy's first excursion into gilded sin, nor a 'We the People' kind of folk-artsy proletarianism."[107] As a fine art, jazz could not remain the special preserve of "a few individuals" but must be available to the widest possible audience. Blesh's San Francisco Museum of Art lectures "had furnished a rallying point for jazz lovers and novices which, as long as it existed, aided in bringing Bunk Johnson out of retirement." His lectures had led to a year of activity for Bunk in San Francisco, but he wanted only a little credit: "I feel that this was not a personal achievement on my part as much as it was a tribute to the power of jazz itself and to the agency of the public museum which Gleason does not consider important enough to mention."[108] The call for activity and cooperation suggested by Gleason was all for the best, but "a call to arms from a featherbed is neither inspiring nor compelling," and he felt compelled to offer his colleague some puzzling advice: "Perhaps he should crawl out of his private one, pack his briefcase with the right contents, and, with better motives than Feather's, hit the trail that Leonard has blazed with such personal, if dubious, success."[109] If Blesh thought that this would be the last word on the subject, he was sadly mistaken.

Two months later, Gleason's response appeared in the *Record Changer* under the banner "That Book Again." He kept his case brief and to the point:

> The inferiority complex of a young but bearded prophet, Mr. Rudi Blesh, was quite aroused by a sentence and a half of mine written 'way last summer saying we didn't need any more books on jazz. . . . I refer to Rudi as "young," purposely. Because back in 1939 and '40 when Gene Williams and I were putting out Jazz Information and telling where Bertha Gonsoulin was, and Woody Broun was putting out the HRS Rag (guys like Ramsey, Smith, Hobson and Sargeant had *already* written books on jazz), Rudi was busily decorating interiors out in San Francisco, his Dartmouth mackinaw shed, his talent hidden, jazz undiscovered and unexplained. The great mass pressure upon him to give up his promising career, publish pamphlets, write columns, a book, give lectures, discover Bunk and devote his life to saying he was the first to write that jazz was a serious art form, had not yet, happily, manifested itself. All this, including a beard, was before him.[110]

Following was an excerpt from the *Herald Tribune* on "Jazz Purism," written by Blesh in March, after which Gleason interjected, "See what I mean?"

But Blesh's suggestion that museum lectures could further the purist cause was not entirely without merit, as others were already proving without his prompting.

On March 17, Dr. Samuel Ichiye Hayakawa (1906–1992), of the Illinois Institute of Technology (later a U.S. senator from California), delivered a lecture at the Arts Club of Chicago. Sponsored by the Poetry Magazine Modern Arts Series, the lecture was entitled *35th and State: Reflections on the History of Jazz* and offered musical demonstrations by New Orleanian Richard M. Jones, Chicagoans Darnell Howard (1895–1966; a clarinetist who had worked with Oliver and Morton) and Jimmy Yancey (1898–1951; a blues pianist favored by purists), and Oro "Tut" Soper (1910–1987; a pianist who had recorded with Baby Dodds for the Steiner-Davis label). Hayakawa's historical survey was a balanced synthesis that would not have pleased Blesh but that aspired to rise above the rancor that predominated in the jazz press. Hayakawa's opening remarks on the New Orleans tradition made his intentions and perspective evident: "Like other American cultural forms, indeed, like the American people themselves, jazz is hybrid."

Building on the work of William Russell and Charles Edward Smith, Hayakawa explained the origins of jazz in New Orleans according to his theory of hybridization. The "ultimate source" of jazz was "Negro folk music," itself a product of the blending of Scottish, Irish, and English balladry in the hands of African Americans. The culture of New Orleans was the key to the transformation of this folk music into jazz: "Enjoying more opportunities and more freedom there than in most other Southern cities, the Negroes got, in a somewhat backhanded way, the impact of the French musical culture of that city."[111] While the body of the lecture followed the earlier histories of Smith and Russell quite closely, Hayakawa emphasized certain points with an insight and clarity that were very much his own. His characterization of early jazz as folk music was masterfully stated:

> The work of these New Orleans musicians represents the first and perhaps only time in which a folk-music was enabled to continue to develop as folk-music, *but* with the technological advantages of modern instruments and their orchestral possibilities. . . . In one way [Negroes] shared the New Orleans culture, but in another way they didn't. They were both within the white culture and outside it. However unjust or unfortunate

this situation may have been (and it continues so to this day), it meant that Negroes were forced back onto their older folk culture and pushed forward into a new culture at one and the same time. They therefore did the only possible thing: they fused the two strains of influence. In so doing, they unwittingly gave to American culture as a whole one of the greatest gifts any minority has brought: a new musical synthesis of urban sophistication with folk feeling.[112]

White musicians in New Orleans responded "immediately" and "added some tricks of their own." In accounting for the rapid spread of jazz throughout the globe, Hayakawa offered a theory tied to the process of urbanization:

Jazz is most popular in the big cities, in Europe and Asia no less than in America. City people, I believe, consciously or unconsciously miss the directness that characterizes folk experience. In our highly technologized urban cultures, we miss that directness most of all. Yet we cannot regress to more unsophisticated modes of feeling. Jazz, therefore, meets a profound need in our civilization because it is a unique fusion of a high degree of technical resourcefulness and inventiveness with the undiluted, elemental down-to-earthness of folk-expression. When that fusion isn't there, so far as I am concerned, it isn't jazz.[113]

The lecture also included descriptions of Chicago rent parties as a "primitive cooperative housing plan," relating the use of pianos in such circumstance to the development of boogie-woogie, with reference to Russell's commentary in *Jazzmen*. At every turn, Hayakawa provided refreshing new angles from which to view the course of jazz history and its meaning.

Particularly noteworthy in this regard is the section entitled "Jazz as an Expression of America," in which Hayakawa argued that "commercial successes, whether in poetry, painting, or jazz, are well known; the original sources of their ideas are often known only to the serious students of the art in question."[114] Yet Hayakawa did not wish to "disparage the importance of popular acclaim," for that was how jazz had become "the art by which America is known." The correlation of this phenomenon to the larger panorama of world events was emphatically stated: "But it is not only the intellectuals who know America by jazz. In some strange fashion, jazz is proving to be a language that people everywhere like to hear." Travelers like

Langston Hughes had heard jazz in Istanbul, and it was no stranger to the cabarets of Moscow, Paris, London, and Melbourne. Hayakawa himself had heard jazz being played on the beaches between Osaka and Kobe when he had last journeyed to Japan in 1935. Authoritarian regimes feared jazz and its implications: "The easy-going manners, the spirit of skepticism, and the spontaneous gaiety which accompanied jazz did not sit well with the protagonists of Emperor-worship and the Old Samurai spirit."[115] Jazz had become "our cultural ambassador to the common people everywhere," representing the essence of the American spirit in a musical language that had universal appeal. While Hayakawa restricted his survey to the early phases of jazz development, he did not feel impelled to condemn more contemporary derivatives. As an exercise in jazz erudition and diplomacy, Hayakawa's reflections were a model for all to emulate. While the message of equanimity presented by the professor may not have received the attention it deserved among the jazz literati, the cue for supplementing the promotion of purism in jazz magazines with lectures to the broader audience of American art lovers did not go unnoticed.

In July, Nesuhi Ertegun addressed a rapt audience at the Pasadena Institute of Art in Los Angeles and was asked to return for more.[116] Such venues provided a more intimate, and infinitely less hostile, environment for traditionalist appeals, providing a welcome alternative to the jazz press. Ironically, Robert Goffin and Leonard Feather had first tested this approach early in 1942, when they inaugurated a lecture series at the New School for Social Research in New York. Such was the success of this first venture that the fifteen-week series was repeated later in the year.[117] Whatever the merits of such presentations, however, the main thrust of traditionalist and modernist proselytism remained firmly entrenched in their respective magazine outlets.

Reaction to the *Esquire* fiasco continued throughout the spring with some very interesting developments. In "Jelly Roll Was Right," one Jazzbo Brown (Nesuhi Ertegun) ridiculed the "surrealist fantasy" contributed to the literary magazine *View* by Barry Ulanov, which included some disparaging remarks directed against Jack Teagarden and Louis Armstrong by the modernist.[118] Also mentioned was a feud with legal implications raging between Robert Goffin and *Esquire.* Jazzbo rejoiced at the news that the Belgian was suing the magazine for $250,000, apparently on the grounds that he "was revolted, as a jazz lover, by the mediocre facsimiles *Esquire* was championing as authentic jazz." To his regret, Jazzbo had learned that this was not, in fact, the case: "Our joy, unfortunately, did not last long. We learned that Goffin was not suing *Esquire* because he was opposed to their manner of promoting jazz." Instead, he was accusing the magazine of having stolen his ideas, in the form of the experts' poll that was now being dominated by Leonard Feather. Jazzbo thought it was exceedingly ironic that the Belgian was bitter, for "if he wants to build up any reputation for himself in this country, he should be as silent as possible about his former connection with *Esquire*." For *Esquire*, he concluded with some cutting advice: "A warning to Arnold Gingrich: Goffin's knowledge of jazz may be small, but he is a most redoubtable lawyer."[119] As late as August, negative references to the *1945 Jazz Book* were abundant in the *Record Changer*. In the editorial section, "Lemme Take This Chorus," attacks on *Esquire* (the *Jazz Book* and the magazine) were combined with an appeal for new blood in the jazz publishing field—specifically someone who would present a forum for modernists *and* traditionalists. Mention was made of George S. Rosenthal Jr. (1922–1967), described as one "who types his own letters, whose family owns a publishing house in Cincinnati, who publishes *Minicam* (read by 75,000), who does not appear to be simply another rich boy eager to 'do something for jazz,' who apparently has studied the jazz field with considerable thoroughness."[120] Rosenthal's "yearbook of hot music" would be called *Jazzways* and was to feature articles by Gene Williams; Fred Ramsey; Rudi Blesh; Art Hodes; Dale Curran; and swing enthusiasts Frank Stacy, Alexander King, and Peter Fischer. Apparently, the purists were not above stacking the deck somewhat themselves when the opportunity presented itself.[121]

By midsummer, a new term had entered the jazz debate. While the origin of the epithet "moldy fig" to refer to purists has often been attributed to Leonard Feather, it was, in fact, provided by Sam Platt, a member of the U.S. Navy, who included it in a letter to *Esquire* printed in June.[122] Feather and Ulanov had no compunction about using it, however, as a quote from the September 1945 *Metronome* makes clear:

> Just as the fascists tend to divide group against group and distinguish between Negroes, Jews, Italians and "real Americans," so do the moldy figs try to categorize New Orleans, Chicago, swing music and "the real jazz." Just as the fascists have tried to foist their views on the public through the

vermin press of *Social Justice*, the *Broom* and *X-Ray*, so have the Figs yapped their heads off in the *Jazz Record, Jazz Session* and *Record Changer*. The moldy figs are frustrated by their inability to foist their idiotic views on the public, and frustrated by the ever-increasing public acceptance of the critics and musicians they hate.[123]

Feather later admitted, with some regret, that "these mean-spirited, clumsily written words were my own."[124] The response from the *Record Changer* was no less inflammatory. Bilbo Brown, a pseudonymous purist, kept the metaphor going with "Rebop and Mop Mop: The New Leftist Rabble Rousers" in the October issue, albeit with a certain sense of humor:

> Led by William Z. Feather (who recently ousted the milder George Browder Simon) and by tempestuous young Barry U. Leninov, the Mop-Mops are not above attacking the pure American teachings in Father Gullickson's jazz justice publication, *The Record Changer*, and Gerald L. Hodes' monthly outcry *The Jazz Record*. . . . With such champions of anti-New Deal bureaucracy, anti-rebop, big business and New Orleans as Eugene McWilliams, Westbrook Blesh, Burton K. Ertegun, "Please hit him again" Avakian, at the helm, the New Orleans First party should have no trouble winning the next national election with Bunk Johnson for president and Bill Colburn for vice-president.[125]

In "Lemme Take This Chorus," editor Gordon Gullickson (1915–1976) countered "moldy figs" with "sour grapes," adding that if Feather ever said anything good about the purists, "I think I will sue him for libel."[126] The editorial recapitulated the war of words as it had transpired, noting Feather's expatriation from England "shortly before war started in Europe," suggesting that his relocation to the United States had not been purely coincidental. In justifying the interest in New Orleans revival, he argued that "the jazzmen of a generation ago have become more than mere substitutes for the current [mediocre] crop. The Sour Grape can't seem to understand this. He believes sincerely that jazz music is a matter of fashion, and seeks to put it on the same level with millinery. This season's music is the rage. He can't understand anyone's preference for music that pre-dates it. That's all there is to it."[127] The next item in the column was an announcement of Bunk Johnson's opening at the Stuyvesant Casino. Interestingly enough, and perhaps lost in the fray, was the appearance of "rebop" (bebop) for the first time in purist attacks on the modernists.

Scholars have come to appreciate that the jazz schisms of the 1940s were a crucial period in the music's history, and rightly so. In *Between Montmartre and the Mudd Club*, Bernard Gendron writes insightfully on the jazz wars of the 1940s, and his analysis of the discursive strategies of the combatants and how they shaped the subsequent construction of jazz history and aesthetics is essential reading. Responding to Scott DeVeaux's *The Birth of Bebop*, Gendron argues, "The historical transition of jazz from an entertainment music to an art music, initiated by the bebop revolution in the mid-1940s, set in motion a fundamental transformation in the way in which the barriers between high and mass culture would henceforth be negotiated," a phenomenon that ushered in a postmodern era in which jazz served the cause of popular culture in aggressively "pilfering" high art, reversing the customary flow.[128] He sees the jazz wars as crucial to the transition: "The bebop revolution . . . was born in the midst of one of the most divisive disputes in the history of jazz, between the partisans of the swing bands and the Dixieland revivalists who wanted to return to early jazz. . . . [The] revivalist controversy and the new aesthetic discourses it generated set the stage for the reception of bebop and made possible the construal of it as an avant-garde music. . . . The discourses of critics were, of course, crucial for alerting an otherwise unsuspecting public that jazz . . . was undergoing a transformation from 'entertainment' to 'art.'"[129] Gendron's incisive discussion of "discursive formations" organized around binary oppositions shows that despite their differences, respective factions shared a broader vision: "The centrality of these binaries to the new aesthetic discourses virtually assured the existence of diametrically opposed aesthetic views that nonetheless belonged to the same discursive world. . . . This means that in the broad sense of 'modernist' that applies to European art discourse, the revivalists were as much 'modernists' as were their swing adversaries."[130]

Despite its value, however, there are some substantial problems with Gendron's reading of the jazz schisms of the 1940s. His contention that jazz became a "post-modern art music" only with the rise of bebop overlooks how New Orleans artists such as Louis Armstrong "pilfered" and "deconstructed" the classical canon in transforming operatic arias into solos in the mid-1920s; even more important, it completely ignores the sustained and very aggressive discursive strategies designed to convince the public that "jazz was art," employed by "hot" collectors in the 1930s.[131] Gendron places the opening salvo of the "first" jazz schism involving "moldy figs" in 1942, citing Ulanov's and Feather's attacks on purists in *Metronome,* but his explanation is too cursory to be convincing.[132] Given that his thesis is predicated on an early (pre-bebop) schism between adherents of swing and those of a New Orleans–style revival, it would make much more sense to identify the book *Jazzmen* and the appearance of the ultrapurist magazine *Jazz Information* in September 1939 as the catalyst for intensification of debate.

Since the term "moldy fig" was not introduced into the jazz wars until June 1945 and was not in circulation until the following September, when purist sights shifted to bebop, applying it to the swing debate is inaccurate. Gendron also misinterprets what the New Orleans–style revivalists were attempting to accomplish. The contention that purists wanted to "identify jazz with the New Orleans style of the 1920s" misses the primary strategic thrust of their efforts as record producers, which was to document what jazz must have sounded like in its *earliest* days, before 1917, as witnessed in the music of Kid Rena, Bunk Johnson, and Kid Ory.[133] Of course, this desire got them into a lot of trouble, but the intent is unmistakable. Furthermore, the statement that "in the mid-1940s, jazz did not yet possess sufficient cultural credentials to draw high art into joint institutional ventures" casts a blind eye on Feather's objective in staging "Jazz at the Met" and Ramsey's vociferous opposition to it.[134] DeVeaux's distinction between art and entertainment misleads Gendron into privileging bebop at the expense of New Orleans style. Had he looked more closely at the debates of the 1930s, he would have been better prepared to situate the jazz wars of the 1940s in historical context and to recognize that acceptance of jazz as art had already been accomplished by 1940.

What set the jazz debates of the 1940s apart was not so much an all-encompassing restructuring of the conventions of jazz discourse as it was a general escalation of hostility among the participants involved, intensified by new factional and institutional affiliations that gave individuals more power. One can argue that the mode of discourse embraced by respective traditionalist and modernist camps was informed by a basically "modernist" perspective, but it is also necessary to recognize that, owing to the vehemence with which respective positions were advanced, the term *modern* would henceforth be associated with "bebop and beyond," while the use of *traditional* was relegated to a localized discourse in New Orleans and effectively removed from the main flow of debate. Because of their extremism, the jazz schisms of the 1940s came to represent the perils of intellectualization within the jazz world.

With a gradual reduction of hostilities among traditionalists and modernists in 1946, however, a new wave of ecumenical thinking entered the jazz discourse, establishing a pluralistic approach to jazz history and criticism that allowed enthusiasts to embrace individual preferences. Of course, this did not always stop the fighting. To some extent this trend represented a reaction against the very idea of jazz expertise and ideology, commingled with nostalgia for the innocence and joy that had accompanied the first flush of discovery in jazz record collecting. On another level, it was a sensible reaction to the proliferation of consumer goods stemming from an ever-widening category still known to the general public as "jazz" (despite the desperate bids for control of definitions). Specialization was inevitable, unless you held the keys to Fort Knox. Purists who had begun their jazz careers as "hot" collectors in the 1930s took stock, and in many cases they saw fit to revise their views. Others did not budge an inch. Abhorrence of conflict not only allowed everyone to disengage and relax a little but also prepared the way for the emergence of synthetic, purportedly inclusive, and self-consciously consensus-oriented historical surveys that promoted the idea of jazz as an organically evolving art form. In retrospect, it is clear that the traditionalists who had argued for diffusionist premises in jazz history won their battle—every jazz history textbook has a chapter on jazz origins in New Orleans and the diaspora that ensued—but otherwise the modernists had taken the field. Even peace in the ranks can be a mixed blessing.

CHAPTER 6

Let the Foul Air Out: The Fun Faction Asserts Itself

In reviewing the proliferation of schismatic forces within the jazz community through the summer of 1945, one can see that there were many: traditionalists versus modernists, contesting the past and future of jazz; debates over emotional versus intellectual content in jazz; adherents of African versus African American versus polyglot origins of jazz; and divisions within each of those cadres based on personality conflicts and ambition as much as on ideology. Yet, amazingly, following the September–October exchange between *Metronome* and the *Record Changer,* a general reduction of invective began to occur. Perhaps this had something to do with the end of the world war, but the real reason might have been that the respective combatants had completely exhausted their vocabulary of insults. Although the mutual hostility between traditionalists and modernists continued to smolder and occasionally reignite, the two camps tended to become increasingly self-absorbed, dedicating themselves to their pet projects with the same vigor with which they had been clubbing each other for more than two years.

Indications that a truce of essentially passive mutual contempt was necessary were already evident in the September issue of the *Jazz Record.* Lieutenant (J.G.) H. M. Apfel's (1923–1996) "Hot Man (Under the Collar)" argued that the time had come to allow each his or her own. Apparently his patience for the continual bickering had been exhausted, for he directed his complaints without discrimination against collectors, critics, and intellectuals of both factions: "I've seen the smart boys who are in the collection business for profit with a Discography in one hand and a price list in the other haggle like fishwives with some other predatory character." The "swing" versus "jazz" battles had become much too personal, and Apfel saw no reason why a preference for Benny Goodman records should brand a collector as being "commercial." Intellectuals were reading too much into music that was simply intended for pleasure: "Webster's hoarse tortured tone a protest against housing conditions in Macon . . . Jazz, the great symbol . . . Ah genius . . . ah rapture . . . (Sorry Saroyan) . . . ah beauty . . . ah Bull."[1] Yet he did have a few kind words for some critics: "There are a few good ones, Hoefer, who plays his beat out ones [records], Avakian, who is sincere, and the historians and biographers of jazz, many of whom are genuinely interested in jazz."[2] Apfel's point was an appeal for tolerance, strongly stated: "If you like it—play it. If you don't—give it away. But why fight about it. Your opinion is as good as mine as to what you like. If you've got any old records to sell for a sawbuck apiece or any criticism of small bands or big bands or you'd like to compare Cezanne to Condon, start a magazine. I don't have to buy it. I'll be at home listening to my records."[3]

Anthropologist Ernest Borneman (1915–1995) provided a similar message in "The Musician and the Critic." In responding to the opinions of Rudi Blesh, he called for an end to ideology in the jazz field. Borneman had discussed the matter of purism with Northwestern University's Melville Herskovits (1895–1963), who was then serving as director of his dissertation on the survival of West African music in the New World. Herskovits emphasized that "a living musical style" is constantly changing and that only "dead" music holds to "pure" form. The opinion that he expressed to Borneman summed up his feeling on the subject: "Purists, it seems to me, are always a little on the unrealistic side, whether they are concerned with jazz or Bach."[4] The anthropologist went on to state that critics like Leonard Feather had much more in common with contemporary musicians "not because Feather's evaluation of the music is more correct than Blesh's but because Feather's standards of value are much more obvious to the musician than Blesh's." Feather and the musicians shared standards of value such as craftsmanship, public acclaim, and financial reward because they were all earning a living in a competitive music market. Blesh's standards were derived from a historical and musicological perspective that, in order to heighten and sharpen its terms of reference, "has to categorize the general and isolate the particular until the total image thus obtained is bound to appear grotesquely distorted and entirely unrealistic to the practicing musician."[5] What Borneman was actually saying was that he agreed with Blesh but that he could understand why musicians did not.

One could not, after all, erase time or the effects of change. New Orleans jazz was the product of a social setting that had existed at a particular time and place, and "to try to recreate the music of that period and that setting now seems as naive and hopeless to me as, say Robert Owen's attempts to recreate the social conditions of primitive communism." Despite differences of taste between himself and Feather, Borneman had to admit that Feather's standards were "much closer to the present social and economic set-up of the band business with its numerous ramifications in the sheet music trade and the radio business than Mr. Blesh's or my own."[6] Borneman's parting words may be seen as reprising the credo that had come to fruition in the discological phase of the New Orleans revival: "Jazz will survive or expire according to whether there is a social demand and an economic basis for it; let us try and help to create this demand and that basis. Mr. Blesh will fulfill his purpose to the extent that he succeeds in making it socially and economically effective; he will fail if he hopes to convince the musicians with an argument which, though rationally correct, has no social and economic evidence to prove itself."[7] In retrospect, one might be tempted to credit Borneman's advice with reorienting Blesh's sense of praxis by recalling the establishment of Circle Records early in 1946 and the *This Is Jazz* radio series soon after. William Russell, for one, had learned early on to substitute action in the field for critical reflection. Despite his somewhat reluctant participation in the 1945 *Esquire* poll, he did not go on record in the jazz press with his complaints, preferring to keep their circulation limited to a few close friends. His energies, like those of Gene Williams, had gone into the promotion of Bunk Johnson's comeback. Indeed, even though he did not perform as a musician on any of the American Music sides (as Feather sometimes did with the groups he was promoting), his favorable review of the Rena Deltas (and Williams's celebration of all Bunk Johnson records in the press) makes it exceedingly difficult to draw absolute distinctions between the behavior of modernist and purist critics. In comparison to Feather, one might only say that Russell's mode of action was extremely "low-profile," while the modernist's was very high.

The degree to which interfactional dispute had dissipated was made evident with the publication of *Esquire's 1946 Jazz Book* and the lack of any substantial reaction to it in the purist press. Gingrich submitted his usual introduction from Switzerland, ostensibly to report on the revival of the European jazz scene but perhaps also to take a sabbatical from the jazz wars at home. As it was, he found a split between the French critics that was roughly equivalent to the traditionalist/modernist feud in America.[8] He could not refrain from commenting on the events of the preceding year entirely, however: "Despite the howls of the righteous, who year by year seem to reduce rather than increase the number of jazz records that they can abide hearing, progress of a sort goes on."[9] Yet the Gold Award winners in the jazz poll remained largely exponents of swing, with several bebop practitioners among the New Star listings, particularly Charlie Parker. Purist experts Russell, Williams, and Avakian were noticeably absent, leaving George Hoefer and Charles Edward Smith as the only traditionalists on the panel. But at least one article appealed to the purist old guard.

Hoefer's "The Collector's Outlook" contained information and a point of view that countered the modernist stranglehold on the *Jazz Book:* "The 'hipped characters' rave and rant at the 'moldy figs' (pre-1940 record collector) but the large companies continue to expand their attention towards the market afforded them by the collector who can no longer find the good old ones in original form. Possibly, the major firms are atoning for the sacrifices made by the old-time collector when all old record piles were sent to the hoppers for reclaiming of the shellac."[10] Hoefer also mentioned that, in addition to the "Big Four" (RCA Victor, Columbia, Decca, and Capitol), some "ninety-four odd labels" had vainly tried to fulfill the tremendous wartime demand. Steve Smith had joined Harry Lim (1919–1990) as a session supervisor for the Keynote label, and numerous reports told of discoveries of caches of old records by servicemen abroad and collectors who had been lucky enough to find them at home.

Yet Leonard Feather's "A Survey of Jazz Today" completely ignored the growing New Orleans revival, except to observe that "something should also be said about those who, through their sincere interest in the best jazz, did much to spread the gospel and counteract the activities of the so-called 'Moldy Fig' coterie, which objects to progress and enlightenment in jazz."[11] Instead, Feather quoted an editorial in *Metronome* by Barry Ulanov to characterize the major accomplishments of the preceding year: "Harmonically jazz is not at all as it was in 1939; its colors are different; its resources are so much broader that comparison with the music of that blissful era is ridiculous. Listen to Duke today, to Woody, to Boyd Raeburn and you'll hear what we mean. Jazz is going brilliantly ahead, utilizing the advances that have been made by the traditional musicians of our day, Bartok, Stravinsky, Schoenberg, Ravel, and adding its own new interpretations. This is the beginning of maturity for America's greatest art. Jazzmen who are still in their musical infancy, childhood or adolescence will be left behind, as the art . . . accepts its adult responsibilities. The *Rampart Street Parade* is over."[12] *Esquire's 1946 Jazz Book* shows that bebop was looming large on the horizon, but the big bands continued to hold sway. Yet within a year, the big swing bands were on the verge of extinction, victims of the economic exigencies accompanying the war, the disruption of personnel that the war had occasioned, and the rise of the star vocalists that continued in the wake of the Petrillo ban. As Ernest Borneman had suggested, it was not purist ideology but changing economic and social conditions that had removed the big band mote from the purist's eye.[13]

The February 1946 issue of the *Record Changer*, which had for the preceding two years provided the opening salvos against the *Esquire* polls, was noticeably free of invective against the modernists. Only the cover, a surrealistic drawing by cartoonist Gene Deitch (1924–), in the form of a "valentine to a moldy fig," offered an indirect and rather arcane slap at the Feather faction. In the March edition, Deitch explained what it all meant in the "Lemme Take This Chorus" column: "Depicted in the lower left is the black tree of protest, with its roots in the old Souf, freed from the manacle of slavery and grasping music, represented by the tone-arm, for support." Just below the tree's elbow lies a "cancerous growth" in the shape of a saxophone, which was intended to represent "'modern' white jazz, that lecherous parasite, forever sucking strength from the main stem." A feather on the ground beneath was "just where it belongs." Other symbols included in the cartoon were the "his master's voice" dog (RCA Victor's logo), representing commercialism, and a crescent moon in honor of Nesuhi Ertegun's recording efforts. And finally: "The limp record suggests the utter exhaustion of it all, jazz records by the juke-box full; labels by the score . . . or possibly it's just a vinylite record. Egad! What drama . . . what conflict . . . what bilge!"[14] Deitch's parody of the state of affairs in the jazz world was an attempt to have some fun with an otherwise deplorable situation.

Carlton Brown expressed a similar point of view in an article entitled "Beware of the Experts" in the same issue. Brown told of a recent conversation he had with a jazzman after a Condon concert at Town Hall, in which the musician lamented the passing of the "good old days":

> He wasn't longing to recapture the days of Buddy Bolden, nor even of Cook's Dreamland Orchestra, yet. His lament was for a spirit that pervaded the jazz scene of no more than five or ten years ago, and is now rarely encountered. "Remember," he said, "when musicians, fans, and yes, even critics, used to think that jazz was for *fun*? Why, when someone got off a fine chorus at a session, you'd actually hear people laugh with enjoyment. Now, most likely, they grimly whip out their chosen music magazine to see if it's all right by the experts to like the stuff."[15]

The message pervading Brown's article echoed Apfel's earlier comments almost exactly, even to the point of listing certain exceptions to the list of villains:

> Some enthusiasts have acquired a knowledge of and feeling for jazz far beyond that of its primary audience, and have used that knowledge and feeling to help others to increase and deepen their enjoyment of the beauties of many kinds of jazz. Such, I think, are the editors and writers of "Jazzmen" and "The Jazz Record Book," who have made their personal partialities secondary to the effort of compiling as clear, thorough and unprejudiced a history and evaluation of jazz as possible. Such informed enthusiasts deserve the greatest credit for the spread of jazz appreciation. They can generally be recognized for their willingness to let listeners and other writers form their own preferences, and by the fact that they refrain from name-calling against those who don't share their preferences and musicians who don't play the way they want them to.[16]

The intellectualization of jazz had spoiled the fun, setting up false and angry gods whose search for greater meaning had obscured the fact that the music was originally intended for the enjoyment of everyday people:

Jazz, as my musician friend maintained in the beginning, is for fun. It is also a fine art, but you should worry who said so first. Before anyone did, jazz was played for the enjoyment, or any variant of the term that you prefer, of people who brought to it no more special equipment than you have in your possession, musically illiterate as you may be, assuming that you have a normal response to rhythm and sound. Jazz was originally and still is played with pleasure by a large number of talented musicians, and danced and listened to by a far greater number of enthusiasts, mostly non-expert.[17]

Here was the essence of jazz, the quality that, after all, accounted for its revolutionary potential and its popularity in the first place. Pedants who demanded adherence to absolute standards were missing the point: just as freedom of expression was intrinsic to a jazz performer, so too was it necessary for the jazz audience, which was entitled to freedom of choice. In response to the incessant quarreling of the Feathers and the figs, the "fun faction" was beginning to make its presence felt.

While the dust was settling in 1946, two books that approached jazz purism from entirely different perspectives made their appearance on the jazz scene. Rudi Blesh's *Shining Trumpets: A History of Jazz* was an expansion of the theories he had originally put forth at the San Francisco Museum of Art, and Mezz Mezzrow's *Really the Blues* (cowritten with Bernard Wolfe, a prominent Trotskyite) was a revealing personal memoir whose exceedingly colloquial approach to language and history contrasted markedly to Blesh's formalism. Both works, however, were ultrapurist, and both enjoyed a considerable popularity, particularly among young converts who accepted them without question, swallowing them whole.[18] As such, they were mutually reinforcing.

The reader of *Shining Trumpets* did not have to venture very far into the book to grasp the underlying theme, which pervaded virtually every page: "Jazz is the music that whites in New Orleans saw only as 'nigger' music, scarcely as important, even, as those silly, shallow, and condescending white imitations of Negro song, the minstrel melody and 'coon' song." Blesh characterized white responses to jazz as fearful and suspicious: "It was something to be listened to with guarded pleasure in the honky tonk or in the Negro street parades that, even today, the white children are not freely allowed to follow; something perhaps even to be danced to if the inferior black men of the orchestra sat on the platform with their faces to the wall." Because jazz was "black" music, it was threatening to the established social order: "The guarded pleasure and the inhibited response are only explainable in part as a fear of the power of the Negro musical genius to break down the social and economic barriers set up against race."[19]

When one compares these words with the opening section of *Really the Blues*, the thematic resemblance is obvious:

MUSIC SCHOOL? Are you kidding? I learned to play the sax in Pontiac Reformatory. . . . They taught me the blues in Pontiac—I mean the blues, blues that I felt from my head to my shoes, really the blues. And it was in Pontiac that I dug that Jim Crow man in person, a motherferyer that would cut your throat for looking. We marched in from the mess hall in two lines, and the colored boys lockstepped into one side of the cellblock and we lockstepped into the other, and Jim Crow had the block, parading all around us, grinning like a polecat. I saw my first race riot there, out in the prison yard. It left me so shaky I almost blew my top and got sicker than a hog with the colic. Jim Crow just wouldn't get out of my face.[20]

The difference is that Mezzrow exemplifies a *positive* white response to black music. The year was 1917, and Mezzrow recalls the racially mixed jam sessions in which he learned to play saxophone, also mentioning his first hearing of the ODJB's "Livery Stable Blues," which sounded to him like the playing of Yellow, the black cornetist in the band.[21] Mezzrow's reaction to the music was anything but "guarded" or "inhibited," and his experience is reason enough to question the credibility of Blesh's unconditional condemnation of "white" responses to jazz. If mixed sessions were permitted in the highly formalized and restrictive environment of the reformatory, it does not take too much imagination to appreciate how many more opportunities for musical amalgamation existed in a city as renowned for casual interaction as New Orleans. Jim Crow had long been resident in the Crescent City, but everybody knew that he took frequent vacations.[22]

What Mezzrow and Blesh shared was an apotheosis of "Crow Jim," a concept that also enjoyed considerable popularity among bebop innovators.[23] Unfortunately, Crow Jim did not transcend the strictures of racist thinking but merely inverted them, positing black superiority in the conception and execution of jazz. Environmental factors were subordinated in *Shining Trumpets* to an overriding preoccupation with race, which was presented in absolute terms—the antithesis of the approach taken in *Jazzmen*. Blesh therefore placed much greater emphasis on African origins than had any of his predecessors, and he relied heavily on information provided by Melville Herskovits in outlining the characteristic features of African music, which he then applied to his discussion of jazz origins in New Orleans.[24] Yet Blesh was well aware of the special conditions of the New Orleans environment, including the existence of a large population of free blacks (*gens de couleur libres*) prior to the Civil War, the importance of the early black brass bands and benevolent societies, and the touchstone of Congo Square. As he put it:

> Logically, we must place the beginnings of jazz very shortly after Emancipation. Later richnesses of the music are to be accounted for by its development in the rich cultural milieu of its birthplace. The Negroid character it has never lost, is accounted for by the earlier date. Not only was Africa nearer in point of time, but in 1870 freshly landed slaves were on hand, the strongly African work-songs were current, and African dancing and ceremonial music were still continued in Congo Square. Much has been made of the fact that Buddy Bolden was a boy when Congo Square activity reached its last stages of decline in the 1880's. What, then, must have been the effect of this African survival at its height, on the children and youths who, in future years, formed the first street bands? May not some of them have danced and sung, drummed or blown wooden trumpets in the historic square?[25]

Blesh was attempting to preempt the authors of *Jazzmen* by placing the origins of jazz some twenty-five years prior to what they had claimed based on the testimony of their informants. Although Blesh's somewhat puzzling "freshly landed slaves" in 1870 might have referred to newly emancipated *former* slaves coming from Cuba, he presented no evidence to back his assertion. As the opening of the quotation reveals, his argument was an ideological construction that did not rest on direct testimony or hard evidence.[26] Such ruminations were typical of Blesh's approach to history, and with its charts illustrating "African Survivals in Negro Jazz" and "Deformations of Negro Jazz," *Shining Trumpets* was more a purist's handbook than a history.

As an example of what Herbert Butterfield has referred to as "presentism," it is without equal in the field of jazz history.[27]

Mezzrow's *Really the Blues,* on the other hand, while never intended as a jazz history, is not without value, despite its limitations. Although Sidney Bechet's influence is unmistakably present throughout the book, it is a much less doctrinaire treatment than *Shining Trumpets.* The discussion of Mezzrow's influence on Panassié is particularly revealing and was later confirmed by Charles Delaunay, who was in a position to know.[28] But when it came to Bechet, Mezzrow was as impressionable as Panassié had been. Here is his account of a shooting incident in Paris, in which Bechet comes off as a martyr to the cause of traditional jazz:

> I remembered a story Sidney had once told me, about the time he was playing with a band in Paris. He had been fighting with the other guys for weeks, trying to get them to work up one big beat and make vibrant organ chords in the background so he wouldn't be alone in his playing, there'd be a real collective spirit. That was the deepest need of his whole being, a musical collectivity; he kept screaming for it, it was an obsession with him. And one night the argument got so violent, one of the guys whom Sidney had been yelling at went and got a gun and came back and took some potshots at him, missing him but winging some innocent bystanders. Both guys were shoved in the Bastille for that, and stayed there for eleven months; Sidney's hair turned completely white in that dungeon.[29]

According to pianist Glover Compton (1884–1964), who was injured in the incident, it was in fact Bechet who started shooting, which calls into question Mezzrow's remark that "Sidney was the supreme example of a man at peace with himself."[30] Mezzrow told the story to draw a contrast between traditionalists and modernists:

> If you let yourself get all split up and pulverized inside, maybe you can make "modern" music, the music of tics, the swing and jump and rip-bop. That's the musical mania of the blowtops, the running-amuck music of guys wrastling with themselves, rolling around on the ground and having fits while their broken-up souls carry on a war inside them. Modern swing and jump is frantic, savage, frenzied, berserk—it's the agony of the

split, hacked-up personality. It's got nothing at all in common with New Orleans, which by contrast is dignified, balanced, deeply harmonious, high-spirited but pervaded all through with a mysterious calm and placidity—the music of personality that hasn't exploded like a fragmentation bomb.[31]

Mezzrow's memoirs, like Blesh's history, did not refrain from stating what were, for their time, sensationalistic points of view, and *Really the Blues* made no attempt to conceal (or apologize for) the author's activities as one of the busiest distributors of marijuana in Harlem.[32] It would perhaps be unfair, however, to account for Mezz's perception of New Orleans music as "mysteriously calm and placid" on that fact alone. Both Mezzrow and Blesh were undoubtedly sincere in their dedication to the cause of African American arts and rights, and while the historical accuracy of their respective works may have suffered as a result, their courage in putting forth such views so strongly cannot be overlooked. Had they only been willing to raise their sights to a higher perspective, both traditionalists and modernists would have realized that on this particular issue they were very much united, and outnumbered.

As it was, the purists continued to find bebop threatening and its growing popularity among young musicians hard to understand. In the May 1946 *Record Changer*, Carlton Brown's "Hey! Ba-Ba-Revolt!" offered a satire on the mannerisms of bebop musicians, particularly with regard to the onomatopoeic character of their song titles, their display of technical virtuosity, and the rapid tempos at which their songs were played (which made dancing virtually impossible). Brown's assessment of the music was roughly equivalent to Mezzrow's: "I heard Woody Herman from half a mile across a subterranean dine-and-danceteria and saw him right up close, and he needs a rest." Brown observed that Herman's brass section played so high "that only a dog can hear it," and his rendition of "Caledonia" was delivered at such a breakneck pace that "they can't sing it, but barely have time to gasp out 'Cal-ia! Cal'ia!' as the number streaks by." With wry humor, he quipped that "there must be a speed at which sound overtakes itself, and the Herd is approaching it so rapidly that—hey, look out! there it *went*!"[33] He also went to see Dizzy Gillespie (apparently not to hear him): "We saw Dizzy fall exhausted into a 52nd Street dungeon and heard him tell the boss that he was too tired to play any more . . . but the boss said some people had read about him in *Gnome* magazine . . . and he Must Go On." Brown felt sorry for Dizzy and suggested that both the music and the environment in which it was being played were decidedly unhealthy: "The bright lights on the stand, turning from red to green to violet in a nest of glittering mirrors, were enough to make anyone scream, through or outside of a trumpet."[34]

Brown also provided a quick summation of the etymology of bebop, with commentary on how it served as a sign of the times:

> The origin of the term "re-bop," for a mop-mop riff with overdrive, is obscure. Some unsung visionary must have seen that mop-mop would wear thin with constant usage and that it would become imperative to re-mop. Why not, then, keep a jump ahead of the pack and *re-bop*? Today the arbiters of advanced jive use the term, and practically nothing else, to describe the playing of Gillespie, whose influence they detect in the bands they admire. Other staples of the vocabulary are "head arrangement," "fabulous," "augmented chords," and "frantic," which has been converted into a term of approval. There is a tendency, among an influential faction of the more daring progressives, to substitute the spelling "be-bop," but at the hour of going to press, returns are not in from the outlying districts and the outcome remains in doubt. This tireless search for the *mot juste* for the music of their choice testifies to the perfectionism of the modernists, but it makes it hard for those outside the inner circle to keep score.[35]

In contrast to the sentiments of the year before, however, Brown made some suggestions in the spirit of compromise: "There is still time for them to abandon their mad course and remain within ear-shot, and maybe if we are kind to them and let them know that we want them to, they will see the advisability of compromise." Of course, some concessions had to be made by the boppers, including a return to "reasonable" chord progressions, moderate dance tempo, and lower volume. In turn, the traditionalist camp must make concessions of its own: "I'm ready with one. It hurts to tamper with tradition, but here, take it, Woody, Dizzy, Stan and Boyd. Little number I just composed called *Ja-Da Ba-Re-Bop*."[36]

Further indications that the purist zeitgeist was shifting were evident in the December announcement that the *Record Changer* was about to launch its first jazz poll. The reasons for doing so, and admission of doubts about its usefulness, were given as follows: "It seems to be fashionable among large-scale music magazines to poll their readers each year so that they can pick an 'All-Star' band. Exactly what is gained by this device is not completely clear to us, but as long as the two great jazz publications (*Down Beat* and *Esquire*) go in for this sort of thing, we may as well have a go at it and see what happens."[37] But as subsequent events proved, the "if you can't lick 'em, join 'em" exterior employed by some purists was in reality a front masking a strategy of subversion that soon had the modernist camp in an uproar. Once again, the bone of contention was *Esquire*'s *Jazz Book*, but this time the tables were turned.

The winners of the 1947 poll were much as they had been in 1946: Gold Star awards went to swing men such as Benny Goodman, Coleman Hawkins, and the Ellington band; Silver Stars (for second place) went to the most popular bebop advocates, like Dizzy Gillespie, George Handy (1920–1997; Raeburn's arranger), and Woody Herman's (1913–1987) orchestra; New Stars were Boyd Raeburn (band), Miles Davis (1926–1991; trumpet), and Sarah Vaughan (1924–1990; female vocalist), representing the new crop of innovators. But Arnold Gingrich had decided to relocate permanently to Switzerland, and Ernest Anderson (1923–1997), Eddie Condon's close personal friend and associate, took over the editing of *Esquire's 1947 Jazz Book* in what amounted to a coup of major proportions. As a result, the book became a publicity vehicle for the traditionalists, effectively eliminating all but the briefest mention of the winners. A letter to *Esquire* from the modernist winners tells the story of what happened: "We, a group of musicians who have won awards in the *Esquire* All American Jazz Polls, hereby protest against the treatment given to the poll in *Esquire's 1947 Jazz Book*." The winners wanted to know why the book had been edited by Eddie Condon's personal manager, who used it as a publicity vehicle for his client, a musician "who has nothing to do with jazz today." They also wanted to know why none of the poll winners had been featured in the book's articles and why no photographs of the New Stars had been included. In sum, the book was "an insult to the musical profession," and the musicians who had helped *Esquire* by taking part in its jazz activities were now divorcing themselves from any association with the magazine: "As long as the present unfair set-up continues, we do not wish to vote in any future polls, and we will refuse to accept any future awards." Among the signatures affixed to the letter were those of Louis Armstrong, Duke Ellington, Big Sid Catlett (1910–1951), Coleman Hawkins, Buck Clayton (1911–1991), Nat King Cole (1919–1965), Dizzy Gillespie, Boyd Raeburn, Miles Davis, Johnny Hodges (1907–1970), Ella Fitzgerald (1917–1996), and Teddy Wilson (1912–1986).[38]

In his autobiography, *The Jazz Years,* Leonard Feather recounts how the panel of experts—save two, Dave Dexter Jr. (1915–1990) and Charles Edward Smith—severed all ties with the magazine in protest. The cumulative effect of the jazz schism had already weakened *Esquire*'s commitment to the promotion of jazz, and the Condon coup served as the proverbial straw that broke the camel's back. According to Feather, the poll had already been weakened beyond salvation:

> Possibly the revolt was inevitable and the poll doomed. The writing had already been visible on the wall: *Esquire* had dropped its regular feature coverage, Gingrich was not around to help us, and as a devastating post-script Robert Goffin sued the magazine, claiming that he had been frozen out of the picture. That I refused to testify on behalf of *Esquire* undoubtedly helped his case. Among the promises supposedly received in the course of the settlement was that *Esquire* would never again run a jazz poll.[39]

The demise of *Esquire*'s jazz policy in early 1947 coincided with the end of the era of the big swing bands, thus eliminating two of the purists' most formidable adversaries. Only bebop remained as a bastion of jazz modernism, but it had the tireless support of *Metronome* and increasing coverage in *Down Beat* to rely on in its bid for public acceptance, which never really worked out anyway. And it was not only the modernists who had been shocked by the fifth-column activities of the Condon clique. Many former traditionalists began to open their minds to bebop, without necessarily sacrificing their love for traditional styles. Within a year of the "victory" over *Esquire*, Bill Grauer Jr. (1923–1963) and Orrin Keepnews (1923–) acquired the *Record Changer* and initiated a much more liberal and inclusive editorial policy toward modern jazz.[40] As with the reissue of "hot" jazz by the majors in the early 1940s, the victories of the purists over their modernist foes were never as satisfying as they were supposed to be. With the modernist menace seemingly diminished, collectors began to fight among themselves, subjecting each other to the same kind of ridicule and derision that had once been reserved for Feather and Ulanov.

A case in point was an article that ran in the September 1947 issue of the *Record Changer,* entitled "I Never Was a Jazz Expert!" Supposedly written by William Genes (as told to Alf Helfensteller), it was a lampoon directed against two of the architects of the Bunk Johnson phase of the New Orleans revival, Gene Williams and Bill Colburn:

> Just like Cole Billborn says, this new kind of music that only he and I can hear because we listen right, will make everybody in the world happy. Then when they all get happy, everybody will be playing this kind of music, and nobody will be unhappy any more. Cole Billborn even says there won't be any more wars when people hear this new music, because the new music will make everybody so happy. Of course I don't say this, because I'm just talking about the music, and I can prove it. But Cole says this, and he should know, because he is the only person besides myself who can hear this happy new music, and he can prove it. The other experts, and the great American public may listen to it, but they listen to it wrong, so they never hear it, and this is a fact, it is important, and it can be proved, and I can prove it by what I am saying, and you can't tell me how wrong I am until you have heard it, too. But you haven't heard it, and you can't hear it, because you don't listen right. Only Cole Billborn and I listen right, and we aren't jazz experts, because there never was any jazz, because nobody ever listened to jazz right.[41]

One can only wonder how Bill Russell, the third member of the Bunk Johnson triumvirate, avoided censure at the hands of Helfensteller, but presumably it was because his contributions to the righteous cause were so substantial, and his demeanor so reticent, that he was granted special immunity.

Russell rarely contributed directly to the debates of the 1940s, and when he did, it was usually as "the voice of reason." His eulogy of Mutt Carey in the November 1948 *Record Changer* demonstrated his ability to avoid being immured in purist doctrine:

> Mutt Carey was more than just a fine trumpet player and well rounded musician. He was an inspirational leader and wise teacher, and even more

important—he had the rare *know how* of putting his music across to the general non-jazz public. Mutt understood that music, to be successful and to survive, must be "commercial." He knew that New Orleans music could be sold to the public and he knew how to present it. It was this special knowledge, in addition to his fine musicianship, that makes his loss especially unfortunate at this time.[42]

Russell was also a master of understatement, allowing him to cloak oblique criticisms of modernist techniques in such a manner as to render them virtually invisible:

Several years ago Mutt advised his son not to take up a tough instrument like the trumpet because "nowadays they expect you to play clarinet parts on the trumpet." He realized that a horn that should be played simply and naturally must be forced and strained to play what could come easily on another instrument. Mutt never made the mistake of trying to imitate the clarinet or piccolo on his trumpet. He knew that the trumpet is the leading melodic voice in the dance orchestra, just as he knew that above all the people like to hear a beautiful melody played or sung. . . . Carey disliked blasting and most enjoyed playing "light-weight swing," and even as Bolden and Oliver did at times, Mutt occasionally played so softly when the band got rocking that the shuffling beat of the dancers' feet all but drowned out the band.[43]

Had Russell chosen dentistry as a profession, he would undoubtedly have been a great success, such was his skill in painlessly attacking "decay." Further commentary revealed his feelings on the impact of the jazz schism on the music scene, Russell once again using appreciation of Papa Mutt as his foil:

Although he sought and received little publicity, Carey was a good enough showman to be a successful leader. He was full of friendliness and good humor. Everyone seemed to have a good word for Papa Mutt. There was no place in his disposition for bitterness or criticism of others, and no one was ever more dependable. With his intelligence and understanding of so many phases of the music business Mutt, if given half a chance, could have helped straighten out the deplorable mess into which, as almost everyone admits, the music racket has fallen today.[44]

198 / NEW ORLEANS STYLE AND THE WRITING OF AMERICAN JAZZ HISTORY

By the time Russell's article appeared in the *Record Changer*, the import of his views could not be lost on the purist collector community, for it was very much in a state of disarray. Internecine strife between old friends such as Hugues Panassié and Charles Delaunay, or between old heroes like Delaunay and ambitious newcomers such as Rudi Blesh, was becoming increasingly commonplace, seriously damaging the spirit of communion on which promotion of the righteous cause had originally been based.

In 1946, just as the jazz schism was dying down in the United States, it was primed to explode in France. Panassié's embrace of purism in *The Real Jazz* soon became an issue in his friendship with Delaunay, whose burgeoning interest in modern jazz, after hearing Dizzy Gillespie and Charlie Parker's "Salt Peanuts" in 1946, was viewed as a defection. In *Jazz 47* (a publication undertaken in 1946 to acquaint potential converts in France with jazz essentials after five years of German occupation), Delaunay and Jean Cocteau (1889–1963) provided a chart constructed by André Hodeir to identify "real" jazz and to differentiate it from commercial imitations, much as Panassié had done in his recent book and reaching similar conclusions about jazz as black music.[45] Delaunay came to the United States later in 1946 to record American musicians for the Swing label, and he absorbed the full range of jazz that was available to him there, modernist and traditional, without bias. Yet his belief that an interest in bebop did not preclude sincere appreciation of traditional jazz was not enough to placate Panassié, and the result was a coup d'état. On October 2, 1947, Panassié presented a "bill of particulars" against Delaunay at the national assembly of the provincial Hot Clubs de France, inaugurating a Gallic schism that mirrored the traditionalist versus modernist debates that had been dividing the American jazz community. Michael Dregni provides a succinct account of what transpired:

> Panassié first accused Delaunay of being a dictator—a role Panassié retained for himself. Then he elaborated the counts of censure. Charge *le premier*: Delaunay hired on September 6, 1946, British jazz aficionado Leonard Feather—"an enemy of the Hot Club," or at least of Panassié—to produce recordings for the Swing label by Louis Armstrong, Panassié's "own" musician. Charge *le deuxième*: Delaunay worked behind the scenes to block Django from recording with Duke Ellington during his U.S. tour—a charge proved untrue by Delaunay's correspondence with Stephen Sholes of RCA. Charge *le troisième*: Delaunay contributed to the

book *Jazz 47* under the Hot Club's name but without its permission; the revue included praise of bebop as well as a contentious article by Jean-Paul Sartre. Charge *le quatrième:* Delaunay was guilty of "pornographic propaganda" exaggerating the value of bebop.[46]

Under duress, and without the votes to make a fight of it, Delaunay resigned from the Hot Club de France, and the partnership in Swing was dissolved. The friendship that had proven so productive and inspirational for "hot" jazz collectors in the mid-1930s was over, providing a very tangible example of what the perils of intellectualization could entail. Panassié and Delaunay never spoke to each other again.

As the end of the decade began to draw near, the supporters of traditional jazz became increasingly concerned with the survival of the music. In "What Is New Orleans Style?" Blesh raised this issue and provided suggestions for the revitalization of the style through extension of the New Orleans tradition by young practitioners. Unfortunately, he chose to demonstrate his plan for further development by criticizing bands like the Yerba Buena, which had a staunch and sizable following. Yet in so doing, he transcended the boundaries of purism established by Russell, Williams, Colburn, and Ertegun in arguing that the style was "wide enough to embrace numberless variants." The problem with the Yerba Buena was "slavish imitation":

Ten years ago the Lu Watters group were avowedly making arrangements from Morton and Oliver records. Many of us believed that the players saw this as a first step to mastering the style and that they would eventually desert imitation for creation. This has never happened. The Watters band now has a wide repertory, great technical proficiency, and a large and consolidated following that is apt to be intolerant, in a provincial way, of all other jazz. Musically the band has stood still and, significantly enough, none of its members like to be compared with the great bands they once were glad to copy. The Watters Band, a few years ago, unquestionably led a jazz renaissance on the Pacific Coast. Today its frozen eclecticism is in danger of holding the movement back.[47]

Blesh saw more hope in Bob Wilber's Wildcats (which he signed to Circle), especially if Wilber could move beyond emulation of his teacher, Sidney Bechet. Also praised was the All Star Stompers, the house band for Blesh's

This Is Jazz radio show, which had been condemned by purists: "It was interesting to note that the many thousands of followers who were attracted to the radio program *This Is Jazz* failed to include a single one of the New Orleans extremists." Apparently, complaints that the band's music was too much like Chicago style did not strike Blesh as ironic in light of his previous writings. He concluded, "These letters will be interesting to look at ten years from now."[48]

On the question of how New Orleans musicians might have changed after coming to Chicago, Blesh averred that "we may never know" but quoted Edmond Souchon, who had heard bands like Oliver's in both places: "Dr. Edmond Souchon of New Orleans writes to me, 'I was one of those "I knew Storyville when . . . " King Oliver,' he continues, 'was at his peak (as a musician . . . and not as the head of a celebrated band as he was later in Chicago) . . . playing in a Negro night club in the "district." . . . Years later, to be exact in 1921–23, I heard him again in Chicago at Lincoln Gardens in front of his celebrated band, and they were definitely *not* as good as before he left New Orleans.'"[49] Blesh felt that basing a rigid doctrine of purism on a few recordings that, in all probability, could not properly "show the infinite variety of mood and inspiration of a great group of artists" was facile in the extreme. New Orleans style was therefore susceptible to progress, variegation, and ultimately modernization, as long as its basic principles were observed. The standards of purism, while inferred from historical recordings, were generally mechanical rather than specifically historical. Given the limitations of the historical record, in other words, theory must prevail.

Having thus disposed of Russell and Williams, Blesh went on the offensive against Delaunay, who may still have been smarting from his falling-out with Panassié. In "Some Thoughts on the Jazz Revival," he lionized Panassié's role in the revival of jazz at the discographer's expense and elaborated on the theories previously presented on New Orleans style:

> The fact has slowly emerged that New Orleans jazz is a genuinely modern music, so modern, in fact, that it is still far in advance of its time, a music so complex in performance and in musical implication that it is still not fully grasped, even by the majority of its adherents. The modernity of New Orleans music can be—and has been—proven musically beyond the possibility of refutation. The necessity, however, of having to go back to

rediscover a music and to discover its modernity, has stamped New Orleans criticism (in the minds of shallow people) as a reactionary process. It has furnished a specious weapon, too, to the proponents of the so-called "modern" jazz. And, no matter how often and how conclusively the myth of bebop and its allied aberrant forms are exploded, like any other fad they must run their course. At the end they will die out, leaving their small residue of experimental discovery to enrich the main stream of development from which they were, on the whole, so far removed. And development, it must be decisively stated, is precisely what is potentially implied in the New Orleans concept.[50]

The jazz schism had distracted critics from the potential for New Orleans–style "progressivism," resulting in a "momentary pause between steps." Delaunay's desertion from the traditionalist camp was for Blesh inconsequential: "Delaunay will be remembered for his prodigious labors in discography, an activity more related to stamp collecting than to science, a form of musical book-keeping important only as an adjunct or tool to musical understanding."

Blesh's theory was that Delaunay was attracted to bebop because there was no place else for him to get "free of Panassié's huge shadow." The pioneer discographer's distaste for critical bickering could thus be explained as transference of an Oedipal impulse directed against Panassié: "And so to bebop he goes and, to justify his move as well as his own critical shortcomings, he now condemns all criticism and all critics."[51] Some choice words were also directed against Ernest Borneman:

The solemn pronouncements of the amateur anthropologists about "social forces that no longer exist" can be dismissed as so much rubbish. The error is one of assuming that the product of a given set of social conditions is unique and producible only by that set. New Orleans music has departed from the bagnios and barrelhouses and the racial discrimination of old New Orleans and, in response to a new set of social forces, is vital today. Artistic traditions may survive—as the social institution of marriage has survived—through a changing society and a changing economy. Jazz, its players, and those who love it seem never to have heard of anthropology.[52]

In closing, and with reference to the "army" of Wildcats, All Star Stompers, and other old-timers like Ory, Blesh urged, "Let's supply and reinforce the progress they have made, which is the progress that we, ourselves, started."[53] It was not made clear whether the "we" mentioned included Panassié or was in the fashion of the royal prerogative.

Blesh's opinions were, however, very much a double-edged sword, and he made the unfortunate mistake of handing it to Delaunay, who was fully capable of wielding it with typically French éclat. In Delaunay's "An Attack on Critical Jabberwocky," the honor of discographers everywhere was suitably avenged. In response to Blesh's claim that the modernity of New Orleans jazz had been established "beyond the possibility of refutation," Delaunay had this to say:

> The meaning of this sort of jabberwocky escapes me. It is bad enough to have the be-bop apostles talk about their music as "modern" or "progressive" instead of saying simply that it is original; if Mr. Blesh now falls into the same trap, he shows merely that he is the opportunist we have suspected him to be all along. New Orleans jazz was an exciting, vigorous music when it was first produced. But it was no better than the musicians who produced it. Mr. Blesh's myth of New Orleans jazz as some kind of abstract phenomenon has no more reality than the disembodied myth of the all-mighty state, or the "modern" state, or other such dehydrated entities.[54]

As for the denigration of the old-guard jazz historians and New Orleans revivalists, Blesh was chided for "calling blame on the heads of other critics who have labored more honestly in the New Orleans vineyards."[55] Delaunay devoted great attention to clarifying his relationship with Panassié as well, and his estimation of his erstwhile colleague's critical prowess toppled the pedestal on which Blesh had placed him:

> Panassié first learned about jazz from Mezzrow and the Chicagoans. His first book was largely an apology for Chicago jazz spiked with special plums of praise for those musicians who were his beloved friends and with special blobs of acid for those who were their enemies. His second book was little more than a reflection of Mezzrow's quarrel with the Chicagoans and Mezzrow's new friendship with Bechet and some of the

New Orleans old-timers. The curious contradictions in Panassié's writings, which have always baffled you in America, are nothing more, and nothing less, than an indication of Panassié's succession of friendships with those American musicians who happened to drift over to Paris. He used to ask them for their preferred musicians, and whatever information they gave him would come out the day after as musical criticism over Panassié's signature. If Hugues had made more friends among be-bop musicians, we would long have had a new "courageous correction" of his previous "stand" on Chicago jazz or New Orleans jazz or whatever his current friends happened to believe in. To think of Hugues as a jazz critic therefore seems to us over here like thinking of a weathervane as a critical instrument.[56]

The problem with pinning all hopes for the survival of New Orleans style on what the young musicians *should* be playing flew in the face of what was actually happening: "For the truth is that be-bop is what the young musicians are trying to play . . . and that bands like Claude Luter, Claude Bolling and Bob Wilber are in a diminutive minority." In addition, there appeared to be no "young Negro musicians" among the revivalists. Delaunay was well aware of the contradiction between Blesh's new pronouncements and his previous position: "To find Mr. Blesh, the old advocate of racism in music, suddenly 'joining the liberals' in a great fanfare about 'the young bands' (all white) . . . is . . . a little comic from the spectator's point of view."[57] Blesh's "army" was, indeed, chimerical, and writers for *Down Beat* supported Delaunay's observations, concerned that the Wildcats and bands like them were marching headlong into a musical cul-de-sac.[58]

Perhaps the statements directed against Panassié enabled a catharsis that allowed Delaunay to jettison the past and move on. Delaunay's *New Hot Discography* in 1948 included entries for bebop and progressive musicians such as Dizzy Gillespie and Stan Kenton, and soon after he was devoting himself to the organization of the first Paris Jazz Festival, in which Sidney Bechet would win the hearts of the audience over Charlie Parker, the leading light of bebop, who was making his European debut. For Delaunay, the power of individuals to *defy* categorization was what now made jazz interesting, reversing the premise that had launched his discographical career. As for Bechet, whose "comeback" with RCA Victor had been hijacked by the New Orleans Revival in 1940, he was struggling heroically to transcend anachronistic typecasting, a point of view that Delaunay applauded. His "victory" over Parker was therefore personally gratifying, but die-hard purists nevertheless preferred to view it as a win for traditionalists against modernists.

Delaunay was certainly not alone in seeking to transcend factionalism in his appreciation of good jazz wherever he found it. Ultimately, purists of the stature of Charles Edward Smith and George Avakian also followed the path to a more latitudinarian approach to jazz. After all, many of the objectives they had set for themselves at the beginning of the decade had been accomplished with the revival of interest in New Orleans style and the increasing availability of both vintage and new recordings, from independents and majors alike. Perhaps it was now time to pause and reflect upon what had been gained by their labors for the righteous cause. It was, in fact, a record of which they could be proud.

By 1947, Charles Edward Smith had fallen upon hard times, and an advertisement in the *Record Changer* offered his prize collection of jazz records to the highest bidder in an attempt to avoid eviction from his New York apartment.[59] One can thus appreciate why he did not resign during the *Esquire Jazz Book* fiasco of 1947—he needed the money. During 1948, he wrote two essays for the *Record Changer* that might best be described as exercises in retrospection. In "Cultural Anthropology and the Reformed Tramp," he reviewed the course of jazz from its supposedly dubious beginnings to its eventual social acceptance, pondering the implications of Borneman's views on purism and cultural dynamics. He was worried about what had happened in the purist camp, noting that the tendency to complain about the decline of jazz was a common failing among collectors: "Healthy as it is in motivation, this has resulted in blind spots and optical illusions amongst the brothers and sisters."[60] He had come to realize that the big swing bands might not have been the villains they were made out to be: "In fact, during the thirties many articles were written *defensively* about men who were in fact taking the initiative in keeping jazz alive. These men weren't always playing in New Orleans combinations, but then, neither were Louis Armstrong and others who have managed to keep up the spirit of the thing often enough to set us on our ears. The small bands simply weren't saleable packages and fell by the wayside much as big orchestras have recently."[61]

The future of jazz had been a common topic of discussion even in those comparatively halcyon days when the collector community was in the process of formation: "Some maintained that the real jazz was created as an expression of life now in the past, that the environment's demise predetermined that of the music. Others held that jazz was adaptable to any environment."[62] The environment for the early New Orleans jazzmen had been a rather hostile one, but that was beginning to change in the mid-1940s: "There is an inevitability and direction in the story of every jazz pioneer. Barriers of prejudice often channel talents into specific directions. Since *Jazzmen* and a much earlier article by this writer, the antagonism of New Orleans' cultural mentors to jazz has been well publicized. Indeed, the city made its implicit apology when it reaffirmed that Basin Street was, in fact, Basin Street. But the early bands went into honky-tonks because, for one thing, there was nowhere else to go if they wanted to play 'ear' music."[63] The salutary influence of the New Orleans environment could be seen in the experience of Leon Roppolo: "Rappolo's ancestry boasted of many fine concert clarinetists and he was given violin lessons to keep away from the clarinet since the latter instrument wasn't paying off so well in the concert field." But since he was a New Orleanian, chances were good that Leon would persist in his desire to play clarinet and that he was likely to play jazz on it. Smith rejoiced in the fact and offered added insight: "Fortunately for us he played it with grace and facility, reminding one less of the influences upon him than of his own contribution to New Orleans music."[64]

The environment, in other words, was conditioned by personality. Recent events had demonstrated the tenacity of those individuals who, through the force of personality, had kept the music alive: "The demise of jazz is, as we must all be aware, not to be a part of the history of the present century. The question as to its adaptability has more or less answered itself." Smith cited the accomplishments of Bunk and Ory, as well as those of Lu Watters and "the Dixielanders of Greenwich Village." While some of this body of work was shoddy or pretentious, "the few that have held to a standard" had made the revival worthwhile. He recalled an all-night listening session in which some inferior Bunk Johnson recordings had been discussed with a friend: " 'But they're important,' my fellow flim-flammer pointed out. 'No one says Bunk is right all the time—the point is, he's *living* history and the more we have of him on records the better.' "[65] There was little reason to fear the competition: "All the deviations that have occurred in jazz . . . from 'symphonic jazz' to the be-bop that is susceptible of analysis and is the new dadaism on our little family tree—all such trends have not kept our jazzmen from their appointed rounds."[66] Smith ended his piece with a quizzical comment— "Imagine that, diary, a laughing jazz critic!"—yet his readers knew what he meant. It was another vote for the fun faction.

What the members of the old guard knew, and what was often lost on the more recent theorists, was that when you felt "blue," you sought refuge in jazz and were duly comforted. This was by far a preferable alternative to using it as a sword of pedantry and slashing the nearest critic with whom you disagreed. As long as such critics continued to rampage, however, it was necessary to keep a wary eye over the shoulder. Perhaps this was the not-so-subliminal message behind the title of Smith's October 1948 article for the *Record Changer,* "Over My Shoulder," a survey of the struggle of "historically-minded" jazz critics to penetrate beneath record labels in their search for historical infrastructure. As Smith stated, "The lofty aim of such ghoulish activity was to find in the past some measurement of the present, reminding one of those who wander about old graveyards making impressions of headstones." To those who pursued this hobby, it was immeasurably important. "So, too," wrote Smith, "is the preoccupation of those who, in their search for the headstones that mark the genealogy of jazz, probe amongst the living, the living dead, and the long-since dead whose headstones are the sidewalk tiles of Basin Street."[67]

Smith admitted the naiveté of the early historians and recalled the policy meetings among the editors of *Jazzmen* ("with and without portfolio— William Russell, Frederic Ramsey, Jr., Stephen W. Smith and myself") in order to hammer out a working consensus to tie divergent opinions together. All in all, they had not been far off the mark:

> A major point of discussion was that of the relative positions of Creole Negro and South Rampart Street jazz, the latter more purely Afro-American in its path of descent. From today's viewpoint we were, musically speaking, properly oriented (for our major aim was to explore the parent style of jazz and its environment). But in the matter of those who played the music only research—and more and more research—could bring into focus the *intermingling* of the musicians themselves: Negro, Creole Negro, and white. This is pretty academic stuff now, but we had the thrill of

those amateur archeologists who take impressions of headstones, with the secure and amazing knowledge that the objects of our research were, in many instances, more alive than we could have hoped.[68]

While Panassié's "ear judgment" had been "excellent," his "historical justification" was "strikingly naive in contrast," meaning that the Americans had to start "from scratch," working their way back to the goose from the golden egg. Slowly, through discussions with Cornish and Lomax's interviews with Morton, and with a willingness to alter previously fixed opinions, the authors of *Jazzmen* had watched the intricacies of the New Orleans cultural landscape and experience emerge. Smith recalled "one who'd had a rather responsible past in jazz but who spent his idle hours griping at 'dam niggers' who got credit for pioneering jazz and, as one might expect, ignored history entirely to blow up his own minor role in the drama."[69] And of course, there was Jelly, whose "urge to write pops was based on the false premise that thereby he could capture the fame denied him and win for himself material security. His own music won out, since his real security was in that music, and that alone."[70]

This was a security in which the authors of *Jazzmen* also shared, for Smith and Smith, Russell, and Ramsey had given to the jazz world a firm foundation on which to build. Basing their work on historical research and devising theories accordingly, they produced a series of books and articles that are still useful as examples of jazz scholarship. While *Jazzmen* and *The Jazz Record Book* were certainly not insusceptible to revision, subsequent histories produced in the 1940s did little to improve on them. That task was to be the prerogative of younger men and women, years later, armed with the insights provided by these pioneer jazz historians. In their documentation of the origins of jazz in New Orleans, Smith and Russell fused their enthusiasm as "hot" record collectors with the painstaking diligence and patience that were required for the job; it was this enthusiasm that sustained their efforts, and had they hesitated, much that was saved would have been lost.

Yet the community of spirit that had nourished the collector-historians was vanishing. The schisms of the 1940s had taken their toll, and by the end of the decade the collector community that had rescued old-timers like Bunk and Ory from oblivion was itself threatened with extinction. To some extent, it was the victim of its own success, as George Avakian affirmed in "The Vanishing American," a kind of "state of the nation" address published in the *Record Changer* in December 1948. His prognosis for the future of the community was not optimistic:

> A vanishing breed, the old-time collectors. Most of them are getting old and fat, though not on their attempted sales of Ace Brigode and Jo Candullo duds. Some of them are sitting back and getting mellow working out astoundingly intricate discographies and histories of obscure recording firms. The research done on Paramount Company and the assorted chain-store labels ("Milling Around with the Mills") is staggering. Without detracting from the work or the incredible patience and devotion that went into it, I must say that I can't help but feel that the same amount of study in something like the stock market would be much more rewarding.[71]

The achievements of the partisans of historical reissues a decade earlier had unleashed a flood of releases that, when combined with the recordings of current bands, made it extremely difficult, and expensive, to collect comprehensively:

> Of course the old-fashioned collector has been snowed right out of existence by the flood of records aimed more or less directly at him. Back in the old days, when my hair was not only un-grey, but actually *was,* you had your pick of only the three major reissue companies to choose from, plus an occasional UHCA and HRS reissue. You could concentrate on current stuff and cut-outs, and be pretty confident that you wouldn't miss a thing. And the cut-outs were far less numerous—at least, what you didn't know about didn't bother you, so life was one blissful paradise of unawareness of such matters as Louis being on a Johnny Dodds *Vocalion,* since no one even knew the *Vocalion* record had ever been made.[72]

Once the economics of the situation got out of hand, collectors were forced to become increasingly narrow in their acquisition habits, specializing in some areas (like the New Orleans revival or bebop) to the exclusion of others.

The correlation of collector specialization identified by Avakian with the division of critics and collectors into exclusive camps during the 1940s is certainly interesting to contemplate. Furthermore, large-scale reissue campaigns by the majors had a deflationary effect on what had previously been extremely rare items. Many collectors thus sought to divest themselves of valued recordings before the bottom dropped out of the market, especially those who fit the profile earlier offered by Apfel in "Hot Man (Under the Collar)." The forces of disintegration—shellac drives, economic deflation, and aesthetic squabbling—had a deleterious effect on the morale of the collector community, taking the fun out of it for some, subtracting the profits for others. One thing was absolutely clear: the golden age of "hot" record collecting was over. What remained was a mass market that catered to the ever-changing and increasingly pluralistic preferences of the American consumer, a great ocean of shifting currents and whirlpools in which the subtleties of historical perspective could easily drown.

The decline of the collector community opened the doors to writers who were unaffiliated within the jazz world. In 1948, Sidney Finkelstein's *Jazz: A People's Music* demonstrated how other doctrines, apart from those developed by jazz critics, could be applied to discussion of the music. As sociologist Morroe Berger's review in the *New York Times* indicated, Finkelstein's book was not so much a history as an attempt to apply Marxian principles to jazz in order to claim it as a vehicle for social protest. A contributor to *Masses* and *Mainstream,* Finkelstein exhibited "too much striving to fit the sociological analysis to the needs of the very special political position to which the author adheres."[73] Berger did not feel that jazz was unsusceptible to sociological analysis, but that "Mr. Finkelstein seems to feel that he must adjust his treatment to a particular (and shifting) brand of social analysis which by its extremism tends to vitiate the validity of the sociological approach in general." In order to illustrate his point, the reviewer sampled passages aimed at representing traditional and modern jazz as reactions against the capitalist system: " 'The old jazz was a protest against the narrowness of semi-feudal Southern life in the years before the first world war, using the idioms and forms given it by semi-feudal life.' " In turn, "modern jazz is a protest against the monopoly control of music and commodity-like exploitation of the musicians, a protest using the idioms and forms given it by commercial music."[74]

As Berger pointed out, little research had been done to actually prove these claims, which detracted noticeably from what would have otherwise been an interesting musicological analysis. Yet *Jazz: A People's Music* was received in some circles as a balanced book because it did not discriminate between the traditionalist and modernist factions in presenting its case. A Marxist perspective enabled Finkelstein to establish organic unity by basing the story in the ineluctable progress of dialectical materialism. Finkelstein thus became a voice of reason in other contributions to the jazz press; in the March 1949 edition of the *Record Changer,* his "Peace in the Ranks" showed how he had come to assume the role of peacemaker. In this article, his approach was historical, and the message he presented was worthy of serious consideration. What he offered was essentially a synthesis of the opinions of previous writers who had grown weary of the jazz feuds: "One of the sad aspects of the jazz scene today, compared to that of a decade ago, is the dissension among its followers." Previously, jazz lovers had been "a united band of young Davids out to battle the sweet and commercial philistines." The jazz community was now divided into three camps—jazz, swing, and bebop—"and the first and last, especially, speak a different and musically antagonistic language. There is as much difference between them as there once was between the followers of hot jazz and sweet."[75]

Finkelstein proposed an interesting thesis concerning the origins of the jazz schism:

It may seem as if the two post-war extremes, bebop and the New Orleans revival, are responsible for the division, but actually the cracks in the ice began to appear in the late thirties, almost at the moment when the battle for hot jazz seemed to be won. One of its signs was the break between Gene Williams, who edited *Jazz Information,* and Steve Smith, who ran HRS. Smith reissued ten rare Bix sides, which Williams denounced as bad music, and then Williams denounced Smith's Spanier-Bechet discs as semi-commercial. Looking back now, we can see in Williams' stand the beginning of the New Orleans revival. He was absolutely sincere with the fanaticism of Carrie Nation wielding an axe in the saloons. And indeed, it was in this spirit that he walked about the living jazz scene of his time. He set himself the task of asserting the values of the old jazz, the great New Orleans jazz which had tended to be weakened in the smooth patterns of Dixieland and forgotten in the rise of the swing bands. . . . But in fighting for the rediscovery of the grass roots of jazz, he felt that he had to cut down everything that seemed to interfere, so that Ellington, Bix and Tesch had to be "debunked," and Basie sneered at.[76]

So it was all Eugene Williams's fault! Was the identity of Alf Helfensteller finally revealed? Finkelstein seemed not to grasp that the hand at the rudder of revival really belonged to Bill Russell, who was not mentioned once in the article. According to Finkelstein, both modernists and traditionalists, "in their embattled state, have lost much critical judgment."

This may have been true, but it was certainly a convenient state of affairs for one who was asserting his personal critical credentials. All of the complaints of the purists directed against the modernists, and vice versa, were included in the survey. Finkelstein was making an appeal for unity:

> With unity among jazz fans who have no axe to grind, long overdue tasks could be taken up. One would be the organization of a body of jazz lovers, on a nation-wide basis, willing both to know the traditional and to encourage new musicians. If such an organization can get started now, it can be the force which will persuade the record companies to reissue some several hundred old discs, as a permanently available history of jazz. It can produce from its ranks some first-rate, impartial criticism. It can give musicians who are eager to play their best the backing they need.[77]

These were laudable sentiments, and it was probably just coincidence that Finkelstein managed to merge into a seamless web arguments that had already been made by Charles Edward Smith, Charles Delaunay, George Avakian, and many others. Was he truly unaware of the prevalence of reissues then available? Or, given his political affiliations, was he merely blowing smoke while busily sharpening his axe? Hypothetically, at least, a united national organization would certainly be easier to infiltrate and control than a situation in which atomistic individualism was rampant. Perhaps Finkelstein wanted to "unite and conquer." As it was, the readers of the *Record Changer* settled for the latest in a long series of appeals for order, for no national organization of the jazz world had ever been able to sustain itself for very long (UHCA immediately comes to mind), and no attempt to establish one resulted from Finkelstein's plea.

As the decade drew to a close, another book arrived on the scene that, at first glance, had nothing to do with the early history of jazz. Leonard Feather's *Inside Be-Bop,* published in 1949, did its best to avoid jazz origins completely, addressing itself instead to the need for a history of modern jazz, which had broken through to national attention only the year before.[78] As Feather put it, "Too many histories of jazz have hit the market in the past decade, most of them devoting a vast proportion of space to the dim and distant past, with very little consideration of the present and no eye at all for the future."[79]A history of the *future* would certainly be novel, but Feather's debut as a historian was fraught with serious implications for the future of jazz scholarship. His skirting of New Orleans can be seen as the first step toward a full-scale challenge to the thesis of New Orleans nativity, a cause to which Feather applied himself with considerable gusto.

When *The Book of Jazz* appeared in 1957, Feather's gauntlet hit the ground with a vengeance. He opened his chapter "Beginnings" accordingly: "Jazz was not born in New Orleans. Jazz is a social, not a racial music. Jazz is written as well as improvised. Jazz can be played in four-four time, waltz time or any other time."[80] To support his assertions, he exploited the writings of traditionalists who had questioned the reliability of informants like Bunk Johnson and then concentrated on the weak links in the arguments of more extreme writers like Rudi Blesh, who were easy targets. What followed, however, was of greater substance. The jazz funeral was not exclusive to New Orleans, as historians and novelists who were preoccupied with "the colorful sociological roots of the music" had contended: "It would be more accurate to estimate that rhythmic funerals were taking place, some years before the turn of the century, all over the South, and, indeed, wherever there was a substantial Negro population."[81]

Was this merely a return to Wilder Hobson's essentialist musings in 1939? Far from it, for Feather had an informant in the Baltimore-born pianist Eubie Blake (1883–1983), who placed such events in Baltimore as early as the late 1880s: "Joe Blow would die, and maybe he belonged to some society, so they would get the money together and have a band for his funeral." Blake described the funeral musicians as nonreaders playing ragtime tunes (specifically mentioning "A Bunch of Blackberries," which in fact was not published until 1899) in an exuberant fashion: "Those trombone slides would be going like crazy. My mother said that nothing but low people followed the parades, and she used to whip me because we played ragtime coming back from the graveyard."[82] Similar testimony about early jazzmen came from W. C. Handy and Willie "The Lion" Smith (1897–1973), with the latter responding to Feather's query about jazz being born in New Orleans as follows: "It's the writers. If you don't think I know what I'm talking about, just look in those books these fellows have written, and see guys like Danny Barker and all of them talking about the bands on the Mississippi riverboats. Man, they've got riverboats all over, right here in Haverstraw, New York. Ever since I can remember, there's been jazz played."[83] These and other comments from sage musicians denied New Orleans' special place in jazz history, leading Feather to conclude that "jazz simply was born in the United States of America."[84]

Yet Feather had left one stone unturned. All of the non–New Orleans musicians recalled as "hot" players by Blake, Handy, Smith, and others were discussed as individuals. Nowhere was there any indication that alternative *styles of interaction* had occurred in the various locations referred to by the informants. Despite the references to "faking" and a diverse assortment of trumpet players and pianists especially, specific clues as to how these early musicians interacted in a band situation were entirely lacking. Nothing resembling the equivalent of New Orleans–style collective improvisation was ever mentioned; what Feather had overlooked in the writings of the traditionalists, and what he had failed to inquire about in conducting his research among the old-timers, was the extremely important issue of how the New Orleans men played *together*. This was the supreme lesson that Bill Russell had learned from Bunk Johnson, and it was a matter of *attitude* as much as mechanics. In the final analysis, New Orleans style was a way of *living* that manifested itself musically in the "City That Care Forgot," and the cooperative approach to performance that evolved there reflected not only the distinctive characteristics of the environment and its people but also, more importantly, the coping mechanisms that allowed such diversity to unify, survive, and flourish in a hazardous location.

In coping with multiple environments over time, New Orleans musicians became masters of adaptation. It was, after all, New Orleans bands that had created an atmosphere of sensation in Chicago and New York during World War I, giving Americans outside of the Crescent City their first sustained taste of jazz, surpassed only by two other New Orleans groups, King Oliver's Creole Jazz Band and the New Orleans Rhythm Kings, with consolidation of those gains in Chicago soon after. Why had so many "hot" record collectors responded intuitively to the early records by New Orleans artists and their disciples well before the establishment of jazz criticism and history, which ultimately suggested that they should do so? And what was the motivation that impelled the collector-historians to spend countless hours documenting the early history of jazz without the slightest hope of financial remuneration? These are questions that Feather left unanswered, but had he been inclined to explore them, he might have seen fit to judge his opponents, and the music they loved, a little less harshly. Clearly, there was something special about the musicians who came from New Orleans. The answer to the riddle of New Orleans style, the secret of its success as a "good-time" music, was the way in which it brought people together, male and female, young and old, blue-collar and white-collar, writer and reader, musician and collector. Liberty, equality, fraternity, and *fun* were the hallmarks of the New Orleans style, which is precisely what had inspired such notable teamwork among "hot" record collectors in the first place. In assessing the impact of "hot" collecting, the publication of *Jazzmen,* the New Orleans revival, and the subsequent schisms within the jazz community, one can readily appreciate that it was not so much the changes in the music as the intellectualization of its reception that imperiled those values in the 1940s.

In reflecting upon the consequences of jazz purism in the 1940s, it is also clear that it served to strengthen the perception of jazz as illustrative of the profound contributions of African Americans to vernacular culture, an idea that was never taken seriously in the cultural mainstream until jazz became recognized as an art music in the 1930s. This was a major accomplishment, necessitating new perspectives involving the investigation of the social and aesthetic implications of black music for American vernacular culture. Yet, in espousing standards of authenticity based on race alone, some "hot" record collectors failed to fully grasp the ways in which the music had cut across racial, ethnic, class, and gender boundaries in impelling young Americans to become advocates for jazz. From its earliest days in New Orleans, for those who were receptive to its message, jazz opened up hopeful possibilities for collaboration, both on and off of the bandstand. One of Sidney Bechet's white students, Bob Wilber, lived with his teacher in Brooklyn in the 1940s and got a "hands-on" education that transcended purely musical considerations, folding him into a tradition that had been worked out years before and thousands of miles away. Because of their flexible attitudes about the tradition, black New Orleans musicians solicited sincere converts of any race—provided they had the desire to *play*. While Rudi Blesh used Wilber to theorize that New Orleans style was ultimately "modern" and susceptible to progress, Wilber was more concerned with learning how to live well in order to play the best music possible, with feeling. Like Sidney had taught him—it was supposed to be "good-time" music, good for the soul.

During the 1940s, anachronistic categories such as "folk," "art," and "popular" no longer adequately described contemporary conditions: jazz was a folk-derived urban music, recognized as an art form, which competed in the popular music market. Musicians such as Bechet and Parker realized this and sought to balance commerce and art, but ideologies celebrating "artistic" or "folk" purity placed theory between the musicians and those who sought to represent them, making communication difficult. By 1950, the jazz world had lost the certainty of consensus that had informed *Jazzmen* a decade earlier. Jazz purism had given way to a relativistic universe in which aesthetics and historiography reflected stylistic pluralism, yet not everyone could adapt to it. Bill Russell never gave up the belief that New Orleans style was the only "true" jazz, a viewpoint that inspired him to make numerous unmediated recordings of Bunk, Wooden Joe Nicholas, and Kid Shots Madison in New Orleans, thus preserving a music that held little interest for the record industry and would otherwise have been lost. In addition, his oral histories with pioneer jazz musicians for Tulane University from 1958 to 1962 reveal a level of selfless advocacy on their behalf that attests to his sincerity. His informants respected him because he arrived with an appreciation of who they were, which is why the interviews are so valuable: they spoke from the heart as if to one of their own.

But most of the "hot" collectors learned to move on. Charles Edward Smith became an advocate for Thelonious Monk (1917–1982) and Charles Mingus (1922–1979), and John Hammond expanded his horizons to include Bob Dylan and Bruce Springsteen, whom he signed to Columbia. George Avakian launched the career of Johnny Mathis with Columbia and continued his abiding dedication to Louis Armstrong and the Duke. In his nostalgic retrospectives for the *Record Changer* in 1948, Smith admitted that many of the assumptions on which purism had been based were contradicted by subsequent research and that, in their eagerness to protect their musical heroes from the contaminating influences of commercialism, purists had often failed to grasp the desire of musicians to play whatever appealed to them. As Ertegun had warned in 1947, intellectualizing the music could take the fun out of it, negating its raison d'être. Nesuhi went on to become a successful entrepreneur of rhythm and blues and jazz with Atlantic Records, producing records for John Coltrane (1926–1967), Charles Mingus, and Ornette Coleman (1930–), and was the man responsible for the Modern Jazz Quartet's success. Even Rudi Blesh eventually outgrew his bête noire role within the jazz community and, together with Harriet Janis, turned to ragtime in 1950. While *Shining Trumpets* is too doctrinaire to be a worthwhile history of jazz, Blesh and Janis's collaboration, *They All Played Ragtime,* became a standard work in the field, opening up new terrain for scholars of American music. Perhaps Blesh's duels with Delaunay had done both of them some good. The greatest danger facing historians in the study of American vernacular culture (or anything else, for that matter) is the assumption that one can possess or monopolize the truth. Of course, as Sasha Frere-Jones reminds us, purism is still with us, but it is reassuring to know that it is not an incurable condition.

CHAPTER 7

The City That Care Forgot Remembers:
The Apotheosis of Jazz in New Orleans

The awakening of American jazz scholarship had many important consequences, but its most lasting contribution was the way it changed perceptions
of the music, both at home and abroad. For better or worse, "jazz shrines"
became a thread in the tapestry of Western civilization with the music's establishment as an internationally recognized art form. In the constellation of
jazz sites glorified by the early histories, New Orleans enjoyed a special position as the place of origin, and exploitation of this advantage became inevitable once the music's pedigree had been authenticated. Orleanians contributed little to the process, relying instead on the writings of William
Russell and Charles Edward Smith to inform them that jazz was art.[1] Beginning in the mid-1940s, however, prominent members of society adopted
purist perspectives in a series of organizations designed to preserve and promote New Orleans jazz. Their motivation was a mélange of altruism, mer-
cantilism, and nostalgia. Obviously, bebop had no place in these strategies,
meaning that the proceeds of such initiatives would not be equally distributed throughout the broader jazz community. Still, a jazz infrastructure
could serve as a foundation that might benefit everyone in the long run.

Prior to the importation of *Jazzmen*, the revival, and the jazz schism,
opinions about jazz in New Orleans were subject to the same disagreements
that had disrupted the nation in the 1920s, but with a few local twists. Yet
tracking early public opinion about jazz in New Orleans is difficult because

the news media of the time did their best to ignore it. Nevertheless, the search for commentary on jazz in the years before 1917 tends to focus on newspapers. This is especially problematic, because prior to the success of the ODJB's "Livery Stable Blues," the term *jazz* had no local currency.[2] One must therefore infer from the descriptions given whether the music under consideration might be "jazz"—akin to asking a blind man for directions in a foreign tongue.

Donald E. Winston, whose conclusions regarding the dearth of newspaper reportage from 1890 to 1917 further complicate the situation, conducted one such study in 1966. According to Winston, "Of the five dailies circulated during the early development of jazz . . . not one gave considerable coverage to newer, 'hot' forms of music."[3] Such imperviousness was the result of several factors involving discrimination: New Orleans journalists "reduced the newer forms of music to an ignominious peg on the musical ladder"; avoided coverage of social events in black neighborhoods because "music, whatever the temperature, was often incidental to some shooting or knifing"; and exhibited an "almost total lack of sophisticated knowledge of music regardless of kind."[4] Elitism interfered with accurate reporting of musical events that fell beyond the pale of respectability.

Yet occasionally, oblique references to "unacceptable" forms of music can be found. With regard to a fire that occurred at "Pig Ankle Corners" (a cluster of saloons located at Franklin and Customhouse, in the District), one report noted the following: "Of the three dives at these corners, 'John the Reek's' is probably the most notorious. The lower floor is used as a dance hall, where the negroes commence to congregate at dark, and to the discordant music of the so-called orchestra they indulge in dancing, drinking and carousing until the light of day drives them back to their hovels."[5] More specific as to instrumentation is a 1902 account by a reporter for the *Item:* "The orchestra consisted of a clarinet, a guitar and a bass fiddle. The guitar was picked by a bullet-headed negro, with a far away look in his eyes, and a molasses-colored musician that blew the clarinet had to brace his feet against the railing of the players' stand to prevent himself from being hurled backward by the strength of his breath, which at each blast into the instrument had the effect of making the player 'kick' back like a shotgun. . . . The Frolics Hall had an orchestra of four instruments. The clarinet was not among them but the raggy ragtime in which the airs were played amply compensated for the lack of the piping noise-maker. Even the music had an indecent ring about it that was disgusting."[6] Although greater care was taken in describing the physical characteristics of the musicians than was devoted to the music, the references to "raggy ragtime," "kick back" clarinet, and a guitarist with "a far away look in his eyes" suggest that the reporter had stumbled upon a band that would not have been out of place in *Jazzmen.*

The insufficiency of newspaper reports as a source for studying early jazz is also borne out by Don Marquis's *In Search of Buddy Bolden,* which relies primarily on *Soards' New Orleans City Directory,* New Orleans vital-statistics records, and oral history interviews.[7] The only newspaper coverage given to Bolden during his lifetime resulted from an attack on his mother-in-law for which he was arrested, thus confirming Winston's contention that the pattern was "one of frugality based on innocence, apathy, and discrimination."[8] Somewhat surprisingly, Winston's study abandons New Orleans in favor of Chicago in 1917, precisely when the term *jazz* begins to show up in the local press. Two brief quips appearing in the *New Orleans Item* in September 1917, overlooked by Winston, still conform to the pattern he describes. In the first, an anonymous writer recounts the exploits of a fisherman who catches a drum, a bass, a croaker, a fiddler, and a needle fish (with which to string them), before noting that "this is the first evidence that the jazz band craze, now an offense to heaven and earth, is spreading to the water under the earth." A week later, with regard to the wildness and rhythmic imprecision of jazz bands, a writer claims that "the trombone player is expected to have a diploma showing that he was graduated from an insane asylum."[9]

The pièce de résistance of New Orleans editorials, however, is undoubtedly "Jass and Jassism," which appeared in the *Times-Picayune* on June 20, 1918, and was intended as a coup de grâce. The unabashedly elitist opinion of its author showed what could happen when ignorance and apathy gave way to malice aforethought: "Why is the jass music, and, therefore, the jass band? As well ask why is the dime novel or the grease-dripping doughnut? All are manifestations of a low streak in man's tastes that has not yet come out in civilization's wash. Indeed, one might go farther, and say that jass music is the indecent story syncopated and counter-pointed. Like the improper anecdote, also, in its youth, it was listened to blushingly behind closed doors and drawn curtains, but, like all vice, it grew bolder until it dared decent surroundings, and there was tolerated because of its oddity."[10] The tendency identified by Winston had reached full maturity, and if one gauges jazz opinion in New Orleans by the views of newspaper editors alone, "Jass and Jassism" provides a very negative judgment.

Fortunately, newspapers have more to offer than editorial opinion, and the public reaction to this indictment indicated mixed sentiments throughout the community, as revealed in the "Letters to the Editor" column of the *Times-Picayune.* "W. T. N." was a staunch defender of jazz, portraying it as "the typical American music—the true music of the hustler—filled with the spirit and bustle of American life." He argued that life would be dull without music, adding, "Jazz has come to stay." Jazz offered "color, passion, savage rhythm" to Americans who needed more than "contemplation and repose." It was valuable because it was so stimulating: "The invigorating music of a good jazz band inspires and that, in part, accounts for its success."[11] Others championed the cause of tolerance, without specifically approving jazz. "Fair Play" accused the editor of "profound shallowness":

> I am no defender of jass, but I think you should recognize it for what it is—a style of playing. . . . Jass may better be compared to the daring style in skirts, which are departures from what was proper a few years ago, and sometimes display things not beautiful. . . . You hint that rhythm can almost be dispensed with. . . . Without structure and pulsation there is no life; human throbbing is necessary even in the classical, otherwise there is no appeal to emotion, and without emotion it becomes nothing. . . . Jass music may call to the sensual in some people, but I prefer to consider it merely the same appeal that makes men want to march, or dance.[12]

From "Encore" came dissatisfaction with the "holier-than-thou" attitude of the *Times-Picayune,* and "M. C." noted that "ignoramuses and giants may acquire tastes, but music has come down through the civilized centuries as something more than an acquired taste, and we don't study, inherit, work on, or compose 'tastes,' but we do with art."[13] Public opinion was thus divided on the question of jazz but differed markedly from the editorial commentary in that it did not call for its extinction. Most of the Orleanians who responded to the editorial seemed to be willing to give the new music a chance to develop, even if they did not personally care for it.

Advertisements in the *Times-Picayune* reflect the positive public response to release of the ODJB's "Livery Stable Blues," which was greeted as a civic accomplishment: "Here is positively the greatest dance record ever issued. Made by New Orleans musicians for New Orleans people, it has all the 'swing' and 'pep' and 'spirit' that is so characteristic of the bands whose names are a by-word at New Orleans dances."[14] Obviously, the sales pitch involved some hyperbole, but the translation of mercantile interest into a kind of cultural boosterism remains noteworthy. The recognition that "spirit" mattered in jazz was exceptional for its time, as was the notion that the music was somehow "characteristic" of local vernacular culture.

Locals took pride in the ODJB's success and were influenced by it. In *Wait until Dark: Jazz and the Underworld, 1880–1940*, Ronald L. Morris argues that Italian American nightclub operators encouraged jazz development in New Orleans and elsewhere.[15] Some segments of the population may have viewed this as a threat. On March 13, 1919, the *Times-Picayune* received a letter from one "jazz fan" whose interest was a bit intimidating, although in a pro-jazz way. Giving his return address as "Hell," the "Axe-man" made a proposal that may have actually frightened people into becoming jazz lovers, at least for a night: "Undoubtedly, you Orleanians think of me as a most horrible murderer, which I am, but I could be much worse if I wanted to. . . . Now, to be exact, at 12:15 (earthly time) on next Tuesday night, I am going to pass over New Orleans. In my infinite mercy, I am going to make a little proposition to you people. Here it is: I am very fond of jazz music, and I swear by all the devils in the nether regions that every person shall be spared in whose home a jazz band is in full swing at the time I have just mentioned. If everyone has a jazz band going, well, then, so much the better for you people. One thing is certain and that is that some of those people who do not jazz it on Tuesday night (if there is any) will get the axe."[16]

This letter coincided with the gruesome murders of a number of Italian grocers throughout the city, so it was not interpreted as a hoax. According to the authors of *Gumbo Ya-Ya*, who recounted the aftermath of the Axe-man's threat, "Cafes all over town were jammed. Friends and neighbors gathered in homes to 'jazz it up.' Midnight found the city alive with the 'canned music' of the period—inner-player pianos and phonographs. In the levee and Negro districts banjos, guitars and mandolins strummed the jazziest kind of jazz. . . . Not a single attack occurred that night."[17] Given the breadth of opinion, ranging from "Jass and Jassism" to the Axe-man, any attempt to characterize reactions to jazz as uniformly positive or negative is counterproductive.

Like most Americans of their day, Orleanians did not agree on how best to cope with change. Unlike most of their compatriots, however, they held a personal stake in the outcome of the debate.

While the Axe-man was apparently sharpening the tool of his trade, the *New Orleans Item* carried a feature under the banner "Orleans' Product: Stale Bread's Fiddle Gave Jazz to the World," defending the city's claim to be the birthplace of jazz. In the article, theatrical impresario Joseph K. Gorham recounted how he had "discovered" Tom Brown's Orchestra early in 1915 and arranged for them to play at Lamb's Café in Chicago.[18] The writer could not resist a certain sarcasm in describing the jazz phenomenon, but his intent to claim it as a local product was clear: "Originating in New Orleans, [it] has aggravated the feet and fingers of America into a shimmying, tickle-toeing, snapping delirium and now is upsetting the swaying equilibrium of the European dance."[19] According to Gorham, the "first and best" jazz had come from New Orleans.[20] New Orleans musicians had less education but more inspiration: "Imitators of the New Orleans boys were springing up. Largely they were educated musicians and while they imitated, to my mind, they have never been able to achieve the effects obtained by players who can't read a note of music."[21] Jazz was important because it was "all the rage," and young people were discovering that it was more fun to dance to it than to judge it. During and after World War I, jazz bands began to show up in the homes and gathering places of the "better sort" of people, transcending to some extent long-standing associations in the public mind with dens of iniquity, poverty, and bad taste.

William "Bébé" Ridgley (1882–1961), the trombonist with the Original Tuxedo Jazz Orchestra, recounted how his band had achieved social acceptance in an interview with William Russell in 1959:

> Ridgley got himself a band headquarters on Howard Avenue, between Dryades and Baronne Streets. He was running a pressing shop and a shoe-black stand. That was their headquarters, and from then on they began to grow faster. In working there, Bébé got to know a white gentleman named Sim Black who was Scoutmaster for Boy Scout Troop 13. He suggested that they wear black tuxedos, derby hats, and white shirts. It was just about time for the debutante season to open up. The late Henry Zeno was playing drums for Ridgley, and he took it upon himself to find the

tuxedo suits. He found them at a tailor shop. They cost the band members $15.00 apiece. From then on "our band just went on like a blaze of fire."[22]

The Tuxedo had worked for white audiences in the District, but after World War I its clientele began to change for the better: "Mr. Black was a big help to them. During his vacation, the band went down to Kentwood and spent the day in the swamps with Mr. Black's Boy Scout troop. When they came back to New Orleans, they played a dance at the house of each of the boys." The Tuxedo was popular at the New Orleans Country Club, the Southern Yacht Club, the St. Charles Hotel, and La Louisiane Restaurant. According to Ridgley, his band "played all the big dances, all the school dances at Tulane and Loyola, and practically everything they could."[23] The Tuxedo also worked the better black dance palaces, such as the Pythian Temple Roof Garden and the Pelican, "where they had the privilege of whipping every band in the city." Great care was taken to ensure that band members conducted themselves in an appropriate manner: "Bébé kept his band on the spot all the time, didn't allow his members to drink until after the dance or at lunch, and no one could smoke, no one could leave their seat till intermission time. Ridgley thinks that this helped to build them up."[24] Other venues included the prestigious Boston Club, "most of all the big white parties and Carnival Balls," and Dr. J. Phares O'Kelley's Twelfth Night Revelers at the Athenaeum. When Ridgley left the Original Tuxedo Orchestra to form a new band in 1925, he was making $25 a night; in the District his usual pay had been $1.50, plus tips. In other words, black jazzmen in New Orleans could rise above not only the stigma of association with vice and poverty but also the material conditions that accompanied it, precisely because of the opportunities that the social acceptance of jazz provided.

The views of the young men and women who attended these events were gathered in May 1958 by Haywood H. Hillyer III, in taped interviews that illuminate opinion from the other side of the bandstand. Mrs. Mary Lucy Hamill O'Kelley recalled that she disliked jazz but found it to be good dance music. Her favorite band for debutante parties and balls was Armand Piron's New Orleans Orchestra, a Creole "society" band that incorporated jazz influences without engaging in much actual improvisation.[25] Elizabeth O'Kelley Kerrigan preferred the bands of Oscar "Papa" Celestin but had

Piron for her debut. She also had fond recollections of the Original Tuxedo Jazz Orchestra, when Ridgley was leading it. Jack Kerrigan, who entered Tulane University in 1918, remembered the popularity of jazz at the subscription dances held on campus at the gymnasium. He felt that Piron had the best jazz band and often stopped by Tranchina's after parties at the Southern Yacht Club to hear him. Kerrigan was also a devotee of Johnny DeDroit and his New Orleans Jazz Orchestra, at Kolbs Restaurant on St. Charles Avenue, and estimated that between 1920 and 1927 jazz bands were used for debutante parties 98 percent of the time. Edmond Souchon spoke from the vantage of a musician as well as a partygoer. He believed that while jazz had emerged from "the lower classes," the middle class accepted it because it was exciting dance music. Hillyer's informants thus agreed that jazz was not looked upon as an art form in the 1920s and that its popularity derived from its functional value in social situations.[26]

Further evidence of the growing social acceptability of jazz comes from the experiences of middle-class youths who became jazz musicians. The New Orleans Owls are a case in point. Although black jazz bands were probably the most popular at parties, white bands like the Owls could rise from amateur to professional status on the basis of social connections. According to Wilfred "Benjie" White, the motivation for forming the band was as much social as it was musical: when they held rehearsals at the West End Roof Garden, half the band danced and socialized with sorority girls while the others played, and then they switched. As White related, "the original Owls had no intention of becoming professional musicians but just sort of drifted into playing for a living."[27] The Owls developed a sound that derived from bands they heard at social events and the big bands that broadcast on radio from cities in the Northeast. In addition to working at the Roosevelt Hotel, the band played many of the same places mentioned by Hillyer's informants and held similar views about how jazz was perceived by young professionals. White felt that "the music they played [wasn't] much for just listening, but it was fine for dancing."[28] By 1928, most of the band's members had moved on to other careers, in White's case because his fiancée "decided he would not play music if he married her."[29] After two years at Tulane's College of Commerce, he became a jeweler. Pianist Siegfried Christensen (1907–1980) went on to practice law. The banjo player, Rene Gelpi (1904–1980), returned to school and became an architect, and the band's original pianist, Edward

"Mose" Ferrer (1894–1966), took Holy Orders. Having had their fun, the Owls relinquished the jazz life to enjoy the fruits of middle-class existence. Yet in White's case, he did so with regret, having "enjoyed playing more than anything he has ever done in his life."[30]

John Wigginton Hyman was another well-born Orleanian who became a professional jazz musician. His grandfather, William Bryan Hyman, was chief justice of the Louisiana Supreme Court and a relative of William Jennings Bryan. Although his mother opposed his desire to play the cornet because "professional artists starved to death in attics," she eventually relented, with the encouragement of his father, and before long he was sneaking off to perform on street corners with young Joseph "Wingy" Manone, a classmate at La Salle School.[31] At age twelve, he relocated to Ocean Springs, Mississippi, when his father bought a farm there to escape the city after some unfortunate business deals. In Ocean Springs, he "played violin with every hillbilly band that would let me sit in, way back in the woods."[32] After the death of his father, he returned to New Orleans, and while living on Audubon Boulevard he renewed his musical contacts, which included several future members of the Owls, often playing parties "just for the fun of it."

Because of his proximity to Tulane University, he attended dances at the gymnasium, where he first heard Joe Oliver: "When I was 16 I heard Joe Oliver's band for the first time at a script dance I had stumbled on. . . . I just could not believe my ears. It was something I had never heard before, and it was very, very great. . . . At those Gym dances the boys would make a buffer zone around the band so the girls could not hear what Happy Bolton was singing—and he was singing the dirtiest songs ever! Bill Kleppinger, Monk Smith and I would stand before Joe's band all night and listen and observe, while the other boys were dancing with the pretty girls."[33] Soon the urge to jazz became irresistible: "In 1917 the Original Dixieland Jazz Band released their first record on Victor. This was too much for the Invincibles and we began to yearn to play 'real jazz.' Monk got a saxophone. We added Earl Crumb on drums (he had observed Happy Bolton very closely), Harry Farrar on piano, Frank Farrar on violin, and I played cornet. This was really the beginning of what turned out to be the New Orleans Owls band."[34] Yet he later declined an offer to join the Owls permanently because "I couldn't keep my job, attend Law School classes at Loyola University and play in a band."[35] A job as a reporter for the *New Orleans Item* in 1919 led to a change in career strategy, and Hyman transferred to Tulane to take classes that would prepare him for the newspaper business. Unfortunately, due to his academic schedule, he kept getting scooped by the competition and had to drop out of school after being fired. He later pursued journalism in New York, following a brief stint in the merchant marine, encountering an editor who advised him to search within "for something that had flowed out of me uncontrollably since childhood." When he returned to New Orleans in 1925, he knew it would be to play music.

His break came when he was asked to replace Emmett Hardy (1903–1925), who was dying of tuberculosis, in Norman Brownlee's (1896–1967) band. While he was with Brownlee, he noted the reception accorded the New Orleans Rhythm Kings upon their return from Chicago: "New Orleans could care less for the second most famous band in jazz history. They could get no jobs here but picked up a few jobs on the Gulf Coast and it was not long before they fell apart."[36] Orleanians took their jazz musicians very much for granted, and whatever notoriety accrued to "home boys" abroad counted for little in the City That Forgot to Care. This lesson was reiterated when Hyman put together a band of his own: "I put together the best band in the city and we made a record in 1927, the best record I ever made. No one ever paid any attention to it. . . . New Orleans is certainly a discouraging city for jazz musicians. My mother was right."[37] He continued as a jazz musician for a number of years, working with Peck Kelley (1898–1980), Tony Parenti (1900–1972), and Ellis Stratakos (1904–1961), before returning to Loyola to earn a music degree that enabled him to teach. He organized bands in elementary schools throughout the city, leading to the establishment of the State Band and Orchestra School, which handled three hundred students a week, including future stars Pete Fountain (1930–) and George Girard (1930–1957), keeping him so busy that he failed to complete his music degree. Eventually he found the strain of running a music school, working for the school board, and attending classes at Loyola overwhelming, so he closed the school, entered Tulane again to study mechanical drawing, and settled into a comfortable life teaching in area high schools in the early 1940s. When he emerged as a jazz musician again during the revival, he changed his name to Johnny Wiggs in order to avoid conflict with the school board.[38]

Hyman's adventures as a jazz musician in New Orleans, like those of the

Owls, illustrate the limits of social acceptance in the Crescent City. Because jazz was appreciated for its functional value as dance music, it was subject to the whims of fashion without recourse to the more purely aesthetic considerations of the "hot" record collectors. The eclipse of New Orleans style, which coincided with the rise of the big bands nationally after 1927, was taken in stride by the dancers, but its effects on jazz musicians were pronounced. As Benjie White admitted, over time his band became increasingly reliant on written arrangements and "began losing its individuality."[39] When placed in the context of changing fashion, the dissolution of the Owls and the lack of interest in Hyman's recordings become part of a larger tableau in which grand aggregations like Paul Whiteman's or Duke Ellington's were dominant. Many local groups sought to follow the national trend. By 1928, Celestin's Original Tuxedo Jazz Band had swelled from seven to fourteen pieces, and Cecil Thornton, an alto-sax player from St. Louis, had been commissioned to do arrangements.[40]

Before long, the belief that New Orleans–style jazz was special was reduced to its bedrock of support—the musicians themselves. Yet for those who cared to notice, these stalwarts were not down for the count. Especially on their home turf, they could be extremely aggressive in their advocacy of "authentic" jazz, as Paul Whiteman found out when he brought his huge concert orchestra to the St. Charles Theatre on October 28, 1928. Bix Beiderbecke and Frank Trumbauer (1901–1956) were with Whiteman, and the musicians who attended the matinee performance knew who they were and expected something special from them—not New Orleans style, but something "real" just the same. Whiteman was a successful entrepreneur, and he was a master at winning over New York critics. His vow to "make a lady out of jazz" had won almost universal acclaim. Unfortunately, the accolades of the pundits did little to prepare him for a night in New Orleans.

According to drummer Arthur "Monk" Hazel (1903–1968), words were exchanged in the alley outside the St. Charles Theatre during intermission:

Well, the whole first thing, they never played one note of jazz. I was delegated to go talk to Whiteman about getting them to play some jazz. I walked up to him, and I said, "Paul, we got to have some jazz." He looked at me—he and Johnny DeDroit were talking there, and they looked at me like that, you know—and I said, "Now I mean it. We're going to have some jazz or else." So he says, "Well, we don't have anything coming up. The only thing we've got, we're going to play things like 'Metropolis' and 'American in Paris.'" It was a big band, a concert band. So I told him, "Uh-uh, man, we gotta have some jazz." So he looked at Johnny, and he looked at me. Johnny said, "Well, the guys are all—man, there's two hundred jazzmen out there! They've come in here to hear Bix and Trumbauer." So he says, "Well, I'll see what I can do."

When the performance resumed, Whiteman addressed the audience: "'Ladies and gentlemen, I have had a lot of requests and threats for Bix and Trumbauer.' And he turns around, and then he looks at them and said, 'Boys, you're on your own,' and he walked off the stage. . . . [Bix and Tram] didn't know what to do. They never had anything like that happen before. First thing you know, Roy Bargy starts vamping 'Singin' the Blues,' so they played. They played 'Singin' the Blues,' and they played 'Melancholy Baby' and a couple of things that Trumbauer played. Everybody was satisfied then."[41] In Hazel's role as ombudsman for local musicians, his "requests and threats" expressed the dissatisfaction they felt about the formalization of their city's music in the hands of outsiders. In making "a lady out of jazz," Whiteman had taken all the fun out of her, and he was getting rich in the process. Well before Charles Edward Smith called attention to "authentic" jazz in *Symposium,* New Orleans musicians were voicing such concerns, but nobody (except Whiteman) heard them. They were too busy trying to find work to write articles, so their purism remained a well-kept secret.

In the spring of 1933, two intrepid newspapermen in New Orleans, one white, the other black, reopened investigation of jazz origins with hopeful intentions. Clarence Orin Blackstone was a transplanted Texan who became a cub reporter at the *Times-Picayune* in 1927. In 1933, he inaugurated a personal project: a magazine dedicated to popular music. The first issue of *Popular Music,* dated March 10, carried the rubric "Leader of First Jazz Band Reviews Rise of New Music." Blackstone had interviewed Nick LaRocca, but he framed the musician's comments in a narrative that was entirely his own. While LaRocca agreed that jazz "first raised its raucous voice" in New Orleans, attempts to garner details were only partially successful: "To LaRocca there is no doubt that New Orleans was the birthplace. He sets no date and he makes no explanations of how it came about. He does not know how long

Negroes had been playing with the weird and unruly monster."[42] LaRocca
was described as "the man who was responsible more than anyone else for its
early acceptance in America and abroad," but he was now "retired, completely out of touch with the modern leaders of the field and even the surviving members of his own outfit." Like many locals, he had become "indiffer-
ent" to jazz.[43] Blackstone's discussion with LaRocca adumbrated many of
the points that later appeared in "hot" collector histories: "A clue to the formative days of that history was supplied in that remark of his that 'you've got
to play with someone who feels as you do.' The birth of jazz, among the Negroes on the plantations of Louisiana and along the wharves of Father Mississippi, was the result of feeling. It was caught up by white musicians who
played on the streets of New Orleans."[44] It was "the prize fight crowd" that
had nurtured LaRocca's first musical enterprises, but "New Orleans hadn't
taken the bunch seriously," so it remained for an outsider—promoter Harry
James—to realize the "furor they might create if transported to new and
more receptive surroundings."[45]

While *Popular Music* highlighted the role of the ODJB in the dissemination of jazz, it placed the origins of the music squarely within the black community. In April 1933, two articles by Edward Belfield Spriggins (1892–1973)
for *Louisiana Weekly,* a black newspaper, provided further support for this
thesis. Under the title "Excavating Local Jazz," Spriggins alluded to local
diffidence as well: "For quite some years now there has been an unusual
amount of discussion concerning the popular form of music commonly called
'jazz.' . . . New Orleans has been either too modest to enter the discussion or
entirely disinterested in the matter."[46] An interview with Willie Cornish had
convinced Spriggins to speak out on jazz origins, leading to the first historical consideration in print of Buddy Bolden's role. Cornish recounted how his
composition of the tune that Jelly Roll Morton later reworked as "Buddy
Bolden's Blues" had been inspired by a night at Odd Fellows Hall when the
heat and humidity combined with certain "foul airs" to create a most inhos-
pitable atmosphere. (The line "let the foul air out," which Morton included
in the lyrics, may also be a reference to Funky Butt Hall, a regular venue for
Bolden that served as a church during the day.) Bolden created a sensation
within the black community at dance halls and at Johnson and Lincoln
parks, propelling him to local celebrity. "Mention is made of Lincoln Park,"
wrote Spriggins, "because it probably made a large contribution to New Or-

leans jazz music. It was here that several other popular bands of the city rendered music for balls, picnics, banquets, and other like affairs."[47]

Spriggins was interested in the preponderance of black jazz bands, and in "Excavating Jazz," he elaborated on this theme. His focus was on the neglected musicians who had launched jazz: "While many lay claim to taking part in the birth of things in the quaint city of New Orleans, some originators are either too modest or they fail to realize that they have made worth while contributions to their chosen fields of endeavor. Such a person is Prof. Arnold Metoyer, one of the city's best cornetists today. It is reliably reported that he was one of the first persons here to play jazz cornet, although today he is unable to play that type of music with any degree of success."[48] Preference was shown for Manuel Perez's Imperial Orchestra, which "was destined to outshine the Bolden band in this free style of music." Spriggins described the Imperial's advantages over Bolden: "While each musician of the group read at sight, all of them put into their scores improvisations that were not written therein and added certain weird sounds that were the fore-runners of modern jazz."[49] Had Rudi Blesh known of this statement, he would undoubtedly have made good use of it! Spriggins's groundbreaking reports were more balanced than those of his "hot" collector contemporaries, but they were submerged in a cultural backwater, remaining hidden until Don Marquis discovered them four decades later.[50]

Blackstone and Spriggins were the first Americans to seriously investigate jazz origins in New Orleans, but they did not follow through. Apparently, Orleanians paid no more attention to local writers on jazz than they did to the music itself, and the task of writing the history of jazz was left to other hands in other places. When "hot" collectors began to descend on the Crescent City in preparation for *Jazzmen* in the late 1930s, they were surprised and dismayed to learn how casually the inhabitants regarded their glorious musical heritage. Charles Edward Smith correctly assessed the situation when he attended Carnival in 1939: "The simple truth of the matter is that the people of New Orleans enjoyed and sustained the music without the music itself getting more than a passing nod from the local guardians of culture. The music was judged by where it was played most. It's an old story now how the trade journals ventured to localize jazz (a year after Storyville closed) and the bigwigs of New Orleans music, who knew their operas but not their four-in-a-bar, utterly disowned it. Through it all the people enjoyed their music and the musical tradition stayed very much alive."[51] New Orleans music was still alive, but it was not entirely well. Most New Orleans jazzmen could not survive on music alone and had to rely on other trades to make ends meet. "No longer," stated Smith, "will the visitor find bands—uptown Negro, Creole Negro, white—at the lake front, at parties, at dances, so many and so varied as to form an unforgettable impression of a city to which music is even more native than Creole cooking."[52] But the collectors were convinced that New Orleans style had sufficient pulse to warrant resuscitation, and the revival was to be the modus operandi, resting as it did on the impact of *Jazzmen*. During the 1940s, the stream of pilgrims to "The Land of Dreams" widened, and accounts of their adventures began to appear in the jazz press with regularity.

Along with coverage of Woody Broun's trip to New Orleans in *HRS Society Rag* in 1940 and the reports of Eugene Williams for the *Record Changer* in 1942, the excursions of Nesuhi Ertegun and Ahmet Ertegun in 1941 exemplify the phenomenon of the "jazz pilgrimage" most effectively. In order to familiarize themselves with the United States, and "with the strong desire to hear good jazz wherever that is possible," the two brothers set out in their roadster on a cross-country trip that took them to San Francisco, Los Angeles, Houston, and New Orleans.[53] Upon arrival in New Orleans, they exhibited the kind of reaction often attributed to Americans in Paris: "And then, New Orleans! For a whole day, we walked up and down the historic streets. To us, it was like an open-air museum."[54] Monk Hazel was their guide, and they "found him to be one of the most intelligent, kind and friendly musicians we had ever met."[55]

As they explored the town with their diminutive Virgil at their side, they were beguiled by the stories he told of days gone by, especially his fond remembrances of Emmett Hardy. He advised the pair to hear Kid Rena and Raymond Burke, a clarinetist who was completely unknown to them. They found Rena playing with a big, "Luncefordish jump band," and he seemed "visibly unhappy in that band; the music became quickly unbearable, and we left to hear Raymond Burke." They did not know what to expect but followed Hazel's suggestion to mention Johnny Dodds:

> We found him in an odd-looking place with a long bar and a few women sitting around it, and an adjoining room where the bandstand was. Here

there were four or five customers. We told Burke that Monk Hazel had sent us and we liked Johnny Dodds. That seemed to make him happy; at once we were friends. He tried to get the band together. A few of its members had disappeared, but still they started to play. Burke at first played very softly, facing the wall. After a few Dixieland tunes the band attacked a slow blues. Burke gradually turned toward us and really got going. The blues must have lasted at least a half-hour. The other musicians left the bandstand one by one and soon only Burke was left, accompanied by drums and piano. All I can say is that Raymond Burke took chorus after chorus of the most extraordinarily poignant blues. Here was a musician, virtually unknown, who is surely one of the important white clarinetists in the history of jazz.[56]

During the performance, Nesuhi became embroiled in a dispute with a stranger at the next table over the relative merits of Bix Beiderbecke and Louis Armstrong. To demonstrate his point on Bix, the stranger grabbed a nearby horn and illustrated with "some very commendable trumpet playing." Nesuhi was awed: "He really had me beat. Afterwards I asked Burke who that character was. 'Oh, just an amateur,' he replied."[57] Without crossing any borders, they had traveled to a very strange land indeed, and as they headed for home the next day, the adage "Land of Dreams" must have seemed very real to them.

Not all jazz pilgrims who came to New Orleans were purists. In 1943, Harry Lim, a Javanese swing enthusiast who worked for Keynote Records, made the trip and reported back to the readers of *Metronome*. Lim made no pretense of his feelings about jazz purism and the conditions prevailing in the Crescent City:

We're all familiar with the great men who gave the city its legendary fame. We also know that today this tourist conscious town has lost almost all of its former glory to the average modern music fan, except the certain fascination it might still hold for a few record collectors who, complete with portable recording equipment, let their "research consciousness" run wild. However, I'm afraid from the musician's standpoint one of the guys down there summed the situation up very aptly with the following: In this man's town you can get high for a quarter, but you just try and get that quarter.[58]

Lim was concerned with "Orleans as it is today," and after noting the "low union scales and other unfavorable working conditions in the French Quarter," he related his surprise at finding "some good Dixieland . . . real authentic Dixieland, because all the boys down there have that 'drop' which you very seldom get in this particular kind of music here in the east."[59]

His enthusiasm stemmed from hearing "a younger white generation of musicians," including trombonist Julian Laine (1907–1957), clarinetist Leonard "Boojie" Centobie (1915–1981), drummer Johnny Castaing (1912–1972), and especially Monk Hazel. Lim explained the absence of a new generation of gifted black players as due to "unprofitable working conditions," and he was unimpressed with the veterans celebrated by the purists: "The older colored boys like Picou, 'Big Eye' Louis and all the other legendary jazz names whose accomplishments are sprinkled all over the early history of jazz and who have decided to stick it out in their home town, have lost all touch with the music as we know it today. You might get some of these men together for a little private session, but the result would only be interesting from an historical standpoint."[60] Ironically, purists and modernists had both found signs of musical vitality in New Orleans and agreed that meeting Monk Hazel was a landmark occasion. Despite their problems, New Orleans musicians retained a creativity and distinctiveness that was immediately recognizable. Like the cuisine, they had a flavor all their own. According to Lim, they played Dixieland jazz "as it really should be played," and if that was not enough for the intrepid jazz pilgrim, other attractions justified a trip to the city: "The food you're going to look for in the first place is bound to be excellent, despite wartime conditions, and even if you won't be able to find the guy who 'taught Louis' you can always send a box of those Pralines to anybody you are trying to impress."[61]

It was clear from the report that Harry Lim enjoyed his sojourn as a jazz tourist, and his depiction of New Orleans as a "tourist conscious town" cut to the heart of the matter. During the war years, an influx of servicemen and transient workers was transforming the city. New Orleans was an army port of embarkation, with attendant navy and coast guard bases, and its population swelled rapidly. In addition, wartime demand for goods expanded manufacturing, attracting workers from upstate Louisiana, Texas, Arkansas, Alabama, and Mississippi. Inflation drove prices upward, making the business of accommodating newcomers more lucrative. While tourism had always been a concomitant of life in the Crescent City, World War II expanded its dimensions in new and unexpected ways. Some jazz pilgrims, in other words, did not come by choice.

Like John Hammond, Ken Hulsizer (1909–1985) was stationed in New Orleans during the war. He wrote of his experiences in "New Orleans in Wartime," published in the English *Jazz Review* in 1945. Perhaps as a result of the circumstances that brought him to the city, or because he was there long enough to see what was happening, Hulsizer displayed little of the enthusiasm that informed Ertegun's and Lim's accounts. He had first come to town in 1933, and the contrasts he witnessed in wartime disturbed him greatly. He was a veteran visitor, and his complaints were many:

> The result of a superimposition of the Armed Forces and industrial workers on a city already crowded and deficient in housing has been to make New Orleans one of the most over-crowded and uncomfortable cities in the country. The rise in prices has been ghastly and the goods and services received for these prices deplorable. In 1933 I could stay in a hotel for a dollar a day. I could get scrambled eggs, grits, biscuits and a cup of good coffee for 5 cents in a clean well-lighted restaurant. In 1941 the same room would cost me $2 and the breakfast 30 cents. In 1944 the room would cost me $5 and the breakfast 75 cents. The hotel and restaurant service would both be poorer than in previous years.[62]

Locals were "reaping a golden harvest . . . as far as the possibilities of extracting money from fools are concerned."[63]

Although Hulsizer described the scene as "Mardi Gras all year long," the benefits for jazz musicians were apparently negligible. "With hordes of people fighting to buy a drink, any kind of drink," Hulsizer stated, "there is no need for the come-on of music as entertainment."[64] Hillbilly bands appealing to transplanted Southern workers and soldiers were becoming prevalent in the French Quarter, reflecting shifting wartime demographics. The new arrivals were placing many of the cherished traditions of New Orleans, including jazz, in jeopardy:

> The attitude of these newcomers toward the Negro is different from that of the native New Orleanians. I don't believe the Negro will be encouraged in any music but church music by these people. The population of

New Orleans used to be 90 per cent Catholic. The newcomers are Protestant. . . . To them religion is not just a Sunday formality, it is a spiritual philosophy that affects their daily lives. This change in religion is sure to affect New Orleans. Never again, I fear, will New Orleans be the pleasantly sinful place it once was.[65]

Nevertheless, the city continued to lure jazz pilgrims, and as Hulsizer noted, "a half dozen came and went while I was there." Unwilling to join the party, he spent most of his time in cozy meetings with Hammond and Orin Blackstone, swapping tales of great collecting "finds" and discussing the inner workings of the music business. His opinion of Blackstone was that "he has done more for New Orleans music and probably for Jazz than any other one man in the country and has seldom been given credit or compensation."[66] Yet even "Blackie" could not reverse the trend: Hulsizer "heard no young musicians playing in traditional fashion here in New Orleans," and the prospects for revival looked dim. He ended his report on a note of despair: "Jazz was born in New Orleans but it doesn't live there any more."[67]

While the New Orleans revival was raging elsewhere, at home the music had reached the nadir. Yet had Hulsizer spent more time in the French Quarter, perhaps to visit a soothsayer to have his tea leaves read, he might have qualified his dire forebodings. Bolstered by the awakening of American jazz scholarship represented in *Jazzmen,* and now concerned about the future of the music they had taken for granted, prominent members of New Orleans society had begun to organize in defense of jazz. The resulting apotheosis of New Orleans style at home was accomplished through the establishment of foundations and clubs, museums and archives, and purist concert halls that catered to a select tourist trade. The creation of a jazz preservation infrastructure took almost two decades to achieve, but the results were noteworthy. New Orleans would re-create itself as the bastion of jazz purism, treating it as a point of civic honor. Purist "missionaries" from around the world came to lend a hand, eager for the chance to "go native." Some, like Bill Russell, Larry Borenstein (1919–1981), and Allan Jaffe (1935–1987), became residents; others returned home to spread the word. But it was the core of prominent Orleanians who provided the enterprise with its momentum and its muscle. If there was an elitist strain within the movement, it was at least dedicated to the cause of the underdog: for the scores of venerable jazzmen whose careers had dwindled since the 1920s, the apotheosis of New Orleans style meant a new lease on life.

First steps often falter, and the initial attempt to provide a support organization for New Orleans jazz was not entirely successful. The National Jazz Foundation (NJF) was established in May 1944 to preserve and promote the city's special musical heritage, and its aims were plainly stated in a circular that was sent to interested parties:

> The Foundation maintains various files on the history of jazz music, on the "oldtimers" in jazz and on their modern counterparts. Through its influence it seeks to maintain a lively interest in jazz music; it seeks to inspire new compositions, and it endeavors to preserve upon phonograph records outstanding examples of music of this type. Recently RCA Victor produced an album of Hot Jazz Recordings by Willie "Bunk" Johnson under the Foundation's sponsorship. . . . One of the primary goals of the Foundation is to establish a jazz museum in New Orleans. The building, tentatively selected (Mahogany Hall on Basin Street), will become the world's depository of any and all information pertaining to jazz and its creators. It will also serve as a clearing-house of such data. It will house the largest collection of jazz records and pictures of jazzmen of yesterday and today.[68]

The Foundation sponsored concerts as a fund-raising device, organized high school competitions, and arranged for jazz bands to visit local hospitals as a morale booster. With the exception of Mrs. Pat Spiess, a paid secretary, all its officers and board members were volunteers, "drawn from business men, members of the press, bankers, doctors, music teachers, record collectors, etc."[69] Jazz was now regarded "as one of the most vital American art forms," appreciated broadly: "The Foundation is non-partisan. Schools of thought from Bolden to Ellington are impartially represented among its officers and members . . . all united in a common purpose . . . in which there can be no barriers of geography, race, or musical style."[70] While New Orleans–style jazz was thus emphasized by the NJF, it was not used as a standard of orthodoxy. After all, the purpose of the organization was to raise money for the support of jazz—adopting a hard line that could alienate potential donors would have been foolhardy. Yet, as events proved, the ecumenical approach was itself not without risk.

The NJF included some of the city's "best" citizens. Edmond Souchon, a founder, was an obstetrician who came from a long line of surgeons and served on the board of directors of the Pan American Life Insurance Company. As a student at Tulane, he had helped to organize subscription dances with Ory, Oliver, and Armstrong, and he heard them again in Chicago while he was attending medical school at Loyola University in the 1920s.[71] President and cofounder Merlin "Scoop" Kennedy (1894–1982) was a newspaperman with the *New Orleans Item*. Although the NJF was essentially his brainchild, Kennedy became an absentee officer after March 1945, when he left for Europe to serve as field director for the Red Cross. He subsequently used his charm and wit to attract European support for the foundation, sending frequent reports back home for inclusion in *Basin Street,* the NJF newsletter. The treasurer was H. Wilson Arnold (1903–1986), of Weil and Arnold Investment Securities. Vice president Henry Alcus (1902–1986) owned Hinderers' Iron Works, producing the ornate grillwork for which the city is famous. Besides Pat Spiess, who handled the newsletter and secretarial duties, the first woman to join the foundation was Myra Menville (1912–1979). Née Myra Eulalie Semmes Walmsley Loker, Mrs. Menville had a family tree that included a Confederate senator, a Rex ("King of Carnival"), a president of the Boston Club (the city's most exclusive society enclave), and a mayor of New Orleans. Among the collectors in the NJF were Orin Blackstone, then city editor of the *Times-Picayune,* and George Blanchin (1905–1980), a clerk whose father had been first violin at the old French Opera. In sum, the membership of the National Jazz Foundation, while not exclusively "blue-blooded," was composed largely of socially prominent individuals, whose very interest in supporting jazz gave the cause an air of respectability.[72]

Translating respectability into dollars, however, was not easy. An anonymous contributor underwrote the office in the Cotton Exchange Building and Mrs. Spiess's salary, keeping expenses minimal. But the fund-raising concerts, featuring Benny Goodman, Louis Armstrong, and Eddie Condon, carried considerable overhead, and as *Basin Street* reported, "As anyone who has given a jazz concert knows, the profit from this is not too large."[73] In March 1945, two months after an Armstrong concert coinciding with the *Esquire* jazz poll celebration, the NJF had four thousand dollars in the bank but needed fifty thousand dollars to establish the Jazz Museum.[74] By April 1946, the goal had still not been met, so other strategies were considered: "Unaccustomed as we are to making public speeches, we are nevertheless willing to do most anything to further the dear old National Jazz Foundation. We have appeared before such august bodies as the Rotary Club, the Cotton Trade Warehouse Association, the Lion's Club, etc. putting on a program in behalf of jazz. But natch, we mentioned the good work the NJF has been doing locally and otherwise."[75] Unfortunately, such appeals were not enough to accomplish the foundation's ambitious program: after June 1946 *Basin Street* ceased publication, and in April 1947 the organization disbanded, just as one of its most intriguing projects was coming to fruition.

The film *New Orleans,* released in 1947, credits the NJF: "With grateful acknowledgment to an organization whose assistance in the production of this picture was invaluable . . . the National Jazz Foundation Inc, New Orleans." Produced by Jules Levey (1896–1975) and directed by Arthur Lubin (1898–1995), the film is a morality tale about the struggle of jazz, portrayed as the "little art form that could," to gain respect from the classical music establishment.[76] The real stars of the film are the jazz artists whose music and activities are nevertheless subordinate to the main love story between the dashing gambler with a heart of gold, Nick Duquesne, and the perky blonde debutante, Miralee Smith, who harbors a not-so-secret desire to frequent his "ragtime" haunts in Storyville, even though she is preparing for a career in opera. The dissonance between a hackneyed storyline and exciting musical interludes by Louis Armstrong, Barney Bigard, Kid Ory, and Zutty Singleton, among others, with Billie Holiday on vocals (as a singing maid), is rather disconcerting, but the manner in which nuggets of information about jazz origins are inserted into the plot is amusing:

MARILI: Why, they almost make their instruments talk! Where does it come from?

NICK: Work songs, gold coast of West Africa, little Christian churches, river boats . . .

Henri Ferber, the local symphony conductor and another closet habitué at Satchmo's jam sessions, exclaims, "You can't lock up ragtime. . . . It makes me feel very well, but mixed up."

Yet Miralee absorbs meaning and direction in life from the music, especially after Satchmo tells her, "Playin' ragtime is like talkin' from the heart, it doesn't lie." Following the death of Grace (Nick's maudlin former flame), Miralee's mother breaks up the budding romance, the Department of the Navy shuts down Storyville, and everybody heads for Chicago (except Miralee, who becomes an opera sensation in Europe). Nick soon learns that there is more joy and money to be made in promoting jazz than there is in gambling. Fast-forward a few years: Satchmo is on the road with a big band, making big money; Nick has cornered the market on jazz talent, including Woody Herman and his Orchestra; and everything hinges on booking Woody into the Metropolitan Opera House in New York. Thanks to Miralee's good graces and her mother's social clout, everything works out beautifully: the couple is reunited, and jazz is vindicated. In its inclusive combination of talents, stereotypes notwithstanding, *New Orleans* effectively illustrated the NJF's ecumenical vision and educational advocacy, and having a Hollywood movie for publicity was certainly unprecedented for a jazz organization. But the film also shows how trite and anemic such policies could seem in comparison to more militant purist perspectives.

Despite the caliber and earnest efforts of its membership, the National Jazz Foundation generated much publicity but little cash or public support. Compounding other problems, its association with *Esquire*'s 1945 jazz poll caused doubts among purists. John Hyman's experience with the foundation revealed another Achilles heel, from the purist perspective: "There was an organization called the National Jazz Foundation, and I innocently tried to get publicity through these people but I learned that this fine group had no use for local musicians. No, they had to have big names like Benny Goodman, Condon, Louie. They spent thousands of dollars on these bands while the New Orleans musicians stayed buried under the rocks."[77] In attempting to walk the tightrope between purists and modernists, the leaders of the NJF ended up walking the plank instead. Yet despite their inability to accomplish stated aims, they made a very significant contribution to the jazz cause in providing a blueprint for further development. Virtually all of the NJF's objectives were ultimately accomplished by the New Orleans Jazz Club, which relied on a greater "purity" of purpose to achieve them.

The New Orleans Jazz Club (NOJC) was conceived on February 10, 1948—Mardi Gras Day—by a coterie of jazz enthusiasts attending the Zulu parade. Present were John Hyman, Don Perry (1928–2003), Gilbert Erskine (1927–), Al Diket (1911–1987), and Babette Diket (1919–2005), who, according to Hyman, were walking along the parade route because "that was the only way we could hear good jazz."[78] During the festivities, Hyman suggested that an organization formed to "help local musicians" might succeed if they called up their friends who liked jazz, and a meeting was held at Orin Blackstone's New Orleans Record Shop, attracting twenty-five prospective members.[79] After a year or two, the membership began to dwindle, until Hyman decided to enlist the assistance of Myra Menville: "You know, in New Orleans everything that succeeds had got to be social. So we got some socialites in and began to attract attention, and on and on the Club went."[80] Hyman recruited many of the former members of the NJF, including Souchon, Blackstone, Blanchin, Kennedy, and Mrs. Menville, and he instilled within them a purist fervor that focused on local musicians and their welfare.

They were paving the road to Preservation Hall and, ultimately, to the New Orleans Jazz and Heritage Festival. While the NOJC was primarily a social and cultural institution organized for the enjoyment of its members, it also got involved in the lives of New Orleans jazz musicians by providing employment through concerts, festivals, recordings, and other fund drives.[81] Like the NJF, the Jazz Club worked to establish a Jazz Museum, which would symbolize official acceptance of jazz as art. New Orleans jazz musicians would be not only fed but also vindicated as artists. In achieving these ends, the NOJC revealed conflicting opinions on issues of race and aesthetics, reflecting divisions present in the general society. The commitment to purism became intrinsic to the organization, and every attempt was made to maintain a balanced racial posture in hiring musicians and providing coverage in the pages of the *Second Line,* the club's magazine. Prevailing conditions, however, limited black membership in the Jazz Club to out-of-town correspondents for many years. To approach the racial question differently would have threatened the agenda to which the club was committed.

Early meetings were limited to record-listening sessions at Kingsley House, a municipally owned social agency, and at members' homes. Musicians such as George Baquet (1881–1949) were invited to attend the presentations and take part in the discussions, but the closest the club came to presenting a program for public consumption was a Sunday-afternoon radio show on WTPS by Al Diket.[82] The response to Diket's program was sufficiently encouraging to stimulate plans for a concert, and on March 23, 1949, a jazz band led by Johnny Wiggs began the shift toward live performance. According to an account published in the *Second Line* in 1950, the impact was catalytic: "Some time after our first few concerts, New Orleans began to become jazz-minded." The Parisian Room, where many of the early NOJC sessions were held, soon had Sunday-afternoon concerts of its own. The Famous Door, on Bourbon Street, was also thriving, and Papa Celestin brought the Tuxedo out of retirement. In addition, there was "a wonderful coincidence on Mardi Gras, 1949: Louis Armstrong was crowned King of the Zulus!!"[83]

The renewal of purism was also evident in newswoman Peggy Mengis's "The Battle against Bebop," appearing on April 10, 1949. Mengis profiled Julian Laine, Armand Hug (1910–1977), Sam DeKemel (ca. 1900–1967), and other Dixielanders who had "determined to blow the socks off the boppers in Sunday afternoon jam sessions."[84] Concern was expressed that youngsters knew little of New Orleans style, which they regarded as "antiquated," and to remedy the situation, "hot jazz is waging a cold war against bebop." The arguments were familiar ones: "The melody [in bebop] is unimportant, fleeting, barely perceptible, if there at all. It is extremely fast with an excessive amount of notes and the beat is not suitable for dancing or marching."[85] By way of contrast, the Dixielanders operated as a team, improvising together on the melody: "The collective improvisation is integrated, yet each musician plays with individuality, weaving subtle emotions into his music. Using their instruments as a medium, the Dixielanders tell the story of jazz in the best way they know how."[86] Yet there was more than a war of words being waged against the New Orleans musicians who were interested in bebop. A sizeable cadre of local modern jazz players arose after World War II, including drummers Earl Palmer (1924–2008), Ed Blackwell (1929–1992), Vernel Fournier (1928–2000), James Black (1940–1988), and Johnny Vidacovich (1949–); trumpeters Dave Bartholomew (1920–), Melvin Lastie (1930–1972), and Clyde Kerr Jr. (1943–); saxophonists Al Belletto (1928–), Alvin "Red" Tyler (1925–1998), Harold Battiste (1931–), Edward "Kidd" Jordan (1935–), Nat Perriliat (1936–1971), and Earl Turbinton (1941–2007); clarinetist Alvin Batiste (1932–2007); bassists Richard Payne (1931–2000), Bill Huntington (1937–), and Julius Farmer (1949–2001); and pianists Ellis Marsalis (1934–), Ed Frank (1932–1997), Wilson Turbinton (1944–2007), and Henry Butler (1949–). They bore no resemblance to the stereotypes that were being foisted upon them, yet purism affected their lives in numerous ways. Although many of these modernists were not yet active in the late 1940s, the ones who were paid an especially high price for their devotion to bebop.[87]

Al Belletto could not find nightclubs willing to hire him, so he was forced to take the engagements that were available: performing for strippers on Bourbon Street. The strippers loved bebop and regarded it as a music created especially for them. The musicians apparently enjoyed the attention but grew restive with the nightly grind and sought refuge on the road.[88] For Earl Palmer, who trained at the Grunewald School of Music on the G.I. Bill after he got out of the service in 1946, the dearth of paying bebop gigs meant that he had to follow the money to rock and roll: he and Dave Bartholomew became integral parts of Fats Domino's money-making machine, and Palmer went on to become the busiest session drummer in Los Angeles in the late 1950s and 1960s.[89] Bartholomew stayed with Fats but later regretted having to turn his back on jazz. Ellis Marsalis, Harold Battiste, and Alvin Batiste abandoned the local scene in 1956 to join Ornette Coleman in Los Angeles. Ornette had landed in the Crescent City in 1949 and found it stifling, but the caliber of musicians he encountered (particularly Ed Blackwell) impressed him. Ellis returned to New Orleans and took a job with Al Hirt (1922–1999) on Bourbon Street. Harold Battiste stayed in Los Angeles, building a career as a producer of pop hits (notably for Sam Cooke, Sonny and Cher, and Dr. John).[90] Alvin Batiste returned to Louisiana and became a respected jazz educator at Southern University, as Marsalis later did at the University of New Orleans.[91]

Modern jazz musicians in New Orleans challenged prevailing assumptions about race and the music business. Harold Battiste founded All for One (AFO) in 1961, a black-owned record company that was intended to control all aspects of production on behalf of the artists. Although it had an early hit with Barbara George's "I Know," AFO failed to meet expectations and eventually languished. In 1961, Al Belletto returned to the city after touring with Woody Herman and Stan Kenton and built a bastion for modern jazz at the Playboy Club in the French Quarter, employing Ellis Marsalis, James Black, Richard Payne, and other modernists for more than a decade. Belletto's presentation of racially mixed combos at the Playboy Club was remarkable, given that the segregated American Federation of Musicians locals in New Orleans did not merge until 1969. Believing that traditional jazz was "entertainment" music that pandered to "Uncle Tom" stereotypes, local modernists aspired to become socially conscious artists who made music according to their own calling. Of course, neither side was blameless in the antagonism, but modernists deserved better treatment than they received from the traditional jazz establishment. Reconciliation would come eventually, but it would take many years.

For New Orleans–style purists, the medium was still the message, and the Jazz Club used concerts to attract new members rather than to raise money. In August 1949, eight open-air concerts were given, leading to more ambitious undertakings by the end of the year. Four months later, the NOJC and the *Times-Picayune* cosponsored a "Battle of Bands" between Celestin and Phil Zito (1914–1998; a pro-LaRocca stalwart) to raise money for the Doll and Toy Fund. Another concert was held at Tulane University, featuring George Lewis's Ragtime Jazz Band: "This was not a public concert. It was fine, and free, entertainment for the faculty members, the student body, and the Club members."[92] Not only did such concerts succeed in employing black and white jazz musicians on a fairly regular basis, but they also swelled the ranks of club membership. By October 1950, the New Orleans Jazz Club had 265 active resident members (with 175 correspondents) and had completed its organization as a nonprofit corporation.[93]

The NOJC agenda, as given in the *Second Line,* included a journal, a weekly radio program, monthly meetings of the "Wax Wing" (collectors), plans for a record label, an annual Jazz Festival, a Jazz Museum, and outreach efforts for musicians in need.[94] The annual Jazz Festival and Jazz Museum became the most challenging objectives, requiring long-range planning and capitalization. For the first two years, the festival consisted of multiple concerts held at Congo Square, but the format soon changed to a single, annual concert on a grander scale. Proceeds from the festival went to charity.[95] The NOJC 1952 Annual Jazz Festival offered George Lewis and his Ragtime Jazz Band, Sharkey Bonano (1904–1972) and his Kings of Dixieland, Paul Barbarin's Jazz Band, and Johnny Wiggs. The festival brochure also contained an appeal to the unaffiliated, along with notice that the NOJC's membership was made up of people from all walks of life—professional people, housewives, students, and musicians: "We heartily welcome any person interested in the preservation of traditional jazz music to join with us in what we feel is a very important civic and cultural undertaking."[96]

Yet in 1953 there was no festival, and Myra Menville, the NOJC secretary, explained what went wrong. Preparations for the event began on April 14, with November 6 as the target date, but D. H. Holmes had already booked the Municipal Auditorium, the usual festival site. Negotiations with the department store eliminated the problem, and a contract was completed with a representative of the auditorium in early June. In September, however, news that a local promoter had hired Nat King Cole for a concert at the same location on the same night created new problems, this time irreconcilable. Faced with the prospect of holding its festival in one part of the building, while a national attraction competed in the other, the NOJC withdrew.[97] The following year's festival was also a disappointment, but for entirely different reasons. A report in the *Second Line* showed that $2,300 had been expended, with a profit of $890, $500 of which went to the Crippled Children's Hospital.[98] Reviewers wrote that "the crowd was big, but should have been bigger in this city where jazz was born," and the *Second Line* correspondent agreed: "Publicity Chairman Scoop Kennedy did a magnificent job—the press and radio cooperation was all that we could have asked." Yet the people of New Orleans were apparently "not interested in buying tickets to see the same bands they can see every night on Bourbon Street."[99] Like the NJF, the NOJC was learning just how risky concert production could be. Unlike their predecessors, however, its members refused to give up.

The "Report on the 1955 Jazz Festival" did little to inspire future confidence. The NOJC had contracted with Helena Rubenstein Cosmetics, then marketing a "Hot and Cool Jazz" lipstick, to help sponsor the festival. It promised to include the event in a national advertising campaign and to underwrite Turk Murphy's (1915–1987) band of West Coast revivalists. Its failure to deliver on both counts—plus problems with musicians about song lists; with the American Society of Composers, Authors and Publisher (AS-CAP); and with stagehands—produced "a bitter pill." Then the rains began, "so that last minute ticket-buyers were kept at home by a sudden downpour." According to the reporter: "This year's Festival promised to be the greatest and most remunerative in the history of the club. It turned out to be the worst."[100] Yet somehow, the NOJC managed to persevere. On the occasion of the eleventh festival, the *Times-Picayune*'s Sim Myers made it clear that progress had been made: "In the 11 years since the first concert, jazz has come a long way. Dixieland has become respectable; jazz has entered the highest planes of our society, and much of this acceptance has come back to

New Orleans. Forward-looking people now regard jazz as something pecu-
liarly American and are pleased that it had its development in New Orleans."[101]

The annual festival had gained the rewards of persistence, proffering jazz
as a civic virtue and forcing the city to remember, but not too much. Eventually, the festival became a possession of the city itself, like Mardi Gras, and
outgrew the NOJC. Coinciding with the 250th anniversary of the founding of
New Orleans, the 1968 festival was spearheaded by the Jazz Club but was actually a municipal undertaking. The *Times-Picayune* announced plans for the
festival on June 8, 1967, and among its subscribers were Joseph W. Simon Jr.,
of the Chamber of Commerce; Henry C. Spicer Jr., public relations director
of International House; Joan M. Vaccaro, of the Louisiana Tourist Development Commission; and Harry M. England, president of the New Orleans
Tourist Commission.[102] To publicize the plan, the Olympia Brass Band
marched into the city council chambers, and council president Maurice
"Moon" Landrieu responded by declaring that "a jazz festival in May will
bring visitors to us in a season that now has no other special celebration to
attract tourists."[103] Pledges from the Anniversary Committee and the Royal
Orleans Hotel, along with public subscriptions, were to raise $75,000, and
anticipated profits were to go to an expansion of the Jazz Museum, an assistance fund for older jazzmen, a perennial fund to underwrite future festivals,
and an international journal.[104] While the 1968 festival yielded barely $1,000
of profit after expenses, it became the prototype for the New Orleans Jazz
and Heritage Festival that began two years later and that routinely attracted
over 250,000 participants by the early 1980s.[105]

The drive to establish a Jazz Museum was another test for the NOJC. Its
progress was piecemeal and protracted yet ultimately successful, especially
once management of the museum was transferred to other hands. The guid-
ing force behind the project was Edmond Souchon, whose grasp of the need
to affiliate with a well-established cultural agency had been born of past experience. Souchon's initial plan was to entice the interest of the New Orleans
Public Library; accordingly, he donated his record collection to the Milton H.
Latter Library in 1952. The *Second Line* carried news of the donation, and librarian John Hall Jacobs commented on the significance of the collection:
"Dr. Souchon's collection of New Orleans jazz is world famous. We feel fortunate that such an important collection is to be made available to serious

students of one of our city's most distinct contributions to contemporary culture."[106] But Souchon's gambit did not pay off. The library was willing to accept the records only; hopes that the donation could serve as a beachhead were soon dashed: "It was at first hoped that the Latter Library would be able to permit the New Orleans Jazz Club to make a sort of Shrine or Museum for the Jazz Greats, but this is not in keeping with the ideas of their Board."[107] Souchon had counted on the "progressive administration of the New Orleans Public Library," citing this factor specifically as a reason for his donation, but he had overestimated their commitment to "progress."[108]

The subject of the Jazz Museum was not seriously raised again until the NOJC board took it up early in 1954. Souchon and Joe Mares Jr. (1908–1991) had obtained "a number of historic instruments used by hot music immortals" and wanted to find "a proper place to display and preserve them."[109] As the brother of Paul Mares (1900–1949), the former leader of the New Orleans Rhythm Kings, Joe enjoyed close ties to the Brunies family and to most of the musicians who had played with Jack Laine. He was also the owner of Southland Records, which recorded many of the bands that were used at NOJC functions, both white and black.[110] The Southland studios in the French Quarter, immediately adjacent to the Mares Brothers Fur Company, became a sort of "Jazz Hall of Fame," with oversized photographs of New Orleans musicians (and the occasional stripper) adorning the walls. Yet discussion at the board meeting provided no leads to a permanent facility, and five years passed before talk gave way to action.

On November 6, 1959, the *States-Item* carried the news that solid plans for a Jazz Museum in the French Quarter were being laid. The site was on Dumaine Street, but the building was to be moved from Bienville, several blocks away. D. H. Holmes was providing $28,000 for its relocation, responding to a unique set of circumstances. In order to enable expansion of a warehouse, the department store had scheduled the demolition of three cottages but had been blocked by the Vieux Carré Commission. A compromise had been arranged whereby the buildings were donated to the NOJC, but only after an appeal to the city council. Souchon reveled in the joys of deferred gratification: "This will be the first jazz museum established in New Orleans, and it represents the fulfillment of a dream the Jazz Club has had for many years. People who come to New Orleans constantly are asking us where they can go to learn about jazz. This will be our answer."[111] Yet the fu-

ture of the Jazz Museum rested on practicalities. Linkage to the tourist economy via paid admissions was essential if it was to survive. During the
groundbreaking ceremony on April 4, 1960, club officials and politicians who
had turned out for the event addressed this connection. Edmond's brother
Harry Souchon (1910–1984), an attorney, was present as master of ceremonies, and he characterized the occasion as "a milestone in the history of
the Jazz Club, a milestone in the history of jazz, and a milestone in the history of New Orleans." Councilman James E. Fitzmorris Jr. concurred: "In
the city where jazz was born, it is appropriate that we should have a jazz museum right here in New Orleans in the center of the French Quarter." Councilman Victor H. Schiro predicted that the Jazz Museum would be a "must"
for tourists.[112] In keeping with the spirit of the ceremony, the Johnny Wiggs
Band provided music, and people danced in the street.

The opening of the Jazz Museum on November 12, 1961, attracted copi-
ous press coverage, including an editorial in the *Times-Picayune* that contrasted markedly with the infamous "Jass and Jassism" jeremiad. In "Jazz
Has Made It," the writer seemed aware of the sins of the past but was
nonetheless barely apologetic: "It's a long way from the shady haunts of Storyville to the respected heights of cultural lore. But Jazz has made it. The
journey has not been quick or easy. Since the musical form emerged out of its
vague origins at some indistinct point in New Orleans' past, jazz and jazzmen
have had their ups and downs. They hit the top Sunday with the opening of
the New Orleans Jazz Museum. It represents some sort of epitome for what
was once considered 'low down.'"[113] The museum was a symbiosis of "aspects of the ivory tower and of the supermarket. There are research facilities
for scholars studying this distinct New Orleans contribution to American
culture, and there are audio outlets for casual sightseers looking for hot
licks."[114]

Frank Gagnard's "A Home For Jazz" approached the potential function
of the museum differently. Focusing on the academic aspects of jazz, Gagnard reflected on what the presence of a research center in New Orleans
might mean with regard to shifting opinions on jazz origins:

Probably nothing in music is debated with greater heat and such contrasting positive attitudes as the birth, growth and dissemination of jazz.
The respectability that the once shady jazz achieved has permitted schol-

arship to rear its disputative head. And where such ephemera as memory and theory provide history, as they do in jazz, there will be as many opinions as there are historians. . . . Such allied authorities as Grove's Dictionary of Music and Musicians and the French critics claim a virtually direct and exclusive line of development from the Congo to the Mississippi, and from New Orleans to Chicago and New York. A later school contests these claims on the basis of broader racial contributions to jazz, a wider play of European influence, and important U.S. developments concurrent with the shaping of the musical form in New Orleans. . . . The location of the museum in this city seems to guarantee a fair shake, if not favoritism, for the position of New Orleans in the formation of jazz.[115]

One suspects from his commentary that Gagnard had read Goffin and Feather but that the purist tendencies in *Jazzmen* had escaped his attention. It was not by coincidence that many members of the Jazz Club carried copies of *Jazzmen* to concerts and meetings.[116] Because William Russell and Charles Edward Smith had familiarized themselves with the local environment, they shared a certain common ground with the members of the NOJC. Their attempt to provide balanced coverage of the early experiences of black, white, and Creole jazzmen in New Orleans was translated into the performance schedules of the annual Jazz Festival, which sought a similar balance, and could also be found in the collection at the Jazz Museum. The celebration accompanying the opening of the museum was more than an apotheosis of New Orleans jazz; it was recognition of the city's multiracial musical heritage. Perhaps understandably, none of the newspaper accounts of the event brought this issue to the fore.[117]

The issue of race was a divisive one for members of the Jazz Club, as it was for most Americans. The range of opinion on the subject within the organization was not readily apparent to outsiders, who therefore tended to portray the NOJC as racist. In *Jazz Masters of New Orleans,* jazz critic Martin Williams (1924–1992) rendered a damning opinion of the New Orleans Jazz Club: "There is a local jazz appreciation club. It is Jim Crow."[118] Yet LaRocca's bitter denunciation of the NOJC as Crow Jim is reason enough to investigate further.[119] More often than not, it fell to Edmond Souchon to clarify the Jazz Club's position on race in the *Second Line,* a chore he did not relish. Responding to allegations that articles in the magazine were "pro-black," Souchon wrote "Was It for This?" in 1954: "We have been accused of a Crow Jim attitude in our writings, to which we do not subscribe. (Meanwhile, at the same time, stressing the catholicity of true jazz)." He was clearly incensed by complaints that the NOJC subscribed to any form of racial bias: "The same accusatory fingers that are pointed at us refuse to wrap themselves around a pencil to write a few lines in their own defense!"[120]

Al Rose tells the story of an integrated jam session featuring Lee Collins (1901–1960) and George Girard at a Jazz Club meeting at the Roosevelt Hotel in 1954. As a producer of the monthly sessions, Rose was in a position to insert Collins into the lineup discreetly after being informed that the NOJC operated under "an unwritten segregation law."[121] His account of the reaction to Collins's appearance on stage reveals how the feelings of the membership could surpass the social strictures that governed Southern attitudes on the eve of desegregation:

> I thought I could hear some sharp intakes of breath, but in a split second I was conscious of applause behind me. As I turned and joined in, I could see George and his band clapping their hands vigorously and smiling broadly. Then the audience joined in the swelling crescendo as Lee walked sedately to the center of the stage, carrying his brilliantly polished, golden horn. . . . The audience, whatever the philosophical flaws of some of its members, was enthralled by the overriding beauty of the performance. They responded with volcanic applause. . . . I never heard a critical word. After that we had mixed groups on the stage right along, and nobody thought anything of it. Their comments always pertained only to the music.[122]

Rose's estimation of Johnny Wiggs in *I Remember Jazz* makes it difficult to ascribe any hint of Jim Crow to the Jazz Club's founder: "He was rabidly anti-capitalist and pro-union. He was a substantial contributor to any cause endorsed by Martin Luther King, whom he considered the greatest living American, an extraordinary view for a white New Orleans jazz musician."[123] Indeed, the NOJC had several factions, some Jim Crow, some Crow Jim, and others striving for moderation. Given the agonies that attended desegregation of the South, the reaction of the membership to the integration of their bandstand was remarkably enlightened.

But there were limits. Berta Wood's "Are Negroes Ashamed of the Blues?" in the May 1957 issue of *Ebony* compelled Souchon to defend the Jazz Club from charges of Jim Crow. His argument did not challenge the inevitability of desegregation, but it was clear that he resented the imposition of policies that failed to take local conditions into account:

> Miss Wood has been shouting from the housetops that we should desegregate *at once, immediately,* and *completely.* We agree with her that this is bound to eventually happen. Even the Supreme Court of the United States of America now is aware of the terrific problem which their sweeping legislation has brought about in our neck of the woods. . . . In New Orleans, for many years, (and we are sure that Miss Wood is unaware of this fact) there are many vicinities where whites and Negroes have been living peacefully and amicably side by side. And with a most pleasant relationship. That is, until desegregation became such a national and "immediate" issue.[124]

Souchon also felt that Wood had not taken the time to acquaint herself with the efforts undertaken by the Jazz Club on behalf of black jazzmen, and so he sought to inform her:

> She does not know that during our "Festivals" they are always included; she has no idea of the innumerable jobs (spot and otherwise) that they have obtained thru the NOJC; of the great number of recording dates that have been thrown their way; of the efforts of *The Second Line* to call the general public's attention to these records and to the Negro musicians on the dates. Nor has she taken the trouble to look over the past files of our little magazine—and actually *count* the articles and pictures of Negro musicians. It would come as a surprise to her, I am sure, to find that the totals add up to almost 50–50 of the two races. For this particular effort in behalf of colored musicians, we are bitterly attacked by a large number of white musicians (and also a large number of NOJC members). So . . . here we are, between a cross-rough . . . Miss Wood belittling our efforts, and local men condemning our "Crow-Jim" attitude.[125]

The New Orleans–style jazz that the NOJC was trying to preserve was, in fact, being undermined by militant desegregation because younger blacks (and modernists) associated it with the Jim Crow practices of the past. Souchon emphasized the irony by noting that "although our pages are open to anyone who will contribute, it is hard for us to recall more than *one* article which was contributed by a Negro."[126] The need to enlist the support of local politicians for projects such as the Jazz Museum and the later versions of the Jazz Festival meant that the Jazz Club could not afford to position itself too far ahead of the pack on controversial issues like desegregation. The essence of Souchon's argument was that, given prevailing conditions, the NOJC was doing the best that it could, which was more than most were willing to do. After all, the Jazz Club had never been intended to revolutionize American society—its mission was to preserve New Orleans–style jazz.

In light of its objectives, the New Orleans Jazz Club was remarkably successful. Beyond accomplishment of its agenda, it created in New Orleans a climate that attracted jazz purists from all parts of the country and the world. In February 1956, William Russell moved to the city from Chicago to open a home base for the American Music label. According to a report in the *Second Line*, his French Quarter shop was situated "in a neighborhood that tourists cannot help finding."[127] The renowned painter and photographer Ralston Crawford (1906–1978) became a frequent visitor during the 1950s and claimed a special distinction: "I am the one northerner who has spent a weekend in New Orleans without becoming an *authority* on New Orleans music."[128] Bob Morris (1924–) was a copy editor with the *Amarillo Daily News* when he accidentally picked up the NOJC radio broadcast from WWL, leading to correspondence with the club's secretary, Myra Menville. In 1955, he applied to the *New Orleans Item* for a position and got it, with telling effect: "Prior to Bob's coming to New Orleans, articles on jazz which appeared in the Item were few and far between. During his all too short stay in New Orleans, he has written at least 20 articles, many of them full length—and with photographs—which the Item printed with much pride."[129]

But perhaps the most dedicated jazz pilgrim was Richard Binion Allen of Milledgeville, Georgia. In 1945, while stationed with the navy in Gulfport, Mississippi, Allen became affiliated with the National Jazz Foundation and began an enduring friendship with Orin Blackstone, eventually becoming his business partner in the New Orleans Record Shop after taking up residence in the city in 1949.[130] As a member of the Jazz Club, Allen made himself indispensable, contributing a record collectors' column to the *Second Line*, assisting Harry Souchon with the WWL radio program, and cataloging the

Souchon collection at the Latter Library. But Allen's entree to New Orleans jazz depended less on his connection to the NOJC than it did on his ability to earn the trust and friendship of the men who made the music. He made a point of seeking them out in even the most remote and seemingly inaccessible locations: "When jazz writers, Northern jazz writers at that time, spoke of New Orleans jazz, they spoke of it as a thing of the past. So it was quite a revelation to me to find out how much jazz there was. See, they'd have bands playing three nights a week, and I'd make all the joints—big barns of dance halls. Some places there wasn't room to swing a trombone."[131] Allen also collaborated with William Russell on various research projects, which proved to be a most effective combination of talents. Shortly afterward, he approached William Ransom Hogan (1908–1971) of Tulane University's Department of History with a proposal to dovetail the oral history work he was doing with Russell with a master's degree. Fortuitously, the Archive of New Orleans Jazz was the unforeseen result.

As a social historian with more than a passing interest in jazz, Hogan realized that Allen's proposal offered potential beyond a degree. He obtained funding from the Ford Foundation to establish an Archive of New Orleans Jazz at Tulane. The project was launched in 1958 and met with almost universal approval, especially from "old-guard" collectors like Ralph Gleason, whose "The Grant to Russell Is All for the Best," appearing in the *San Francisco Chronicle*, was ecstatic: "When the award was announced there was an almost unanimous expression of approval on the part of the jazz musicians and fans who have known Russell. Bill Russell is exactly the kind of man who deserves such financial help." Gleason recounted how Russell had devoted himself unselfishly to the needs of jazz musicians for more than twenty years, "helping them in every way he could." His efforts to preserve New Orleans jazz were legendary, and Gleason used the occasion of the grant to eulogize his old friend: "Russell, if I may be corny for a moment, is the nearest thing to a saint I have ever known. His absolute honesty and integrity is so immediately discernible that he has the trust of everyone who knows him."[132] The association of New Orleans jazz with the Ford Foundation and the city's most prestigious academic institution combined with the establishment of the Jazz Museum to complete the apotheosis of jazz in New Orleans in 1961. Like the Jazz Museum, the Archive of New Orleans Jazz became a clearinghouse for information on jazz, and tourists used these resources to find out where the "real" jazz was being played.

Russell and Allen had been serving privately in this capacity long before the Archive of New Orleans Jazz was established. The exploits of Alden Ashforth (1933–) and David Wyckoff (1933–), two of the busiest jazz pilgrims to come to New Orleans in the 1950s, provide a telling example of how their influence could extend into even the most carefully guarded preserves of American privilege.[133] Ashforth was the scion of Boston Brahmins, and Wyckoff came from a respectable Connecticut family. The boys met in 1946 while attending St. Paul's boarding school in Concord, New Hampshire, where fellow students were circulating the American Music recordings of Bunk Johnson—along with the addresses of William Russell and Dick Allen. In May 1950, the duo decided that a trip to New Orleans would be much more stimulating than studying, and so off they went. By the time they arrived in New Orleans, Ashforth's father had hired a detective agency, and having discovered a letter from Allen in Wyckoff's room, school officials knew where to find them. Alden negotiated a deal with his father permitting the boys to spend the weekend before returning to Concord: on Friday they heard Papa Celestin at the Paddock on Bourbon Street and the next night caught George Lewis and his band at Manny's Tavern. A sizeable donation to St. Paul's obviated their expulsion, but if anyone thought that the boys had learned their lesson, they were sadly mistaken.

Ashforth and Wyckoff began classes at Harvard in fall 1950; in January 1951, they were back in New Orleans. Local contacts led them to black jazz musicians and, inevitably, to trouble with the authorities. The friends had plans on two fronts: to record bands that had been overlooked by Russell and to take lessons from black musicians (Alden took clarinet from George Lewis, and Wyckoff tried trumpet). Associating with African Americans in New Orleans was exceedingly risky, and the two were arrested on trumped-up charges almost immediately, facing a judge who began his interrogation by asking them why they were seated in the "nigger" section. Explaining that they were Harvard students conducting research on New Orleans jazz was not enough to pacify the judge, but twenty dollars, on loan from Dick Allen, sufficed to free them. With the promise of returning to college if his father would buy him a tape recorder, Ashforth assembled the resources necessary to achieve the first goal. Documentation of the Eureka Brass Band occurred on August 25, followed by recordings of clarinetist Emile Barnes (1892–1970) and trumpeter Kid Thomas Valentine (1896–1987) on August 30 and September 3, 1951.[134]

Once Ashforth had obtained a clarinet, the second goal also seemed within grasp. Alden was summoned to the bandstand by George Lewis one night to sit in with his band, playing for a white audience. When a customer objected, the proprietor told Lewis that the "white boy" would have to step down. Lewis announced that the "white boy" was "with us," and if he had to step down, they all would. With a packed house, the owner relented and invited the offensive patron to leave, after refunding the price of his drink. Ashforth remained on stage. The next tune called was one that usually goes by the title of "Pork Chop Rag" but is better known in some circles as "Kiss My F——ing Ass." When his big moment came and Lewis beckoned for him to take a chorus, Alden froze—no sound came out. According to legend, from that time on, whenever George Lewis's bands performed that number, they would always leave one chorus "silent" as a testament to Ashforth's first "solo" and the circumstances that had permitted it.

These experiences illustrate how interest in New Orleans jazz and association with the men who made it could engender activism against segregation. Ashforth became a musicologist and composer with a Ph.D. from Princeton and maintained an abiding interest in jazz throughout a long career at UCLA; Wyckoff became a psychiatrist. Two years prior to the George Girard–Lee Collins precedent alluded to by Al Rose, they had conspired with Bill Huntington (at the time a traditional banjoist) to join trumpeter Percy Humphrey (1905–1995) of the Eureka on stage at a New Orleans Jazz Club event. Some people walked out, but others, such as Doc Souchon and Myra Menville, remained. The adjustment of attitudes on race was perhaps the most difficult challenge facing anyone seeking to erect institutions celebrating jazz in New Orleans, but ever so gradually, almost imperceptibly, progress was made. Ashforth's assessment of the New Orleans Jazz Club was that some of the members, such as Joe Mares, were not receptive to outsiders but that most were gracious and solicitous of their interest. At Manny's Tavern and Luthjens, much more than at NOJC concerts, one could still experience traditional jazz as dance music functionally tied to community life, but the neighborhood bar scene was not for everyone. Proprietors catering to the tourist trade were less concerned with authenticity than they were with exploiting the jazz revival monetarily: at the Paddock, Celestin's band was elevated behind the bar and encouraged to "Tom" as much as possible. The city needed a performance site that could offer unadulterated New Orleans–style jazz on a continuous basis without deferring to commercial imperatives, and it was out of this need that Preservation Hall grew, officially commencing operations on June 19, 1961.

The Hall evolved from a series of "pass-the-hat" sessions initiated by art dealer E. Lorenz "Larry" Borenstein at his Associated Artists Studio in 1956. A native of Milwaukee who had relocated to the French Quarter during World War II, Borenstein found that running a gallery left too little time for listening to jazz at dance halls like Luthjens and the Moulin Rouge, so he arranged for the musicians to play private concerts at his establishment on off nights, which were many. Occasionally, these sessions inspired the ire of the authorities and landed everybody in court:

> These were changing times in New Orleans and the mood was reflected in night court. A certain judge managed to combine the judicial dignity of a kangaroo court and the philosophy of lynch law with the humor of Milton Berle. An archconservative, the judge was outraged at any racial mixing. . . . One night in 1957 Kid Thomas and several musicians, white and colored, stood before him. In stern tones the judge delivered a lecture. "We don't want Yankees coming to New Orleans mixing cream with our coffee." He went on to say that Thomas Valentine was well liked by decent folks in nearby Algiers and also appreciated as a "good yard boy." People thought well of him for giving cornet lessons to West Bank kids, and if he would remember his place in the future and not get "uppity," the judge would let him go this time.[135]

When Preservation Hall opened in 1961, it was under the auspices of the Society for the Preservation of Traditional New Orleans Jazz, a short-lived organization with plenty of enthusiasm but little business acumen. As Borenstein later recalled, "I realized that the only hope was to put the activity on a businesslike basis."[136] He enlisted the services of Allan Jaffe and Sandra Jaffe, a husband-and-wife team that had come to New Orleans from Pennsylvania the previous year.

Allan Jaffe was a graduate of the Wharton School of Finance, but "for his business success in a variety of fields, including real estate, he was less inclined to credit his training at the Wharton business school than the common sense learned from early years of hanging around his father's paint and wallpaper shop."[137] The Jaffes held full-time jobs in order to subsidize the Hall, revealing their dedication to the musicians who were its beneficiaries. The turning point came when they discovered that touring could be more lucrative than running the Hall, and after 1963 Jaffe used this formula to expand the roster of players to over a hundred and to bring them to receptive audiences all over the world, transforming Preservation Hall into an international phenomenon in less than a decade.[138] He often sat in on brass bass with the bands and, according to William Russell, soon became "one of the best brass band parade sousaphonists in town."[139] Yet in spite of the Jaffes' crucial role, the success of Preservation Hall rested on the spirit of cooperation and commitment demonstrated by others as well. Russell contributed as the kindly "bouncer," as an usher, and as the violinist with the New Orleans Ragtime Orchestra. Richard Allen stimulated interest among Tulane students and credited them with playing an important role in the resurgence of jazz in New Orleans as well.[140]

But the ones who really gave Preservation Hall meaning were the elderly African American and Creole musicians who performed there. Writer and clarinetist Tom Sancton's (1949–) memoir, *Song for My Fathers: A New Orleans Story in Black and White,* recounts his experiences as a teenager who discovered the appeal of traditional jazz at a time when the Beatles and the Rolling Stones were captivating most of his classmates. Tom's father (a journalist and writer) was a radicalized Southern liberal whose commitment to social justice had led him to the musicians at Preservation Hall, an interest that he shared with his son. George Lewis became young Sancton's mentor, assisted by banjoist George Guesnon (1907–1968) and saxophonist Harold Dejan (1909–2002), the leader of the Olympia Brass Band. Together, they worked him hard. Sancton came to revere Lewis and company as gracious, generous, and gifted human beings who valued traditional jazz as a means of conferring dignity and prosperity upon its practitioners, despite the ever-present threat of racism. The old men found the boy's interest at first mysterious, then amusing, and finally gratifying, especially once he started making progress on the clarinet. Sancton later attended Harvard, became a Rhodes scholar, and ended up as the bureau chief for *Time* magazine in Paris, but he never forgot the lessons his black "fathers" had taught him, and he still plays beautifully, as a standard-bearer of the New Orleans jazz tradition. His experience with George Lewis in the 1960s was not unlike William Russell's with Bunk two decades earlier, both cases demonstrating how jazz could efface seemingly impenetrable social and racial barriers.[141]

What the founders of Preservation Hall gained was the same insight that had sustained the collector independents and the revivalists of the 1940s: "noncommercial" music could find a market when correctly presented. The lack of appurtenances at the Hall—the absence of alcohol, air-conditioning, and luxurious appointments—reminded the audience that it was the music that mattered. Whether the bands were playing "authentic" jazz in the manner of its first practitioners was seemingly beside the point and, at best, debatable, as the jazz schisms of the 1940s had shown. It was the *expectation* that they were that kept the audiences clamoring for more. New Orleans–style jazz, like Plymouth Rock, had intrinsic appeal as a touchstone of the American experience. Audiences believed that what they were hearing was authentic, and therefore profound, because that was what they wanted. Yet in the final analysis, it was the musician's power to generate joy and move audiences that made such belief possible.

The revival of traditional jazz came late to New Orleans, following trends started elsewhere, but its effects were deeper and more abiding. The awakening of American jazz scholarship elevated the music to the stature of a "serious" art form and subjected it to considerable intellectualization, but the survival of New Orleans style acted like a conscience to remind the intellectuals that jazz should also be fun, rooted as it must be in a sense of play that is basic to the human experience.[142] Once jazz had "made it," the original urge to advocacy that had attracted many "hot" collectors to the left in the 1930s seemed incongruous in a canon-driven jazz establishment that relied on capitalism to realize most of its ambitions. Experiments in "noncommercial" music such as Preservation Hall provided a convincing illusion of devotion to such communitarian ideals, but the reality still boiled down to sound business practices, albeit tempered by a kind of benign aesthetic vigilance and sincere concern for the musicians' welfare.

The work of the New Orleans–style purists who pioneered the writing of jazz history has since been revised, especially with regard to the myopia that purism entails, but many of the other lessons they taught are timeless. Perhaps the most valuable lesson learned from the awakening of American jazz scholarship, the New Orleans revival, and the jazz wars that followed is that reconciliation is always a possibility and that it is usually worth the effort. On May 19, 2007, Tulane University held its commencement at the New Orleans Arena, adjacent to the Superdome. It was a memorable occasion for many reasons: as an opportunity to call attention to the large number of graduates who had engaged in community service post-Katrina; as a way to celebrate the return of families that had been dispersed by the storm; and as a chance to recognize heroism within a city that had come very close to drowning in a sea of incompetence, racial discord, and fear. One of the highlights of the commencement was the awarding of an honorary doctorate to Ellis Marsalis, who looked magnificent in his regalia. Dr. Michael White's Liberty Jazz Band, a traditional ensemble, was performing for graduation as usual, but he had some surprise ringers in the band. Ellis's sons Jason (1977–; drums) and Delfeayo (1965–; trombone) were present, and there was also a prerecorded greeting from Wynton Marsalis (1961–) on the huge video monitors that were strategically placed around the arena.

Wynton's message was an expression of gratitude for the education he had received from Ellis, coupled with the pride he felt in his father's accomplishments. Like most New Orleans jazz musicians, he had benefited from "hands-on" instruction. Yet perhaps Wynton deserved some gratitude as well. All of the young Marsalises grew up as modernists, but it was Wynton, in the guise of a "neoclassicist," who did the most to repair the damage caused by the rift between traditionalists and modernists in New Orleans. By recognizing the New Orleans jazz tradition as a continuum of innovation in his programs at Jazz at Lincoln Center, Wynton had revealed himself to be a peacemaker. Now half his family was sitting in with the Liberty Jazz Band, waiting for the downbeat. This was the best way for them to express what they were feeling at that moment, and they came together effortlessly. It was a magic moment for all in attendance, demonstrating the healing power of New Orleans jazz.

Epilogue

One must now reiterate what should always have been obvious: New Orleans–style jazz still matters. Scholars need to recognize that the complacency often attached to the interpretation of New Orleans jazz history—the inclination to treat it as a story that has already been told—is premature. Fascination with bebop, or perhaps the desire to get Louis Armstrong to Chicago as quickly as possible, may account for the canon-driven dearth of coverage of jazz in New Orleans during the 1920s and following. This is an oversight that renders most jazz history textbooks, "official" or not, much less useful than they ought to be.[1] Somewhat more disturbing is the invisibility of important New Orleans voices in Eric Porter's *What Is This Thing Called Jazz? African American Musicians as Artists, Critics, and Activists,* an otherwise valuable scholarly representation of jazz musicians as articulate and self-directed artists. With the exceptions of Louis Armstrong and Wynton Marsalis, a century of commentary by Sidney Bechet, Jelly Roll Morton, Barney Bigard, Lee Collins, Baby Dodds, George "Pops" Foster (1892–1969), Joe Darensbourg (1906–1985), Danny Barker, and Earl Palmer is completely ignored.[2] The investiture of bebop as *the* jazz art music within academia may provide a partial explanation, and if that is the case, one can appreciate why purists fought so hard to contain its influence in the 1940s. What is more troubling is the suspicion that contemporary scholars have ceased to see New Orleans jazz as something that matters beyond the accomplishments of Armstrong and Marsalis—twin historical bookends with nothing in between.[3]

Perhaps we can blame organic, evolutionary historical perspectives for the oversight, while also recognizing that it was the triumph of bebop as the dominant paradigm in jazz studies after the 1940s that created those perspectives in the first place.

It may be fashionable these days to criticize Ken Burns for yielding to the temptations of the "official" historical canon and the teleological comfort that derives from it, but it is also true that his *Jazz* series stimulated increased interest in early New Orleans jazz among some scholars, and one can thank him for that. Like the "hot" collectors and New Orleans purists of yore, he meant well, and something positive was accomplished. But that is not the equivalent of getting the story right or embracing it holistically. All scholars who profess to love jazz need to revisit the achievements of the New Orleans pioneers and their progeny, whose vision continues to inspire. We owe them that much. This statement applies to so-called traditionalists and modernists. A singular story that has remained largely untold is the saga of New Orleans' modern jazz players: drummers Ed Blackwell, Earl Palmer, and James Black; trumpeters Dave Bartholomew, Melvin Lastie, and Clyde Kerr Jr.; saxophonists Nat Perriliat, Al Belletto, Edward "Kidd" Jordan, Harold Battiste, Alvin "Red" Tyler, and Earl Turbinton; clarinetist Alvin Batiste; bassists Richard Payne, Bill Huntington, and Julius Farmer; and pianists Ellis Marsalis, Ed Frank, Wilson "Willie Tee" Turbinton, and Henry Butler, to name only a few.[4] These men beat the odds by creating memorable music in a town that refused to respect them, largely because of jazz purism. Perhaps now we can shine the spotlight on all the players who deserve it and renew our understanding of why the jazz tradition has remained vital and communally connected in New Orleans for more than a century, despite the well-intentioned efforts of purists to preserve it.

Notes

Introduction

1. Al Rose and Edmond Souchon, *New Orleans Jazz: A Family Album*, 3d ed., rev. and enlarged (Baton Rouge: Louisiana State University Press, 1984), ix.

2. Sasha Frere-Jones, "Pop Music: True Grime—A Genre's Magic Moment," *New Yorker*, Mar. 25, 2005, 86–87. On defining "hot," see *The New Grove Dictionary of Jazz*, 2d ed., vol. 2, ed. Barry Kernfeld (London and New York: Macmillan, 2002), s.v. "Hot (i)," by Eric Thacker, 281. Thacker places the origin of the term within tune titles of the ragtime era, such as Theodore Metz's "A Hot Time in the Old Town Tonight" (1886), and notes that application of the term is "generally confined to music of the early and swing periods and the continuation of styles emanating from that time." It should be appreciated from the outset that "style" is an inherently ambiguous designation, defined as "a mode of expression or performance," possibly referring to "a musical composition, types of composition, methods of composition, media, nations, periods, or [all of these] in combination." See *Harvard Dictionary of Music*, 2d ed., rev. and enlarged (Cambridge: Belknap Press of Harvard University Press, 1974), s.v. "Style," 811–12.

3. Scott DeVeaux, "Constructing the Jazz Tradition: Jazz Historiography," *Black American Literature Forum* 25, no. 3: 525–60, quotes on 525, 553.

4. See *New Grove Dictionary of Jazz* (2002), s.v. "New Orleans Jazz," by Lawrence Gushee, 887–88. Gushee discusses performance practices associated with New Orleans style in considerable detail, including distinctions between bands that remained in New Orleans and those that traveled, white and black traditions, and the variance in degrees of improvisation and command of the lead among early New Orleans bands. Anyone wishing to familiarize themselves with the origins of jazz in New Orleans should consult Gushee's work on the subject. On the extremely thorny issue of early chronology, for example, his "The Nine-

teenth-Century Origins of Jazz," *Black Music Research Journal* 14 (Spring 1994): 1–24, is indispensable.

5. The "Jass and Jassism" editorial of June 20, 1918, discussed later in the introduction, should suffice to represent the attitudes emanating from the *Times-Picayune*. For the antipathy of Creole pedagogues to jazz, see p. 89 in Bruce Boyd Raeburn, "King Oliver, Jelly Roll Morton, and Sidney Bechet: Ménage à Trois, New Orleans Style," in *The Oxford Companion to Jazz,* ed. Bill Kirchner (New York and London: Oxford University Press), 88–101. See also Raeburn, "Dancing Hot and Sweet: New Orleans Jazz in the 1920's," *Jazz Archivist* 7, nos. 1–2 (1992): 10–13. For a succinct theoretical perspective on creolization, see Roger D. Abrahams, with Nick Spitzer, John F. Szwed, and Robert Farris Thompson, *Blues for New Orleans: Mardi Gras and America's Creole Soul* (Philadelphia: University of Pennsylvania Press, 2006).

6. Jared Snyder's yet unpublished work on Henry Peyton's Accordiana Band promises to significantly expand appreciation of the use of the accordion in early "hot" music. On the Golden Rule Orchestra, see Johnny St. Cyr, interview by William Russell, with Manuel Manetta, Aug. 27, 1958, tape recording, Hogan Jazz Archive, Tulane University (henceforth HJA).

7. See Richard Campanella, *Geographies of New Orleans: Urban Fabrics before the Storm* (Lafayette: Center for Louisiana Studies, 2006), which provides an excellent and supremely useful overview of demographic configurations throughout the city over the course of the nineteenth and twentieth centuries.

8. Karl Koenig, "The Plantation Belt Brass Bands and Musicians, Part 1: Professor James B. Humphrey," *Second Line* 33 (Fall 1981): 24–40.

9. See Richard Knowles, *Fallen Heroes: A History of New Orleans Brass Bands* (New Orleans: Jazzology Press, 1996).

10. See Michael G. White, "The New Orleans Brass Band: A Cultural Tradition," in *The Triumph of the Soul: Cultural and Psychological Aspects of African American Music,* ed. Ferdinand Jones and Arthur C. Jones (Westport, Conn.: Praeger, 2001), 69–96.

11. Rudi Blesh, *Shining Trumpets: A History of Jazz* (New York: Alfred A. Knopf, 1946), 179. For the advertisement, see *New Orleans States,* Jan. 17, 1924. Charlie Bocage, interview by Richard B. Allen and Herb Friedwald, July 18, 1960, tape recording, HJA.

12. Peter Bocage, interview by William Russell and Richard B. Allen, Jan. 29, 1959, tape recording, HJA.

13. Max Harrison, Charles Fox, and Eric Thacker, *The Essential Jazz Records: Volume I: Ragtime to Swing,* Discographies 12 (Westport, Conn.: Greenwood Press, 1984), 47–48. The essential thrust of Harrison's statement was earlier presented by Lawrence Gushee in the liner notes for *Steppin' on the Gas: Rags to Jazz, 1913–1927* (New World Records NW 269/Recorded Anthology of American

Music, 1977), in which he states that "the Morgan Band was, I think, modern in New Orleans terms. This 1927 rhythm section sounds amazingly like those of the 1940s revival (or survival) bands of Bunk Johnson and George Lewis" (5).

14. Ed Kirkeby worked for the Columbia Phonograph Company in 1917 and recalled how company officials "tore their hair out" over Victor's success with the ODJB. He was ordered to find jazz bands, but "this older [New Orleans] style was kind of raw, and very few people could play it, especially the New Yorkers." W. E. T. Kirkeby, interview by John Steiner, June 28, 1961, tape recording, HJA. See also Gushee, "Nineteenth-Century Origins," 2, 9–10, on Walter Kingsley's articles based on conversations with New Orleans musicians, published in the *New York Sun* in 1917 and the *Dramatic Mirror* in 1918.

15. Lawrence W. Levine, *Highbrow/Lowbrow: The Emergence of Cultural Hierarchy in America* (Cambridge: Harvard University Press, 1988). See especially the chapter "Order, Hierarchy, and Culture," 169–242.

16. Henry F. May, *The End of American Innocence: A Study of the First Years of Our Own Time, 1912–1917* (Chicago: Quadrangle Books, 1964), 30.

17. John A. Kouwenhoven, *The Arts in Modern American Civilization* (New York: W. W. Norton, 1967), 13 (originally published as *Made in America* [Doubleday, 1948]). For Kouwenhoven's views on jazz, see "What's American about America?" in *Literary Types and Themes,* ed. Maurice B. McNamee, James E. Cronin, and Joseph A. Rogers (New York: Holt, Rinehart and Winston, 1960), 247–55. The blurring of boundaries among art, popular, and folk categories was not new with jazz; for nineteenth-century antecedents, see Michael Broyles, "Immigrant, Folk, and Regional Musics in the Nineteenth Century," in *The Cambridge History of American Music,* ed. David Nicholls (Cambridge: Cambridge University Press, 1998), 135–57. Yet jazz did more than blur boundaries. In his discussion of classical ("authenticity" in composer authority), popular ("accessibility" in adaptive, audience-oriented performance), and traditional (orally transmitted folk music tied to lifestyle) categories post-1860, in *America's Musical Life: A History* (New York and London: W. W. Norton, 2001), Richard Crawford states: "The idea of three spheres—classical, popular, and traditional—offers an image of American music making that is richer and more flexible than the familiar binary view of classical versus popular music (or the cultivated versus the vernacular, or highbrow versus lowbrow)" (229); see also 228–30. The "hot" collectors' concept of jazz as an authentic folk music relying on spontaneous composition in performance (live or on record) subverted such distinctions by conflating all three spheres.

18. Lawrence W. Levine, "Jazz and American Culture," *Journal of American Folklore* 102 (Jan.–Mar. 1989): 6–22, quote on 7.

19. Levine, "Jazz and American Culture," 10–11; Levine, *Highbrow/Lowbrow,* 221–23.

20. Levine, "Jazz and American Culture," 12. See also Guthrie P. Ramsey Jr., "Cosmopolitan or Provincial? Ideology in Early Black Music Historiography, 1867–1940," *Black Music Research Journal* 16 (Spring 1996): 11–43.

21. Levine, "Jazz and American Culture," 13. See also Lewis Porter's chapter "Responses to Early Jazz, 1919–1934," in *Jazz: A Century of Change* (New York: Schirmer Books, 1997), 121–58, in which Porter argues that responses to jazz "ran the gamut from the insulting to the surprisingly understanding" (127).

22. Levine, "Jazz and American Culture," 19–20.

23. Kathy J. Ogren, *The Jazz Revolution: Twenties America and the Meaning of Jazz* (New York: Oxford University Press, 1989), 138.

24. Ogren, *Jazz Revolution*, 7.

25. Ogren, *Jazz Revolution*, 139–40. See also H. O. Brunn, *The Story of the Original Dixieland Jazz Band* (Baton Rouge: Louisiana State University Press, 1960); Horst H. Lange, *The Fabulous Fives*, rev. ed. by Ron Jewson, Derek Hamilton-Smith, and Ray Webb (Chigwell, England: Storyville Publications, 1978), v–vi.

26. Ogren, *Jazz Revolution*, 142. See also Reid Badger, *A Life in Ragtime: A Biography of James Reese Europe* (New York: Oxford University Press, 1995); Ron Welburn, "James Reese Europe and the Infancy of Jazz Criticism," *Black Music Research Journal* 7 (1987): 35–44. Inspection of "A Negro Explains Jazz," *Literary Digest,* Apr. 26, 1919, yields no concrete information on jazz origins. See also Guthrie Ramsey, "Cosmopolitan or Provincial?" 31.

27. Ogren, *Jazz Revolution*, 142. See also Martin Williams, *Jazz Masters of New Orleans* (New York: Macmillan Company, 1967), 28; Dick Holbrook, "Mister Jazz Himself—The Story of Ray Lopez," *Storyville,* no. 64 (Apr.–May 1976): 135–51; Oro, "United We Stand—Hot," *Billboard,* Dec. 26, 1936.

28. Ogren, *Jazz Revolution*, 160. See also Samuel B. Charters and Leonard Kunstadt, *Jazz: A History of the New York Scene* (Garden City: Doubleday, 1962), 139–42.

29. MacDonald Smith Moore, *Yankee Blues: Musical Culture and American Identity* (Bloomington: Indiana University Press, 1985), 106.

30. Moore, *Yankee Blues,* 119.

31. The first response from the audience at the ODJB's debut in New York City was, "Tell those farmers to go home!" Once the patrons were instructed that the music was for dancing, their attitude changed dramatically, and the jazz craze was on. See Dominic James "Nick" LaRocca, interview by Richard B. Allen, May 26, 1958, tape recording, HJA. See also Holbrook, "Mister Jazz Himself," 142.

32. Moore, *Yankee Blues,* 131.

33. Morroe Berger, "Jazz: Resistance to the Diffusion of a Culture Pattern," *Journal of Negro History* 32 (1947): 461–94; Neil Leonard, *Jazz and the White Americans: The Acceptance of a New Art Form* (Chicago: University of Chicago Press, 1962).

34. James Lincoln Collier challenges Leonard's conclusions in *The Reception*

of Jazz in America—A New View, I.S.A.M. Monographs 27 (Brooklyn: Institute for Studies in American Music, 1988). For a critique of Collier's analysis, see Lawrence Gushee, review of *The Reception of Jazz in America—A New View,* by James Lincoln Collier, in *Ethnomusicology: A Journal of the Society for Ethnomusicology* 33 (Spring–Summer 1989): 352–54.

35. Leonard, *Jazz and the White Americans,* 155–56.

36. "Jass and Jassism," *New Orleans Times-Picayune,* June 20, 1918.

37. See Charles Suhor, "Jazz and the New Orleans Press," *Down Beat* 36 (June 12, 1969): 18.

38. Ronald G. Welburn, "American Jazz Criticism, 1914–1940" (Ph.D. diss., New York University, 1983), 14–15.

39. Welburn, "American Jazz Criticism," 36–43, 52. See also Collier, *Reception of Jazz,* 35–40; B. H. Haggin, *Music on Records: A New Guide to the Music, the Performances, the Recordings,* 4th rev. ed. (New York: Alfred A. Knopf, 1945); Haggin, *Music in the Nation* (Freeport, N.Y.: Books for Libraries Press, 1971). For contextual information on the quest for an indigenous American music, see Gilbert Chase, *America's Music: From the Pilgrims to the Present* (New York, Toronto, and London: McGraw-Hill, 1955), especially the chapter entitled "Nationalism and Folklore," 385–402. Given the dearth of references to this context in the writings of "hot" collectors, however, one must assume that they were not cognizant of it. Frederic Ramsey Jr. described Roger Pryor Dodge as "the first *true* intellectual to write about jazz"; see Frederic Ramsey Jr., "An Interview with the Historian, Writer, Photographer," interview by Pete Whelan, Federal Twist, N.J., July 28, 1988, *78 Quarterly* 1 (1989): 32–39. See also Pryor Dodge, ed., *Hot Jazz and Jazz Dance: Roger Pryor Dodge Collected Writings, 1929–1964* (New York: Oxford University Press, 1995).

40. Welburn, "American Jazz Criticism," 55.

41. John Gennari, *Blowin' Hot and Cool: Jazz and Its Critics* (Chicago and London: University of Chicago Press, 2006), 22, 25, 27.

42. Leonard Feather, response to questionnaire, June 11, 1981, in Welburn, "American Jazz Criticism," 204.

43. Warren I. Susman, "Culture and Commitment," in *Culture as History: The Transformation of American Society in the Twentieth Century* (New York: Pantheon Books, 1984), 185. See also Lewis A. Ehrenberg, *Swingin' the Dream: Big Band Jazz and the Rebirth of American Culture* (Chicago and London: University of Chicago Press, 1998), on jazz's associations with the left in the 1930s.

44. Collier disputes the idea "that the American people, until relatively recently, have ignored or despised jazz" (*Reception of Jazz in America,* 1).

45. Susman, *Culture as History,* 203.

Chapter 1

1. Charles Edward Smith, "Jazz: Some Little Known Aspects," *Symposium: A Critical Review* 1 (Oct. 1930): 502–17. Despite its importance, Smith's article

has not been included in anthologies of early jazz writing and criticism. For information on Burnham, see Samuel Francis, *Thinkers of Our Time: James Burnham* (London: Claridge Press, 1999). Burnham's gradual odyssey into Marxism (which he abandoned in 1940) can be traced in the pages of the *Symposium*, especially his exchanges with Leon Trotsky in the July 1932 issue (503–5) and the journal's publication of his revolutionary manifesto "Thirteen Propositions" in Apr. 1933 (127–34). For a statement of editorial policy, see *Symposium* 1 (Apr. 1930), 3; on readership, see *Symposium* 4 (Oct. 1933), 403.

2. Al Rose, interview by author, New Orleans, July 29, 1989, tape recording, HJA. Collier names Van Vechten as one of the best, and one of the earliest, American jazz critics of the 1920s (*Reception of Jazz in America*, 34).

3. Smith also had business relationships with various record companies (see chap. 3).

4. Charles Edward Smith, "Jazz: Some Little Known Aspects," 502.

5. Charles Edward Smith, "Jazz: Some Little Known Aspects," 505.

6. Charles Edward Smith, "Jazz: Some Little Known Aspects," 505, 506.

7. Charles Edward Smith, "Jazz: Some Little Known Aspects," 507. See also Ed Salzman, "There's Money in Jazz 78s (Some)," unidentified clipping, n.d., in Nick LaRocca scrapbook, HJA.

8. Charles Edward Smith, "Jazz: Some Little Known Aspects," 508, 509.

9. Charles Edward Smith, "Jazz: Some Little Known Aspects," 509.

10. Charles Edward Smith, "Jazz: Some Little Known Aspects," 513.

11. Charles Edward Smith, "Jazz: Some Little Known Aspects," 514.

12. S. Frederick Starr, *Red and Hot: The Fate of Jazz in the Soviet Union, 1917–1980* (New York: Oxford University Press, 1983). See also Francis Newton, *The Jazz Scene* (London: Macgibbon and Kee, 1959); Gene Lees, *Meet Me at Jim and Andy's: Jazz Musicians and Their World* (New York: Oxford University Press, 1980); James Lincoln Collier, "The Faking of Jazz: How Politics Distorted the History of the Hip," *New Republic*, Nov. 18, 1985, 33–40; Collier, *Reception of Jazz*.

13. Starr, *Red and Hot*, 94–96. See also Michael H. Kater, "Forbidden Fruit? Jazz in the Third Reich," *American Historical Review*, 94, no. 1 Feb. 1989, 11–43. According to Kater, the Nazis' inability to properly define what jazz was created a policy of confusion that was self-defeating.

14. Starr, *Red and Hot*, 101–6. See also Mark Naison, *Communists in Harlem during the Depression* (Urbana: University of Illinois Press, 1983), 68–71.

15. Starr, *Red and Hot*, 106.

16. Starr, *Red and Hot*, 99–100; Irving Howe and Lewis Coser, *The American Communist Party: A Critical History, 1919–1957* (Boston: Beacon Press, 1957), 275; Daniel Aaron, *Writers on the Left: Episodes in American Literary Communism* (New York: Harcourt, Brace and World, 1961). For more detail on Gold, see

Alan M. Wald, *Exiles from a Future Time: The Forging of the Mid-Twentieth-Century Literary Left* (Chapel Hill and London: University of North Carolina Press, 2002), 39–70.

17. See Michael Gold, "The Skunks of Jazz," in "What a World," *Daily Worker,* Aug. 29, 1933; Gold's response to reactions to the poem, in "What a World," *Daily Worker,* Sept. 6, 1933; "A Reader Points Out Michael Gold's Errors on the Negro Question," *Daily Worker,* Sept. 18, 1933.

18. Charles Edward Smith, "Class Content of Jazz Music," *Daily Worker,* Oct. 21, 1933. For Communist Party interest in jazz throughout the 1930s, see Naison, *Communists in Harlem,* 211–19. See also Dale Curran's novels *Piano in the Band* (New York: Reynal and Hitchcock, 1940) and *Dupree Blues* (New York: Alfred A. Knopf, 1948), which locate the "fundamental reality of American life" in the stories of jazz musicians. This is a far cry from sociological portrayals of jazzmen as deviants, a trend that began with Carlo L. Lastrucci, "The Professional Dance Musician," *Journal of Musicology* 3 (Winter 1941): 168–72, and led to Howard S. Becker, *Outsiders: Studies in the Sociology of Deviance* (New York: Free Press of Glencoe, 1963), especially 82–119.

19. Charles Edward Smith, "Class Content of Jazz Music." Smith's emphasis on the poly-racial origins of jazz sets him apart not only from Gold but also from John Hammond, whom Gennari sees as the most influential jazz writer of his time (*Blowin' Hot and Cool,* 11, 19, 24–26, 34–37, 68).

20. Susman, "The Culture of the Thirties," in *Culture as History,* 134.

21. Starr writes: "Smith was forcing jazz into the procrustean bed of Marxist ideology and his American readers knew it. . . . Many Soviet critics accepted his theories enthusiastically, although they had little opportunity to test them and despite the fact that Smith never had even half the Russian following of . . . Michael Gold." Gold believed that jazz was the product of a Negro-Jewish nexus, a mutuality born of oppression. See *Red and Hot,* 99–100. The coincidence of Gold's views with those of Daniel Gregory Mason did not escape MacDonald Smith Moore's attention. See Moore, *Yankee Blues,* 127.

22. Judging from Daniel Aaron's characterization of Gold in *Writers on the Left,* his interests were far more literary than musical, with the possible exception of "Yiddish folksongs and Hebrew hymns" (85). For Gold, jazz was fodder for propaganda.

23. The title of this essay is a pun on Collier's survey of jazz history, *The Making of Jazz: A Comprehensive History* (Boston: Houghton Mifflin Company, 1978). See also Starr, *Red and Hot:* "Closely linked with the unfolkish tendencies of radio and phonograph, jazz was commercial from the outset. Had it been otherwise, the emigration of New Orleans musicians to Chicago, Chicagoans to New York, of New Yorkers to Europe, and all of them to recording studios would never have occurred" (97–98).

24. Collier, "Faking of Jazz," 34. It should be noted, however, that first impressions of New Orleans bands were often negative. See Holbrook, "Mister Jazz Himself," 142–43.

25. Collier, "Faking of Jazz," 37.

26. Collier uses the interviews contained in the appendix of "American Jazz Criticism" extensively in framing his argument in "The Faking of Jazz," but he does so selectively. For example, Collier quotes Walter Schaap (1917–2005) on p. 39 of his essay, except that the last line is omitted: "This was also the Depression, and the left-wing movement was sometimes pro-Communist and sometimes not." See Walter Schaap, interview by Ronald G. Welburn, Mar. 17, 1982, transcript of tape recording, in Welburn, "American Jazz Criticism," 269.

27. B. H. Haggin, letter to the editor, "The Politics of Jazz," *New Republic,* Dec. 16, 1985, 6.

28. John Henry Hammond Jr., interview by Ronald G. Welburn, June 3, 1980, transcript of tape recording, in Welburn, "American Jazz Criticism," 206–7.

29. Collier, "Faking of Jazz," 39.

30. See Howe and Coser, *American Communist Party,* 37, 60–61, 99, 144–46, 156, 169, 483–90. During the 1930s, competing leftist factions often abandoned discourse in favor of violence. See Hal Libros, "Styles in Political Reform Organizations," in *Our Sociological Eye: Personal Essays on Society and Culture,* ed. Arthur B. Shostak (Port Washington, N.Y.: Alfred Publishing Company, 1977), 243–53. What Libros objected to was the Communists' lack of a democratic spirit: "The Communist movement, on the other hand, was undemocratic. Its political line was handed down. . . . Members usually accepted the decision, going to sleep one night believing in a particular policy and awakening the next morning to find out (after they read the *Daily Worker*) that they believed the opposite" (250). Libros was a friend of Al Rose's from days at Temple University.

31. Much of what follows is based on the author's interview with Al Rose, cited earlier (July 29, 1989). Although Rose's claims that he was the scion of an aristocratic Creole family (not Jewish), that he ran guns during the Spanish Civil War, and that he served as Trotsky's bodyguard are spurious, his experience and recollections regarding jazz and the left are credible. See his son's account: Rex Rose, "Al Rose, His Secret Life," http://rexrose.com.

32. Rose was recruited for membership in the Lovestoneite movement by Israel Zimmerman. Jay Lovestone was the head of the dominant faction within the Communist Party of the United States until he was expelled by Stalin following the Sixth Congress of the Comintern in 1928. In the early 1930s, he went on to establish the Opposition Communist Party of the United States, usually referred to as the Right Opposition. See Robert J. Alexander, *The Right Opposition: The Lovestoneites and the International Communist Opposition of the 1930s* (Westport, Conn.: Greenwood Press, 1982). For information on Rose's jazz activities,

see Al Rose, *I Remember Jazz: Six Decades among the Great Jazzmen* (Baton Rouge: Louisiana State University Press, 1987).

33. Rose, interview by author, July 29, 1989.

34. Rose, interview by author, July 29, 1989.

35. John Hammond, interview by Welburn, June 3, 1980, 209, 214.

36. Rose stated in an interview that he was out with Hammond the night before he was to join the Communist Party. If this was the case, he apparently changed his mind, and there is considerable doubt that he would have even entertained the idea, given the following statement: "It was important for anyone interested in the struggle for civil and social justice to understand the dangers communism had for Negroes. . . . The result for most Negroes who turned to communism in that turbulent decade was frustration, disillusionment and final rejection." See Alan Pomerance, *Repeal of the Blues: How Black Entertainers Influenced Civil Rights* (Secaucus, N.J.: Citadel Press, 1988), 35.

37. See Ralph de Toledano, *Lament for a Generation* (New York: Farrar, Strauss and Cudahy, 1960), 21–45, on the disenchantment of young Columbia University students, several of whom became notable jazz writers, with Stalinism. Toledano studied at Juilliard and was editor of the *New Leader* before defecting from the Socialist Party of America as part of the "old guard" faction of anti-Communists led by Louis Waldman. He graduated from Columbia in 1938 and became a founding editor of *Jazz Information* in 1939.

38. Toledano, who later became Richard Nixon's biographer, is specifically mentioned by Rose as one who made this journey. See Toledano's account in *Lament for a Generation.*

39. Rose, interview by author, July 29, 1989. See also Russell Sanjek, interview by Ronald G. Welburn, Feb. 11, 1982, transcript of tape recording, in Welburn, "American Jazz Criticism," 247.

40. Collier, "Faking of Jazz," 39. Regarding Collier's "The Faking of Jazz" and *The Reception of Jazz in America*, one might argue that "myths" are not always intentionally manufactured for ideological or other purposes but are often the consequence of the difficulties inherent in trying to render complex cultural processes intelligible. For a critique of Collier along these lines, see Gushee, review, 353–54.

41. See Krin Gabbard, *Black Magic: White Hollywood and African American Culture* (New Brunswick and London: Rutgers University Press, 2004), 199–234, quote on 204. For the discussion following, see Gabbard, *Black Magic*, 210–12, quote on 212.

42. See Jed Rasula, "The Media of Memory: The Seductive Menace of Records in Jazz History," in *Jazz among the Discourses,* ed. Krin Gabbard (Durham and London: Duke University Press, 1995), 134–64, quotes on 134, 136, 140; see also 146.

Chapter 2

1. Lawrence Gushee, "A Preliminary Chronology of the Early Career of Ferd 'Jelly Roll' Morton," *American Music* 3 (Winter 1985): 389–412. See also Alan Lomax, *Mister Jelly Roll: The Fortunes of Jelly Roll Morton, New Orleans Creole and "Inventor of Jazz"* (New York: Grossett and Dunlap, 1950).

2. "Jelly Roll Morton Symposium," tape recording, May 7, 1982, HJA.

3. One such acolyte was Bix Beiderbecke. See Jean Pierre Lion, *Bix: The Definite Biography of a Jazz Legend,* trans. from the French by Gabriella Page-Fort, with Michael B. Heckman and Norman Field (New York: Continuum International Publishing Group, 2005), 12.

4. Much of the foregoing account of "hot" collecting origins in the Ivy League is taken from Stephen W. Smith, "Hot Collecting," in *Jazzmen,* ed. Frederic Ramsey Jr. and Charles Edward Smith (New York: Harcourt, Brace and Company, 1939), 288–89. See also John Hammond, "An Experiment in Jazz History," in *Black Music in Our Culture: Curricular Ideas on the Subjects, Materials and Problems,* ed. Dominique-Rene de Lerma (Kent: Kent State University Press, 1970), 43.

5. Albert J. McCarthy, "A Questionnaire: Charles Edward Smith," in *This Is Jazz,* ed. Ken Williamson (London: Newnes, 1960), 246.

6. Derek Langridge, *Your Jazz Collection* (Hamden, Conn.: Archon Books, 1970), 27.

7. Langridge, *Your Jazz Collection,* 23.

8. On "second lines," see Helen A. Regis, "Blackness and the Politics of Memory in the New Orleans Second Line," *American Ethnologist* 28, no. 4 (2001): 752–77; Helen A. Regis, "Second Lines, Minstrelsy, and the Contested Landscapes of New Orleans Afro-Creole Festivals," *Cultural Anthropology* 14, no. 4 (1999): 472–504.

9. Langridge, *Your Jazz Collection,* 31–32.

10. For Sam Morgan's Jazz Band, see Jeanette Kimball, interview by William Russell, Feb. 10, 1962, and Isaiah Morgan, interview by William Russell and Richard B. Allen, Dec. 1, 1958, tape recordings, HJA. For Celestin, see William "Bébé" Ridgley, interview by William Russell and Ralph Collins, June 2, 1959, tape recording, HJA.

11. "New Orleans Funeral," 16-mm. film, narrated by Matthew Houston, filmed by Jules Cahn, written and produced by Dolores Arodoyno, 1962, HJA.

12. William J. Schafer and Richard B. Allen, *Brass Bands and New Orleans Jazz* (Baton Rouge: Louisiana State University Press, 1977); Knowles, *Fallen Heroes.* See also Louis Armstrong, *Swing That Music* (London, New York, and Toronto: Longmans, Green and Co., 1936). Armstrong mentions "lodge parades and things like that" and contends that "hot" New Orleans brass bands were stylistically and functionally unlike their Northern counterparts (15–16).

13. For *Down Beat,* see Welburn, "American Jazz Criticism," 79–103; Gennari, *Blowin' Hot and Cool,* 67, 88, 90–94, 103, 174.

14. Charles Edward Smith, "Collecting Hot," abridged reprint in *Esquire's Jazz Book,* ed. Paul Eduard Miller (Chicago: Esquire, 1943–44), 15–16.

15. Ramsey and Smith, *Jazzmen,* 289.

16. Archie Green, "Graphics #68: Winding Down," *JEMF Quarterly* (Fall/Winter 1985; published Spring 1990): 99–107, quote on 101.

17. Merrill M. Hammond, "Crusader—'To the Beat of a Drum,'" *Second Line* 2 (Aug. 1951): 9, 8.

18. Charles Edward Smith, "Collecting Hot," 15.

19. Charles Edward Smith, "Collecting Hot," 15.

20. Charles Edward Smith, "Collecting Hot," 16.

21. Whitney Balliett, "Panassié, Delaunay et Cie," in *American Musicians: Fifty-six Portraits in Jazz* (New York: Oxford University Press, 1986), 3–11; Neil Leonard, *Jazz: Myth and Religion* (New York: Oxford University Press, 1987), 138. Hugues Panassié, *Hot Jazz; The Guide to Swing Music,* trans. Lyle and Eleanor Dowling (New York: M. Witmark & Sons, 1936).

22. On "primitivism" in the works of Panassié and Goffin, see John Gennari, "Jazz Criticism: Its Development and Ideologies," *Black American Literature Forum* 25, no. 3 (1991): 449–523, especially 465–67; Welburn, "American Jazz Criticism," 117–23.

23. Charles Delaunay, interview by Ronald G. Welburn, Sept. 24, 1980, transcript of tape recording, in Welburn, "American Jazz Criticism," 198. See also Charles Delaunay, *Delaunay's Dilemma: De la Peinture au Jazz* (Mâcon: Éditions W, 1985), 47.

24. Balliett, "Panassié, Delaunay et Cie," 6. For exposition of how the subjective decisions of discographers affect historical conceptualization, see William Howland Kenney, "Historical Context and the Definition of Jazz: Putting More of the History in 'Jazz History,'" in Gabbard, *Jazz among the Discourses,* 100–117.

25. William Russell recalls that Hilton R. Schleman's *Rhythm on Record* (London: Melody Maker Publications, 1936) was also widely used. See William Russell, interview by Richard B. Allen and John Perhonis, Feb. 16, 1976, tape recording, HJA. See also George Hoefer, "Collectors: Personalities and Anecdotes," in Paul Eduard Miller, *Esquire's Jazz Book* (1943–44), 29.

26. Stephen W. Smith, "Hot Collecting," 293.

27. Quotes are from translated excerpts in Lion, *Bix,* xv. Panassié was not the first to write on jazz for *La Revue Musicale.* In the bibliography to André Coueroy and André Schaeffner, *Le Jazz* (Paris: Éditions Claude Aveline, 1926), there is a citation of Marion Bauer, "L'influence du Jazz-Band," *Revue Musicale,* Apr. 1924. Also, Coueroy and Shaeffner's first chapter within the section "D'Afrique en Amérique" is "Musique Pure et Musique Élémentaire," indicating

a kind of proto-purism already in place in France in 1926, one that made direct connections to Africa. Like Panassié 's *Le Jazz Hot,* however, this book was not well grounded historically.

28. For more on the organization of the Hot Club de France, see Michael Dregni, *Django: The Life and Music of a Gypsy Legend* (New York: Oxford University Press, 2004), 75–79.

29. Georges Hilaire, "Hugues Panassié," *Hot Jazz,* Mar. 1935, 14, 16. For additional information on French reception of jazz, see Ludovic Tournès, *New Orleans sur Seine: Histoire du jazz en France* (Paris: Librairie Arthème Fayard, 1999).

30. For the quote, see Balliett, "Panassie, Delaunay et Cie," 6. For Panassié's critique of essentialism, see Gennari, "Jazz Criticism," 465–68. See also Ted Gioia, *The Imperfect Art: Reflections on Jazz and Modern Culture* (New York: Oxford University Press, 1988), 29.

31. Hoefer, "Collectors," 30. See also Thomas J. Hennessey, "The Black Chicago Establishment, 1919–1930," *Journal of Jazz Studies* 2 (Dec. 1974): 15–45, in which he points out that "the New Orleans contingent controlled the cabarets and recording sessions" (21).

32. Hoefer, "Collectors," 30. Hoefer began writing for *Tempo* in 1938 and was with *Down Beat* for twenty-eight years. The evolution of his monthly "Hot Box" column (beginning Oct. 1, 1939) illustrates the natural progression from "hot" collecting to history, as stated in his obituary in *Down Beat* 34 (Dec. 28, 1967): "Originally a column for collectors, it was later expanded to include all facets of jazz history" (13).

33. Hoefer, "Collectors," 30.

34. Leonard, *Jazz and the White Americans,* 138.

35. Sanjek, interview by Welburn, Feb. 11, 1982, 247–49, 250. Archie Green also names artist E. Simms Campbell as an influence; see "Graphics #68," 101.

36. Charters and Kunstadt, *Jazz,* 319; Arnold Shaw, "The Expanding Jazz Bookshelf," *Saturday Review,* Jan. 25, 1958, 63–65; Welburn, "American Jazz Criticism," 136.

37. Gilbert Millstein, "The Commodore Record Shop and Milt Gabler," in *Eddie Condon's Treasury of Jazz,* ed. Eddie Condon and Richard Gehman (New York: Dial Press, 1956), 83.

38. As quoted in Leonard, *Jazz: Myth and Religion,* 148.

39. Sanjek, interview by Welburn, Feb. 11, 1982, 250–51.

40. Sanjek, interview by Welburn, Feb. 11, 1982, 250, 257.

41. Welburn, "American Jazz Criticism," 100–103.

42. "The History of Swing Music," 20 parts, *Down Beat* 3 (June 1936): 4; 3 (July 1936): 4; 3 (Aug. 1936): 3; 3 (Sept. 1936): 6; 3 (Nov. 1936): 8; 4 (Jan. 1937): 6; 4 (Feb. 1937): 8; 4 (Mar. 1937): 10; 4 (Apr. 1937): 8; 4 (May 1937): 10; 4 (June 1937): 10; 4 (July 1937): 12; 4 (Aug. 1937): 10; 4 (Sept. 1937): 14; 4 (Oct. 1937): 12; 4 (Nov.

1937): 16; 4 (Dec. 1937): 17; 5 (Jan. 1938): 17; 5 (Mar. 1938): 13; 5 (Apr. 1938): 12.

43. Marshall Stearns, "The History of Swing Music," *Down Beat* 3 (Aug. 1936): 6–7; Marshall Stearns, "The History of Swing Music (Chapter IV: The White Tradition in Chicago—Did Rhythm Kings Borrow Ideas from Negroes?)," *Down Beat* 3 (Sept. 1936): 6, continued in *Down Beat* 3 (Oct. 1936): 6.

44. Lawrence Gushee, *Pioneers of Jazz: The Story of the Creole Band* (New York: Oxford University Press, 2005).

45. Nick LaRocca, letter, *Down Beat* 3 (Sept. 1936): 1; Nick LaRocca, "Jazz Stems from Whites, Not Blacks," *Metronome* 52 (Oct. 1936): 20, 51, 53; Nick LaRocca, "History of the Original Dixieland Jazz Band," *Tempo* 4 (Oct. 1936): 4, 11–12.

46. Welburn, "American Jazz Criticism," 93.

47. Marshall Stearns, New Haven, Conn., to Nick LaRocca, Washington, D.C., Jan. 11, 1937, unpublished vertical file, Nick LaRocca Collection, HJA.

48. For a comparison of Hammond's *Down Beat* reportage of Smith's death and accounts of eyewitnesses, see Chris Albertson, *Bessie* (New York: Stein and Day Publishers, 1972), 216–26. See also Dave Oxley, interview by William Russell, Jan. 6, 1965, tape recording, HJA.

49. For LaRocca's claim to be an originator of jazz, see Nick LaRocca, interviews by Richard B. Allen, May 21, May 26, June 2, June 9, and June 16, 1958, and Nick LaRocca, interview by William Ransom Hogan, Oct. 26, 1959, tape recordings, HJA. For reassessment of this claim, see Richard M. Sudhalter, *Lost Chords: White Musicians and Their Contributions to Jazz, 1915–1945* (New York: Oxford University Press, 1999); Bruce Boyd Raeburn, "Jazz and the Italian Connection," *Jazz Archivist* 6, no. 1 (1991): 1–6; Jack Stewart, "The Original Dixieland Jazz Band's Place in the Development of Jazz," *Jazz Archivist* 19 (2005–6): 16–25; Lynn Abbott and Doug Seroff, "'Brown Skin, Who You For?' Another Look at Clarence Williams's Early Career," *Jazz Archivist* 8, nos. 1–2 (1993): 1–15.

50. See Irving Kolodin, "Number One Swing Man," in *Jam Session: An Anthology of Jazz*, ed. Ralph J. Gleason (New York: G. P. Putnam's Sons, 1958), 67–86, a reprint of an article that first appeared in *Harper's* (Sept. 1939). For details on Hammond and Goodman, see also John Hammond, "Experiment in Jazz History," 51–54; George Frazier, "Take Thirty," *Esquire*, June 1968, 97. Although Goodman married Hammond's sister in the early 1940s, their relationship did not remain indefinitely cordial. See John McDonough, review of *Hammond on Record*, by John Hammond, in *Down Beat* 45 (Jan. 12, 1978): 58–60.

51. Hammond actually censored release of the Glenn Miller (1904—44) recording of "W.P.A." because he considered it degrading to blacks; see George T. Simon, *Glenn Miller and His Orchestra* (New York: Thomas Y. Crowell Company, 1974), 214. For Miller's mercurial rise to fame and the impact of racism on the dance band business, see Irving Kolodin, "The Dance Band Business: A Study in Black and White," *Harper's*, June 1941, 72–82.

52. Kolodin, "Number One Swing Man," 68. See also Ernest P. Dryson, "The Man Who Discovered Everybody," *Washington Post*, Feb. 1, 1970.

53. This was one of three concerts featuring all-black talent held under the auspices of Popular Front policies between the fall of 1938 and the spring of 1939 in which communist organizations participated. Negative reactions in the *Daily Worker* so incensed Hammond that he demanded, and received, an apology from the newspaper. See Naison, *Communists in Harlem*, 211–13. Naison's coverage of these events fails to mention any New Orleans acts. Although *New Masses* sponsored "From Spirituals to Swing," Hammond insisted the concert was not politicized in any way. See John Hammond, interview by Welburn, June 3, 1980, 209.

54. Helen Lawrenson, "Black and White and Red All Over," *New York Magazine*, Aug. 21, 1978, 36–43, gives the inside story. See also John S. Wilson, "Obituaries: Barney Josephson, Owner of Cafe Society Jazz Club, Is Dead at 86," *New York Times*, Sept. 30, 1988; David W. Stowe, "The Politics of Café Society," *Journal of American History* 84 (Mar. 1998): 1384–1406.

55. Lawrenson, "Black and White," 36.

56. See Charles Edward Smith, "Heat Wave," *Stage*, Sept. 1935, 45–46, quote on 45. Much of this article is taken from LaRocca's letters, illustrating how interaction with musicians confirmed historical details that had previously been extrapolated. Smith corresponded with LaRocca from late 1933 and was publishing information thus obtained by 1935. See Charles Edward Smith, New York, to Nick LaRocca, New Orleans, Nov. 21, 1933; Nick LaRocca to Charles Edward Smith, Nov. 30, 1933; Charles Edward Smith to Nick LaRocca, Dec. 7, 1933; Nick LaRocca to Charles Edward Smith Dec. 10, 1933; and Charles Edward Smith to Nick LaRocca, June 29, 1936, all unpublished vertical file, Nick LaRocca Collection, HJA. Regarding the influence of Negro folk music, LaRocca remained impervious to Smith's arguments.

57. Charles Edward Smith, "Swing," *New Republic*, Feb. 16, 1938, 39–41.

58. Charles Edward Smith, "Swing," 40.

59. Charles Edward Smith, "Swing," 40.

60. Charles Edward Smityh, "Swing," 41.

61. Smith wrote about this first trip to New Orleans in " 'It's Tough—Trying to Run Down Jazz Facts': But Smith Digs 'Em from Vets like Papa Laine in Orleans," *Down Beat* 7 (Jan. 1, 1940): 8. Jack Laine came to his attention (for the first time) on a tip from Walter Pichon that led to Ernest Giardina and hence to an interview with Laine: "Laine knew that the chief inspiration for Dixieland style came from Negro bands like that of Buddy Bolden's because he was there when it happened. I learned from him, as I had from Willy Cornish of the Bolden band, that most of the New Orleans sessions were not hit-or-miss jam sessions but had been worked out by ear at informal rehearsals." Smith also relates how Russell and Ramsey "trudged the streets of Harlem, ringing doorbells," in search of Oliver's relatives when they were researching *Jazzmen*.

62. See Armstrong, *Swing That Music*, 12–13. Armstrong introduced most of the tropes that were later used in the construction of Bolden as the original cornet hero in *Jazzmen*, including allusions to power and volume ("loud and strong . . . hear him a mile away"), primacy ("the first of them all . . . as early as 1905"), and his nervous breakdown and subsequent incarceration. An almost sycophantic and historically implausible characterization of the ODJB's influence in New Orleans from 1913 (likely ghost-written) may account for the book's apparent lack of credibility among collectors. See William Howland Kenney, "Negotiating the Color Line: Louis Armstrong's Autobiographies," in *Jazz in Mind: Essays on the History and Meaning of Jazz*, ed. Reginald T. Buckner and Steven Weiland (Detroit: Wayne State University Press, 1991), 38–59. News of Bunk circulated quickly: see Park Breck, "This Isn't Bunk; Bunk Taught Louis," *Down Beat* 6 (June 1939): 4, which quotes a letter from Russell on Bunk and his mention of King Bolden.

63. Russell began writing music about 1929. When Henry Cowell published some of his compositions in 1933, he felt "the use of the name Wagner on music would be about equal to writing a play and signing it 'Henry Shakespeare,' so he changed his name." See William Russell, interview by William Ransom Hogan and Paul R. Crawford, Aug. 31, 1962, tape recording, HJA. See also Bruce Boyd Raeburn, "The Musical Worlds of William Russell," *Southern Quarterly* 36 (Winter 1998): 10–18.

64. Russell, interview by Hogan and Crawford, Aug. 31, 1962; see also "Bill Russell Reminisces," interview by George W. Kay, *Mississippi Rag* 6 (Sept. 1979): 1–4.

65. Kay, "Bill Russell Reminisces," 1.

66. Russell, interview by Hogan and Crawford, Aug. 31, 1962.

67. Russell, interview by Hogan and Crawford, Aug. 31, 1962.

68. Kay, "Bill Russell Reminisces," 1.

69. Stephen W. Smith, "Hot Collecting," 294. This was a reference to Edward Noyes Westcott's novel *David Harum: A Story of American Life* (New York: Appleton and Company, 1898), about a perspicacious lad who makes good.

70. Sanjek, interview by Welburn, Feb. 11, 1982, 252; Russell, interview by Hogan and Crawford, Aug. 31, 1962. Russell refers to Rosenberg as "a friend and fabulous guy around New York" in this interview, confirming the opinion presented by Sanjek that he was one of the major unsung heroes in the spread of jazz information.

71. See "Collectors' Items," *Jazz Information* 1 (Nov. 24, 1939): 2, 4; Charles Edward Smith, "I Thought I Heard Buddy Bolden Play," *HRS Society Rag*, July 1938, 8; Walter E. Schaap, "Jazzmen Abroad," *Jazz Information* 1 (Nov. 1, 1939): 2, 8; Walter Schaap, "Jazzmen Abroad," *Jazz Information* 1 (Nov. 24, 1939): 2, 4; Walter Schaap, "Jazzmen Abroad," *Jazz Information* 1 (Dec. 8, 1939): 4; Margaret Kidder, "Americana in Paris," *HRS Society Rag*, Jan. 1939, 16–20; James

Higgins, "George Frazier," *HRS Society Rag,* July 1938, 1–4; Otis Ferguson, "John Hammond," *HRS Society Rag,* Sept. 1938, 1–7. The final issue of *Jazz Information* (Nov. 1941) includes a history of the magazine written by Gene Williams, emphasizing its ultrapurist rationale: "J.I. took the basic theory and background of jazz much as it was established in *Jazzmen,* forsaking the amorphous, too eclectic methods of earlier French and American writers. But it went further than *Jazzmen;* it pointed out the very tenuous link between the swing movement of today and the genuine, exciting music of the folk blues and the New Orleans jazz tradition."

72. Winthrop Sargeant, *Jazz: Hot and Hybrid* (New York: Arrow Editions, 1938); Wilder Hobson, *American Jazz Music* (New York: W. W. Norton, 1939; reprint, New York: Da Capo Press, 1976).

73. In *Blowin' Hot and Cool,* Gennari describes *Hot and Hybrid* as "the first U.S. book to apply the scrutiny of a professional music critic to jazz, describing chord structures, scale systems, and rhythmic patterns in a way that gave 'hot jazz' meaning as a complex musical language rather than as a vague emotional state" (119).

74. Frank Norris, "Wilder Hobson," *HRS Society Rag,* Jan. 1939, 4.

75. Norris, "Wilder Hobson," 4.

76. Hobson, *American Jazz Music,* "Acknowledgments." Hobson was given access to Sargeant's manuscript before publication, thus accounting for the similarity of musicological analysis. D.E.D's review, "Hobson's 'American Jazz Music' Traces Rise of Pop Music," *Down Beat* 6 (May 1939), finds the first three chapters "dull and uninformative" and opines, "One of these days someone is going to write a terrific book on hot jazz. Hobson came close" (4).

77. Hobson, *American Jazz Music,* 92.

78. Hobson, *American Jazz Music,* 39, 93. Fate Marable did not employ black New Orleans musicians until 1917–18; see William Howland Kenney, *Jazz on the River* (Chicago and London: Chicago University Press, 2005), 38–50. The racially mixed nature of some of Jack Laine's Reliance bands may have been what misled Hobson.

79. Ramsey had an interesting family background. His father was the abstract painter Charles Frederic Ramsey (1875–1951), the son of painter Milne Ramsey (1846–1915). Charles was dismissed as director of the Minneapolis School of Art "for socialist views" in 1917 and moved to New Hope, Pa., where he founded the New Group in 1930 to combat the dominance of New Hope Impressionists over the Phillips Mill exhibitions. By 1932 the group was known as the Independents, and in 1938 Ramsey joined the Cooperative Painting project, "in which artists sought to submerge their singular identities in joint artistic ventures . . . influenced by improvisational jazz and collective political theories." See http://www.michenermuseum.org/bucksartists.

80. William Russell, "Boogie Woogie," *Hot Jazz,* June–Sept. 1938. For an in-

teresting comparison of Russell's views with an account by Sidney Martin printed in the July 1938 *Down Beat,* see "Boogie Woogie: Notes and Nuts," *HRS Society Rag,* Sept. 1938, 10–11. For an account of how Russell came to be recruited for *Jazzmen,* see Russell, interview by Hogan and Crawford, Aug. 31, 1962.

81. Russell, interview by Hogan and Crawford, Aug. 31, 1962.

82. Russell, interview by Hogan and Crawford, Aug. 31, 1962.

83. Russell, interview by Hogan and Crawford, Aug. 31, 1962.

84. See Frederic Ramsey Jr., "Grand Lama of Jazz," *HRS Society Rag,* Aug. 15, 1940, 2–6.

85. Russell, interview by Allen and Perhonis, Feb. 16, 1976. In this interview, Russell states that he did most of the writing because Smith was "too busy" running the Hot Record Exchange.

86. Ramsey and Smith, *Jazzmen,* xi.

87. William Russell and Stephen W. Smith, "New Orleans Music," in Ramsey and Smith, *Jazzmen,* 9.

88. Russell and Smith, "New Orleans Music," 10. Russell romanticized the propensity for "faking" as arising from a supposed lack of musical training within the black community—an erroneous assumption. See Charles Kinzer, "The Tios of New Orleans and Their Pedagogical Influence on the Early Jazz Clarinet Style," *Black Music Research Journal* 16 (Fall 1996): 279–302. Charles Edward Smith was more balanced: "Almost from its inception, there have been two types of jazzmen, those who could read and consequently formed a bridge between jazz and popular music as such, and the jazzmen, from Bolden to Bechet, who have always represented an improvisational trend closer to folk music than to written music" ("'It's Tough,'" 8).

89. Russell and Smith, "New Orleans Music," 15.

90. Russell and Smith, "New Orleans Music," 23.

91. Russell and Smith, "New Orleans Music," 30–31.

92. Russell and Smith, "New Orleans Music," 33.

93. William Russell, interview by William Ransom Hogan and Paul R. Crawford, Sept. 4, 1962, tape recording, HJA.

94. Russell and Smith, "New Orleans Music," 36. In an interview with William Russell years later, however, the wife of Joe Oliver stated that the couple could live "very well" on one dollar a night. See Stella Oliver, interview by William Russell and Ralph Collins, Apr. 22, 1959, tape recording, HJA.

95. Hot Jazz Society of San Francisco to William Russell, Dec. 1, 1943, unpublished vertical file, William Russell Collection, HJA.

96. Charles Edward Smith, "New Orleans: 'Callin' Our Chillun Home,'" in Ramsey and Smith, *Jazzmen,* 3–6.

97. Charles Edward Smith, "White New Orleans," in Ramsey and Smith, *Jazzmen,* 40.

98. Charles Edward Smith, "White New Orleans," 41.

99. Charles Edward Smith, "White New Orleans," 42.

100. Charles Edward Smith, "White New Orleans," 44.

101. Charles Edward Smith, "White New Orleans," 57.

102. Charles Edward Smith, "Land of Dreams," in Ramsey and Smith, *Jazzmen*, 266–67.

103. Charles Edward Smith, "Land of Dreams," 268.

104. On Morton in Harlem, see Charters and Kunstadt, *Jazz*, 236–37. On adaptation to Swing Era conventions, see Barney Bigard, *With Louis and the Duke: The Autobiography of a Jazz Clarinetist*, ed. Barry Martyn (London: Macmillan Press, 1985). On Luis Russell and Bob Crosby, see John Chilton, *Ride, Red, Ride: The Life of Henry "Red" Allen*, with a selected discography compiled by Brian Peerless (London and New York: Cassell, 1999), 58–63; *Stomp Off, Let's Go! The Story of Bob Crosby's Bob Cats & Big Band* (London: Jazz Book Service, 1983). On Don Albert, see Christopher Wilkinson, *Jazz on the Road: Don Albert's Musical Life* (Berkeley: University of California Press, 2001). Both the ODJB and Jelly Roll Morton tried to adapt to Swing Era conventions (unsuccessfully) in offering compositions or arrangements for big band during attempted "comebacks" in the 1930s.

105. Charles Edward Smith, "Land of Dreams," 283.

106. Stella Oliver contradicts numerous "facts" found in Ramsey's account; e.g., he was born in Abend, La., not on Dryades Street in New Orleans; he was a "yard boy" for a Jewish family, not a "butler." See Stella Oliver, interview by Russell and Collins, Apr. 22, 1959.

107. For development of this point, see Leonard, *Jazz: Myth and Religion*, 118–22, 132–33.

108. Paul Barbarin (Oliver's drummer at the Royal Gardens) stated that Oliver was crowned "King" in Chicago, not New Orleans. See Paul Barbarin, interview by William Russell, Richard B. Allen, and Robert Campbell, Mar. 27, 1957, tape recording, HJA; Gene Anderson, "The Genesis of King Oliver's Creole Jazz Band," *American Music* (Fall 1994): 283–303.

109. Several authorities have shown that the exodus from New Orleans was not the product of the closing of Storyville, which was already moribund by 1913. See Al Rose, *Storyville, New Orleans* (Tuscaloosa: University of Alabama Press, 1974), especially 213–15. According to Oliver's wife, his arrest during a cabaret police raid was the cause for the move. See Stella Oliver, interview by Russell and Collins, Apr. 22, 1959; Raeburn, "Ménage à Trois," 88–94.

110. Frederic Ramsey Jr., "King Oliver and his Creole Jazz Band," in Ramsey and Smith, *Jazzmen*, 66.

111. Ramsey, "King Oliver," 70.

112. Baby Dodds contradicts Ramsey's depiction of Oliver as "a band man, and a band man only," stating that after the recordings made the band famous, what had been conceived as a cooperative group became "Oliver's band," which

was why he and his brother quit. See Warren "Baby" Dodds, interview by William Russell, May 31, 1958, tape recording, HJA. See also Raeburn, "Ménage à Trois," 94.

113. Ramsey, "King Oliver," 91.

114. William Russell, "Louis Armstrong," in Ramsey and Smith, *Jazzmen*, 120–22. This was luck, for if Armstrong had been arrested two years before, there would not have been a band for him to play in. See Abbey "Chinee" Foster, interview by William Russell and Ralph Collins, Mar. 21, 1961, tape recording, HJA.

115. Russell, "Louis Armstrong," 139.

116. Russell, "Louis Armstrong," 139.

117. Russell, "Louis Armstrong," 130.

118. Russell, "Louis Armstrong," 132.

119. DeVeaux, "Constructing the Jazz Tradition," 532–33. DeVeaux differentiates between the "Tragic" tone of *Jazzmen* and the contrasting "Romantic" narrative strain in the "official" historical surveys.

120. Guthrie Ramsey, "Cosmopolitan or Provincial?" 34.

121. Gennari, *Blowin' Hot and Cool*, 122–30, quotes on 123.

122. Gennari, *Blowin' Hot and Cool*, 123–24.

123. Gennari, *Blowin' Hot and Cool*, 129.

124. DeVeaux, "Constructing the Jazz Tradition," 533.

125. Arthur F. Wertheim, "Constance Rourke and the Discovery of American Culture in the 1930s," in *The Study of American Culture: Contemporary Conflicts*, ed. Luther S. Luedtke (Deland, Fla.: Everett/Edwards, 1977), 49–61, quote on 50.

126. Daniel Aaron, "An Approach to the Thirties," in Luedtke, *Study of American Culture*, 1–17, especially 12–14.

127. For further critique of "myths" contained in *Jazzmen*, see Daniel F. Havens, "Up the River from New Orleans: The Jazz Odyssey—Myth or Truth?" *Popular Music and Society* 11 (Winter 1987): 61–74. Of course, the authors of *Jazzmen* knew there would be omissions: "Those of us who worked on *Jazzmen* had no illusion that we should or could say the last word on a subject that had so many ramifications. We therefore determined to throw the emphasis on enough significant individuals in hot jazz (the Bolden tradition) to make clear what happened to jazz in this or that environment" (Smith, "'It's Tough,'" 8).

Chapter 3

1. "Discology" describes a wider phenomenon than "discography" (writing about records), recognizing the shift from consumption to production of records that occurred in the late 1930s. Orin Blackstone used the term in *Playback* magazine (1949–52; continuing *The Jazzfinder*). His *Index to Jazz* (1945–48, in four parts) was the only major discography produced by an American during the

1940s. In 1943 an American edition of Charles Delaunay's *Hot Discography*, by the Commodore Record Shop, came out; in 1948 Delaunay's *New Hot Discography* became available, with the aid of George Avakian.

2. Tom Stagg and Charlie Crump, *New Orleans, the Revival: A Tape and Discography of Negro Traditional Jazz Recorded in New Orleans or by New Orleans Bands, 1937–1972* (Dublin: Bashall Caves Publishers, 1973); Teizo Ikegami, *New Orleans Renaissance on Record* (Tokyo: Alligator Jazz Club, 1980).

3. How the aims of the phonograph industry changed between 1890 and 1950 is a study in adaptation to new technologies and ever-widening and pluralistic popular tastes. Compare the conclusions reached by Hughson Mooney, "Years of Strain and Stress: 1917–1929 in the Whitburn Record Charts," *Popular Music and Society* 12 (Summer 1988): 1–20, to *New Grove Dictionary of Jazz* (1988), s.v. "Recording: Technological Developments: Recording and Playback after 1947," by Gordon Mumma, in which Mumma describes public tastes after World War II: "Finally the record-buying public was larger, more affluent, and, as a result of wartime travel and radio broadcasting, more catholic in its musical taste that it had ever been" (354).

4. See Tim Brooks, *Lost Sounds: Blacks and the Birth of the Recording Industry* (Urbana: University of Illinois Press, 2004), especially 83–92. See also Dan Weisman, "The Louisiana Phonograph Company," *Jazz Archivist* 4, no. 2 (Dec. 1989): 1–5

5. In the two months of Apr. and May 1891, one New Orleans coin-slot machine took in the "incredible sum" of one thousand dollars. Recordings of Louis Vasnier, a local Creole minstrel, made in 1891, may have been among the cylinders played on that machine (Weisman, "Louisiana Phonograph Record Company," 2–3).

6. Roland Gelatt, *The Fabulous Phonograph: From Tin Foil to High Fidelity* (New York: J. B. Lippincott Company, 1955), 188–91.

7. *New Grove Dictionary of Jazz* (1988), s.v. "History of Jazz Recording: Early Recordings," by Chris Sheridan. For the story of how this situation was reversed by the OKeh Record Company in 1920, with sales of Mamie Smith's "You Can't Keep a Good Man Down" (750,000 sold) and "Crazy Blues" (1,500,000 sold), see Ed Kirkeby, in collaboration with Duncan P. Schiedt and Sinclair Traill, *Ain't Misbehavin': The Story of Fats Waller* (New York: Dodd, Mead and Company, 1966), 63–67. As one Richmond, Va., record dealer told Ralph S. Peer, an OKeh agent: "The colored folk are buying record players like crazy. They don't really have that kind of money to spend. It's these records of Mamie Smith's" (Kirkeby, *Ain't Misbehavin'*, 67).

8. In 1902, external-horn Victors could be had for $15 to $35, but prices then began to rise. In 1916, enclosed-horn Victrolas and Edison Amberol consoles retailed for about $200, while Vocalion "art models" ranged from $375 to $2,000. By the mid-1920s, "flat-top" console phonographs were available for $100. See

Gelatt, *Fabulous Phonograph*, 191–93. See also William Howland Kenney, *Recorded Music in American Life: The Phonograph and Popular Memory, 1890–1945* (New York: Oxford University Press, 1999), which quotes *Talking Machine Weekly* (Aug. 1919): "The future of our industry lies in encouraging the sale of high-priced goods and the best records. It emphatically does not lie in pushing cheap machines and jazz records" (63).

9. See Gelatt, *Fabulous Phonograph*, 191. For discussion of how advertising portrayed the phonograph as a status symbol, see Paul Carter, *Another Part of the Twenties* (New York: Columbia University Press, 1977), 133.

10. See Gelatt, *Fabulous Phonograph*, 212–13.

11. See *New Grove Dictionary of Jazz* (1988), s.v. "Victor," by William S. Brockman. See also Kenney, *Recorded Music in American Life*, which argues that from 1917 to 1926, Ed King "promoted a musical synthesis of jazz with late Victorian sentiment and propriety" (63). King was with Victor from 1913 until Nov. 1926, when he switched to Columbia.

12. Gelatt gives the causes for the decline: "Radio broadcasting undoubtedly figured as the major cause. . . . But radio alone could not have brought the phonograph to such a sorry plight, nor could the indifference and apathy of RCA, nor the inflated prices at which most records and equipment continued to be quoted. These were surely contributory. But there was in addition something else, something intangible: a sudden disenchantment on a country-wide scale with phonographs, needles, records, and the whole concept of 'canned music.' The malaise broke out in 1929 and spread devastatingly to every city and state in America" (*Fabulous Phonograph*, 255–56).

13. See *New Grove Dictionary of Jazz* (1988), s.v. "Columbia," by Howard Rye and Barry Kernfeld. For information on the Columbia 13000-D and 14000-D series, see Dan Mahony, *The Columbia 13/14000-D Series: A Numerical Listing*, rev. 2d ed. (Stanhope, N.J.: Walter C. Allen, 1966).

14. See Brunn, *Story of the Original Dixieland Jazz Band*, 64–73, for the reasons why the ODJB went to Victor.

15. For information on Ralph Peer, see Alan Ward, "New Orleans Blues—The Story of Ralph Peer," *Footnote* 20 (June–July 1989): 15–17; Mike Hazeldine, "Record Reviews: 'New Orleans, 1924–1925, No. 2,'" *Footnote* 20 (Apr.–May 1989): 25–27; James S. Griffith, "Notes from an Interview with Marion Maxwell," *JEMF Quarterly* 21 (Spring–Summer 1985; published Spring 1989): 63; Kirkeby, *Ain't Misbehavin'*, 63–71. See also Nolen Porterfield, *Jimmie Rodgers: The Life and Times of America's Blue Yodeler* (Urbana: University of Illinois Press, 1979); Russell Sanjek, *American Popular Music and Its Business: The First Four Hundred Years* (New York: Oxford University Press, 1988).

16. Edison continued to produce blank cylinders for such purposes until 1929. See Mumma, "Recording."

17. Hazeldine, "Record Reviews," 26.

18. Saxophonist and leader White recalled that Columbia wanted an original number at the first session, but "other than 'Eccentric' and 'West End Romp,' the numbers recorded at the latter session were numbers Columbia ordered the band to play, things they hadn't played before." See Benjie White, interview by Richard B. Allen and Paul R. Crawford, Mar. 16, 1961, tape recording, HJA. See also Isaiah Morgan, interview by Russell and Allen, Dec. 1, 1958; Andrew Morgan, interview by William Russell, July 4, 1961, tape recording, HJA.

19. For information on Gordon, see Debora Kodish, *Good Friends and Bad Enemies: Robert Winslow Gordon and the Study of American Folksong* (Urbana: University of Illinois Press, 1986). For a broad survey of early folklorist collecting and field recording, see Joseph C. Hickerson, "American Folksong: Some Comments on the History of Its Collection and Archiving," in *Music in American Society, 1776–1976: From Puritan Hymn to Synthesizing,* ed. George McCue (New Brunswick: Transaction Books, 1977), 107–17.

20. This story is recounted in Ruth A. Banes, David A. Bealmear, and Kent Kaster, "Florida Bound Blues," *Popular Music and Society* 12 (Winter 1988): 43–58.

21. See R. Serge Denisoff, *Great Day Coming: Folk Music and the American Left* (Urbana: University of Illinois Press, 1971), especially 70–74, 109–11, 136–39, 168–70; Robbie Lieberman, *My Song Is My Weapon: People's Songs, American Communism, and the Politics of Culture, 1930–50* (Urbana: University of Illinois Press, 1989); Joe Klein, *Woody Guthrie: A Life* (New York: Alfred A. Knopf, 1980). For the Lomaxes' relations with Leadbelly, see John A. Lomax and Alan Lomax, *Negro Folk Songs as Sung by Lead Belly* (New York: Macmillan Company, 1936), especially 47–64.

22. See Russell, interview by Allen and Perhonis, Feb. 16, 1976, for the story of Martin's involvement in alerting Morton to Lomax's activities. It should be noted that Lomax interviewed only one other jazzman, James P. Johnson, and it did not go well.

23. "Jelly Roll Morton Symposium," May 7, 1982.

24. "Jelly Roll Morton Symposium," May 7, 1982.

25. For Morton's life and career, see William Russell, *"Oh Mister Jelly": A Jelly Roll Morton Scrapbook* (Singapore: Jazz Media Aps, 1999); Phil Pastras, *Dead Man Blues: Jelly Roll Morton Way Out West* (Berkeley: University of California Press, 2001); Gushee, "Preliminary Chronology"; Laurie Wright, *Mr. Jelly Lord* (Chigwell, England: Storyville Publications, 1980); Whitney Balliett, "Profiles: Ferdinand La Menthe," *New Yorker,* (June 23, 1980), 38–49; Kenneth Hulsizer, "Jelly Roll Morton in Washington," in Williamson, *This Is Jazz,* 202–16.

26. For Russell and Rose, see "Jelly Roll Morton Symposium," May 7, 1982. For Smith and Martin, see Russell, interview by Allen and Perhonis, Feb. 16, 1976. A general description of others can be found in Hulsizer, "Jelly Roll Morton in Washington."

27. See statements made in "Jelly Roll Morton Symposium," May 7, 1982; Russell, interview by Allen and Perhonis, Feb. 16, 1976.

28. See, e.g., Jelly Roll Morton, "I Discovered Jazz in 1902 (from *Downbeat*)," in *Frontiers of Jazz*, ed. Ralph de Toledano (New York: Oliver Durrell, 1947), 104–7 (originally published in *Down Beat* 5 [Aug. 1938]).

29. This fact was apparently overlooked by Martha Gravois and Martin W. Andresen, "The Senior Officer Oral History Program: There's More To It Than 'Have Tape Recorder, Will Travel,'" *International Journal of Oral History* 9 (Nov. 1988): 227–33. Gravois and Andresen claim that the U.S. Army pioneered the methodology several years prior to Allan Nevins's work at Columbia University from 1948 (227–28). For a thoughtful discussion of the benefits and liabilities of jazz oral history, see Burton W. Peretti, "Oral Histories of Jazz Musicians: The NEA Transcripts as Texts in Context," in Gabbard, *Jazz among the Discourses*, 117–33.

30. See, e.g., some of the quotations from the *Chicago Tribune* and the *San Francisco Chronicle*, in Alan Lomax, *Mister Jelly Roll*, front matter. See also Balliett, "Profiles: Ferdinand La Menthe," 38. For the response to the Circle release of the Library of Congress recordings (in abridged form), see Rudi Blesh, "An Open Letter to Jazz Record Readers," *Jazz Record*, no. 60 (Nov. 1947): 17–18, in which Blesh answers complaints about the high cost of the records, questions about how the rights were acquired from the Morton estate, and other charges suggesting pecuniary motives.

31. Russell, interview by Allen and Perhonis, Feb. 16, 1976.

32. Lomax, *Mister Jelly Roll*, xvi and 12–14, 43–52.

33. Lomax, *Mister Jelly Roll*, 64, 66.

34. Lomax, *Mister Jelly Roll*, 102.

35. Lomax, *Mister Jelly Roll*, 67–109.

36. Lomax, *Mister Jelly Roll*, xv.

37. Lomax, *Mister Jelly Roll*, xv.

38. *The Cultural Approach to History*, ed. Caroline F. Ware (New York: Columbia University Press, 1940).

39. B. A. Botkin, "Folklore as a Neglected Source of Social History," in Ware, *Cultural Approach to History*, 308–15, quote on 311.

40. Charles Seeger, "Folk Music as a Source of Social History," in Ware, *Cultural Approach to History*, 316–23, quote on 319. Note the following from Denisoff, *Great Day Coming*: "The WPA in the late thirties exhibited a number of folkloristic interests, many of which fed into the radical subculture of New York City. Some of these undertakings were the Folklore Studies of the Federal Writers' Project under B. A. Botkin; the Index of American Design of the Federal Art Project; the folk music recordings and social music activities of the Federal Music Project, directed by Charles Seeger; the Folksong and Folklore Department of the National Service Bureau of the Federal Theater Project; and the Lomax-di-

rected Folk Music Archives of the Library of Congress. These projects both injected new material into the radical milieu and recorded a number of proletarian singers as folk artists" (70).

41. Neil Leonard explains how centralization of the recording industry during the latter 1920s curtailed jazz releases, especially with the onset of the Depression (*Jazz and the White Americans,* 95, 103–4), contributing to the dearth of new jazz releases by 1934. See also Gelatt, *Fabulous Phonograph,* 265.

42. Gelatt, *Fabulous Phonograph,* 265.

43. See *New Grove Dictionary of Jazz* (1988), s.v. "Bluebird," by Howard Rye and Barry Kernfeld. For other short-lived RCA Victor subsidiaries, see *New Grove Dictionary of Jazz* (1988), s.v. "Victor."

44. Gelatt, *Fabulous Phonograph,* 266–67.

45. Gelatt, *Fabulous Phonograph,* 265–77.

46. See Lomax, *Mister Jelly Roll,* 302.

47. See Gelatt, *Fabulous Phonograph,* 267–72.

48. Details of this arrangement are given in Millstein, "Commodore Record Shop," 83–85.

49. See Delaunay, *Delaunay's Dilemma,* 230–35. Dregni emphasizes Delaunay's role to the virtual exclusion of Panassié: "Delaunay wrote in January 1937 to Jean Bérard, the new Gramophone label director at Pathé-Marconi, to suggest creating a jazz line under his control to produce recordings and license American releases for France. To Delaunay's great surprise, Bérard approved his proposal, and the two met to discuss the project on February 6. Pathé-Marconi would provide studios, engineers, and record-pressing and engineering services; Delaunay and the Hot Club would have a free hand in selecting artists and repertoire. Thus was born Swing, the first record label in the world loyal solely to jazz" (*Django,* 124).

50. Commodore Reissues brochure, 1941, from "Discology" vertical file: "Commodore Records," HJA.

51. See Millstein, "Commodore Record Shop," 96–97, for the story. Louis Armstrong was aware that the UHCA promoted its cause; see his chapter "Record Fans and Hot Clubs," in *Swing That Music,* 103–9.

52. Millstein, "Commodore Record Shop," 97. The latter idea was the brainchild of Richard Edes Harrison, a cartographer for *Time* who was also on the board of directors at UHCA.

53. See Eddie Condon and Thomas Sugrue, *We Called It Music: A Generation of Jazz* (New York: Henry Holt and Company, 1947), 237–38.

54. Condon and Sugrue, *We Called It Music,* 259–60.

55. Condon and Sugrue, *We Called It Music,* 262–68. See also Bill Esposito, "Commodore, Gabler, and Crystal," *IAJRC Journal* 23 (Winter 1990): 32–34. For the Peterson photographs and the promotion of Commodore, see "Swing: From a Dark Past It Comes into Its Golden Age," *Life,* Aug. 8, 1938, 50–60, especially 58–59.

56. Brian Rust, *The American Record Label Book* (New Rochelle, N.Y.: Arlington House Publishers, 1978), 85.

57. Rust, *American Record Label Book,* 165.

58. Stephen W. Smith, "Surface Noise: Commodore Classics in Swing???" *HRS Society Rag,* Sept. 1938, 17.

59. This is based on a comparison of the aforementioned Commodore brochure (which lists all UHCA releases and Commodore reissues) with titles of HRS reissues given in *HRS Society Rag* (Aug. 1938–Oct. 1940) and *Jazz Information* (Nov. 1939–Oct. 1940).

60. See "Reissue Agreement Reached by Hot Record Society and Columbia," *HRS Society Rag,* Nov. 1940, 22–23.

61. HRS, however, did not advertise Commodore.

62. This is not surprising, given the fact that the Hot Record Exchange was the headquarters for the authors of *Jazzmen.* See Sanjek, interview by Welburn, Feb. 11, 1982, 246–47, 252–53. Sanjek mentions the HRS crew's emphasis on "black music" (as opposed to *Jazz Information*'s interest in "JAZZ"), along with Eugene Williams's reference to Jelly Roll Morton as making "clown music" (251).

63. See the commentary cited in *New Grove Dictionary of Jazz* (1988), s.v. "Hot Record Society," Howard Rye.

64. Steve Smith, liner notes, *Bechet-Spanier Big Four, Vol. 1* (HRS 2000–2001, 1940).

65. Steve Smith, liner notes, *Bechet-Spanier Big Four, Vol. 2* (HRS 2002–3, 1940). Smith's dedication to "hot" collecting was not inexhaustible, however. He sold the Hot Record Shop in 1941, and Caidin Records purchased the HRS label in 1948, after which the Smiths retired to Valley Falls, N.Y., where they bought a cattle ranch.

66. Rust, *American Record Label Book,* 165.

67. Lomax, *Mister Jelly Roll,* 317.

68. Lomax, *Mister Jelly Roll,* 317.

69. *HRS Society Rag,* Aug. 1940, 36.

70. Rust, *American Record Label Book,* 128.

71. Quoted in *The Blue Note Label: A Discography,* comp. Michael Cuscuna and Michel Ruppli (Westport, Conn.: Greenwood Press, 1988), xii. Compare the Blue Note manifesto with Delaunay's preface to *De la Vie et du Jazz,* written in 1938 and published during the German occupation of France. Because jazz was widely seen as an antidote to Fascist tyranny, its spiritual content had to be safeguarded to ensure potency. See Delaunay, *Delaunay's Dilemma,* front matter.

72. Michael Cuscuna states this in Cuscuna and Ruppli, *Blue Note Label,* xi.

73. This story and considerable biographical detail can be found in J. Lee Anderson, "The Blue Note Story," *Mississippi Rag* 16 (Oct. 1989): 1–6.

74. Cuscuna and Ruppli, *Blue Note Label,* xi.

75. V-Discs were issued in twelve-inch format because the ten-inch presses at

RCA Victor and Columbia were busy supplying the expanding popular market for dance music and jazz; twelve-inch presses were mostly idle as the result of diminished demand for classical records. See Leonard, *Jazz and the White Americans:* "In 1939 Americans bought 45,000,000 'popular' records and only 5,000,000 'classical,' a ratio of 9:1" (92). The V-Disc program included record company officials and jazz experts who had joined the military, such as Stephen Sholes (Victor A&R), George Simon (*Metronome*), Tony Janak (Columbia), and Morty Palitz (Decca). V-Discs were issued from 1943 until 1949. See Richard S. Sears, *V-Discs: A History and Discography* (Westport, Conn.: Greenwood Press, 1980).

76. As stated by Lion in J. Lee Anderson, "Blue Note Story," 4.

77. Quoted in Cuscuna and Ruppli, *Blue Note Label,* xii.

78. Many jazz musicians incorporated elements of the classical tradition into their music; the Ellington-Strayhorn arrangement of *The Nutcracker* and the activities of the "progressive" big bands of the 1940s (Boyd Raeburn, Stan Kenton, Claude Thornhill, Woody Herman, and Earl Spencer) were, perhaps, more successful attempts at wedding jazz and classical concepts than the "symphonic" jazz of Paul Whiteman in the 1920s.

79. See Cuscuna and Ruppli, *Blue Note Label,* xii; J. Lee Anderson, "Blue Note Story," 4.

80. Quoted in Cuscuna and Ruppli, *Blue Note Label,* xiii.

81. See *New Grove Dictionary of Jazz* (1988), s.v. "Blue Note (ii)," by Howard Rye and Barry Kernfeld.

82. Hugues Panassié, liner notes, *The Panassié Sessions* (RCA Victor LPV-542, 1967), as well as Hugues Panassié, *Monsieur Jazz* (Paris: Editions Stock, 1975), 160.

83. Panassié, liner notes, *Panassié Sessions.* See also Hugues Panassié, Foreword, in *Hugues Panassié Discusses 144 Hot Jazz Bluebird and Victor Records,* ed. John Reid (Camden, N.J.: RCA Manufacturing Company, 1940), especially this note to readers from RCA Victor: "Your comments on this booklet will be of great interest to the Hot Jazz Record Department. Mention of Victor and Bluebird records (now unavailable) which you would like to see reissued, if possible, will be of great assistance in preparing future Hot Jazz releases" (end matter).

84. See *Setting the Tempo: Fifty Years of Great Jazz Liner Notes,* ed. and intro. Tom Piazza (New York: Anchor Books, 1996).

85. Lomax, in *Mister Jelly Roll,* states that the 1939 Jelly Roll Morton Victor session was "part of a series of hot jazz revival recordings which Panassié, the French critic, had arranged" (312). For Ramsey's account, see 313–17.

86. "Jelly Roll Morton Symposium," May 7, 1982.

87. "Jelly Roll Morton Symposium," May 7, 1982.

88. "Jelly Roll Morton Symposium," May 7, 1982.

89. For an example of some of Jelly Roll's tall tales told in New York, see Albert Nicholas, interview by Richard B. Allen and Lars Edegran, June 26, 1972,

tape recording, HJA. For information concerning Jelly Roll's arguments with New York bandleader Chick Webb, see Barney Bigard, interview by Floyd Levin, July 25, 1969, tape recording, HJA.

90. "Jelly Roll Morton Symposium," May 7, 1982.

91. "Jelly Roll Morton Symposium," May 7, 1982.

92. Tape recording of conversation among Sidney Bechet, "Big Eye" Louis Nelson Delille, Alphonse Picou, Peter Bocage, and John Reid, ca. June 1944, HJA.

93. The most reliable biography of Sidney Bechet is John Chilton, *Sidney Bechet: The Wizard of Jazz* (London: Macmillan Press, 1987). See pp. 130–48 for details of Bechet's signing to RCA Victor.

94. Chilton, *Sidney Bechet*, 131.

95. Among them was the Haitian Orchestra, with Willie "The Lion" Smith (recorded for Variety in 1939), which musicologist Ernest Borneman has called "the first deliberate reunion of jazz and Afro-Spanish folk music in history" (quoted in Chilton, *Sidney Bechet,* 124).

96. Chilton, *Sidney Bechet,* 135–42.

97. Chilton, *Sidney Bechet,* 134.

98. The school had two students, Bob Wilber and Richard Hadlock. For details, see Bob Wilber, interview by William Russell, May 1, 1961, tape recording, HJA.

99. See Sidney Bechet, *Treat It Gentle* (London: Cassell and Company, 1960), 170–71, 175, 179, 181.

100. Russell, interview by Hogan and Crawford, Sept. 4, 1962. See also "The Great Victor Bootleg Expose," in Orrin Keepnews, *The View from Within: Jazz Writings, 1948–1987* (New York: Oxford University Press, 1988), 52–59.

101. Russell, interview by Hogan and Crawford, Sept. 4, 1962. See also Chilton, *Sidney Bechet,* which describes Camp Unity: "It was a vacation centre with swimming and boating facilities on nearby Lake Ellis; it also offered tennis courts, horseback riding, hikes through the Berkshire countryside and camp-fire sing-songs. The only aspect of Camp Unity that irked some of the musicians who worked there was that its organizers made a point of propounding left-wing political ideas" (144)

102. For insight into the affiliation of jazz enthusiasts and the OWI, see Frederic Ramsey Jr., "Those Washington, D.C. Blues," *Record Changer,* Sept. 1945, 4–7, which discusses appropriation problems during the war; fear for the preservation of jazz recordings made by the OWI; and the generally "reactionary" policies of congressional authorities toward the program, akin to the spirit that had dissolved the Federal Art Project, selling its paintings as "scrap canvas."

103. John Hammond, "Experiment in Jazz History," 49.

104. John Hammond, "Experiment in Jazz History," 51, 53.

105. For a full account, see John Hammond and Irving Townsend, *John Hammond on Record: An Autobiography* (New York: Ridge Press, 1977). For empha-

sis on Hammond's role in working for civil rights within the entertainment industry (and in the army), see Pomerance, *Repeal of the Blues.*

106. See "Reissue Agreement."

107. Heywood Hale Broun, "Editorial," *HRS Society Rag,* Feb. 1941, 6.

108. "Reissue Agreement," 22–23. See also "Columbia Reissues Start in October," *Jazz Information* 2 (Sept. 20, 1940): 3–5.

109. "John Hammond Says," *HRS Society Rag,* Dec. 1940, 19–20.

110. "John Hammond Says," 20.

111. See Charles Miller, "George Avakian," *Jazz Information* 2 (Feb. 7, 1941): 9–11. See also Leonard Feather, *The New Yearbook of Jazz* (London: Arthur Barker, 1959), 85. Insights into Avakian's present interest in New Orleans music appear in Vincent Fumar, "New Orleans to Moscow?" *Wavelength,* no. 114 (Apr. 1990): 4.

112. John Hammond, liner notes, *Frank Teschemacher* (Columbia Album C-43, 1941). For an announcement of the "Jazz Masterworks Series," see "Columbia Introduces New Jazz Label," *Jazz Information* 1 (Dec. 22, 1939): 1.

113. Charles Edward Smith, liner notes, *New Orleans Jazz* (Decca Album A-425, 1940).

114. Charles Edward Smith, with research by Stephen H. Sholes and William Russell, liner notes, *The Hot Jazz of Louis Armstrong* (RCA Victor Album HJ-1, 1945).

115. See *New Grove Dictionary of Jazz* (1988), s.v. "History of Jazz Recording: The War Years and the AFM Recording Ban," by Chris Sheridan. The ban on recording instigated by James C. Petrillo, president of the American Federation of Musicians, was intended to gain royalty payments for union members from record manufacturers, largely to offset loss of income due to the popularity of radio. The union ban lasted from Aug. 1942 until Victor and Columbia finally settled in Nov. 1944 (Decca and Blue Note settled in Sept. and Nov. 1943, respectively). Information on the V-Disc program is also provided. For a contemporaneous account of the effects of wartime, the Petrillo ban, and the adaptive powers of the record industry, see Harold Humphrey, "The Disk Business Digs In," *Band Year Book,* Sept. 26, 1942, 1.

116. See Sheridan, "History of Jazz Recording: The War Years," which observes: "The crucial event was the war. Its immediate effects on the American treasury led to several significant fiscal and other measures. Driving for pleasure was banned to save gasoline; a cabaret tax of 30% (later reduced to 20%) was imposed, making smaller, cheaper bands a more attractive booking proposition; and for a time a midnight curfew was introduced. In addition, the stresses of wartime, as though echoing those of the Depression, increased popular demand for the sentimental and the reassuring; this in turn boosted the standing of vocalists, who very soon began to see their names appearing in headlines at the top of the bill"

(259). See also Mumma, "New Techniques after 1947," on the impact of tape recording and microgroove pressing with the emergence of the 33 1/3 r.p.m. LP by Columbia in 1948 and the 45 r.p.m. single by RCA Victor the following year (353–54). Oliver Read and Walter I. Welch, *From Tin Foil to Stereo: The Evolution of the Phonograph* (New York: Bobbs-Merrill Company, 1959), 333–42, discusses changes in the materials used in record manufacture (the switch to plastics) and provides additional detail on the Petrillo ban. On the extent of consumer demand, see Hilmer Stark, "Keep 'Em Spinning in the Homes," *Band Year Book,* Sept. 26, 1942, 18–19.

Chapter 4

1. Heywood Hale Broun, "Down in New Orleans," *HRS Society Rag,* Sept. 1940, 8–12, gives details; see p. 12 for quote.

2. William Russell, "Delta—New Orleans," *HRS Society Rag,* Oct. 1940, 28–30, especially 28.

3. Russell, "Delta," 29–30.

4. Russell, "Delta," 30.

5. Rudi Blesh, liner notes, *Kid Rena's Delta Jazzband* (Circle Album S-10, 1948).

6. Blesh, liner notes, *Kid Rena's Delta Jazzband.* For "The Circle Story," see Rudi Blesh, liner notes, *Baby Dodds Trio—Jazz a la Creole* (GHB 50, 1970), recounting its founding in 1946 and how it was named by Marcel Duchamp: " 'Call it Circle,' he said. 'Records *are* circles and, besides, no one can call you squares.' "

7. For challenges to Bunk's veracity, see Lawrence Gushee, "When Was Bunk Johnson Born and Why Should We Care?" *Archivist,* Nov. 2, 1987, 4–5, 6; Morroe Berger, "Jazz Pre-history—and Bunk Johnson," in Toledano, *Frontiers of Jazz,* 91–103; Donald M. Marquis, *In Search of Buddy Bolden: First Man of Jazz* (Baton Rouge: Louisiana State University Press, 1978), especially 4, 76–77. Mike Hazeldine and Barry Martyn support Bunk's claims in *Bunk Johnson, Song of the Wanderer* (New Orleans: Jazzology Press, 2000).

8. The sixty dollars required for Bunk's new set of teeth came from Ramsey and Russell, while the twenty-five dollars for the trumpet and cornet came from Lu Watters. See Paul A. Larsen, "Bunk Is History!" *Storyville,* no. 43 (Oct. 1972): 4–7.

9. Edmond Souchon, M.D., "Weeks Hall and Bunk Johnson," *Second Line* 15 (Sept.–Oct. 1964): 15–17, 20, especially 15.

10. The story appeared in the May 15, 1941, issue of *Down Beat;* see Larsen, "Bunk Is History!" 4.

11. As transcribed in Larsen, "Bunk Is History!" 6.

12. Larsen, "Bunk Is History!" 6.

13. See "Jazz Information Enters Reissue Field," *Jazz Information* 2 (Dec. 6,

1940): 1, 7 (for description of "Limited Edition No. 1"). Ralph de Toledano, a founder of the magazine, stated, "As no other generation, we made an intellectual cult of jazz" (*Lament for a Generation*, 18).

14. Kay, "Bill Russell Reminisces," 2.

15. Letter from David Stuart, Los Angeles, to "Big Eye" Louis Nelson, New Orleans, July 25, 1941, in "Persons" file: "Delille, 'Big Eye' Louis Nelson," HJA.

16. V-Discs and American Music records were also pressed on vinylite because there was less breakage in shipment (Sears, *V-Discs*, ix).

17. Christopher Hillman, *Bunk Johnson: His Life and Times* (New York: Universe Books, 1988), 52. For a report on the mission by William Russell, see "I Ain't Gonna Study War No More," *Jazz* 1 (Aug. 1942): 22–23.

18. Hillman, *Bunk Johnson*, 51–52.

19. Nesuhi Ertegun, "Record Review," *Record Changer*, Jan. 15, 1943, 1. The son of the Turkish ambassador to the United States, Ertegun had resided since 1941 in Washington, D.C., where he promoted integrated jazz concerts and worked for the *Record Changer*. In 1947, he founded Atlantic Records (with brother Ahmet). See *New Grove Dictionary of Jazz* (1988), s.v. "Ertegun, Nesuhi," by Howard Rye.

20. Between 1942 and 1944, Nesuhi Ertegun resided simultaneously in Los Angeles and Washington, D.C. For speculation on how he obtained Morton masters made by the United Record Company released on Jazz Man, see Roy Carew, interview by Johnson McRee and George Kay, Nov. 28, 1964, tape recording, HJA. For additional information, see "Nesuhi Ertegun," *Second Line* 3 (Nov.–Dec. 1952): 1, 16–17.

21. Russell, interview by Hogan and Crawford, Aug. 31, 1962.

22. Albert Warner (1890–1966) replaced Robinson on trombone, Chester Zardis (1900–1990) played bass, and Edgar Mosley (1895–1962) was the drummer.

23. See "From Gene Williams in New Orleans," *Record Changer*, Oct. 15, 1942, 2. Williams contributed regularly to this magazine; see his "J.I. in Exile" column, from Apr. through Sept. 1943. See also Eugene Williams, "Conscientious Objection," *Record Changer*, Feb. 1943, 4.

24. "Jazz Man Records Presents Bunk Johnson and His Original Superior Band," Jazz Man Records brochure, 1942, from "Discology" vertical file: "Jazz Man Records," HJA.

25. Hillman, *Bunk Johnson*, 52.

26. "Old New Orleans Jazz by Bunk Johnson's Jazz Band," Jazz Information Records brochure, 1943, from "Discology" vertical file: "Jazz Information Records," HJA.

27. "Old New Orleans Jazz."

28. Quoted in Peter Martin, "Lu Watters: The Legend, the Man," *Mississippi Rag* 12 (May 1985); 1–6, especially 4. In 1946, Watters was indicted for income-tax evasion on the proceeds from the Dawn Club. The corporation owed thirty thou-

sand dollars, but jail time was averted due to Watters's service in the navy. For information on sidemen, including Benny Strickler (also with Bob Wills's Western swing band), see Jim Goggin, *Turk Murphy—Just for the Record* (San Leandro, Calif.: San Francisco Traditional Jazz Foundation, 1982), where Murphy is quoted: "Bill Colburn played a tape for Bunk Johnson made by Benny Strickler and Bunk swore up and down it was King Oliver" (3). See also Bill Colburn and Gene Williams, "That Frisco Jazz Band," *Jazz* 1 (Aug. 1942): 10–16.

29. Emelia Hodel, "Hot Jazz Lectures Have S.F. Popeyed," *San Francisco News*, Apr. 12, 1943.

30. Hodel, "Hot Jazz Lectures."

31. Hodel, "Hot Jazz Lectures."

32. "Bunk Johnson Rides Again," *Time*, May 24, 1943, clipping from "Persons" file: "Johnson, Willie Geary 'Bunk,'" HJA.

33. This information is given in Rudi Blesh, "Willie 'Bunk' Johnson: Last of the Olympians," *Record Changer*, Sept. 1949, 12.

34. Hot Jazz Society of San Francisco, newsletter, July 19, 1943, in "Persons" file: "Johnson, Willie Geary 'Bunk,'" HJA. The man who made the hall available was Harry Bridges, a famed union organizer; the FBI attempted to deport him to his native Australia in 1939 for communist affiliation but was blocked by the Supreme Court. For the connection to the Bunk Johnson concerts, see Alice Thompson, "Re-Birth of the Blues," *San Francisco News*, Nov. 18, 1943.

35. Quoted in Hot Jazz Society of San Francisco, newsletter, July 28, 1943, in "Persons" file: "Johnson, Willie Geary 'Bunk,'" HJA. Basie had heard Bunk at the Yellow Front Cafe in Kansas City some thirteen years before.

36. Virgil Thomson, "Music at the Golden Gate," *New York Herald Tribune*, Aug. 8, 1943.

37. Thomson also mentions Bridges as "a patron of cultural activities," and there is discussion of difficulties with the local musicians union, until he intervened.

38. Kay, "Bill Russell Reminisces," 2. For additional information on Russell's 1943 trip, see William Russell, "New Orleans News Letter," *Record Changer*, Aug. 1943, 11, 16. Russell stayed on the home front as "an avowed pacifist, [he] did not fight in that war (or in any war preceding or since) but he remained convinced that passive resistance and conscientious objection was the way to go about things." See "The 'Grand Lama of Jazz'," *Baton Rouge Morning Advocate Sunday Magazine*, Oct. 11, 1981, in "Persons" file: "Russell, William," HJA.

39. Kay, "Bill Russell Reminisces," 2.

40. None of Bunk's recordings in San Francisco was released while he was alive, but in Los Angeles he recorded at the Decca studios for the World Transcription Service, where he was teamed with Lee Young (1914–2008) on drums and Red Callender (1916–1992) on bass, two modernists. This was a mixed session in other ways: trombonist Floyd O'Brien (1904–1968), formerly with Bob

Crosby, played, as did New Orleans stylists Wade Whaley, pianist Fred Washington (ca. 1888–?), and guitarist Frank Pasley (1904–1968). Bill Colburn had selected the musicians, supposedly on Bunk's behalf. See Hillman, *Bunk Johnson,* 59–60.

41. Hillman, *Bunk Johnson,* 63. Also see comments by Francis Squibb in "A Life Devoted to Jazz History," *New Orleans Times-Picayune,* Aug. 14, 1982.

42. Kay, "Bill Russell Reminisces," 2.

43. From Mar. 1944, Hammond was stationed in New Orleans, attached to the army's Information and Education Section, and given the task of ensuring "just treatment" for black troops. He staged a number of shows for integrated audiences at Camp Plauché, including Ella Fitzgerald, Louis Jordan, and Jan Garber. See Hammond and Townsend, *John Hammond on Record,* 248–56. See also Hillman, *Bunk Johnson,* 69.

44. See "GHB Jazz Foundation Acquires American Music," *Jazz Beat,* Aug. 16, 1989, 3.

45. Russell built the band according to Bunk's conception. The notes for the album were dedicated to Hoyte Kline, who had died in Italy just before discharge. See William Russell, liner notes, *New Orleans Parade* (American Music Album 101–103, 1945), in "Persons" file: "Johnson, Willie Geary 'Bunk,'" HJA.

46. Bechet, *Treat It Gentle,* 170–72.

47. Mike Hazeldine, "Dear Wynne," *Footnote* 15 (June–July 1984): 4–29, especially 7.

48. See James Lincoln Collier, *Louis Armstrong: An American Genius* (New York: Oxford University Press, 1983), 297. Armstrong's career was in the doldrums by 1946, before the All Stars formula returned him to popularity, which some saw as a return to "real" jazz (308–12).

49. See "Voila Le Jazz Originale," *Basin Street* 1 (Mar. 1945): 2–3.

50. For information on Jack Crystal (father of comedian Billy Crystal) and his close association with the Commodore enterprises, see "Biggest Little Man of Jazz Dies in Long Beach, N.Y.," *Second Line* 15 (Mar.–Apr. 1964): 13–14, 18.

51. See various letters in Hazeldine, "Dear Wynne." See also Hillman, *Bunk Johnson,* 75–78.

52. The Wildcats were the East Coast equivalent of the Yerba Buena revivalists. See Whitney Balliett, "The Westchester Kids," in *Improvising: Sixteen Jazz Musicians and Their Art* (New York: Oxford University Press, 1977), 235–53. See also Wilber, interview by Russell, May 1, 1961; Orrin Keepnews, "Wilber's Wildcats—Youthful Jazz Veterans Are Giving Old Forms New Life," *Record Changer,* May 1948, 8–9.

53. Jean Gleason, "Bunk Storms 52nd Street," *Record Changer,* Apr. 1945, 7.

54. Hazeldine, "Dear Wynne," 12–13.

55. Hazeldine, "Dear Wynne," 15–16.

56. Hazeldine, "Dear Wynne," 17.

57. Hazeldine, "Dear Wynne," 20–21. Paris was the official with the Boston Jazz Society who had booked the Savoy Cafe engagement.

58. Hazeldine, "Dear Wynne," 24.

59. Russell, interview by Hogan and Crawford, Aug. 31, 1962.

60. Quoted in Hazeldine and Martyn, *Bunk Johnson,* 264.

61. For details on Ory's prerevival career, see Edward "Kid" Ory, interview by Nesuhi Ertegun and Bob Campbell, Apr. 20, 1957, tape recording, HJA. A good synopsis can also be found in Nesuhi Ertegun, liner notes, *Kid Ory's Creole Jazz Band* (Good Time Jazz L-12022, 1957).

62. Nesuhi Ertegun, liner notes, *Kid Ory's Creole Jazz Band.*

63. Philip Elwood, liner notes, *Kid Ory's Creole Jazz Band* (Folk Lyric Records 9008, 1975).

64. Nesuhi Ertegun, liner notes, *Kid Ory's Creole Jazz Band.* See also Nesuhi Ertegun, "New Orleans on the Air," *Jazz Record,* no. 20 (May 1944): 6–7, in which he refers to "thousands" of letters (7).

65. Orson Welles, "Foreword," in Dave Dexter Jr., *Jazz Cavalcade: The Inside Story of Jazz* (New York: Criterion, 1946), vi.

66. William Russell, "Notes, 1942–1949," unpublished manuscript, William Russell Collection, HJA, Box II, p. 504. This manuscript is tantamount to a diary of Russell's relationship with Bunk Johnson, and more.

67. Elwood, liner notes, *Kid Ory's Creole Jazz Band.* On Ory's success at the Jade in Los Angeles from Apr. 1945, see Alma Hubner, "Kid Ory," in *Selections from the Gutter: Jazz Portraits from "The Jazz Record,"* ed. Art Hodes and Chadwick Hansen (Berkeley: University of California Press, 1977), 112–15, especially a letter from Marili Morden (dated June 25, 1945) in which she states: "It is now quite impossible to have anything resembling solitude when listening to Kid Ory's band—in fact, one is lucky to get a seat within listening distance. . . . Many people have been telling me for months that the band was fine but wouldn't draw enough business for anyone to risk hiring them. Other night club owners . . . are now trying to lure them away from the Jade."

68. George Montgomery, "Jazz in Los Angeles," *Record Changer,* Apr. 1945, 33.

69. Marili Ertegun, "New Orleans Jazz," *Clef* 1 (Aug. 1946): 5, 28–32, especially 32. Nesuhi and Marili divorced in 1951.

70. Nesuhi Ertegun, "New Orleans on the Air," 7.

71. Crescent Records advertisement, *Record Changer,* Nov. 1945, 3.

72. Crescent Records advertisement.

73. Eugene Williams, "Bunk Johnson—American Music," *Record Changer,* Apr. 1945, 4.

74. Russell, "Notes, 1942–1949," Box I, p. 296.

75. Exner's approach to the record business was akin to Bill Russell's: "I want

nothing out of them but to come somewhere near breaking even. Anything in the way of profit over and above the reasonable costs of production and distribution belong to the great men who made the music." See Dr. F. B. Exner, "Crusader for Jazz," *Second Line* 4 (Jan. 1953): 3, 10, 12–13, quote on 13. See also Paul Ashford, "Dr. Exner—Jazz Connoisseur," *Playback* 2 (Aug. 1949): 19–20, where the recordings are described as "less commercial than artistically satisfying in their intention and fulfillment" (19).

76. See George Avakian, liner notes, *Kid Ory and His Creole Jazz Band* (Columbia Records Album C-126, 1947); Rudi Blesh, liner notes, *This Is Jazz, Vol. 2: Kid Ory and His Creole Jazz Band* (Circle Records Album S-11, 1947).

77. As quoted in Al Otto and Ben Marble, "What Did Ory Say?" *Clef* 1 (Mar. 1946): 4–5, 14.

78. Otto and Marble, "What Did Ory Say?" 14.

79. Blesh, liner notes, *Kid Ory and His Creole Jazz Band*.

80. Rose and Souchon, *New Orleans Jazz*, 132–33.

81. According to Blesh, "he is the only survivor of the early classic period of jazz not only to retain his technical and inventive powers but actually to be, today, at his mature greatest" (liner notes, *Kid Ory and His Creole Jazz Band*). Hugues Panassié called Ory's band "artistically as well as commercially, the most successful of all the 'New Orleans Revival' bands. One is even tempted to say: the *only* 'revival' band that was a hundred per cent successful in bringing back to life real New Orleans jazz." See Stanley Dance, *Jazz Era: The Forties* (New York: Da Capo Press, 1988), 190.

82. Otto and Marble, "What Did Ory Say?" 4.

83. Another Bunk biography is Austin M. Sonnier, *Willie Geary "Bunk" Johnson: The New Iberia Years* (New York: Crescendo Publishing, 1977). California grew in the migration to the "Sunbelt," which accelerated during and after World War II, but the concentration of entertainment media remained in New York, close to major business and industrial corporations and their advertising budgets. For details, see David R. Goldfield and Blaine A. Brownell, *Urban America: From Downtown to No Town* (Boston: Houghton Mifflin Company, 1979), 303, 332–39.

84. The Stuyvesant Casino was a rental hall usually used for weddings and union meetings. Sam Augenblick and Ben Menschel were the proprietors. From 1945 on, however, it became the site for numerous jazz sessions. See Maury Cagle, "The Stuyvesant Casino in the Early 1950s," *Tailgate Ramblings* 20 (Mar. 1990): 8, 10.

85. Hillman, *Bunk Johnson*, 90.

86. Hillman, *Bunk Johnson*, 90–91. For an interesting discussion of appropriate settings for jazz, see Francis Newton (Eric Hobsbawm), "Jazz Concerts," in Williamson, *This Is Jazz*, 11–16: "At their gloomiest they remind the critic of those mediaeval divorce trials in which husbands accused of impotence were sup-

posed to disprove the charge by making love to their wives in front of the judges. It could be done . . . but, taking all in all, the atmosphere was just not right for this kind of activity" (11).

87. Williams committed suicide on May 5, 1948. See "Final Bar," *Down Beat* 16 (June 2, 1948): 10. The jazz press lamented his death at age thirty, especially his friend Ralph de Toledano, who stated: "When Gene found jazz, it was more than music to him. It was mother, father, wife and kids to him, something to give his life direction and meaning" (Ralph de Toledano, "Eugene Williams," *Record Changer,* July 1948, 18). It was later reported that Williams had lost $25,000 on Bunk and Ory (Ralph J. Gleason, "Bunk's an Amazing Story," *Down Beat* 16 [Aug. 26, 1949]: 6–7, especially 7).

88. Ralph J. Gleason, liner notes, *Bunk Johnson—An American Original* (RCA Victor Album HJ-7, 1946).

89. New Orleans musicians often became homesick and found reasons to abandon the road, even if it meant giving up financial rewards. This is why members of Piron's band deliberately scuttled a New York audition for George White's "Scandals" in 1923. See Charlie Bocage, interview by Allen and Friedwald, July 18, 1960.

90. Harold Drob and Barry Martyn, "Bunk at the Stuyvesant," *New Orleans Music* 1 (Oct.–Nov. 1989), 6–14, quote on 7.

91. Drob and Martyn, "Bunk at the Stuyvesant," 7.

92. Drob and Martyn, "Bunk at the Stuyvesant," 8, 10.

93. Drob and Martyn, "Bunk at the Stuyvesant," 12.

94. Drob and Martyn, "Bunk at the Stuyvesant," 12–13.

95. Ahmet Ertegun, "Bunk Back at Casino," *Record Changer,* June 1946, 18.

96. Russell, "Notes, 1942–1949" Box I, p. 179.

97. Russell, "Notes, 1942–1949," Box I, pp. 153–37.

98. Eugene Williams, liner notes, *New Orleans Revival* (Decca Records Album A-549, 1947).

99. This figure is taken from Russell, "Notes, 1942–1949," Box I, p. 259.

100. Don C. Haynes, "Bunk's Concert a Miserable Mess: His Ork Hall Bash a Complete Snafu," *Down Beat* 13 (Sept. 23, 1946); clipping in "Persons" vertical file: "Johnson, Willie Geary 'Bunk,'" HJA.

101. Bob Aurthur, "Jazzorama," *Jazz Record,* no. 60 (Nov. 1947): 15–17, quote on 15–16.

102. Aurthur, "Jazzorama," 16–17.

103. George Hoefer, "Fans Who Misinterpreted Now Are Forgetting Bunk," *Down Beat* 15 (Dec. 15, 1948): 6.

104. See Russell, "Notes, 1942–1949," Box I, pp. 28–85.

105. Russell, "Notes, 1942–1949," Box I, pp. 28–85; letter from John T. Schenck, Chicago, to Bill Russell, Pittsburgh, Aug. 17, 1946, p. 276, Hogan Jazz Archive, Tulane University.

296 / NOTES TO PAGES 138–42

106. See Russell, "Notes, 1942–1949," for details. See also Hazeldine, "Dear Wynne," 14–16, 20–25.

107. This movie was made at Dave Bell's apartment by Phil Featheringill (his partner in the Session Record Shop in Chicago) and is a part of the film holdings of the Hogan Jazz Archive.

108. André Hodeir, *Jazz: Its Evolution and Essence,* trans. David Noakes (London: Secker and Warburg, 1956), 24, 32–33, quote on 32–33.

109. Dance, *Jazz Era,* 20.

110. Rasula, "Media of Memory," 150.

111. See "GHB Jazz Foundation," 3. For additional proof, see Thomas A. Sancton, "Play It Again, Woody," *Time,* Oct. 23, 1989, 4, 76–78.

112. It should be noted that Rudi Blesh recorded the Original Zenith Brass Band, another heuristically "reconstituted" brass band, for his Circle label in 1946.

113. Hazeldine, "Dear Wynne," 22.

114. Hazeldine, "Dear Wynne," 20, 23. The quotation on racial essentialism is from Sherrie Tucker, "Big Ears: Listening for Gender in Jazz Studies," *Current Musicology,* nos. 71–73 (Spring 2001–Spring 2002): 375–408, quote on 380–81. See also Guthrie Ramsey, "Cosmopolitan or Provincial?" 30–37.

115. See Jim Goboldt, *A History of Jazz in Britain, 1919–50* (London: Quartet Books, 1984): "This was the Trad Boom. . . . Hundreds of young men assiduously copied and, to a certain extent, absorbed the jazz of New Orleans pioneers. . . . Apart from the musicality of these pioneers, their racial and social background had a particularly romantic appeal. Young white men readily identified with black players three thousand miles distant and living in an entirely different environment" (266). See also James Lincoln Collier, *Making of Jazz,* which states that "almost at the same moment traditional bands were being put together in London, Paris, Melbourne, Stockholm, Rome, and San Francisco" (331).

Chapter 5

1. "Diffusionism" describes "achieved cultural transmission" in which a discrete creation spreads to other groups through a process of "acculturation." Diffusionists use historical methods to reconstruct acculturation and to study the permutations that occur. "Evolutionism" is a brand of "functionalism" that concentrates on institutions and studies their development via "progress" from primitive to more sophisticated stages. As Melville J. Herskovits explained: "The culminating argument against cultural evolutionism derived from the refusal of the evolutionists to take into account those considerations of time and place that, as we have seen, are so important in any study of the dynamics of culture." See Melville J. Herskovits, *Cultural Dynamics* (New York: Alfred A. Knopf, Inc., 1967; an abridgement of *Cultural Anthropology,* 1947), quotation from p. 137; see also 130–38, and 159–81.

2. The correspondence of a concept like "progress" with the record indus-

try's novelty-oriented marketing strategies is largely rooted in a dependence on advertising that began in the 1920s. For discussion of advertising as a social force in U.S. history, see Paul Carter, *Another Part of the Twenties,* 123–44; Stuart Ewen, *Captains of Consciousness* (New York: McGraw-Hill, 1976). Advertisers often present the quality of "newness" as a value in and of itself, subordinating other factors such as historical significance or aesthetic merit.

3. The jazz schism began with opposition to the "modernity" of the big swing bands, but bebop's novelty, the behavior of its practitioners, and its espousal by critics who were already disliked made it especially unpalatable to the purists. Progressive big bands like those of Stan Kenton (1911–1979) and Boyd Raeburn (1913–1966) combined the worst features of modernism in the eyes of the purists, because they fused the two strains and expanded instrumentation toward symphonic levels. Let me state emphatically that I find bebop and progressive jazz to be highly exciting and entertaining music and do not share the opinions put forth by traditional purists. See Scott DeVeaux, *The Birth of Bebop: A Social and Musical History* (Berkeley: University of California Press, 1997); Frank Tirro, "The Silent Theme Tradition in Jazz," *Musical Quarterly* 53 (July 1967): 313–30.

4. Henry F. May, *The Enlightenment in America* (New York: Oxford University Press, 1976), 64. See also Dickson K. Bruce Jr., *And They All Sang Hallelujah: Plain-Folk Camp-Meeting Religion, 1800–1845* (Knoxville: University of Tennessee Press, 1974), 6–11, for a discussion of emotion versus intellect in the history of American revivalism. For an exploration of the "religious" aspects of jazz appreciation and production, see Neil Leonard, *Jazz: Myth and Religion;* William L. Grossman and Jack W. Farrell, *The Heart of Jazz* (New York: New York University Press, 1956).

5. For a selective sampling of such articles, see Dick Rieber, "First Thrills in Beulah-Land," *HRS Society Rag,* July 1938, 9–11; Charles Edward Smith, "How To Be A Collector," *HRS Society Rag,* Aug. 1940, 24–28; Russell Sanjek, "The Swing Critic Murders—Part 1," *HRS Society Rag,* Sept. 1940, 23–26; Marni de Kay Rous, "Des Vues Sociales du Jazz," *HRS Society Rag,* Mar. 1941, 18–23. In his reiteration of editorial policy in the last issue of *Jazz Information* (Nov. 1941), Gene Williams emphasized the magazine's serious intellectual intent: "J.I.'s policy had begun to crystallize by the end of its first year. We took the risk of talking about jazz seriously, and in terms that seemed strange to many. We held the position, obvious enough to anyone who knows the music, that the real jazz is the stuff that came out of New Orleans, flavored with ragtime and rooted in the blues; that this music is as valid today as it ever was, and that the best hope for jazz is to recover those roots." This admission would suggest that the rift between the Commodore Record Shop and the Hot Record Exchange dissolved in a purist impulse that united members of the two factions in the fall of 1940.

6. See George T. Simon, *The Big Bands* (New York: Macmillan Company,

1967); Gunther Schuller, *The Swing Era: The Development of Jazz, 1930–1945* (New York: Oxford University Press, 1989).

7. DeVeaux, *Birth of Bebop,* especially 39–49, 157–64; John S. Wilson, *Jazz: The Transition Years, 1940–1960* (New York: Appleton-Century-Crofts, 1966), 17–18. See also Dizzy Gillespie with Al Fraser, *To Be, or Not . . . to Bop* (New York: Doubleday and Company, 1979), on difficulties Gillespie experienced in recruiting musicians who could play the new style for his big bands.

8. For details on Russell's Tempo Music Shop ("patterned after Commodore") and how Russell was "gradually weaned over" to modernism, see Robert Gordon, *Jazz West Coast: The Los Angeles Jazz Scene of the 1950s* (New York: Quartet Books, 1986), 9–11.

9. As it is used today, the term *modern jazz* refers to bebop and the styles that followed it. See DeVeaux, *Birth of Bebop;* Wilson, *Jazz: The Transition Years,* 7–24; Arnold Shaw, *The Street That Never Slept: New York's Fabled 52nd St.* (New York: Coward, McCann and Geoghegan, 1971), especially 251–83. Thus, when purists complained about "modernism" before 1945, they meant swing; although bebop was already being played, relatively few purists were aware of it.

10. Bill Russell gives the impression that *Jazzmen* did not generate much revenue at first. Russell recalls a two-hundred-dollar advance that translated into thirty dollars each. The first royalties were used up in gift copies and editing of the galleys, which cost fifty cents a word to change. See Russell, interview by Allen and Perhonis, Feb. 16, 1976. Distribution received a huge boost when Editions for the Armed Services, Inc., "a non-profit organization established by the Council on Books in Wartime," sponsored the pocket-sized paperback edition of *Jazzmen* for soldiers. For information on Armed Forces Radio Service, see Jerry Valburn, "Armed Forces Transcriptions as Source Materials," in *Studies in Jazz Discography I,* ed. Walter C. Allen (New Brunswick: Rutgers University Press, 1971), 47–52.

11. Englishmen Max Jones and Sinclair Traill (1904–1981) recalled receiving copies of *Jazzmen* as early as Jan. 1940. See Max Jones and Sinclair Traill, "A Good Book—But Too Late," *Melody Maker,* June 15, 1957. For information on how jazz aided Europeans seeking to thwart Nazi oppression, see Ernest Borneman, "The Jazz Cult," in Condon and Gehman, *Eddie Condon's Treasury of Jazz,* 33–67.

12. For reactions of young collectors and dealers to the shellac drive, see Paul Bacon, "Jazz Fan," in Frank Driggs and Harris Lewine, eds., *Black Beauty, White Heat: A Pictorial History of Classic Jazz, 1920–1950* (New York: William Morrow and Company, 1982), 8–18, especially 18.

13. Charles Edward Smith and William Russell, "New Orleans Style," *Modern Music* 18 (May–June 1941): 235–41, quote on 238.

14. Smith and Russell, "New Orleans Style," 239.

15. Smith and Russell, "New Orleans Style," 241.

16. Louis Harap, "The Case for Hot Jazz," *Musical Quarterly* 27 (Jan. 1941): 47–61, especially 49–50. Harap's interest in "noncommercial" music was hardly fortuitous. He was a staunch Marxist (with a Ph.D. in philosophy from Harvard University) who wrote on philosophy and musicology, while also editing *Jewish Survey* (1939–42) and *Jewish Life* (1948–57).

17. Harap, "Case for Hot Jazz," 51.

18. Harap, "Case for Hot Jazz," 52.

19. See Alan Levy and Barbara L. Tischler, "Into the Cultural Mainstream: The Growth of American Musical Scholarship," *American Quarterly* 42 (Mar. 1990): 57–73, especially 63–68.

20. See Arnold Gingrich, "Introduction," in *Esquire's 1945 Jazz Book,* ed. Paul Eduard Miller (New York: A. S. Barnes and Company, 1945), v.

21. Charles Edward Smith, with Frederic Ramsey Jr., Charles Payne Rogers, and William Russell, *The Jazz Record Book* (New York: Smith and Durrell, 1942), xiv.

22. Charles Edward Smith, *Jazz Record Book,* xi, xiii.

23. Charles Edward Smith, *Jazz Record Book,* 1.

24. Charles Edward Smith, *Jazz Record Book,* 1.

25. Charles Edward Smith, *Jazz Record Book,* 2.

26. Charles Edward Smith, *Jazz Record Book,* 3.

27. Charles Edward Smith, *Jazz Record Book,* 3–5.

28. Charles Edward Smith, *Jazz Record Book,* 7–8.

29. Charles Edward Smith, *Jazz Record Book,* 10–24.

30. Charles Edward Smith, *Jazz Record Book,* 25–39.

31. Charles Edward Smith, *Jazz Record Book,* 117.

32. Hugues Panassié, *The Real Jazz,* trans. Anne Sorelle Williams, adapted for U.S. publication by Charles Edward Smith (New York: Smith and Durrell, 1942), xi–xiv. Nesuhi Ertegun, in "The Real Jazz?" *Record Changer,* Feb. 1943, 1–2, states: "Old-time collectors will find really nothing of great interest or originality in it. The information it contains is not new" (2). Gennari cites *Real Jazz* as an example of racial essentialism in *Blowin' Hot and Cool* (57). Guthrie Ramsey interprets Panassié's intent differently; see "Cosmopolitan or Provincial?" 33.

33. In the preface, Panassié states that "since jazz is a music created by the black race, it is very difficult and, in fact, almost impossible for a white man to get to the heart of it at first shot. A period of slow assimilation is required, and this period may well extend through several years. I had not yet achieved the necessary degree of assimilation at the time my first book was finished in 1934" (*Real Jazz,* vii). See also Balliett, "Panassié, Delaunay et Cie," 10–11.

34. Panassié, *Real Jazz,* 56. Panassié did see merit in Ellington's bands, admitting that others offered "interesting innovations," but felt that most did not approach Duke's standards.

35. Panassié, *Real Jazz,* 56–57. Panassié had made similar arguments earlier,

but without the purist trappings; see his "Panassié Decries Plight of Critics!!" *Down Beat* 6 (Mar. 1939): 3.

36. Panassié, *Real Jazz*, 60.

37. Panassié, *Real Jazz*, 65.

38. Alderson Fry, Max Kaplan, and William C. Love, *Who's Who in Jazz Collecting* (Nashville: Hemphill Press, 1942), 5.

39. Fry, Kaplan, and Love, *Who's Who in Jazz Collecting*, 5–6.

40. Fry, Kaplan, and Love, *Who's Who in Jazz Collecting*, 9–46. The "swing matinee idol" preference is what Gabbard identifies as "emotional" record collecting, a "feminine" strategy. See "Black Magic," 199.

41. Fry, Kaplan, and Love, *Who's Who in Jazz Collecting*, 21, 27, 13, 16, 19 (following the sequence of quotes).

42. For more on collectors in the 1940s, see Bacon, "Jazz Fan"; Thurman Grove and Mary Grove, "Jazz and the Collector," in *Jazz Review*, ed. Max Jones and Albert McCarthy (London: Jazz Music Books, 1945), 14–18; Charles F. Huber II, "King of the Canvassers," *IAJRC Journal* 22 (Fall 1989): 44–47; James H. Lavely, "Collecting Jazz," *Playboy*, Sept. 1955, 9–10, 12. For European activities, see Borneman, "Jazz Cult"; *National Federation of Jazz Organizations of Great Britain Blue Book*, comp. James Asman (London: J. D. Garrod, 1952).

43. Gennari, *Blowin' Hot and Cool*, 19–25; Gabbard, "Revenge," 202–3. See also Tucker, "Big Ears," especially 395–96.

44. Fry, Kaplan, and Love, *Who's Who in Jazz Collecting*, 41.

45. Bechet, *Treat It Gentle*, 173, 183.

46. Bechet, *Treat It Gentle*, 174, 183. For a full account of the incident, see Hazeldine, "Dear Wynne," 10–19.

47. "Rita, who was getting more and more disgusted with Bunk's shenanigans every minute, said 'I hope the Union fixes him good if he walks out,' etc. And I laughed and said Bunk never worries about little things like the Union." See Russell, quoted in Hazeldine, "Dear Wynne," 23. It would appear that Temple was both pro-union and ethical.

48. This characterization is consistent with the paradigmatic framework with which Barbara Smuts interprets the role of male bonding in hostility against women, in "Male Aggression against Women: An Evolutionary Perspective," in *Human Nature: An Interdisciplinary Biosocial Perspective* 3 (1992): 1–44. I would like to thank Linda L. Carroll for providing this reference.

49. Gene Williams, New York, to Bill Russell, Pittsburgh, Mar. 26, 1945, in Hazeldine, "Dear Wynne," 14.

50. Rudi Blesh, *This Is Jazz: A Series of Lectures Given at The San Francisco Museum of Art* (San Francisco: privately printed, 1943), 3. Interestingly enough, Bunk's statement is identical to the one by LaRocca cited by Charles Edward Smith in his *New Republic* essay of Feb. 16, 1938.

51. Blesh, *This Is Jazz*, 3.

52. Blesh, *This Is Jazz*, 4.

53. Blesh, *This Is Jazz*, 4.

54. Blesh, *This Is Jazz*, 8.

55. Blesh, *This Is Jazz*, 8.

56. Blesh, *This Is Jazz*, 16. Blesh's accusation that NORK purloined this tune is contradicted by Frederic Ramsey in *Chicago Documentary: Portrait of a Jazz Era* (London: Jazz Sociological Society, 1944), 12.

57. Blesh, *This Is Jazz*, 16.

58. Blesh, *This Is Jazz*, 33.

59. Jake Trussell Jr., "Why Fusion?" *Jazz Music* 2 (Sept. 1943): 4–5.

60. Trussell, "Why Fusion?" 4–5. See also John Hammond, "Is the Duke Deserting Jazz?" *Jazz Record*, Feb. 15, 1943, 4–5: "During the last ten years he has been adding men to his once compact group, has introduced complex harmonies solely for the effect. . . . The more complicated his music becomes the less feeling his soloists are able to impart to their work" (4).

61. John Hammond, "About the Author," is included among the prefaces to Leonard Feather, *The New Edition of the Encyclopedia of Jazz* (New York: Bonanza Books, 1960), 17–18.

62. On Feather's influence after the 1940s, see Gary Giddins's statement in Gennari, *Blowin' Hot and Cool*, 23; for Feather's contributions to the jazz schism, see 109, 120.

63. Ulanov was a New Yorker who studied with Franz Boas and Lionel Trilling at Columbia, receiving his A.B. in 1939. After completing his Ph.D. in English literature at Columbia in 1955, he held appointments at Princeton University (1951–53) and Barnard College (1953–88). He was offered the editorship of *Metronome* in 1943, after serving as editor of *Swing* (1939–41) and the *Review of Recorded Music* (1941–43).

64. Max Jones, "U.S. Commentary," *Jazz Music* 2 (Sept. 1943): 11–13, quote on 12.

65. For attacks by servicemen on Dizzy Gillespie, see Shaw, *Street That Never Slept*, 252–56. For threats to members of the Raeburn band in 1945, see David Allyn's comments and Buddy De Franco's account of the beating of Dodo Marmarosa by sailors, in Ira Gitler, *Swing to Bop: An Oral History of the Transition in Jazz in the 1940s* (New York: Oxford University Press, 1985), 208, 209.

66. Edwin Hinchcliffe, "No Laughing Matter," *Jazz Music* 2 (Nov. 1943): 44–45, especially 44.

67. Hinchcliffe, "No Laughing Matter," 44 (Armstrong, Bessie Smith, Ellington).

68. Hinchcliffe, "No Laughing Matter," 44.

69. Hinchcliffe, "No Laughing Matter," 44–45.

70. R. G. V. Venables, "In Self Defence," *Jazz Music* 2 (Nov. 1943): 45.

71. Arnold Gingrich, "Introduction," in *Esquire's Jazz Book*, ed. Paul Eduard

Miller (New York: Smith and Durrell, 1944), v–ix. See also Charles Edward Smith, "Collecting Hot: 1944," *Esquire,* Feb. 1944, 27, 98–100, a retrospective on the tenth anniversary of his 1934 article that had popularized "hot" collecting. The essay's congratulatory tone—"jazz collecting has taken its place alongside Sandwich glass and Currier & Ives prints as significant Americana"—and celebration of "hot" jazz as an aspect of heroic individualism—"a part of American life"—and evidence of "the coming of age of American music, all the way from its folk roots to its philharmonic fulfillments," may be seen as the apogee of the consensus wrought during the 1930s.

72. "Esquire's All-American Band," in Paul Eduard Miller, *Esquire's Jazz Book* (1944), 114.

73. For information on Roger Kay, an Egyptian critic, see Leonard Feather, *The Jazz Years: Earwitness to an Era* (New York: Da Capo Press, 1987), 80.

74. Wilson, *Jazz: The Transition Years,* 18.

75. For comparison of *Down Beat* and *Metronome* polls, see Woody Woodward, *Jazz Americana* (Los Angeles: Trend Books, 1956), 96–101. *Esquire's* poll differed from those of the trade magazines in using a panel of critics instead of relying on readers' votes. While purists routinely dismissed *Down Beat* and *Metronome* polls as popularity contests, their reactions to the *Esquire* polls were based on the high expectations that they placed on supposedly "expert" opinion.

76. Pvt. Bob Aurthur, "The Great Enlightenment," *Jazz Record,* no. 17 (Feb. 1944): 4–5, quote on 4.

77. Aurthur, "Great Enlightenment," 5.

78. Aurthur, "Great Enlightenment," 5.

79. Frederic Ramsey Jr., "Jazz at the Met," *Jazz Record,* no. 17 (Feb. 1944): 6–7, quote on 6.

80. Ramsey, "Jazz at the Met," 7. See also Jimmy Butts, "Harlem Speaks," *Jazz Record,* no. 12 (Sept. 1, 1943): 2, 5. See also the qualifications offered by Ramsey in "The Mail Box," *Jazz Record,* no. 13 (Oct. 1943): 13. The event was staged for the sale of war bonds and sponsored by the National Women's Council of the Navy League of the U.S.; see "Editorial: The Upward Journey of Hot Jazz, from the Junkshops to the Met," *Esquire,* Feb. 1944, 6.

81. Ramsey, "Jazz at the Met, " 7. See also Bruce Boyd Raeburn, "Early New Orleans Jazz in Theaters," *Louisiana History* 43 (Winter 2002): 41–52, for contrary opinions. For reactions to *Esquire's Jazz Book,* see Jake Trussell Jr., "Jim Crow—Upside Down," *Jazz Record,* no. 19 (Apr. 1944): 4–5, which accuses the panel of experts of reverse racism. Trussell attracted controversy; his "To the Editor," *Jazz Record,* no. 13 (Oct. 1943): 6, proposed that collectors knew more about jazz "purity" than "hot" musicians. Fats Baker contradicted him in "Let the Foul Air Out," *Jazz Record,* no. 13 (Oct. 1943): 8–10, warning against setting musicians and collectors against each other. Leonard Feather did not heed the warning. See his *The Book of Jazz* (New York: Meridian Books, 1959), 30–38.

82. Alma Hubner, "Must Jazz Be Progressive?" *Jazz Record*, no. 19 (Apr. 1944): 8–9, especially 8; Alma Hubner, "Of Chile and Jazz," *Jazz Record*, no. 14 (Nov. 1943): 6–7.

83. Hubner, "Must Jazz Be Progressive?" 8.

84. Hubner, "Must Jazz Be Progressive?" 8.

85. Hubner, "Must Jazz Be Progressive?" 9.

86. Hubner, "Must Jazz Be Progressive?" 9.

87. Hubner, "Must Jazz Be Progressive?" 9.

88. Pat Richardson, "Of Jazz And Intellectuals," *Jazz Record*, no. 20 (May 1944): 10–11, especially 10.

89. John Lucas, "Young Cats Going to the Dogs," *Jazz Record*, no. 21 (June 1944): 4–5.

90. Fred E. Glotzer, "On Jazz Critics," *Metronome* 60 (July 1944): 7.

91. Bill Swenton, "And He for Raeburn," *Metronome* 60 (July 1944): 7. Leonard Feather, "Dizzy Is Crazy like a Fox," *Metronome* 60 (July 1944): 16, 31. This was Feather's first piece on Dizzy; note Gillespie's comments in Shaw, *Street That Never Slept:* "Like when Leonard Feather first came, he completely ignored me. He was interested in Billie Holiday, Al Casey, Oscar Pettiford. The cats that people were talking about, the Gold Award Winners for *Esquire,* he wrote about" (257).

92. Anton Stepanek, "Jazz and Semantics," *Jazz Record*, no. 26 (Nov. 1944): 5. See also Ralph Berton, "A Critique for Critics," *Jazz Record*, no. 25 (Oct. 1944): 7–8, which argues that specialization of tastes and factionalism were diverting the jazz community from its true mission.

93. John Lucas, "More on Semantics," *Jazz Record*, no. 27 (Dec. 1944): 4. See also the letter to the editor by Pfc. Gerald L. Landau, "The Mail Box," *Jazz Record*, no. 26 (Dec. 1944): 12–13: "I am convinced that there are kicks to be had in both types of music. . . . The quality of music depends on the sincerity, imagination, technique and emotional intensity applied to it by the musician involved."

94. Gingrich, "Introduction," in *Esquire's 1945 Jazz Book*, ed. Paul Eduard Miller (New York: A. S. Barnes and Company, 1945), v.

95. Gingrich, "Introduction" (1945), vi–vii.

96. See "Backstage with the Experts," in *Esquire's 1945 Jazz Book*, 253–56, for panelist profiles. Representatives of *Billboard* and *Variety* were eliminated., and the number of blacks was increased from one to two. Letters written by Gene Williams and William Russell contain information on how Feather used devious strategies to subvert the power of "traditionalists" within the poll. See Hazeldine, "Dear Wynne," 24–25.

97. See "Esquire's All-American Band," in Paul Eduard Miller, *Esquire's 1945 Jazz Book*, 48–108, especially 61–62, 79–80.

98. Nesuhi Ertegun, "Esquire 1945," *Record Changer*, Feb. 1945, 3–5, quote on 3. Ertegun had also reacted negatively the year before as Jazzbo Brown; see "The

Esquire Farce," *Record Changer*, Mar. 1944, 23–24, 29. See also John Steiner, "Esquire in Shreds," *Record Changer*, Feb. 1944, 5–6.

99. Ertegun, "Esquire 1945," 4.

100. Ertegun, "Esquire 1945," 4–5.

101. George Avakian, "Philippine Philippic," *Record Changer*, Feb. 1945, 12, 42–46.

102. Avakian, "Philippine Philippic," 12, 42.

103. Avakian, "Philippine Philippic," 45–46.

104. Art Hodes, "Editorial," *Jazz Record*, no. 29 (Feb. 1945): 16.

105. See Rudi Blesh, "Esquire's Second Swing Concert," *Jazz Record*, no. 29 (Feb. 1945): 8–9.

106. As quoted in Rudi Blesh, "Crawl Out of Bed—Winter Is Over," *Record Changer*, Mar. 1945, 7, 15, especially 7. See also Ralph J. Gleason, "Featherbed Ball," *Record Changer*, Sept. 1944, 48, 54–55.

107. Blesh, "Crawl Out of Bed," 7.

108. Blesh, "Crawl Out of Bed," 7, 15.

109. Blesh, "Crawl Out of Bed," 15.

110. Ralph J. Gleason, "That Book Again," *Record Changer*, May 1945, 26. See also the letter from MM (Marili Morden), in "Let That Foul Air Out!" *Record Changer*, July 1945, 32.

111. Dr. S. I. Hayakawa, *35th and State: Reflections on the History of Jazz* (Chicago: privately printed, 1945), 1. Elements of this lecture were also printed in Hayakawa's column for the *Chicago Defender* in 1945.

112. Hayakawa, *35th and State*, 2.

113. Hayakawa, *35th and State*, 2.

114. Hayakawa, *35th and State*, 5.

115. Hayakawa, *35th and State*, 6.

116. See Montgomery, "Jazz in Los Angeles," *Record Changer*, Aug. 1945, 32.

117. Feather, *Jazz Years*, 77–79.

118. Jazzbo Brown, "Jelly Roll Was Right," *Record Changer*, May 1945, 6–7, 24–25., especially 6.

119. Jazzbo Brown, "Jelly Roll Was Right," 7, 24. Goffin's *Jazz: From the Congo to the Metropolitan*, trans. Walter Schaap and Leonard Feather (New York: Doubleday, Doran and Company, 1944), was the only other jazz history besides *Jazzmen* to be distributed to American troops during World War II. Some collectors saw the work as derivative, relying too heavily on *Jazzmen*. See Morroe Berger, "Early New Orleans Jazz Bands," *Jazz Record*, no. 19 (Apr. 1944): 6–7. Other saw Goffin's book as "reasonably accurate." See Rita Temple, "Folk Roots of Jazz," *Jazz Record*, no. 23 (Aug. 1944): 8.

120. Gordon Gullickson, "Lemme Take This Chorus," *Record Changer*, Aug. 1945, 34.

121. Gullickson, "Lemme Take This Chorus" (Aug. 1945), 34, quotes Rosen-

thal: "We have tried to make our staff of writers as well balanced as the book will allow." A review of *Jazzways,* ed. George S. Rosenthal, Jr. and Frank Zachary, in collaboration with Frederic Ramsey Jr. and Rudi Blesh (London: Musicians Press, Ltd., 1946), shows that despite Rosenthal's intentions, the book was heavily weighted toward the purist audience, with a majority of articles and photographs devoted to traditional jazz and New Orleans. Rosenthal and Zachary later collaborated on *Portfolio* (1949–51), an important graphic arts magazine.

122. See Feather, *Jazz Years,* 88. See also Arthur McAuliffe, "A Treatise on Mouldy Figs," *Metronome* 61 (Aug. 1945): 13, 21. Excerpts from Platt's letter are on p. 13.

123. Quoted in Feather, *Jazz Years,* 88–89.

124. Feather, *Jazz Years,* 89. According to John Hammond, Feather's animosity toward the purists mellowed in later years as the result of an accident in San Francisco. See John Hammond, "About the Author," 17–18.

125. Bilbo Brown, "Rebop and Mop Mop: The New Leftist Rabble Rousers," *Record Changer,* Oct. 1945, 34.

126. Gordon Gullickson, "Lemme Take This Chorus," *Record Changer,* Oct. 1945, 35.

127. Gullickson, "Lemme Take This Chorus" (Oct. 1945), 35.

128. Bernard Gendron, *Between Montmartre and the Mudd Club: Popular Music and the Avant-Garde* (Chicago and London: University of Chicago Press, 2002), 121–41, quote on 121.

129. Gendron, *Between Montmartre and the Mudd Club,* 122.

130. Gendron, *Between Montmartre and the Mudd Club,* 140.

131. See especially Joshua Berrett, "Louis Armstrong and Opera," in *The Louis Armstrong Companion: Eight Decades of Commentary* (New York: Schirmer Books, 1996), 24–29.

132. Gendron, *Between Montmartre and the Mudd Club,* 123, 336. Gendron selected 1942 as the onset of schism and relates "moldy figs" to it because "this date and metaphor were offered to me by Dan Morgenstern," (note 7, 336). Citing Ulanov in 1942 as the opening salvo in a war of words that had been going on since the late 1930s requires a more detailed explanation.

133. Gendron, *Between Montmartre and the Mudd Club,* 126.

134. Gendron, *Between Montmartre and the Mudd Club,* 122.

Chapter 6

1. H. M. Apfel, "Hot Man (Under the Collar)," *Jazz Record,* no. 36 (Sept. 1945): 7–8, quote on 8.

2. Apfel, "Hot Man," 8.

3. Apfel, "Hot Man," 8.

4. Ernest Borneman, "The Musicians and the Critic," *Jazz Record,* no. 36 (Sept. 1945): 9–10, quote on 9. Born Ernst Wilhelm Julius Bornemann, Borneman

was a German crime writer, ethnomusicologist, filmmaker, musician, and psychoanalyst specializing in sexology. Before he fled to England to escape the Nazis in 1933, he was active in the German Communist Party.

5. Borneman, "Musicians and the Critic," 9.

6. Borneman, "Musicians and the Critic," 10.

7. Borneman, "Musicians and the Critic," 10.

8. See Gingrich, "Introduction," in *Esquire's 1946 Jazz Book,* ed. Paul Eduard Miller (New York: A. S. Barnes and Company, 1946), v–ix.

9. Gingrich, "Introduction" (1946), viii–ix.

10. George Hoefer, "The Collectors' Outlook," in Paul Eduard Miller, *Esquire's 1946 Jazz Book,* 145–50, quote on 145.

11. Leonard Feather, "A Survey of Jazz Today," in Paul Eduard Miller, *Esquire's 1946 Jazz Book,* 151–63, quote on 161.

12. Quoted in Feather, "Survey of Jazz Today," 152. Ulanov extolled progress in liner notes for Boyd Raeburn: "Jazz today is no longer three, four or a half-dozen men blowing, each man for himself. . . . The Original Dixieland Jazz Band . . . King Oliver's Creole Band . . . all these are honored names in jazz. They started something . . . but their day is over. . . . Though the foundation has not been forgotten, a great deal has been added." See Barry Ulanov, liner notes, *Innovations by Boyd Raeburn* (Jewel Records Album D-1, 1946). According to Bill Russell, Bill Colburn used these recordings as examples of "the sort of music he didn't like." Russell also mentions an occasion when Bunk Johnson was caught listening to these recordings, apparently with pleasure, at Gene Williams's apartment, at which point his host promptly confiscated them. See Russell, "Notes, 1942–1949," Box I, p. 192; Bill Russell, New Orleans, to Bruce Boyd Raeburn, New Orleans, Nov. 13, 1984.

13. See Simon, *Big Bands,* 31–32. See also Hsio Wen Shih, "The Spread of Jazz and the Big Bands," in *Jazz,* ed. Nat Hentoff and Albert McCarthy (New York: Rinehart and Company, 1959), 186–87, for an alternative perspective on what killed the big bands.

14. See Gordon Gullickson, "Lemme Take This Chorus," *Record Changer,* Mar. 1946, 7, 45, which quotes Deitch. For more information on Deitch, see Gordon Gullickson, "Lemme Take This Chorus," *Record Changer,* Aug. 1946, 8, 18, where the artist gives biographical details. For a selection of his artwork, with a commentary by George Avakian, see Gene Deitch, *The Cat* (New York: Changer Publications, 1948).

15. Carlton Brown, "Beware of Experts!" *Record Changer,* Mar. 1946, 8, 10–11, quote on 8.

16. Carlton Brown, "Beware of Experts!" 11.

17. Carlton Brown, "Beware of Experts!" 11.

18. See Sally-Ann Worsfold, "Book Reviews," *Jazz Journal International* 32 (Oct: 1979): 21, for Worsfold's first response to *Shining Trumpets,* which she later

viewed as "circumscribed and myopic": "[For] an impressionable fourteen year old [the book] was taken at face value, merely serving as a handbook of the records to be avoided rather than enjoyed." For an alternative view of Blesh's influence, see George H. Buck Jr., "Rudi Blesh, 1899–1985," *Collector's Record Club Newsletter* 11 (Sept.–Dec. 1985): 1–2. For reviews of *Shining Trumpets* and *Really the Blues* by collectors, see Ernest Borneman and Hugues Panassié, "The Record Changer Book Review," *Record Changer*, Dec. 1946, 12–15, which is essentially favorable. See also John McNulty, "Hot Music and Hopheads," *New York Herald Tribune*, Oct. 27, 1946, on Mezzrow: "Now these many years ago, jazz music mixed together white man and Negro; made teams of Irish, Jews, Dutch, and African. . . . The wild and certainly crazy cult of jazz music became, that long ago, a spearhead of tolerance. That historic fact comes up out of this curious book, and it is good to read."

19. Blesh, *Shining Trumpets*, 3–4.

20. Mezz Mezzrow, with Bernard Wolfe, *Really the Blues* (New York: Random House, 1946), 3–4. Bernard Wolfe (1915–1985) was a Yale graduate who had contributed articles to the *New International* in the mid-1930s and served on Trotsky's secretarial staff in Mexico in 1937. *Really the Blues* was the beginning of his creative writing career, which included *Limbo* (1952), a sensational science-fiction thriller, and *The Great Prince Died* (1959), a novel about Trotsky. See Carolyn Geduld, *Bernard Wolfe* (New York: Twayne, 1972).

21. Mezzrow, *Really the Blues*, 11–13.

22. Edmond Souchon and Johnny Wiggs both recalled the thrill of hearing black bands in New Orleans when they were very young. See Edmond Souchon, interview by Haywood H. Hillyer III, May 7, 1958, and Johnny Wiggs, interview by William Russell, Aug. 26, 1962, tape recordings, HJA, for details on early experiences and the popularity of black bands at white high school and college fraternity parties.

23. For a discussion of Crow Jim, see Leonard Feather, "Jazz in American Society," in *The New Edition of the Encyclopedia of Jazz* (New York: Bonanza Books, 1960), 79–88. While Crow Jim has most often been associated with the modernist perspective, Blesh's racial thesis and Mezzrow's aspiration to live his life as a black man show the power of this concept within the traditionalist fold.

24. Blesh, *Shining Trumpets*, xi, 25–80. Blesh's exposition of the African background influenced future jazz historians; see especially Marshall W. Stearns, *The Story of Jazz* (New York: Oxford University Press, 1956), 11–32.

25. Blesh, *Shining Trumpets*, 157–58. Blesh, like the authors of *Jazzmen*, was operating under the misapprehension that activity in Congo Square had continued into the 1880s. Jerah Johnson, "New Orleans's Congo Square: An Urban Setting for Early Afro-American Culture Formation," *Louisiana History* 32 (Spring 1991): 117–57, places termination of the ring shouts by 1856. For links between New Orleans and Cuba in the nineteenth century, see Rebecca J. Scott, *Degrees*

of Freedom: Louisiana and Cuba after Slavery (Cambridge and London: Belknap Press of Harvard University Press, 2005). Blesh's desire to place jazz origins earlier is contravened by the recent tendency among historians to bring that chronology forward, closer to 1915. See Gushee, "Nineteenth-Century Origins," 1–24.

26. Typical of this approach was the way he dismissed the testimony of the informants of *Jazzmen,* many of whom he had interviewed himself: "Having suffered, as many of them had, from neglect and misunderstanding, they may well have had the psychological need to consider themselves creators, not of a stage, but of jazz itself. Deeper still is the general social need of the Negro to justify himself and to escape from the false stereotype that white 'superiority' has cast upon him" (Blesh, *Shining Trumpets,* 158).

27. "Presentism" is a tendentious approach to history that seeks to justify a priori conclusions through a selective use of factual information. In *Shining Trumpets,* Blesh went one step further in making statements for which there was no factual basis whatsoever. See Herbert Butterfield, *The Whig Interpretation of History* (London: G. Bell and Sons, 1951).

28. Mezzrow, *Really the Blues,* 194–97. See also Charles Delaunay, "An Attack on Critical Jabberwocky," *Record Changer,* Mar. 1949, 13–14.

29. Mezzrow, *Really the Blues,* 326.

30. Mezzrow, *Really the Blues,* 327. For an eyewitness account, see Glover Compton, interview by William Russell, June 30, 1959, tape recording, HJA.

31. Mezzrow, *Really the Blues,* 327.

32. See Rose, *I Remember Jazz,* 17–19, for information on Mezzrow's marijuana trade.

33. Carlton Brown, "Hey! Ba-Ba-Revolt!" *Record Changer,* May 1946, 12, 26, quote on 12.

34. Carlton Brown, "Hey!" 12.

35. Carlton Brown, "Hey!" 26.

36. Carlton Brown, "Hey!" 26.

37. See the advertisement for "The Record Changer All-Star Band," *Record Changer,* Dec. 1946, 21. The results of the poll were announced in "The Record Changer's All-Star Band," *Record Changer,* Feb. 1947, 6–7. For "World's Greatest Authority," George Avakian placed first, with 31,683 points; William Russell second, with 29,588; Charles Edward Smith third, with 25,517; and Rudi Blesh fourth, with 23,713.

38. See Feather, *Jazz Years,* 89–93, for discussion of *Esquire's 1947 Jazz Book* and a photographic reproduction of the letter. See also "Esquire's Winners Protest," *Metronome* 63 (Apr. 1947): 26–27.

39. Feather, *Jazz Years,* 92.

40. Coverage of bebop in the pages of the *Record Changer* began in Apr. 1946 with the addition of Bill Gottlieb (1917–2006) to the staff, but it was limited. Gottlieb had worked as a jazz columnist for the *Washington Sunday Post* and *Down*

Beat and was a renowned jazz photographer. See "Contributors," *Record Changer,* June 1946, 8. When Nesuhi Ertegun took over the editorship of the magazine in Aug. 1947, he made it clear that it would no longer be a sectarian publication: "First, let's stop being unduly serious about jazz. It's supposed to be a lively art, remember? You want solid documentation? Fine. You want honest criticism? Great. But no more obscurantist quarrels between critics, between groups, between schools and styles. No more insults. Fights between critics do nothing but increase the notoriety of those critics. Enough of this type of self-promotion." See "Ertegun," *Record Changer,* Aug. 1947, 4, 13, quote on 4. The reaction to the Condon coup was also revealing. In A. Condom, "The Record Changer's Book Review: Esquire's 1947 Jazz Book," *Record Changer,* Mar. 1947, 8–9, 15, the contents were listed as thirty-one features on Eddie Condon, with an afterthought: "Of course, there are one or two other things in the Year Book too, but you know how it is in the advertising business: you always have to throw in some fillers with your plugs" (15). For information on the Grauer-Keepnews takeover, see Keepnews, *View from Within,* 4–8.

41. William Genes (as told to Alf Helfensteller), "I Never Was a Jazz Expert!" *Record Changer,* Sept. 1947, 11.

42. Bill Russell, "Mutt Carey," *Record Changer,* Nov. 1948, 7.

43. Russell, "Mutt Carey," 7. Ironically, "playing clarinet parts on the trumpet" is one of the practices that Brian Harker identifies as basic to Louis Armstrong's early stylistic development in New Orleans. See Brian Harker, "The Early Musical Development of Louis Armstrong, 1901–1928" (Ph.D. diss., Columbia University, 1997).

44. Russell, "Mutt Carey," 7.

45. See André Hodeir, "La Charte du Jazz," in *Jazz 47: America: Cahiers France-Amérique-Latinite, no. 5.* (Paris: Éditions Pierre Seghers, 1947), 23–24.

46. See Dregni, *Django,* 238–40, quote on 238–39.

47. Rudi Blesh, "What Is New Orleans Style?" *Record Changer* (Mar. 1948), 11, 16, quote on 11.

48. Blesh, "What Is New Orleans Style?" 16. Purists were not the only ones who had criticisms of "This Is Jazz." See Bill Gottlieb, "If New Orleans Jazz Isn't Dead Now, Blesh Faddists Are Killing It," *Down Beat* 14 (Feb. 26, 1947): 3. See also Michael Levin, "Jazzman Blasts Blesh As Phoney: Blesh Trying to Corner Monopoly on N.O. Jazz: Three Stars Quit Program," *Down Beat* 14 (Oct. 8, 1947): 1, 12–13.

49. Blesh, "What Is New Orleans Style?" 11.

50. Rudi Blesh, "Some Thoughts on the Jazz Revival," *Record Changer,* Nov. 1948, 14, 23, quote on 14.

51. Blesh, "Some Thoughts," 14.

52. Blesh, "Some Thoughts," 14, 23.

53. Blesh, "Some Thoughts," 23.

54. Delaunay, "Attack on Critical Jabberwocky," 13.

55. Delaunay, "Attack on Critical Jabberwocky," 13.

56. Delaunay, "Attack on Critical Jabberwocky," 13–14.

57. Delaunay, "Attack on Critical Jabberwocky," 14. Claude Luter (1923–2006); Claude Bolling (1930–).

58. See Amy Lee, "Figs Might Do Well to Take a Hint from Bop—Make New Dixie Sounds," *Down Beat* 16 (May 16, 1949): 2.

59. See Gordon Gullickson, "Lemme Take This Chorus," *Record Changer,* Aug. 1947, 4, which states: "Charles Edward Smith writes that he has fallen upon evil times and must dispose of his records. He says that if he doesn't get cash in a flash, he and his records will be out on the curb, and the residents of Christopher Street will be seeing flying discs instead of flying saucers. A great joker, that boy."

60. Charles Edward Smith, "Cultural Anthropology and the Reformed Tramp," *Record Changer,* June 1948, 11–12, 24, quote on 11.

61. Charles Edward Smith, "Cultural Anthropology," 11.

62. Charles Edward Smith, "Cultural Anthropology," 11.

63. Charles Edward Smith, "Cultural Anthropology," 11–12.

64. Charles Edward Smith, "Cultural Anthropology," 12.

65. Charles Edward Smith, "Cultural Anthropology," 12.

66. Charles Edward Smith, "Cultural Anthropology," 12.

67. Charles Edward Smith, "Over My Shoulder," *Record Changer,* Oct. 1948, 13–14, quote on 13.

68. Charles Edward Smith, "Over My Shoulder," 13.

69. Charles Edward Smith, "Over My Shoulder," 14. Smith showed that, unlike LaRocca, he was willing to change his mind: "The chief handicap we early American writers on jazz had to face was that our awareness of the music far outweighed considerations of the environment. We conceived of the Bolden Band as playing to-hell-and-gone style . . . raucous on stomps, speaking a deep savage sorrow in the blues. And this was, according to the most valid oral testimony then obtainable, the music. But *now* we know that Cornish (who could read) and a friend from the Robichaux outfit (which played quadrilles and rags for patrons of Antoine's in the gaslight era) combined to introduce into the Bolden repertoire music that was already on paper. Until we began patiently to explore that sort of background, we wrote from what seemed a secure vantage point, for example, Louis Armstrong's Hot Five and Hot Seven. We didn't quite grasp the significance of Jelly's statement that Tony Jackson played everything from 'opera to the blues.' That's a mighty wide swath, with plenty of corn waving in amongst the golden grain!"

70. Charles Edward Smith, "Over My Shoulder," 14.

71. George Avakian, "The Vanishing American," *Record Changer,* Dec. 1948, 14, 22, quote on 14.

72. Avakian, "Vanishing American," 14. Both Charles Edward Smith and

George Avakian became involved with modernists in later years. Note Smith's response to McCarthy, "Questionnaire," in Blesh, *This Is Jazz*, 236–56, in which Smith states: "Of moderns I like so many, not only Monk but even Mingus, and in work of the past I rate very highly the arranging of certain men—Basie, Fletcher, and, not to forget the distaff on the down beat, Mary Lou Williams" (247). Avakian later became the Columbia Records official in charge of Boyd Raeburn's return to the dance band field in 1956.

73. See Morroe Berger, "Hot, Sweet and Social," *New York Times*, 1948, in "Subjects" vertical file: "Book Reviews," HJA.

74. Quoted in Berger, "Hot, Sweet and Social." See also Sidney Finkelstein, *Jazz: A People's Music* (New York: Citadel Press, 1948), 233. While Finkelstein's social interpretation of jazz history was obtrusive, his critique of the strengths and weaknesses of jazz literature was fundamentally sound. He correctly identified the "primitivist" perspectives that connected Blesh with Panassié, noting that *Shining Trumpets* "carried the 'folk,' 'primitive' and 'African' theory of jazz to its furthest extreme. Its most worthwhile quality was that it carried the exploration of the roots of jazz back into the blues and spirituals of the past century" (6). Finkelstein's appreciation of *Jazzmen* was concise: "[It] carried understanding of jazz a step forward. In this book, unlike Panassié's, jazz appeared as the creation of an entire people more than of a few representative musicians. The authors were able to recreate in words a musical life, mainly of New Orleans, which was only faintly represented on records. Today there seems in the book to be too poetic a nostalgia thrown about the life of the Negro people in the South, and it is now apparent that the movement was a necessary step forward for jazz. But the book is still the best documentary history of the early days of jazz" (3–4). Favorable commentary was also given to the *Jazz Record Book* (5). As a critic, Finkelstein displayed considerable talent. See Max Jones, *Jazz Retrospect* (Boston: Crescendo Publishing, 1976), in which he refers to *Jazz: A People's Music* as "the first mature statement of jazz criticism" (146).

75. Sidney Finkelstein, "Peace in the Ranks," *Record Changer*, Mar. 1949, 11–14, quote on 11.

76. Finkelstein, "Peace in the Ranks," 11.

77. Finkelstein, "Peace in the Ranks," 12. For Finkelstein's views on bebop and the pitfalls engendered by its popularity in 1948, see Sidney Finkelstein, "Jazz Reaches a Turning Point," in *The Jazzfinder '49* (New Orleans: Orin Blackstone, 1949), 5–14.

78. Finkelstein, "Peace in the Ranks," 5. See also Wilson, *Jazz: The Transition Years*, which states: "By 1949 the general public was still putting up a strong resistance to bop and even the jazz audience was wearying of repeated servings of what had become cliches. Gillespie by then had reached a point of desperation in his attempts to develop an audience for the big band he was leading" (23). Also see Feather, *Jazz Years*, in which Feather recalls "that I was able to record Sarah

Vaughan, Dizzy Gillespie and Charlie Parker before any of them had secured a contract with any company was naturally a source of special pleasure to me; so was my series of Carnegie Hall concerts from 1947–9 in which, with the help of the young jazz promoter Monte Kay and the popular bebop disc jockey Symphony Sid Torin, I was able to prove the existence of a substantial audience for the music of Dizzy (and, on the first concert, Bird)" (103).

79. Leonard Feather, *Inside Be-Bop* (New York: J. J. Robbins and Sons, 1949), 3.

80. Feather, *Book of Jazz*, 8.

81. Feather, *Book of Jazz*, 22.

82. Feather, *Book of Jazz*, 22. Feather's use of Blake's testimony contrasts with that provided by Eubie's biographer, Al Rose, in *Eubie Blake* (New York: Schirmer Books, 1979), in which the pianist's recollections are less sure: "It's hard to say when I first started hearing this syncopated kind of music" (12).

83. Quoted in Feather, *Book of Jazz*, 26.

84. Feather, *Book of Jazz*, 29. While Feather was adept at musicological analysis, the ultimate expression of evolutionist critical theory came with Andre Hodeir's *Jazz: Its Evolution and Essence* (1956), which tackled the problem of permanence versus change in jazz. See Dr. Louis Gottlieb, "The Beginning of Method in Jazz Criticism," *Jazz: A Quarterly of American Music*, no. 1 (Oct. 1958): 19–26.

Chapter 7

1. Eric Porter argues that Louis Armstrong's *Swing That Music* (1936) deserves consideration as an early history of jazz, and one would have to agree. However, "hot" collectors did not seem to take much note of it. See Eric Porter, *What Is This Thing Called Jazz? African American Musicians as Artists, Critics, and Activists* (Berkeley: University of California Press, 2002), 43.

2. Most New Orleanians referred to what later became known as "jazz" as "ragtime," "gutbucket," or "ratty music." For discussion of the etymology of the word, see Peter Tamony, "Jazz, the Word," *Jazz: A Quarterly of American Music*, no. 1 (Oct. 1958): 33–39, 42. See also facsimiles of E. T. Gleeson's article of Mar. 16, 1913, with his retrospective account of Art Hickman's use of the term: "I Remember: The Birth of Jazz," *San Francisco Call-Bulletin*, Sept. 1938, 40–41; Lewis Porter, *Jazz: A Century of Change*.

3. Donald E. Winston, "News Reporting of Jazz Music from 1890 to 1927" (M.A. thesis, University of Oklahoma, 1966), 26.

4. Winston, "News Reporting of Jazz Music," 28.

5. *New Orleans Item*, Nov. 10, 1900, quoted in Winston, "News Reporting of Jazz Music," 31–32.

6. *New Orleans Item*, Nov. 16, 1902, quoted in Winston, "News Reporting of Jazz Music," 33.

7. Marquis, *In Search of Buddy Bolden*, 1–28.

8. Winston, "News Reporting of Jazz Music," 37. For an account of the attack on the mother-in-law, see Marquis, *In Search of Buddy Bolden*, 112–14.

9. See *New Orleans Item*, Sept. 7, 14, 1917.

10. "Jass and Jassism," *New Orleans Times-Picayune*, June 20, 1918.

11. See W. T. N. to Editor of *Times-Picayune*, July 2, 1918, undated clipping, in LaRocca clippings file, HJA.

12. See Fair Play to Editor of *Times-Picayune*, June 20, 1918, undated clipping, in LaRocca clippings file, HJA.

13. See Encore to Editor of *Times-Picayune*, June 29, 1918, and M. C. to Editor of *Times-Picayune*, June 29, 1918, both in LaRocca clippings file, HJA.

14. See Maison Blanche Music Department advertisement, *New Orleans Times-Picayune*, Apr. 15, 1917.

15. See Ronald L. Morris, *Wait until Dark: Jazz and the Underworld, 1880–1940* (Bowling Green: Bowling Green University Popular Press, 1980), especially 87–102.

16. The letter from the Axe-man was dated Mar. 13, 1919, and appeared in the *New Orleans Times-Picayune* the next day.

17. See Lyle Saxon and Robert Tallant, *Gumbo Ya-Ya: A Collection of Louisiana Folk Tales* (Boston: Houghton Mifflin Company, 1945), 87.

18. For alternative explanations of how Brown's band was discovered by out-of-town promoters, see Brunn, *Story of the Original Dixieland Jazz Band*, 26–27; Holbrook, "Mister Jazz Himself," 131–51.

19. "Orleans' Product: Stale Bread's Fiddle Gave Jazz to the World," *New Orleans Item*, Mar. 9, 1919.

20. For discussion of Chicagoan Bert Kelly's claims to have started the jazz craze by contemporary New Orleans musicians, see the letters to the *New York Dramatic Mirror* in 1919, in the appendix to Samuel B. Charters, *Jazz: New Orleans, 1886–1963: An Index to the Negro Musicians of New Orleans*, rev. ed. (New York: Oak Publications, 1963), 156–58, which deny his claim.

21. "Orleans' Product."

22. See Ridgley, interview by Russell and Collins, June 2, 1959. The account is given in the third person by the transcriber of the interview.

23. Ridgley, interview by Russell and Collins, June 2, 1959.

24. Ridgley, interview by Russell and Collins, June 2, 1959.

25. As an interesting aside, during retrieval of a collection of vintage 78s for the Hogan Jazz Archive, the Piron orchestra came up in conversation with an elderly Garden District socialite, for whom the orchestra had played in the very ballroom where the records were stored. I said: "Oh, how wonderful! You must have hired the band for its exquisite dance tempos." "No," she said. "We hired them because they were cheap."

26. Souchon stated: "The social question never occurred in their mind. Jazz

was not considered as an art which started in New Orleans or as a form" (interview by Hillyer, May 7, 1958). See also Mrs. Mary Lucy Hamill O'Kelley, May 4, 1958, tape recording, HJA; Elizabeth O'Kelley Kerrigan, May 4, 1958, tape recording, HJA; Jack Kerrigan, May 4, 1958, tape recording, HJA; Mrs. Evelyn Sinclair Moyar, May 6, 1958, tape recording, HJA; Dr. Homer J. Dupuy, May 6, 1958, tape recording, HJA; Mrs. Esther Dupuy Breckenridge, May 14, 1958, tape recording, HJA; Charles L. Dufour, May 12, 1958, tape recording, HJA. In addition to the interviews conducted by Hillyer, see George Blanchin, interview by Richard B. Allen, Nov. 13, 1959, tape recording, HJA, which is also helpful in characterizing the reactions of young Orleanians to early jazz bands, both black and white.

27. Benjie White, interview by Allen and Crawford, Mar. 16, 1961.

28. Benjie White, interview by Allen and Crawford, Mar. 16, 1961.

29. Benjie White, interview by Allen and Crawford, Mar. 16, 1961.

30. Benjie White, interview by Allen and Crawford, Mar. 16, 1961.

31. For biographical information on John Hyman, see Myra Menville, "Wiggs—Self-Explained," *Second Line* 29 (Spring 1977): 3–13; Al Rose, "Both of Johnny Wiggs," *Second Line* 12 (Sept.–Oct. 1961): 11–14, 24; Peter R. Haby, "Johnny Wiggs," *Footnote* 9 (Oct.–Nov. 1977): 4–14; Wiggs, interview by Russell, Aug. 26, 1962.

32. Menville, "Wiggs," 4.

33. Menville, "Wiggs," 4–5. Bill Kleppinger (1899–1982); Lester "Monk" Smith (1898–1952); James "Red Happy" Bolton (ca. 1885–1928).

34. Menville, "Wiggs," 5. Earl Crumb (1899–1979); Frank Ferrer (1896–1969). "Harry" Ferrer is the same person as "Mose."

35. Menville, "Wiggs," 5.

36. Menville, "Wiggs," 6.

37. Menville, "Wiggs," 6.

38. As Hyman put it, "I had to change my name because the School Board would not permit anybody to play that old bad music called jazz, so I used the first part of my middle name and called myself Johnny Wiggs" (Menville, "Wiggs," 12–13).

39. Benjie White, interview by Allen and Crawford, Mar. 16, 1961.

40. For details from two members of Celestin's band, see Jeanette Kimball, interview by Russell, Feb. 10, 1962; Narvin H. Kimball, interview by William Russell, Nov. 25, 1961, tape recording, HJA.

41. See Arthur "Monk" Hazel, interview by William Russell and Richard B. Allen, July 16, 1959, tape recording, HJA. For further detail on the matinee, see Will Specht, "King of Jazz Royally Received," *Prelude* 2 (Dec. 1928): 8–9, which states that "the gentle hand of 'symphonic' jazz too often obliterates the vitality of a type of music which has coarse virility." For newspaper reviews that support Hazel's account, see Althea Wuerpel, "Whiteman Still Wizard at Jazz," *New Or-*

leans States, Oct. 29, 1928, which confirms that numbers such as "Crazy Rhythm" and "That's My Weakness Now,"which were "very popular but not on the program," had also been performed; W. Boyd Gatewood, "King of Jazz Confesses 'That's My Weakness Now' and Names Orleans Food," *New Orleans Times-Picayune,* Oct. 29, 1928, which describes the interview as taking place "back in the wings of the St. Charles Theater while his orchestra played without him," during which "a cornet virtuoso had just finished a sobbing cacophony in solo that brought down the house out front." Roy Bargy (1894-1974).

42. See Orin Blackstone, "Leader of First Jazz Band Reviews Rise of New Music," *Popular Music,* Mar. 10, 1933, 1, 7-8, quote on 7.

43. Blackstone, "Leader of First Jazz Band," 1.

44. Blackstone, "Leader of First Jazz Band," 7.

45. Blackstone, "Leader of First Jazz Band," 7.

46. E. Belfield Spriggins, "Excavating Local Jazz," *Louisiana Weekly,* Apr. 22, 1933. For additional information on Spriggins, see Lynn Abbott, "E. Belfield Spriggins: Pioneer African-American Discoverer of Buddy Bolden and Others," *78 Quarterly* 1, no. 10 (1999): 13-53.

47. Spriggins, "Excavating Local Jazz."

48. E. Belfield Spriggins, "Excavating Jazz," *Louisiana Weekly,* Apr. 29, 1933. Arnold Metoyer (ca. 1876-1935).

49. Spriggins, "Excavating Jazz."

50. See Marquis, *In Search of Buddy Bolden,* 2, 4, 109.

51. Charles Edward Smith, "Land of Dreams, " 265-85, quote on 268.

52. Charles Edward Smith, "Land of Dreams," 267-68.

53. Nesuhi Ertegun, "Real and Fake," *Record Changer,* May 1943, 2-4.

54. Nesuhi Ertegun, "Real and Fake," 3.

55. Nesuhi Ertegun, "Real and Fake," 3.

56. Nesuhi Ertegun, "Real and Fake," 4.

57. Nesuhi Ertegun, "Real and Fake," 4.

58. See Harry Lim, "Way Down Yonder," *Metronome* 59 (Oct. 1943): 36, 38.

59. Lim, "Way Down Yonder," 36.

60. Lim, "Way Down Yonder," 36.

61. Lim, "Way Down Yonder," 38.

62. See Ken Hulsizer, "New Orleans in Wartime," in Jones and McCarthy *Jazz Review,* 3-6, quote on 3.

63. Hulsizer "New Orleans in Wartime," 3.

64. Hulsizer, "New Orleans in Wartime," 4.

65. Hulsizer, "New Orleans in Wartime," 6.

66. Hulsizer, "New Orleans in Wartime," 5.

67. Hulsizer, "New Orleans in Wartime," 6. For accounts by other "jazz pilgrims" on the state of jazz in New Orleans during the mid-1940s, see George Hartman, "New Orleans Today," *Jazz Record,* no. 28 (Jan. 1945): 4-6, which

states that "it is really a shame that the general public in New Orleans doesn't go for real good jazz from 'way back, the real jazz. New Orleans music has been so highly publicized and the city turned out so many good bands from the old days, but the people down there nowadays are just not educated to jazz" (4). See also Eugene Williams and Skippy Adelman, "New Orleans Today," in *Jazzways,* ed. George S. Rosenthal and Frank Zachary (London: Musicians Press Ltd., 1946).

68. National Jazz Foundation leaflet, in "Subjects" vertical file: "Foundations, Local—National Jazz Foundation," HJA. For additional perspective on the NJF, see Charles Suhor, *Jazz in New Orleans: The Postwar Years through 1970* (Lanham, Md., and London: Scarecrow Press, 2001), 22–27. See also George Hoefer, "Hot Box: National Jazz Foundation," *Down Beat* 12 (Feb. 1, 1944): 11.

69. NJF leaflet.

70. "Big Night for Basin Street," brochure (ca. 1945), in "Subjects" vertical file: "Foundations, Local—National Jazz Foundation," HJA.

71. For biographical information on Edmond Souchon, see "Biographical Data on Dr. Edmond Souchon, II," *Second Line* 20 (Sept.–Oct. 1968): 97–98, 104, 107; Carolyn Kolb, "He Will Be Missed," *Second Line* 20 (Sept.–Oct. 1968): 95–96; George Kay, "To Doc from a Friend," *Second Line* 20 (Sept.–Oct. 1968): 105; Myra Menville, "Penny Whistle—Last Letter," *Second Line* 20 (Sept.–Oct. 1968): 99–100; Merrill Hammond, "A Jazz Catalyst," *Second Line* 20 (Sept.–Oct. 1968): 101–2; Souchon, interview by Hillyer, May 7, 1958.

72. For information on Myra Menville, see "Crusader—Myra Menville," *Second Line* 2 (Dec. 1951): 1, 12, 17; Myra Menville, "A Secretary's Saga (or Myra's Farewell Blues or Nostalgia Run Rampant)," *Second Line* 7 (Nov.–Dec. 1956): 29–32; "A Special Memorial Tribute Section," *Second Line* 31 (Spring 1979): 5–12. For information on Merlin "Scoop" Kennedy, see "Editor's Note: Scoop," *Second Line* 2 (Sept. 1951): 16. Information on the other members of the NJF was derived from names appearing on the foundation's letterhead and in *Basin Street* and locating them in *Polk's New Orleans City Directory, Vol. LXV, 1945–46* (New Orleans: R. L. Polk and Company, 1946).

73. See "Facts on the Foundation," *Basin Street* 1 (Aug. 1945): 3.

74. See "Conditions That Prevail," *Basin Street* 1 (Mar. 1945): 1.

75. See untitled statement, *Basin Street* 2 (Apr. 1946): 2.

76. *New Orleans,* dir. Arthur Lubin, prod. Jules Levey (United Artists, 1947). For a full analysis of this film, see Krin Gabbard, *Jammin' at the Margins: Jazz and the American Cinema* (Chicago: University of Chicago Press, 1996).

77. Menville, "Wiggs," 8.

78. Menville, "Wiggs," 9.

79. Blackstone had opened a record store in 1945 after leaving the *Times-Picayune* to pursue his various interests in jazz. See "Calling All Collectors," *Basin Street* 1 (Oct. 1945): 2; Richard B. Allen, "Orin Blackstone—1907–1980—A Personal Tribute," *Second Line* 32 (Fall 1980): 33–35; "Blackstone," 1, 8–9. See

also "New Orleans Jazz Club Celebrates 20th Birthday," *Second Line* 19 (Jan.–Feb. 1968): 1, 3.

80. Menville, "Wiggs," 9.

81. Like the NJF, the NOJC established a fund to help Oscar Celestin reform his band.

82. See "The Jazz Club Story—Our Birth," *Second Line* 1 (June 1950): 1; "The Jazz Club Story—In the Beginning," *Second Line* 1 (July–Aug. 1950): 5; "The Jazz Club Story—We Come of Age," *Second Line* 1 (Sept. 1950): 3.

83. "Jazz Club Story—We Come of Age," 3. Both Panassié and Leonard Feather were in New Orleans for the concerts and other activities accompanying Armstrong's reign as Zulu.

84. See Peggy Mengis, "The Battle against Bebop," *Times-Picayune New Orleans States Magazine,* Apr. 10, 1949. According to Suhor, New Orleans purists were highly successful in monopolizing press coverage of their events to the detriment of modernists, whose activities often went unreported ("Jazz and the New Orleans Press," 18–19).

85. Mengis, "Battle against Bebop."

86. Mengis, "Battle against Bebop."

87. For a basic introduction and "timeline chart" to what Charles Suhor calls "an invisible generation" of modernists in New Orleans, see *Jazz in New Orleans,* 192–290.

88. One of Belletto's earliest gigs was in a racially mixed band with Earl Palmer and Ed Frank in New Orleans, an association that was terminated when they were arrested for breaking segregation laws. See Jason Berry, "Bandstand: The Return of Jazz Pioneer Belletto," *New Orleans Times-Picayune,* Oct. 19, 1984. Regarding playing for strippers and life on the road, see Jon Pult, "Fest Focus: Al Belletto," *OffBeat,* May 2000, 160, 165.

89. For the jazz background of Dave Bartholomew, see Rick Coleman, *Blue Monday: Fats Domino and the Lost Dawn of Rock 'n' Roll* (Cambridge: Da Capo, 2006), 35–41 (the book as a whole discusses his subsequent career with Fats). For Palmer's affiliation with Fats Domino, see Tony Scherman, *Backbeat: Earl Palmer's Story* (Washington, D.C.: Smithsonian Institution Press, 1999), 62–101; for his list of sessions as a drummer for hire, see 170–88.

90. See Jason Berry, Jonathan Foose, and Tad Jones, *Up from the Cradle of Jazz: New Orleans Music since World War II* (Athens: University of Georgia Press, 1985), 48–49, 152–53, 184–86.

91. For information on Marsalis, Battiste, and Batiste, see D. Antoinette Handy, *Jazz Man's Journey: A Biography of Ellis Marsalis, Jr.* (Lanham, Md.: Scarecrow Press. 1999).

92. "Jazz Club Story—We Come of Age," 3.

93. "Jazz Club Story—Today," *Second Line* 1 (Oct. 1950): 3.

94. "Jazz Club Story—Today," 3.

95. See Myra Menville, "Now It Will Be Told (Why There Was No 1953 Festival)," *Second Line* 5 (Mar.–Apr. 1954): 14–15.

96. Brochure for the New Orleans Jazz Club 1952 Annual Jazz Festival, Sept. 28, 1952, in "Subjects" vertical file: "Concerts and Festivals, Local—New Orleans Jazz Festival, 1952," HJA.

97. Menville, "Now It Will Be Told," 14–15.

98. "1954 Jazz Festival," *Second Line* 5 (Nov.–Dec. 1954): 7–8, 27.

99. "1954 Jazz Festival," 7.

100. "Report on the 1955 Jazz Festival," *Second Line* 6 (Nov.–Dec. 1955): 30–31, quote on 30.

101. Sim Myers, "It's Jazz Time," *New Orleans Times-Picayune*, Oct. 10, 1959.

102. Stanley Resnick, "Plans for Jazz Festival Here in 1968 Announced," *New Orleans Times-Picayune*, June 8, 1967.

103. Resnick, "Plans for Jazz Festival."

104. For information on proceeds of the 1968 festival, see Jazzfest Talent Committee, Minutes of Meeting, Jazzfest '68, in "Subjects" vertical file: "Concerts and Festivals, Local—New Orleans Jazz Heritage, 1968," HJA. For prior expectations, see Resnick, "Plans for Jazz Festival." Despite the inability to fund an ambitious agenda due to limited 1968 profits, the support shown by municipal government, especially Mayor Victor Schiro, helped to ensure an encore the following year.

105. For discussion of the connections between the 1968–69 festivals and the birth of the New Orleans Jazz and Heritage Festival, and of the role played by Richard B. Allen of the Hogan Jazz Archive, see Vincent Fumar, "Jazz Fest 1989: It Was Twenty Years Ago Today," *Wavelength*, no. 103 (May 1989): 29–31. For information on the growth of Jazz Fest, see Geraldine Wyckoff, "Louisiana—A Decade of Music," *Gambit*, Jan. 1, 1991, 35–37.

106. See "New Orleans Public Library Receives Jazz Collection," *Second Line* 3 (Sept.–Oct. 1952): 8–9.

107. "New Orleans Public Library," 8–9.

108. The New Orleans Public Library eventually found the maintenance of the Souchon collection too burdensome and transferred the donation to the Hogan Jazz Archive in 1976.

109. Untitled news item, *Second Line* 5 (Mar.–Apr. 1954): 15.

110. See George Kay, "Joe Mares' Southland," *Mississippi Rag* 11 (July 1984): 1–3, for details.

111. Quoted in "Reveal Plans for Quarter Jazz Museum," *New Orleans States-Item*, Nov. 6, 1959.

112. "Jazz Museum Ground Broken," *New Orleans Times-Picayune*, Apr. 5, 1960.

113. "Jazz Has Made It," *New Orleans Times-Picayune*, Nov. 11, 1961. Also see Suhor, "Jazz and the New Orleans Press," 18.

114. "Jazz Has Made It."

115. Frank Gagnard, "A Home for Jazz," *New Orleans Times-Picayune*, Feb. 12, 1961.

116. In private conversation, Don Perry has emphasized the importance of *Jazzmen* as the bible of the NOJC. See also Menville, "Secretary's Saga," 30, and "Crusader—Myra Menville," which mentions "the battered copy of 'Jazzmen' that Myra carries with her to every concert, festival and jazz meeting" (12).

117. See Stella Martin, "Parade Opens Music Center," *New Orleans Times-Picayune*, Nov. 13, 1961; Mark Dean, "Jazz Renaissance," *Tulane Hullabaloo*, Nov. 17, 1961; Beth Bagby, "Mayor Schiro Proclaims Jazz Week Parade, Ceremony Opens Museum," *Tulane Hullabaloo*, Nov. 17, 1961. Perhaps surprisingly, some of the best reportage of the inauguration of the Jazz Museum is to be found in the Tulane student newspaper. For information on the vagaries attending NOJC administration of the museum, and on its ultimate transfer to the Louisiana State Museum in 1977, see Donald M. Marquis, "New Orleans Jazz Club Collections of the Louisiana State Museum," *Second Line* 41 (Fall 1989): 8–9. As an interesting aside, the iconic role played by the Jazz Museum in developing jazz purism may be seen in its entry into American epic subliterature: the comic book. See "The King of New Orleans," in *Strange Adventures*, no. 147 (Dec. 1962), in which relics from the Jazz Museum reawaken doctors subjected to a sleeping spell by King Zero in a post–nuclear holocaust America. Traditional jazz delivers the population from the grasp of the evil Zero, thus enabling the residents to "build a new life here in New Orleans."

118. Martin Williams, *Jazz Masters of New Orleans*, xvii.

119. See Nick LaRocca, interview by Allen, June 2, 1958; Nick LaRocca to William R. Hogan, June 18, 1958, in Nick LaRocca correspondence file, HJA.

120. Edmond Souchon, "Was It For This?" *Second Line* 5 (Apr.–May 1954): 20.

121. Rose, *I Remember Jazz*, 66.

122. Rose, *I Remember Jazz*, 67.

123. Rose, *I Remember Jazz*, 149.

124. Edmond Souchon, "Chameleon in Wood," *Second Line* 8 (Sept.–Oct. 1957): 3–5, 18, quote on 3–4.

125. Souchon, "Chameleon in Wood," 3.

126. Souchon, "Chameleon in Wood," 3. In 1971, Mrs. Charlotte McCullum Boutney became the first black admitted to the NOJC board. The following year, Nelson Jean Jr. became the club's first black secretary. Souchon's complaint that blacks seemed disinterested in contributing to the exploration of jazz history was reiterated by Billy Taylor in "Negroes Don't Know Anything about Jazz," in *The Jazz Word*, ed. Dom Cerulli, Burt Korall, and Mort Nasatir (New York: Ballantine Books, 1960), 40–45. Since that time, Dr. Taylor has done much to remedy the situation.

127. See "Bill Russell Moves to New Orleans," *Second Line* 7 (Mar.–Apr.

1956): 5. For insight into Russell's photographic pursuits in New Orleans during this period, see Jonathan Williams, "Music Is to Make People Happy," *Black Mountain Review*, no. 7 (Fall 1957): 83–85; William Russell, "Eight Photographs," *Black Mountain Review*, no. 7 (Fall 1957): 86–94.

128. See "Ralston Crawford's Photographs," *Second Line* 4 (July–Aug. 1953): 1–2, 12, quote on 2. See also J. Lee Anderson, "The Painter as Photographer," *Mississippi Rag* 18 (Aug. 1990): 1–5. Interestingly enough, Crawford had been a member of the Independents with Charles Frederic Ramsey, Fred Ramsey's father.

129. See "Bob Morris Leaves New Orleans," *Second Line* 9 (Sept.–Oct. 1958): 12, 21, quote on 12.

130. For information on Richard B. Allen, see Allen, "Orin Blackstone," 34; Carolyn Kolb, "Dick Allen: Mr. Jazz Music," *Southern Living* 6 (June 1971): 46, 48, 50, 52, 54–55; Whitney Balliett, "Mecca, La.," in *Such Sweet Thunder: Forty-Nine Pieces on Jazz* (New York: Bobbs-Merrill Company, 1966), 298–334; and a posthumous retrospective by Butch Thompson, "The Legacy of Jazz Historian Dick Allen," *Mississippi Rag* 34 (May 2007): 8–11. Allen came from a long line of psychiatrists, who ran a sanitarium in Milledgeville, prompting him to say of his childhood environment, "It was just a small insane asylum, but it was always home to me."

131. Quoted in Kolb, "Dick Allen," 48.

132. Ralph J. Gleason, "The Grant to Russell Is All for the Best," *San Francisco Chronicle*, undated clipping, in "Persons" vertical file: "Russell, William," HJA. For additional information on the Hogan Jazz Archive, see S. Frederick Starr, "Scholars at Tulane Are Building an Archive on Jazz," *Smithsonian* 11 (Nov. 1980): 100–102, 104.

133. Alden Banning Ashforth, interview by Bruce Boyd Raeburn, Sept. 2, 2007, tape recording, HJA. The information following is taken from the interview.

134. For details on the Barnes and Thomas sessions, see *Bill Russell's American Music*, ed. and comp. Mike Hazeldine (New Orleans: Jazzology Press, 1993), 143–53.

135. Larry Borenstein, "Introduction," in *Preservation Hall Portraits* (Baton Rouge: Louisiana State University Press, 1968), 1–6, quote on 2. The name of the judge in question was Edwin A. Babylon.

136. Borenstein, "Introduction," 3.

137. William Carter, "Thanks, Allan," *Jazz Archivist* 2, no. 2 (Nov. 1987): 1–3, quote on 2.

138. William Carter, "Thanks, Allan," 2–3. For a history of Preservation Hall and insight into the Jaffes' relationships with the black musicians who worked there, see William Carter, *Preservation Hall: Music from the Heart* (New York: W. W. Norton, 1991).

139. Bill Russell, "The Proprietors," in *Preservation Hall Portraits*, 7–9, quote on 9.

140. Kolb, "Dick Allen," 54–55.

141. Thomas Sancton, *Song for My Fathers: A New Orleans Story in Black and White* (New York: Other Press, 2006). A parallel memoir, written by Barry Martyn (1941–), a transplanted Londoner and New Orleans–style drummer since the 1960s, is also enlightening. Martyn recounts how a 1959 George Lewis concert in England changed his life, drawing him to New Orleans. See Barry Martyn, *Walking with Legends: Barry Martyn's New Orleans Jazz Odyssey,* ed. Mick Burns (Baton Rouge: Louisiana State University Press, 2007). The expansion of the New Orleans revival as an international phenomenon after 1950, due to the recordings and touring of George Lewis, Kid Thomas Valentine, Emanuel Paul, Kid Sheik Colar, and others, is an important topic beyond the scope of this study, and Martyn's book provides a useful introduction to it.

142. For a similar line of reasoning, see Dale Cockrell, "Nineteenth-Century Popular Music," in Nicholls, *Cambridge History of American Music,* 158–85: "While this is a story about the American veneration of the marketplace . . . the quasi-industrial product seemed then (and seems yet today) to lie near the primal point where human beings found identity, community, meaning, and happiness . . . and often does mark for the cultural historian those gripping moments when social or intellectual pretensions were dropped in favor of visceral joy and pleasure, thus (unintentionally?) revealing baseline human (and historical) truths and values, moments in musical lives when fun should be taken with profound seriousness" (185).

Epilogue

1. See, e.g., the paucity of coverage of New Orleans jazz at home in the 1920s, in Alyn Shipton, *A New History of Jazz,* rev. and updated ed. (London and New York: Continuum, 2007); Geoffrey C. Ward and Ken Burns, *Jazz: A History of America's Music* (New York: Alfred A. Knopf, 2000); Lewis Porter and Michael Ullman, with Edward Hazell, *Jazz: From Its Origins to the Present* (Englewood Cliffs, N.J.: Prentice Hall, 1993); Ted Gioia, *The History of Jazz* (New York and Oxford: Oxford University Press, 1997). Gioia has one sentence (45) on New Orleans as a jazz environment in the 1920s, which is more than any of the others.

2. See the bibliography for citations to these memoirs.

3. See Eric Porter, *What Is This Thing Called Jazz?,* especially 43–44, on Louis Armstrong, and the later chapter devoted to Wynton Marsalis.

4. Scholars have not given New Orleans jazz modernists their just due. The two primary exceptions are Berry, Foose, and Jones, *Up From the Cradle of Jazz;* and Suhor, *Jazz in New Orleans,* but greater breadth and depth are needed.

Bibliography

The chapter notes contain complete bibliographic citations, and it would be redundant to repeat them here. The following list of books and articles provides suggestions for collateral readings germane to this study.

New Orleans Style

Brothers, Thomas. *Louis Armstrong's New Orleans*. New York: W. W. Norton and Company, 2006. Brothers contributes fresh perspectives on New Orleans as an early jazz environment, inquiring into how performance styles were originally configured and situating young Armstrong in a social and musical milieu that is full of paradox and possibility.

Harker, Brian. "The Early Musical Development of Louis Armstrong, 1901–1928." Ph.D. dissertation, Columbia University, 1997. Harker investigates Armstrong's associations with young contemporaries and how this interaction affected his stylistic development.

Russell, William. *New Orleans Style*. Comp. and ed. Barry Martyn and Mike Hazeldine. New Orleans: Jazzology Press, 1994. This is a compendium of transcribed interviews on performance style that Russell conducted with New Orleans musicians (arranged by instrument).

Creoles

The works below provide basic information and interesting theoretical perspectives.

Ake, David. "'Blue Horizon': Creole Culture and Early New Orleans Jazz." In *Jazz Cultures*. Berkeley and London: University of California Press, 2002, 10–41. Ake questions simplistic racial characterizations in assessing ethnic diversity in New Orleans and uses the experiences of Creole musicians to challenge the conceptualization of early jazz as folk music.

Anthony, Arthé Agnes. "The Negro Creole Community in New Orleans, 1880–1920: An Oral History." Ph.D. dissertation, University of California at Irvine, 1978. Anthony tracks permutations of Creole culture in the early twentieth century, noting stability in neighborhood demographic patterns and institutional affiliations.

Fiehrer, Thomas. "From Quadrille to Stomp: The Creole Origins of Jazz." *Popular Music* 10 (January 1991): 21–38. Fiehrer challenges jazz origins in American vernacular culture, arguing that Creole music traditions are the wellspring.

Logsdon, Joseph, and Arnold R. Hirsch, eds. *Creole New Orleans: Race and Americanization.* Baton Rouge: Louisiana State University Press, 1992. This collection provides an overview of Creole history through essays by Karen Cosse Bell, Arnold Hirsch, Jerah Johnson, Joseph Logsdon, and Joseph Tregle.

Scott, Rebecca J. *Degrees of Freedom: Louisiana and Cuba after Slavery.* Cambridge and London: Belknap Press of Harvard University Press, 2005. Scott compares the aftermath of emancipation in Cuba and New Orleans, emphasizing the political advocacy of Creoles for blacks.

Thompson, Shirley. "'Ah Toucoutou, ye conin vous': History and Memory in Creole New Orleans." *American Quarterly* 53, no. 2 (2001): 232–62. Thompson examines the constituencies that compete for control of Creole identity.

Discography

Atkins, Jerry. "Discographies and Discographers." *IAJRC Journal* 22 (Fall 1989): 55–61.

Booth, Mark. *American Popular Music: A Reference Guide.* Westport, Conn.: Greenwood Press, 1983.

Hazeldine, Mike, ed. and comp. *Bill Russell's American Music.* New Orleans: Jazzology Press, 1993. This is a history of one revivalist record label.

Rust, Brian. *Brian Rust's Guide to Discography.* Westport, Conn.: Greenwood Press, 1980. Rust's work is the best history of discography available.

Discographies of the New Orleans Revival

Ikegami, Teizo. *New Orleans Renaissance on Record.* Tokyo: Alligator Jazz Club, 1980.

Stagg, Tom, and Charlie Crump. *New Orleans, the Revival: A Tape and Discography of Negro Traditional Jazz Recorded in New Orleans or by New Orleans Bands, 1937–1972.* Dublin: Bashall Caves Publishers, 1973.

Memoirs

Before consulting the works below, an acquaintance with Kathy Ogren's work is recommended: Kathy Ogren, "'Jazz Isn't Just Me': Jazz Autobiographies as Performance Persona." In *Jazz in Mind: Essays on the History and Meaning of Jazz,* ed. Reginald T. Buckner and Steven Weiland. Detroit: Wayne State University Press, 1991. 112–27.

Barker, Danny. *A Life in Jazz.* Ed. Alyn Shipton. New York: Oxford University Press, 1986.

Barker, Danny. *Buddy Bolden and the Last Days of Storyville.* Ed. Alyn Shipton. London: Cassell, 1998.

Bechet, Sidney. *Treat It Gentle.* London: Cassell, 1960.

Bigard, Barney. *With Louis and the Duke: The Autobiography of a Jazz Clarinetist.* Ed. Barry Martyn. London: Macmillan Press, 1985.

Collins, Lee. *Oh, Didn't He Ramble: The Life Story of Lee Collins as Told to Mary Collins.* Ed. Frank Gillis and John Miner. Urbana-Champaign: University of Illinois Press, 1974.

Darensbourg, Joe. *Telling It Like It Is.* Ed. Peter Vacher. London: Macmillan Press, 1987.

Foster, George. *Pops Foster: The Autobiography of a New Orleans Jazzman.* Ed. Tom Stoddard. Berkeley: University of California Press, 1971.

Gara, Larry. *The Baby Dodds Story.* 1959. Rev ed., Baton Rouge: Louisiana State University Press, 1992.

Lomax, Alan. *Mister Jelly Roll: The Fortunes of Jelly Roll Morton, New Orleans Creole and "Inventor of Jazz."* New York: Grossett and Dunlap, 1950.

Louis Armstrong, in His Own Words: Selected Writings. Ed. Thomas Brothers. Index Charles Kinzer. New York and London: Oxford University Press, 1999.

Manone, Wingy, with Paul Vandervoort II. *Trumpet on the Wing.* Garden City: Doubleday and Company, 1948.

Martyn, Barry. *Walking with Legends: Barry Martyn's New Orleans Jazz Odyssey.* Ed. Mick Burns. Foreword by Bruce Boyd Raeburn. Baton Rouge: Louisiana State University Press, 2007.

Sancton, Thomas. *Song for My Fathers: A New Orleans Story in Black and White.* New York: Other Press, 2006.

Scherman, Tony. *Backbeat: Earl Palmer's Story.* Washington, D.C.: Smithsonian Institution Press, 1999.

Oral Histories

The William Ransom Hogan Archive of New Orleans Jazz at Tulane University is the primary repository for oral history related to New Orleans jazz. The archive maintains an index of interviews, listed alphabetically by informant surname, at http://www.library.tulane.edu. Oral histories provide the best access to the biographical details, thoughts, and feelings of the musicians who created the New Orleans jazz tradition. While transcripts are invariably useful as guides, the interviews yield the most information as audio documents, in which the informant's full powers of expression are manifested.

Peretti, Burton. "Oral Histories of Jazz Musicians: The NEA Transcripts as Texts in Context." In *Jazz among the Discourses*, ed. Krin Gabbard. Durham and London: Duke University Press, 1995. 117–33. Peretti provides a thoughtful discussion of the benefits and liabilities of jazz oral history.

Recommended Audio Collections

The Atlantic New Orleans Jazz Sessions (4 CDs). Mosaic MD4-179. 1998: USA.
Breaking Out of New Orleans, 1922–1929 (4 CDs). JSP921. 2004: UK.
The Complete Original Dixieland Jazz Band 1917–1936 (2 CDs). RCA 66608.2. 1995: USA.
Jelly Roll Morton, 1926–1930 (5 CDs). JSP 903. 2000: UK.
Louis Armstrong, The Hot Fives and Sevens (4 CDs). JSP100. 1999: UK.
New Orleans: Great Original Performances 1918–1934 (CD). Louisiana Red Hot 613. 1998: USA.

Index

George H. Buck (GHB) Foundation, 296n111
Gershwin, George, 16, 17
Gillespie, John Birks "Dizzy," 145, 168, 169,
192–93, 198, 203, 301n65, 303n91, 312n78;
on Feather, 303n91
Gingrich, Arnold, 162–63, 164, 165, 168–69;
Ertegun's criticism of, 170, 177; *Esquire's
1946 Jazz Book* and, 185; *Esquire's 1947
Jazz Book* and, 194
Gioia, Ted, 48
Girard, George, 226, 249
Gitler, Ira, 100
Gleason, Jean (née Rayburn), 124, 155
Gleason, Ralph, 124, 132, 155, 172–73, 252
Glotzer, Fred E., 167
Goffin, Robert, 46, 169, 248, 304n119; suit
against *Esquire* by, 176–77, 195
Gold, Michael, 28–29, 31, 35, 267n21
Golden Rule Orchestra, 8
Gonsoulin, Bertha, 118
Goodman, Benny, 50, 53, 54, 92–93, 146, 152,
237; Hammond and, 106, 273n50
Gordon, Robert Winslow, 86–87
Gorham, Joseph K., 222
Gorky, Maxim, 28
Gottlieb, Bill, 308n40
"Grant to Russell Is All for the Best, The"
(Gleason), 252
Grauer, Bill, Jr., 195
Green, Abel, 163
Green, Archie, 45
Grennard, Elliott, 163
Grunewald School of Music (New Orleans),
242
Guesnon, George, 256
Guild Records, 145
guitar, 66
Gullickson, Gordon, 178
Gumbo Ya-Ya (Saxon and Tallant), 221
Gushee, Lawrence, 3–4, 38, 52, 261n4, 262n13

Haggin, Bernard H., 20, 31–32, 33, 35
Halfway House Orchestra, 9, 85
Hall, Weeks, 65, 113
Hammond, John, 60, 147, 215, 292n43; on
"Black, Brown, and Beige," 160; as collec-
tor, 41, 154; at Columbia Records, 53–54,
92–93, 105–8; *Esquire* jazz polls and, 163;
Feather and, 160; Gennari on, 20–21;
Goodman and, 273n50; HRS label and, 97;

Hulsizer and, 234, 235; leftist politics of,
31–32, 33, 269n36; "Lettre D'Amérique,"
49; Lion and, 99; major record companies
and, 5–6; in New Orleans, 292n43; on race,
71; reformism and, 82; Rose and, 34; Rus-
sell on, 58; on Russell's Johnson record-
ings, 122; "Spirituals to Swing" concert
and, 73; Stalinism and, 35; UHCA label
and, 95
Hammond, Merrill, 45, 58
Handy, W. C., 213
Harap, Louis, 147, 299n16
Hardin, Lil, 74, 75, 152
Hardy, Emmett, 226, 231
Harker, Brian, 309n43
Harlem Renaissance, 14
Harrison, Max, 10–11
Hawkins, Coleman, 94, 96, 163, 167, 194, 195
Hayakawa, Samuel Ichiye, 174–76
Haynes, Don C., 136
Hazel, Arthur "Monk," 227–28, 231–32, 233
Hazeldine, Mike, 122, 131
"Heat Wave" (Smith), 54
Helfensteller, Alf, 196, 211
"Hellfighters" orchestra, 15
Hennessey, Thomas J., 272n31
Hentoff, Nat, 78
Herman, Woody, 186, 192, 194, 239, 242,
286n78
Herskovits, Melville, 183, 190, 296n1
"Hey! Ba-Ba-Revolt!" (Brown), 192–93
Higginbotham, J. C., 169
*Highbrow/Lowbrow: The Emergence of Cul-
tural Hierarchy in America* (Levine), 11–14
Hilaire, Georges, 48
Hillman, Christopher, 116, 122, 131, 132
Hillyer, Haywood H., III, 223
Hinchcliffe, Edwin, 161–62
Hines, Earl, 105, 145
Hirt, Al, 242
Hobsbawm, Eric (Francis Newton), 294n86
Hobson, Wilder, 41, 59–60, 97, 212
Hodeir, André, 139–40, 141, 198
Hodel, Emelia, 118–19
Hodes, Art, 164, 172, 177
Hoefer, George, Jr., 49–50, 137–38, 147, 183,
185, 272n32
Hogan, William Ransom, 252
Hogan Jazz Archive (Tulane University), 38,
318n108

Jazzmen (*continued*)
and, 150; jazz schism and, 180; jazz scholarship hegemony and, 151; Johnson's information in, 56, 113; "myths" in, 279n127;
New Orleans style in, 76–80; NOJC and,
248; publication of, 60–61; Ramsey and,
56, 60–62, 73–76; RCA Victor's Morton
sessions and, 101–2; Russell and, 56–58,
60–67, 75–76, 298n9; Charles Edward
Smith and, 60–61, 67–73; Lee Smith and,
155; Stephen W. Smith and, 56, 60–62
Jazz Museum, 236, 252, 319n117; NJF and,
237; NOJC and, 240, 243, 245–48, 251
jazz organizations, 217; NJF, 7, 236–40, 251.
See also New Orleans Jazz Club (NOJC)
jazz origins, 53, 67; Blackstone and Spriggins
on, 230; race and, 4, 34, 68–71
jazz pilgrims, 56, 232–33, 234–35, 253–54
jazz polls, 6, 143, 160, 164, 193–94, 302n75.
See also *Esquire's Jazz Books* (jazz polls)
Jazz Record Book, The (Smith and Russell),
6, 147–50, 151, 207
"Jazz: Resistance to the Diffusion of a Cultural Pattern" (Berger), 18
*Jazz Revolution, The: Twenties America and
the Meaning of Jazz* (Ogren), 14–16
jazz schism, 6–7, 143–81; big bands and,
144–45; collector community on, 161–62;
Esquire jazz polls and, 162–71; in France,
198; Gendron and, 179–80; jazz polls and,
160; *Jazz Record Book* and, 147–50; lectures and, 173–76; modernists and, 143–44,
145, 163, 167; *Modern Music* article and,
146–47; *Real Jazz* and, 150–51; religious revivalism and, 143–44; *This is Jazz* and,
157–59; traditionalists and, 143–44, 163,
167, 181, 258; *Who's Who in Jazz Collecting* and, 151–55; women and, 153, 155–57.
See also Leonard Feather; purism; Barry
Ulanov
jazz scholarship, 150, 151, 212, 259–60
"Jazz: Some Little Known Aspects" (Smith),
23–27, 35
Jazzways yearbook, 177, 305n121
Jazz Years, The (Feather), 195
Jelly Roll Morton and his Red Hot Peppers,
9
"Jelly Roll Morton Symposium, The," 38–39,
102
"Jelly Roll Was Right" (Brown), 176

"Jim Crow," 189, 248–50
Jimmy Ryan's, 123, 124, 137
John the Reek's, 218
Johnny Wiggs Band, 247
Johnson, Bill, 61–62
Johnson, James P., 53, 282n22
Johnson, Willie "Bunk," 6, 111–27, 129–41;
Bechet and, 122–27, 139; controversy of,
139; death of, 137, 138; downturn of,
136–38, 139–40; at *Esquire* concert, 169–70;
first recordings of, 112–13, 114–16;
Jazzmen and, 56, 113; Karoley and, 155; on
New Orleans Revival, 136; New Orleans
style and, 126, 213; new teeth and trumpet
for, 113, 289n8; NJF and, 236; Oliver and,
73, 75; as originator of revival, 111; Ory's
recordings and, 129–30; Raeburn and,
306n12; Reid and, 105; Russell and, 6, 65,
134, 138–39, 213; Russell's recordings of,
114–16, 120–22; San Francisco recordings
of, 118–21, 291n40; Smith on, 205;
Stuyvesant Casino concerts and, 131–35;
subsequent recordings of, 116–17; Temple
and, 156–57; Williams, Eugene and,
114–17, 122–25, 130, 138–39
Jones, Claude, 102
Jones, Max, 161, 298n11
Jones, Richard M., 174
Jones and Collins Astoria Hot Eight, 9
Jordan, Edward "Kidd," 241, 260
Josephson, Barney, 54
Joy, Leonard, 102, 103

Kaminsky, Max, 171
Kaplan, Max, 151–52
Kapp, Jack, 92, 93
Karoley, Mary, 105, 114, 155
Kay, George, 120–21
Kay, Roger, 163
Keepnews, Orrin, 195
Kelley, Peck, 226
Kennedy, Merlin "Scoop," 237, 244
Kenney, William Howland, 271n24, 275n62,
276n78, 281n8
Kenton, Stan, 193, 203, 242, 286n78, 297n3
Keppard, Freddie, 64
Kerr, Clyde, Jr., 241, 260
Kerrigan, Elizabeth O'Kelley, 223
Kerrigan, Jack, 224
Keynote label, 185, 232

Noone, Jimmie, 128
Nordskog label, 127
Norris, Frank, 59

O'Brien, Floyd, 291n40
ODJB. *See* Original Dixieland Jazz Band (ODJB)
Office of War Information (OWI), 105, 119, 123, 145, 287n102
Ogren, Kathy J., 14–16, 19
OKeh label, 51, 74, 85–86, 107; "race" series of, 40
O'Kelley, Mary Lucy Hamill, 223
Oliver, Joe, 62, 96, 127, 147, 200, 278n108, 278n112; commercialism and, 30; Hyman and, 225; King Oliver's Creole Jazz Band and, 9, 27, 55, 74, 85, 152, 199, 200, 213–14; Ramsey and, 73–76, 77; on RCA Victor, 84
Olympia Brass Band, 245, 256
Onward Brass Band, 9
oppression, 31, 35; jazz as response to, 90
oral history, 91
Orchestra Hall (Chicago), 136
Original Creole Orchestra, 52, 61–62, 64
Original Dixieland Jazz Band (ODJB), 11, 54–55, 83, 189, 218, 225, 278n104; audition for Columbia by, 85; Laine's bands and, 69; New York City debut of, 264n31; public response to, 220–21; Stearns on, 52–53
Original Tuxedo Jazz Orchestra, the, 9, 43, 222–24, 241
Original Zenith Brass Band, 296n112
Ory, Edward "Kid," 74, 116, 127–31, 135, 136, 140, 238; on Columbia, 108, 130; in Los Angeles, 293n67; Morton and, 102, 103; Panassié and, 294n81; in San Francisco, 119, 122
Osgood, Henry, 13
Otto, Al, 130

Paddock, the, 253, 255
Paley, William S., 92–93
Palmer, Earl, 241–42, 259, 317n88
Panassié, Hugues, 6, 46, 82, 147, 150–51, 317n83; Blesh on, 200–201, 202; Delaunay and, 47–49, 198–99, 202–3; HRS label and, 97; Mezzrow and, 101, 191, 202; Ory and, 294n81; RCA Victor and, 101; reemergence of swing and, 94; Smith on, 207;

Swing label and, 284n49; UHCA label and, 95
Paramount label, 40
Parenti, Tony, 226
Paris, Wynne, 123
Paris Jazz Festival, 203
Parisian Room, the, 241
Parker, Charlie, 145, 185, 198, 203, 204, 215, 312n78
Pasadena Institute of Art, 176
Pasadena Jazz Society, 129
Pasley, Frank, 292n40
Pathé-Marconi label, 94
Patterson, Albion, 41
Paul Barbarin's Jazz Band, 243
Pavageau, Alcide "Slow Drag," 121, 131, 134, 135
Payne, Richard, 241–42
Peer, Ralph, 85–86
Peerless Orchestra, 8
Pelican Dance Hall, 223
Peretti, Burton, 283n29
"perfectionists," 163
Perkins, Dave, 69
Perriliat, Nat, 241, 260
Perry, Don, 239
Peterson, Charlie, 96
Petrillo, James C., 288n115
Petrillo ban, 121, 186, 288n115
Pettiford, Oscar, 163, 303n91
Peyton, Dave, 13
Peyton, Henry, 262n6
"Philippine Philippic" (Avakian), 171–72
phonograph industry, 83–84, 280n3, 280n8; radio and, 40, 84, 92, 281n12
piano, 66, 67, 149
Picou, Alphonse, 43–44, 105, 112, 233
Pig Ankle Corners, 218
Pioneers of Jazz: The Story of the Original Creole Band (Gushee), 52
pirating, 105
Platt, Sam, 177
Playboy Club, 242
Popular Music (magazine), 228–29
Porter, Eric, 259
Porter, Lewis, 264n21, 312n2
Preservation Hall, 1, 7, 240, 255–58
pricing of records, 46
Princeton University, 41, 60